THE CENTURY PSYCHOLOGY SERIES

James J. Jenkins
Walter Mischel
Willard W. Hartup
Editors

HUMAN INFERENCE:

strategies
and shortcomings
of social judgment

RICHARD NISBETT
University of Michigan

LEE ROSS
Stanford University

PRENTICE-HALL, INC., *Englewood Cliffs, New Jersey 07632*

Library of Congress Cataloging in Publication Data

Nisbett, Richard E
  Human inference.

  Bibliography: p.
  Includes indexes.
  1. Cognition   2. Inference (Logic)   3. Judgment.
I. Ross, Lee, joint author.   II. Title.
BF311.N57   153.4′32   79–20945
ISBN 0-13-445130-9

© 1980 by PRENTICE-HALL, INC., *Englewood Cliffs, N.J. 07632*

Printed in the United States of America

10   9   8   7   6   5   4   3   2   1

editorial production/supervision and interior design: CATHIE MICK MAHAR
manufacturer buyer: HARRY P. BAISLEY

PRENTICE-HALL INTERNATIONAL, INC., *London*
PRENTICE-HALL OF AUSTRALIA PTY. LIMITED, *Sydney*
PRENTICE-HALL OF CANADA, LTD., *Toronto*
PRENTICE-HALL OF INDIA PRIVATE LIMITED, *New Delhi*
PRENTICE-HALL OF JAPAN, INC., *Tokyo*
PRENTICE-HALL OF SOUTHEAST ASIA PTE. LTD., *Singapore*
WHITEHALL BOOKS LIMITED, *Wellington, New Zealand*

for
SUSAN ISAACS NISBETT
and
JUDITH ROSS

contents

II

Inferential Tasks:
Normative Principles and Lay Practice

preface

One of philosophy's oldest paradoxes is the apparent contradiction between the great triumphs and the dramatic failures of the human mind. The same organism that routinely solves inferential problems too subtle and complex for the mightiest computers often makes errors in the simplest of judgments about everyday events. The errors, moreover, often seem traceable to violations of the same inferential rules that underlie people's most impressive successes.

The paradox persists in contemporary psychological theory and research. In European psychology it is the work of Piaget and Freud that perhaps provides the best illustration. Piaget's elegant and provocative theories of cognitive development offer an account of the stages through which the initially helpless and ignorant human infant passes on its journey to become an adult. And what a piece of work is Piaget's adult—so impressively armed with problem-solving tools and insights into the social and physical world. In contrast, the adult human to which Freud introduced us is far less notable for mature rationality and sophistication than for the vestiges of its infancy. In everyday thought and action, and in the greatest personal and social crises, Freud's adult is governed by unconscious strivings and by primitive, often irrational inferential processes. Can the Piagetian adult, the master of formal operations, be the same organism as the Freudian adult whose mental life and behavior are so compromised by the thought processes and unfulfilled needs of the infant?

The same paradox is apparent in contemporary North American social psychology. Many social psychologists are preoccupied with the irrational or destructive elements of social life—with intergroup conflict, with the deficiencies of the "group mind," with social apathy and pathology, with ethnic and racial prejudice, biased cognitive processes by which dissonance between action and belief is reconciled and on those that allow illusions of personal merit to be sustained in the face of manifestly contradictory facts. At the same time, another cadre of scientists explores the rational capacities and insights that allow people to decipher the meaning and the causes of social events and that bring coherence, harmony and predictability to social life. Again, the reconciliation seems difficult and tenuous. How can any creature skilled enough to build and maintain complex organizations, or sophisticated enough to appreciate the nuances of social intercourse, be foolish enough to mouth racist clichés or spill its lifeblood in pointless wars?

The position of this book is integrative; it maintains that people's inferential failures are cut from the same cloth as their inferential successes are. Specifically, we contend that people's inferential strategies are well adapted to deal with a wide range of problems, but that these same strategies become a liability when they are applied beyond that range, particularly when they are applied to problems requiring some appreciation of the normative principles that help to guide the professional scientist's more formal inferences. We should warn the reader that the following pages give relatively more attention to shortcomings, and less to triumphs, than any balanced survey of everyday judgments would justify. This emphasis on error follows from much the same premise that leads many of our colleagues to study perceptual illusions or thinking disorders—the belief that the nature of cognitive structures and processes can be revealed by the defects which they produce.

The human adult portrayed in this book does solve difficult problems, sometimes using deceptively simple strategies first learned in early childhood. At the same time, this human also makes egregious judgments and ill-considered decisions, harming himself and others through the misapplication of informal, but usually helpful strategies and through the inability or unwillingness to apply more formal inferential principles.

We believe this characterization will prove to be less paradoxical figure than does the Piagetian portrait of a sophisticated paragon who nevertheless somehow lapses into specific errors inconsistent with his general capacities.

We also believe it is also less paradoxical than the Freudian portrait of a tormented creature whose errors are largely motivational, the product of buried needs, wishes, conflicts, traumas, and defense mechanisms. Finally, we believe our portrait of lay inference helps to tie together a considerable body of work in contemporary social psychology. Research and theory dealing with such classic social psychological phenomena as attitude change, social influence, and prejudice are presented along with more recent efforts of the attribution theorists and their kin in the "cognitive-social" area. Our intent is to show the continuity between those processes underlying intellectual and social achievements and with those underlying judgmental errors and social conflicts on the other.

The organization of the book merits a brief introduction. In the initial section (chapters 1 to 3), we introduce the reader to the analogy between the inferential tasks of the layperson or "intuitive scientist" and those of the formal scientist, an analogy that figures heavily in the plan of the book. We then discuss the simplistic but generally helpful cognitive strategies used by the intuitive scientist and show how their overapplication or misapplication can result in major judgmental or inferential errors. In the middle section (chapters 4 through 8), we deal with specific inferential tasks, from the initial collection and coding of the data, to the testing and revision of informal psychological theories, that people perform so imperfectly. Throughout this section we discuss the formal or "normative" rules of inference of which people sometimes seem ignorant, rules which they understand primarily in particular narrow and familiar contexts or which they understand only in the abstract, without, really being able to apply them appropriately and broadly. In the final section (chapters 9 through 12), we first treat two specific issues in more detail: the special case of inferences about oneself and one's own behavior (chapter 9) and the general problem of distinguishing between motivationally based errors and intellectually based ones (chapter 10). Then, in the last two chapters, we cover the personal and social costs of human inferential shortcomings (and the factors limiting such costs), and the possibilities of improving people's inferential strategies.

acknowledgments

Our earliest and most abiding intellectual debt is owed to Stanley Schachter, who was our graduate advisor in Columbia's social psychology program. He showed us the continuity of between everyday judgmental strategies and the formal rules of science It was from him that we learned that when the social scientist is most serious and creative he thinks and talks like a layperson, using familiar intuitive strategies and focusing always on the phenomena of daily social existence. He made us understand that while the formal tools of the scientist are essential, they generally serve the goal of verifying insights, not of producing them.

Our second great debt is to Amos Tversky. It soon will be apparent to the reader that this book could not have been written without the foundations laid by Daniel Kahneman and Amos Tversky in their work on judgmental heuristics. That work alone would not have made this book possible. Our conversations with Tversky (and on a few delightful occasions with Kahneman, as well) were essential to helping us appreciate the implications of their work for the immediate concerns of our own research and for the broader concerns of social psychology. In earlier drafts we tried to indicate the specific ideas whose origins could be traced to these informal conversations. But in order to spare the reader from seeing over and over again in each chapter the refrain, "We are indebted to Amos Tversky for this idea," we now simply acknowledge, with gratitude, the magnitude of our personal and professional debt.

Another important debt is to two philosophers, Alvin Goldman and Steven Stich. Their vigorous criticism helped us to clarify our arguments and, even more importantly, helped us to recognize this book's relevance to traditional epistemological concerns.

Our colleague and academic editor, Walter Mischel, also merits special mention. His early encouragement, and his unfailingly helpful suggestions for revision, have well justified our intention to publish under his distinguished editorship in the Century Series.

Many other people—too many to acknowledge each without risking an embarrassing omission—have generously donated their time to commenting on earlier versions of the book or on our earlier research reports. Some of these informal reviewers, however, have exerted such an impact on so many chapters or saved us from such serious errors, that their help must be acknowledged publicly. This list of generous colleagues includes Robert Abelson, Teresa Amabile, Daryl Bem, Eugene Borgida, Philip Brickman, Gordon Bower, Robyn Dawes, Phoebe Ellsworth, Patricia Gurin, Tory Higgins, Dennis Jennings, Edward E. Jones, Harold Kelley, David Krantz, Ronald Lemley, Richard Lempert, Mark Lepper, Hazel Markus, Shelley Taylor, and Timothy Wilson. We also are deeply indebted to the dozens of fine graduate students and to our stimulating colleagues at Michigan and Stanford who have helped us over the last several years to formulate and clarify the ideas presented in this book. The authors' research reported in this book was greatly facilitated by generous research support from the National Science Foundation and the National Institute of Mental Health.

No book reaches publication without much painstaking preliminary work, including typing and retyping endless drafts, countless hours proofreading and reference finding, and scores of tactful suggestions about errors in grammar and incomprehensible sentences. The contributions of Joy Davis, Sharon Frey, Lois Govaere, and Shelagh Towson are gratefully acknowledged. We are similarly indebted to Margaret Yamashita for her superb job in copy editing and to Charles Lord for his painstaking preparation of the subject index.

Finally, we wish to express our gratitude, and our love, to those who collaborate not in our writing or in our research, but in our lives: To Susan and Judy, and to our children, Matthew Nisbett and Joshua, Timothy and Rebecca Ross.

part I

INTUITIVE STRATEGIES OF INFERENCE

1

an introduction
to the
intuitive scientist

> The logic of science is also that of business and life.
> *John Stuart Mill.*

This book is about human inference and human error. It portrays people as intuitive scientists who are gifted and generally successful, but whose attempts to understand, predict, and control events in the social sphere are seriously compromised by specific inferential shortcomings. In part, these shortcomings reflect people's failure to use the normative principles and inferential tools that guide formal scientific inquiry. They also reflect people's readiness to apply more simplistic inferential strategies beyond their appropriate limits.

The book will document both underutilization of normatively appropriate strategies and overutilization of more primitive intuitive strategies. Part 1 describes some of the intuitive strategies and illustrates their overuse. Part 2 draws an analogy between the inferential tasks of the formal scientist and those of the layperson and documents the layperson's errors made by failing to employ normatively correct strategies in daily life judgments. Part 3 examines the origins of inferential failings, the costs of these failings, and the possibility of improving people's inferential strategies.

THE FRAMEWORK OF THE BOOK

In many ways, this book represents a return to a currently unfashionable tradition in Western thought—the epistemological tradition of simultaneous concern with psychological description and with normative prescription. The early epistemologists, for example, Bacon, Descartes, Locke, and Spinoza, were as much psychologists as philosophers. Much of their work was concerned with describing, in the form of empirically testable propositions, the structures and processes of human thought. These descriptions then were used as departure points for criticism and for proposing more appropriate and effective habits of thought. This tradition of equal concern with description and prescription was continued in the work of such later philosophers as Hume, Kant, and Mill.

Around the turn of the century, philosophers began to abandon descriptive work, leaving this to the new discipline of psychology, which was developing empirical methods for describing thought processes. There was a new division of labor, in which psychologists focused on the essentially empirical task of description and philosophers focused on the normative tasks of criticism and prescription. The predominantly normative emphasis is already evident in the work of such early twentieth-century epistemologists as Russell, Carnap, and Popper.

Lately, some epistemologists, notably Alvin Goldman (1978, 1979), have begun to recognize that normative issues are illuminated by the recent descriptive work of cognitive psychologists and have devoted themselves to learning this work. The literature of cognitive psychology presents evidence of the sorts of mental processes that people use for particular problems and provides strong hints of the limits of human cognitive capacities. Goldman (1978) has argued that it makes little sense for philosophers to ignore such work and to propose cognitive procedures which people may be incapable of actually using, and he and other epistemologists have recognized that it is similarly pointless to criticize cognitive procedures that people do not actually use.

The concerns of this book are complementary. Recent descriptive work by cognitive psychologists and by social psychologists concerned with inference has unearthed cognitive procedures ranging from the dubiously effective to the patently inadequate. It makes little sense simply to describe such procedures and move on; they cry out for criticism. Indeed, some psychologists working in this tradition have assumed the critic's role. Beginning with classic work on decision making (Edwards 1954) and on clinical versus statistical prediction by Meehl (1955), psychologists in the judgment and decision-making traditions have allowed their empirical work to be guided by normative models and have compared both the layperson and the scientist to formal canons of inference. Investigators working in this newer, critical tradition include Herbert Simon and his collaborators, Daniel Kahneman and Amos Tversky, and the Oregon Decision Research Group of Paul Slovic, Sarah Lichtenstein, Robin Dawes, and Baruch Fischhoff. This book grows out of this critical tradition and draws heavily on the ideas and research of these investigators.

An equally important influence on the book comes from the cognitive tradition within social psychology. This tradition was founded in America by the neo-Gestaltist Kurt Lewin. Lewin's chief concern was with the cognitive structures and processes that produce actions in the social sphere. His representation of these structures and processes was quasi-geometrical, stemming perhaps from Gestalt psychology's spatial perception concerns. Lewin's representational mode depicting the "life space" of the individual by goal regions, barriers, forces, and vectors did not prove useful to investigators working in the tradition he established and, for the most part, has been abandoned. It has been replaced by more purely verbal concepts and relations such as those proposed by Fritz Heider in his classic book *The Psychology of Interpersonal Relations*. Heider proposed a very small list of subject terms (for example, *person, other, life space*) and predicate relations (for example, *can, ought, tries, suffers, benefits, harms, causes, wants*) to describe the phenomenology of person perception and the processes of interpersonal relations. Heider also introduced the notion of causal attribution as a fundamental process underlying much of social perception and action. Harold Kelley (1967), building on Jones's and Davis's (1965) earlier efforts, formalized Heider's conceptions of causal inference and drew the parallel between the layperson's methods of analysis and the scientist's.

Kelley's formulation of attribution theory brought the study of causal inference to the center stage of social psychology. What Kelley proposed, essentially, is that the layperson makes causal inferences using criteria analogous to those used by the trained social scientist. The layperson notes the covariation between particular "effects" (social acts and outcomes) and potential "causes" (the presence or absence of specific actors and particular features of the situation). From such observations, the layperson arrives at roughly the same conclusions that the academically tutored scientist would reach through more formal statistical analyses and more rigorously applied logical principles. For example, Sally infers that the "cause" of Jane's enthusiastic recommendation of Chez Paris was the quality of the restaurant rather than Jane's undiscriminating palate, ulterior motives, or chance, to the extent that certain essentially statistical criteria are met: Specifically, the recommendation should show *consistency* (Jane makes the same recommendation on many occasions and in many contexts), *distinctiveness* (Jane does not make similarly enthusiastic recommendations of all restaurants), and *consensus* (other patrons of Chez Paris seem to share Jane's enthusiasm).

The layperson, in traditional attribution theory, is capable of applying psychological, as well as logical and statistical insights. The layperson seems to know much about the situational pressures and constraints that influence human behavior, and causal attributions reflect such knowledge. Thus, a dollar given to a panhandler is apt to be attributed to the giver's generosity only to the extent that the situational context is free of the usual reasons for eliciting such gifts from "people in general." If the panhandler's demeanor suggested that a less generous "gift" might bring insults or physical abuse, or if the panhandler's plight seemed particularly sad, the intuitive psychologist would be far less likely to assume that the giver is particularly generous or to assign a critical causal role to such "generosity."

Kelley, in his 1967 article and in subsequent contributions (1972, 1973), cited many studies showing that lay causal attributions do correspond to normative standards of inference. Subsequent investigators (notably McArthur, 1972, 1976) also supported this view.

Kelley's formulation of attribution theory and his parallel between the inferential tasks of the layperson and those of the scientist provided the impetus for the present book. Each of us has done research on causal attribution processes. But through that work we have become increasingly more impressed with the evidence of people's departures from normative standards of inference and less impressed with the evidence of their adherence to them (Ross, 1977a). This concern has been augmented by our contact with researchers, most notably Amos Tversky and Daniel Kahneman, who are concerned with informal judgment. Their work has revealed profound, systematic, and fundamental errors in judgments and inferences. These errors are the major concerns of this book. We will consider the ways in which these errors deviate from normative standards of logical and scientific inference, the origins and underlying causes of these errors, and the implications of these errors both for social psychological theory and for the problems of everyday social life.

THE TOOLS OF THE INTUITIVE SCIENTIST

This book contends that the seeds of inferential failure are sown with the same implements that produce the intuitive scientist's more typical successes. These intuitive implements are of two broad types— "knowledge structures" which allow the individual to define and interpret the data of physical and social life and "judgmental heuristics" which reduce complex inferential tasks to simple judgmental operations.

Few, if any, stimuli are approached for the first time by the adult. Instead, they are processed through preexisting systems of schematized and abstracted knowledge—beliefs, theories, propositions, and schemas. These knowledge structures label and categorize objects and events quickly and, for the most part, accurately. They also define a set of expectations about objects and events and suggest appropriate responses to them. A price is paid for this mental economy, however. The knowledge structures themselves are not infallible guides to the nature of physical or social reality. Some beliefs, theories, and schemas are relatively poor and inaccurate representations of the external world. More dangerous, objects and events are not always labeled accurately and sometimes are processed through entirely inappropriate knowledge structures. Without these structures stored in memory, life would be a buzzing confusion, but their clarity is helpful only in proportion to their validity and to the accuracy with which they are applied to the data at hand.

Besides knowledge structures, people also use a few simple judgmental heuristics. These cognitive strategies, or rules of thumb, are the layperson's tools for solving a variety of inferential tasks. The two heuristics on which Kahneman and Tversky focused are the representativeness heuristic and the availability heuristic.

The representativeness heuristic allows the individual to reduce many inferential tasks to what are essentially simple similarity judgments. An object is assigned to one conceptual category rather than to another according to the extent to which its principal features represent or resemble one category more than another. A botanist assigns a plant to one species rather than another by using this judgmental strategy. The plant is categorized as belonging to the species that its principal features most nearly resemble. The problem with the heuristic is that it is sometimes used as the only judgmental strategy when it cannot alone provide an accurate judgment. When the known features of an object cannot categorize it definitely, statistical considerations become important to correct categorization. In particular, the relative frequency of the categories in the population under consideration becomes the normatively appropriate guide to categorization to the extent that the known features of the object are ambiguous guides to categorization. The work of Kahneman and Tversky (1973) shows that people have little understanding of these statistical considerations or of how to combine the statistical considerations with representativeness considerations.

The availability heuristic is used when judging frequency, probability, and even causality. Objects or events are judged as frequent, probable, or causally efficacious to the extent that they are readily "available" in memory. The heuristic is a fallible guide for such judgments because many factors besides actual frequency, statistical probability, or true causal efficacy affect the memorial availability of objects and events.

A final intuitive strategy involves weighting the relevance of one's data. We argue that people effectively assign inferential weight to physical and social data in proportion to the data's salience and vividness. Information is heeded, processed, stored, and retrieved in proportion to its sensory, cognitive, and affective salience. By default, more vivid information is more likely to enter inferential processes than is less vivid information. This strategy of evidential weighting is dangerous because the vividness of information is normally related only obliquely at best to its true value as evidence.

Thus, the layperson approaches the inferential tasks of everyday life armed with knowledge and with strategies that, for all their general helpfulness and efficiency, have many flaws. These flaws are compounded by the knowledge and the strategies that the layperson does *not* possess, or at any rate fails to use in many inferential tasks to which they are essential.

INFERENTIAL PROBLEMS AND THE FORMAL SCIENTIFIC REQUIREMENTS FOR THEIR SOLUTION

The formal inferential rule system followed by professional scientists is the standard against which the layperson is compared throughout this book. We believe that this comparison is not forced or artificial, nor is it entirely unfair to the layperson. Many of the inferential tasks that confront the layperson are directly analogous to those that confront the scientist. In addition, the layperson's inferential failings, we believe, often can be traced directly to ignorance of the formal scientific requirements for solving these inferential problems. It will be useful, therefore, to describe some of the inferential tasks confronting both the formal and the lay scientist.

The most basic inferential tasks are *descriptive*. The formal scientist must be able to characterize and describe accurately the individual *datum*—object, or event. When, as is usually the case, there is more than one object or event to be considered, the scientist must accurately characterize the *sample* of data, a task which entails several, mainly arithmetic operations. Often the sample of objects or events is treated as the evidential base for generalizing to some *population* of objects or events, a task which entails several statistical as well as arithmetic operations.

Many tasks require more than the mere description of single events (or samples or populations of a single type of event) and are concerned primarily with relationships between different types of events. The scientist often needs to observe *covariation* between events and to measure the magnitude of the covariation in terms of some defined criterion. If possible, principles or theories capable of *causally explaining* the covariation are formulated. The observed covariation and the postulated causal explanations then are used as the basis for *predicting* future events. For the formal scientist, all three tasks are governed by fixed statistical and logical principles.

Finally, the formal scientist adheres to a set of general rules for *theory testing*, which operate at every stage of the inquiry. There are rules for testing whether a given characterization of the datum, sample, or population is correct, whether events covary as believed, whether causal explanations are adequate, and whether predictions are valid guides to future events.

We argue that, in the context of daily life, the intuitive scientist is prone to make certain errors in solving the analogous inferential problems. These errors do not result from any inability to comprehend the principles of scientific inference. Indeed, almost all of the most frequently violated principles can be described on some level of abstraction and can be illustrated in some particular context that would be readily understood and accepted by any bright adolescent. The intuitive scientist, moreover, *does* readily apply many of the principles under certain circumstances—for example, when an appropriate "problem-solving set" is established and when the data and problem format prompt appropriate strategies and discourage inappropriate ones. Conversely, even the formal scientist is susceptible to many of the failings we shall describe, in everyday life and occasionally even in scientific endeavors. We will preview the intuitive scientist's shortcomings, each of which will be examined in later chapters.

DESCRIPTION. In characterizing the single *datum*, the intuitive scientist often is misled by prior theories of the object or event in question. Preexisting knowledge structures influence unduly, and often without the individual's awareness, the characterization of a given event. In characterizing *samples,* the lay scientist usually is at the mercy of the sample of events that can be retrieved from memory. This would present little difficulty if the only determinant of the memorability of events was their relative frequency. This clearly is not the case, however, since salience, retrievability, and other factors unrelated to true frequency, often influence the make-up of the sample of events that the individual can recall. Such biases in the "read-out" will create distortions in characterizing the sample. When the individual attempts to generalize from the characteristics of the sample to those of the *population,* two considerations become paramount—the size of the sample and its freedom from bias. The evidence indicates, however, that people have little understanding of the importance of either consideration. They seem to have little conception of the relative stability to be expected of the characteristics of a large set of observations or, conversely, of the instability and unreliability of the characteristics displayed in a small set of observations. More seriously, people seem to have little conception of the damage done by sample bias. They seem to be almost as willing to generalize from samples known to be biased in crucial parameters as to generalize from samples known to be unbiased.

DETECTION OF COVARIATION. There is no assumption as critical to contemporary attribution theory (or to any theory that assumes the layperson's general adequacy as an intuitive scientist) as the assumption that people can detect covariation among events, estimate its magnitude from some satisfactory metric, and draw appropriate inferences based on such estimates. There is mounting evidence that people are extremely poor at performing such covariation assessment tasks. In particular, it appears that a priori theories or expectations may be more important to the perception of covariation than are the actually observed data configurations. That is, if the layperson has a plausible theory that predicts covariation between two events, then a substantial degree of covariation will be perceived, even if it is present only to a very slight degree or even if it is totally absent. Conversely, even powerful empirical relationships are apt not to be detected or to be radically underestimated if the layperson is not led to expect such a covariation.

CAUSAL INFERENCE. When people have managed a detect a pattern of covariation, they still may fail to analyze correctly the possible causes of the covariation. In some instances, strong prior theories of causality may override the implications of the covariation pattern. In other instances, peoples' inferences about causality appear almost arbitrary or capricious because they are so heavily influenced by the perceptual salience of particular causal candidates. In still other instances, causal "schemas" or analytic strategies appropriate in some domains may "intrude" into domains to which they are inappropriate, causing more appropriate and helpful schemas to be overlooked.

PREDICTION. Even when people have recognized the true degree of covariation in a data set and have made correct causal inferences about the basis for the covariation, they may make normatively inappropriate predictions about future cases. Most critically, people appear to have little concept of the relevance of population base rates in general and regression phenomena in particular. When required to predict the outcome of an event, people tend to ignore the base rates, or relative frequencies of the outcome possibilities. When dealing with parametric observations, people tend to make "nonregressive" predictions that would be justified only if the empirical covariation were far greater than is usually the case in the social domain.

THEORY TESTING. People have few of the formal scientist's skeptical or disconfirmatory skills. Once formulated or adopted, theories and beliefs tend to persist, despite an array of evidence that should invalidate or even reverse them. When "testing" theories, the layperson seems to remember primarily confirmatory evidence and to ignore potentially disconfirmatory evidence. When confronted forcibly by disconfirmatory evidence, people appear to behave as if they believed that "the exception proves the rule."

JUDGMENT AND BEHAVIOR

Part 2 of the book documents errors in each of the judgmental domains just described. The reader not familiar with the research on judgment and inference might wonder whether people's *behavior* reflects the type of judgmental errors we discuss. We hasten to assure such readers that there is substantial evidence showing that behavior often reflects, indeed sometimes amplifies, these judgmental errors.

The attribution literature shows that people do not merely verbalize dubiously correct causal explanations but express them behaviorally both inside and outside the laboratory (when they often are unaware that they are subjects in an experiment). Behaviors which have been shown to reflect prior causal attributions include insomniacs' sleeplessness, stutterers' verbal productions, nursery-school children's willingness to cheat at games and college students' willingness to cheat on examinations, adults', adolescents', and children's time spent working on and playing at various activities, elementary school students' littering of school grounds, and housewives' willingness to place an ugly billboard advertising natural beauty on their lawns!

In the literature on judgment and decision making, the connection is even stronger since the judgments studied *are themselves* typically behaviors of very great importance: judgments by clinicians of the degree of patients' mental illness, judgments by social workers of a client's inclination toward child abuse, judgments by parole officers of convicts' likelihood of recidivism, judgments by faculty admissions committees of acceptance of applicants for graduate school, and judgments by stockbrokers of the advisability of purchasing particular stocks.

We do not emphasize these real-world, behavioral effects in our review of the literature because we believe the main points are not in dispute: People's judgments often affect their behavior, and both their judgments and their behavior reflect inferential errors outside the laboratory as well as in it.

We also say little about precisely *how* people's judgments affect their behavior. This is neither an oversight nor a deliberate choice. We simply acknowledge that we share our field's inability to bridge the gap between cognition and behavior, a gap that in our opinion is the most serious failing of modern cognitive psychology. The problem was perhaps first noted by E. R. Guthrie in his famous gibe at E. C. Tolman, who may be considered the founder of modern cognitive psychology. Professor Tolman's rat, Guthrie joked, can never reach the goal at the end of the maze but rather, is left at the start box—with its hypotheses, theories, and expectations—"buried deep in thought." Cognitive psychologists had made so little progress in treating behavioral matters that, decades later, Daryl Bem was obliged to admit that cognitive theories, including his own self-perception theory, "remain mute about any phenomenon in which the noncognitive response classes play the dependent variable role; as dependent variables such response classes are extra-theoretical. . . . How do attributional models account for noncognitive response classes? They do not" (1974, p. 217).

There is surely no more important task for cognitive psychologists than to bring these noncognitive response classes under their theoretical umbrella—to provide a way of explaining the circumstances under which, the manner in which and the degree to which, particular judgments influence particular behavior. Had we ourselves been able to make even tentative inroads into these problems, we would have done so.

COGNITIONS HOT AND COLD

Since this book is about inferential errors, the authors are bound to be asked whether such errors are not also the products of people's *motivational* and *emotional* make-up. We should confess from the outset the prejudice in our viewpoint. We proceed from the working hypothesis that inferential and judgmental errors arise primarily from nonmotivational—perceptual and cognitive—sources. Such errors, we contend, are almost inevitable products of human information-processing strategies. In ordinary social experience, people often look for the wrong data, often see the wrong data, often retain the wrong data, often weight the data improperly, often fail to ask the correct questions of the data, and often make the wrong inferences on the basis of their understanding of the data. With so many errors on the cognitive side, it is often redundant and unparsimonious to look also for motivational errors. We argue that many phenomena generally regarded as motivational (for example, self-serving perceptions and attributions, ethnocentric beliefs, and many types of human conflict), can be understood better as products of relatively passionless information-processing errors than of deep-seated motivational forces.

We have no wish, however, to deny that motives and emotions can influence human inference or to assert that all human follies can be explained by program error. Indeed, the perceptual and cognitive biases that we have described often operate on social data biased already by motivational and emotional factors. One's choice of friends, residence, occupation, news media, topics for reading and conversation, and perhaps even the social theories and theorists to whom we expose ourselves, all show the impact of such factors. To the extent that motives dictate social behavior, which in turn influences one's samples of information about the world, there is ample opportunity for social inferences to be distorted by needs and wishes. Our working assumption, therefore, is simply that self-serving motivational factors need not be introduced to explain most of the fundamental inferential or judgmental biases discussed in this book. In fact, as we shall see, the erroneous judgments, predictions, and causal assessments reached by the intuitive psychologist—far from being self-serving—often *undermine* self-esteem and *limit* the individual's capacity to satisfy personal needs.

THE QUESTION OF NORMATIVENESS: THE SCIENTIST AS CRITIC

Since this book is about inferential error, the question bound to arise in the minds of many readers is just how one knows that certain inferences are "erroneous," or, to turn the question around, how one knows that a given inferential strategy is "correct" or normatively appropriate. Our answer to this question is straightforward: We follow conventional practice by using the term "normative" to describe the use of a rule when there is a consensus among formal scientists that the rule is appropriate for the particular problem (cf. Stich & Nisbett, 1979). Some of the problems that we discuss, however, are relatively novel, and such "consensus" as exists is confined to the authors and the few colleagues with whom we have discussed the problems. In some cases, the term "normative" means "what the authors (and at least some other people) take to be the appropriate strategy." In these cases, the judgment that a given strategy is normatively appropriate is a tentative one that ultimately must be upheld or reversed by the court of informed opinion.

We do not doubt that many of our own current judgments about what is normatively appropriate will be overturned. In writing the book, we have changed our minds about too many normative questions too often to be under any illusions of the durability of these judgments. Moreover, we have become increasingly aware of the difficulty of defining what is "normative" when one moves beyond the relatively simple question of how to solve correctly some particular problem. "Normatively appropriate" strategies for the solution of some problems are extremely time consuming and expensive. It may be clear what must be done if one wishes a correct answer to such problems, but sometimes it may be even clearer that the correct solution is not worth the effort. This gives rise to more important questions of normativeness which are not fundamentally empirical in nature: How much effort, for what kinds of problems, should be expended to obtain a correct solution?

We have become excited by such normative questions and are pleased that our book highlights them. We have not been able to make much progress toward their solution, however, and do not return to them until the final chapters, in which they are discussed only briefly. It is our hope that others, particularly philosophers who are more comfortable with such questions, will be motivated to pursue them.

We wish to say something else about the role of scientist as critic. We know from past experience in presenting this material that some people are offended by the spectacle of their fellow human beings caught in inferential traps designed by smarter-than-thou psychologists. It may be helpful in forestalling this understandable response to emphasize that this book was written in a spirit of genuine humility. We have found that our richest source of data demonstrating human inferential failings comes not from the undergraduates in our experiments or classrooms but from ourselves and our friends, most of whom are trained social scientists. Consistent with this belief, we have mixed personal anecdotes with formal data throughout the book. For us, and we trust for the reader as well, these anecdotes often will prove more disconcerting than the formal empirical work.

A second reason for our humility is that we remain enormously impressed with the power and accomplishments of the human mind. In writing this book, we began to feel that workers in human inference are now in a position akin to that of investigators of human perception. Perception researchers have shown that in spite of, and largely because of, people's exquisite perceptual capacities, they are subject to certain perceptual illusions. No serious scientist, however, is led by such demonstrations to conclude that the perceptual system under study is inherently faulty. Similarly, we conclude from our own research that we are observing not an inherently faulty cognitive apparatus but rather, one that manifests certain explicable flaws. Indeed, in human inference as in perception, we suspect that many of people's failings will prove to be closely related to, or even an unavoidable cost of, their greatest strengths.

Our respect for intuitive inferences, however, should not obscure our conviction that there is considerable room for improvement. That improvement in inferential abilities can result from formal training, especially training in statistics, is readily documented. The general question of prophylaxis and cure for inferential shortcomings is the topic of our final chapter.

We wish, finally, to address a quite different kind of reader. In our experience, some people respond to the material in this book with the attitude "Well, I always knew most people were stupid, and this just proves it." We hope to show that this comforting attitude is not tenable. We hold a contrary view, expressed by Amos Tversky, that there is *no* inferential failure that can be demonstrated with untrained undergraduates that cannot also (at least with a little ingenuity) be demonstrated in somewhat more subtle form in the highly trained scientist. For any readers who may be inclined to exempt themselves from the inferential failings cited in this book, we present the following thought-experiment, which will serve as a touchstone for us at several points.

Let us suppose that you wish to buy a new car and have decided that on grounds of economy and longevity you want to purchase one of those solid, stalwart, middle-class Swedish cars—either a Volvo or a Saab. As a prudent and sensible buyer, you go to *Consumer Reports,* which informs you that the consensus of their experts is that the Volvo is mechanically superior, and the consensus of the readership is that the Volvo has the better repair record. Armed with this information, you decide to go and strike a bargain with the Volvo dealer before the week is out. In the interim, however, you go to a cocktail party where you announce this intention to an acquaintance. He reacts with disbelief and alarm: "A Volvo! You've got to be kidding. My brother-in-law had a Volvo. First, that fancy fuel injection computer thing went out. 250 bucks. Next he started having trouble with the rear end. Had to replace it. Then the transmission and the clutch. Finally sold it in three years for junk." (Nisbett, Borgida, Crandall, & Reed 1976, p. 129)

The logical status of the cocktail party information is that the number of Volvo-owners has increased from several hundred to several hundred and one, and that the frequency-of-repair record perhaps should be changed by an iota on a few dimensions. We trust that readers will recognize that their own response to the encounter would not be so trivial a statistical adjustment or be the calm observation that "every now and again one does sample from the tails of the distribution." We hope that the following chapters offer several such glimpses of the shortcomings of human inference in everyday life, and we are confident that the reader's response to some of these portraits will be a sheepish grin.

SUMMARY

The book traces the source of many inferential errors to two tendencies: the overutilization of certain generally valid, intuitive, inferential strategies and the underutilization of certain formal, logical, and statistical, strategies. The intuitive strategies include the application of preexisting "knowledge structures"—schemas, beliefs, and theories—and the utilization of the "representativeness" and "availability" heuristics.

The tasks of lay inference are compared with the tasks of the formal scientist, including characterization of events, samples and populations; assessments of covariation, causal analysis, prediction, and theory testing. The layperson's characterizations of events often are unduly influenced by prior beliefs or knowledge structures. Characterization of samples is distorted by the differential "availability" in experience and memory of various events. Characterization of the population is compromised by ignorance of statistical considerations, chiefly those of sample size and sample bias. Covariation assessment is overly influenced by prior theories of expected covariation and is insufficiently influenced by actual data configurations. Causal analysis suffers from a similar overutilization of prior theories and from overreliance on the sheer conspicuousness of potential causal candidates. People have little knowledge of the regression considerations underlying prediction tasks and substitute simple similarity or representativeness judgments. Finally, people have little appreciation of strategies for disconfirmation of theories and often persist in adhering to a theory when the number of exceptions to the theory exceeds the number of confirmations.

It is argued that people's behavior often reflects the errors apparent in their verbal judgments and that the erroneous judgments are best understood as cognitive failings rather than as motivational ones. The book raises, but makes little attempt to answer, important "normative" questions.

2

judgmental heuristics and knowledge structures

> The most characteristic thing about mental life, over and beyond the fact that one apprehends the events of the world around one, is that one constantly goes beyond the information given.
>
> *Jerome Bruner.*

The perceiver, as Bruner (1957) recognized, is not simply a dutiful clerk who passively registers items of information. Rather, the perceiver is an active interpreter, one who resolves ambiguities, makes educated guesses about events that cannot be observed directly, and forms inferences about associations and causal relations. In this chapter we explore the strategies that permit and encourage the perceiver to "go beyond the information given," that is, to venture beyond the most immediate implications of the data. We sketch some of the "knowledge structures" applied to understanding the world. These range from broad propositional theories about people in general to more schematic representations of objects, events, and actors. These structures house the person's generic knowledge and preconceptions about the world and provide the basis for quick, coherent, but occasionally erroneous interpretations of new experience.

Before discussing these structures, we will introduce the reader to the "availability heuristic" and the "representativeness heuristic"—two simple judgmental strategies on which people seem to rely, and by which they sometimes are misled, in a variety of inferential tasks. In so doing, the chapter introduces the reader to a set of extraordinarily important contributions by Daniel Kahneman and Amos Tversky (1972, 1973, in press; Tversky & Kahneman, 1971, 1973, 1974). We will draw continually upon these contributions in subsequent chapters of the book.

The heuristics to be explored are relatively primitive and simple judgmental strategies. They are not irrational or even nonrational. They probably produce vastly more correct or partially correct inferences than erroneous ones, and they do so with great speed and little effort. Indeed, we suspect that the use of such simple tools may be an inevitable feature of the cognitive apparatus of any organism that must make as many judgments, inferences, and decisions as humans have to do. Each heuristic or, more properly, the misapplication of each heuristic, does lead people astray in some important inferential tasks. Since this book is particularly concerned with inferential failings, it is the misuse of the heuristics—their application in preference to more normatively appropriate strategies—that we will emphasize.

Although we characterize the heuristics as "judgmental strategies," the term is misleading in that it implies a conscious and deliberate application of well-defined decision rules. The heuristics to be explored should be distinguished from straightforward computational or judgmental "algorithms" (such as the method for finding square roots or deciding whether one's bridge hand merits an opening bid), which generally are explicit and invariant both in the criteria for their use and the manner of their application. The intuitive psychologist probably would not assent to, much less spontaneously express, any general formulation of either heuristic. Instead, the utilization of the heuristics is generally automatic and nonreflective and notably free of any conscious consideration of appropriateness. As we shall see, the heuristics are not applied in a totally indiscriminate fashion. In many contexts in which a given heuristic would promote error, people refrain from using it and probably could articulate why its use would be foolish. On other logically equivalent and equally unpropitious occasions, people readily apply the same heuristic and may even attempt to justify its use.

THE AVAILABILITY HEURISTIC

When people are required to judge the relative frequency of particular objects or the likelihood of particular events, they often may be influenced by the relative *availability* of the objects or events, that is, their accessibility in the processes of perception, memory, or construction from imagination (cf. Tversky & Kahneman 1973). Such availability criteria often will prove accurate and useful. To the extent that availability is actually associated with objective frequency, the availability heuristic can be a useful tool of judgment. There are many factors uncorrelated with frequency, however, which can influence an event's immediate perceptual salience, the vividness or completeness with which it is recalled, or the ease with which it is imagined. As a result, the availability heuristic can be misleading.

Availability Biases in Frequency Estimation

Let us proceed first by introducing and then exploring in some detail three judgmental tasks for which application of the availability heuristic might lead one to biased estimates of the relative frequency of various objects or events. The first two examples are hypothetical (although we shall document closely related experimental results in later chapters).

(1) A pollster who asks a sample of American adults to estimate the "percentage of the work force who are currently unemployed" finds an "egocentric bias." That is, currently unemployed workers tend to overestimate the rate of unemployment, but currently employed workers tend to underestimate it.

(2) An Indiana businessman confides to a friend, "Did you ever notice how many Hoosiers become famous or important? Look anywhere—politics, sports, Hollywood, big business, even notorious bank robbers—I couldn't guess the exact figures, but I bet we Hoosiers have far more than our fair share on just about any list in *Who's Who.*"

(3) A group of subjects consistently errs in judging the relative frequency of two kinds of English words. Specifically, they estimate the number of words beginning with particular letters (for example, *R* or *K*) to be greater than the number of words with those letters appearing third, although words of the latter type actually are far more numerous.

Examples 1 and 2 seem to present common and familiar errors, although one might not immediately recognize the role of availability factors in producing them. In fact, some readers might hasten to cite motivational or even "psychodynamic" factors that could induce unemployed workers to overestimate the commonness of their plight or that could prompt proud Indiana residents to exaggerate their share of the limelight. Example 3 seems less intuitively obvious and at first seems quite unconnected to the other two examples. Nevertheless, the chief source of error in all three cases seems to us to be the availability heuristic.

Consider Example 1, about estimates of unemployment. Here the bias in subjective availability can be traced to a bias in initial sampling. Unemployed people are more likely to know and meet other unemployed people than are job-holders, and vice versa. The reasons for such a sampling bias are hardly mysterious: The unemployed individual is likely to share the neighborhood, socioeconomic background, and occupation of other jobless individuals. He also is likely to encounter other unemployed people in such everyday endeavors as job-hunting, visiting employment agencies, collecting unemployment benefits, and shopping at stores offering cut-rate prices or easy credit. Indeed, he even may seek out such individuals for social comparison, information exchange, or general commiseration. Thus, to the extent that the unemployed person relies upon the sample generated by his personal experience, he will be misled about the commonness of unemployment. In the same manner, employed people, who are apt to live, work, and shop near one another, are apt to err in the opposite direction.

It is important to emphasize that the people in this hypothetical example would not be compelled to rely upon biased availability criteria in estimating the frequency of unemployment. They could try to recall media presentations of data, could apply some popular rule of thumb ("When there's an energy shortage, jobs disappear"), or could employ some more appropriate "sampling procedure" ("How many people have I seen lining up outside my neighborhood unemployment office on the first of the month this year as compared with last year?"). They even could attempt to compensate for the biases distorting their samples of available data ("Hardly anyone I know is jobless, but of course, I don't get to meet many unemployed people, do I? I guess I'd better adjust my estimate upward!"). Indeed, it is quite likely that some people *would* avoid availability criteria or at least would attempt the necessary adjustments. Throughout this book, however, we present experimental evidence showing that simple, tempting, availability criteria are used in contexts in which availability and frequency are poorly correlated and are used without appropriate adjustments for the factors that bias subjective experience.

Now let us consider Example 2, about the relative prominence of Indiana natives. The Hoosier's egocentric estimate clearly contains some of the same features as in our initial example. That is, people from Indiana are disproportionately likely to know or hear about famous fellow Hoosiers. Beyond such biases in initial exposure, however, this example introduces the potential influence of additional biases in *storage*. When a national sportscaster says "Myra Swift of Grandville, Indiana and Mary Speed of Bigtown, Florida won gold medals in the Olympics yesterday," it is the accomplishment of his fellow Hoosier that the Indiana businessman is more likely to notice and to remember. Accordingly, the sample of famous people he subsequently can recall from memory will reflect biases at the "storage" stage as well as at the sampling stage.

Biases in exposure, attention, and storage can arise, of course, from many factors besides the kinship between the perceiver and the object. As we shall see in later chapters, for instance, oddity or newsworthiness could accomplish the same end. Thus, people from all states might overestimate the number of very big, very small, very young, very pretty, or very hirsute Olympic gold medalists because such factors would bias the rater's likelihood of sampling, storing, and recalling the pertinent instances.

Example 3, about estimates of the frequency of the letter *R* in the first versus the third position, is subtler. In fact, readers who try the experiment themselves may find that they make the same incorrect assessments of relative frequency as did the original subjects. Once again, an inappropriate application of the availability criterion is the source of the difficulty. Like the subjects in Tversky's and Kahneman's (1973) demonstration, the reader probably finds that instances of words beginning with *R* are easier to generate spontaneously (at least in a casual first attempt) than are instances of words that have *R* as their third letter. But the differences in ease of generation do not reflect corresponding differences in word frequency. Any truly *random* sample of English words would reveal words beginning with *R* to be much *less* common than words with *R* as their third letter. The relative difficulty of generating words like "care," "street," and "derail," may give interesting hints of the storage and retrieval of one's vocabulary, but it says virtually nothing about objective word frequencies.

An analogy may be instructive here: In a quick search of the library, one would find it easier to find books by authors named Woolf than by authors named Virginia, or to find books about Australia than books by authors born in Australia. Such differences obviously would indicate little about the relative frequencies of such books in the library's collection. Instead, they would reflect the library's system for referencing books and granting access to them. By the same token, first letters apparently are more useful cues than third letters are for referencing and permitting access to the items in one's personal word collection. Once again, the use of criteria other than the subjective ease of generation (or, alternatively, recognition of relevant biases and adequate compensation) could lead people to a more accurate estimate.

Availability of Event Relationships and of Causal Explanations

Kahneman's and Tversky's work has been largely on the use of the availability heuristic in judgments involving the frequency or probability of individual events. Other research indicates that subjective availability may influence judgments of *relationships* between events, particularly *causal* relationships.

Jones's and Nisbett's (1972) account of the divergent causal interpretations of actors and observers—from which observers cite "dispositional" factors (traits, abilities, attitudes, etc.) to explain behaviors and outcomes that the actors themselves attribute to "situational" factors—is one case in point. For example, the actor who gives a dollar to a beggar is apt to attribute his behavior to the sad plight of the beggar, but the observer of the behavior is apt to attribute it to the actor's generosity. From the actor's perspective, it is the constantly changing features of the environment that are particularly salient or "available" as potential causes to which his behavior can be attributed. From the observer's perspective, the actor is the perceptual "figure" and the situation merely "ground," so that the actor himself provides the most available causal candidate. Indeed, by altering actors' and observers' perspectives through videotape replays, mirrors, or other methods, one can correspondingly alter the actors' and observers' causal assessments (cf. Arkin & Duval 1975; Duval & Wicklund 1972; Regan & Totten 1975; Storms 1973).

Subsequent research by a number of investigators, most notably Taylor and her associates (for example, Taylor & Fiske 1975, 1978), has demonstrated a more general point regarding availability and causal assessment. It appears that almost *any* manipulation that focuses the perceiver's attention on a potential cause, for example, on a particular participant in a social interaction, affects causal assessment. Whether the attentional manipulation is achieved by a blunt instruction about which participant to watch, subtle variations in seating arrangement, or by "solo" versus "nonsolo" status of, for example, female or black participants, the person made disproportionately "available" to onlookers is seen to be a disproportionately potent causal agent. (See also McArthur & Post 1977; McArthur & Solomon 1978.)

Availability effects also may account for other biases involving perceived causality. Consider Fischhoff's (1975; Fischhoff & Beyth 1975) reports on the subjective certainty of hindsight knowledge. These reports show that outcomes often seem in retrospect to have been inevitable. This may be because the antecedents and causal scenarios that "predicted" such outcomes have far greater "after-the-fact" availability than do antecedents or scenarios that predicted alternative outcomes that did not in fact occur. In a smilar vein, Ross, Lepper, Strack, and Steinmetz (1977) demonstrated that *explaining* why some event is consistent with known preceding events (for example, explaining the suicide of a clinical patient whose case history one has examined) tends to increase the subjective likelihood that the event actually did occur. Again, the relevant mechanism appears to be the availability heuristic. The explanation creates a particular causal scenario, and its causal factors are disproportionately available to the perceiver when predictions are made later

In both hindsight and explanation, the subjective ease of generation appears to be important. The subjects seem to respond not only to the mere presence of potential causal scenarios but also to the relative ease with which they were detected or invented. People probably implicitly assume this subjective ease of generation to be somehow symptomatic of the scenario's likelihood or of the explanation's aptness.

Appropriate and Inappropriate Applications of the Availability Heuristic

An indiscriminate use of the availability heuristic clearly can lead people into serious judgmental errors. It is important to reemphasize that in many contexts perceptual salience, memorability, and imaginability may be relatively unbiased and therefore well correlated with true frequency, probability, or even causal significance. In such cases, of course, the availability heuristic often can be a helpful and efficient tool of inference.

The same jobless individuals whose estimates of unemployment rates were distorted by the availability heuristic could make a reasonably accurate estimate of the preponderance of oak trees to maple trees in their neighborhood by using the same strategy. In estimating the frequencies of various types of trees, the individual's personal experiences and subsequent recollections would constitute generally unbiased samples. Similarly, the Indiana resident who was misled by the disproportionate availability of instances of famous fellow Hoosiers might have fared quite well if the same heuristic had been applied in estimating the success of German Olympians relative to Italian Olympians. Furthermore, the "ease of generation" criterion would have helped rather than hindered Tversky's and Kahneman's subjects if the experimental task had been to estimate the relative frequencies either of a) words beginning with R versus words beginning with L, or b) words with R versus L in the third position. In either of these cases, differences in the relative ease of generation would have reflected differences in frequency quite accurately.

The normative status of using the availability heuristic, and the pragmatic utility of using it, thus depend on the judgmental domain and context. People are not, of course, totally unaware that simple availability criteria must sometimes be discounted. For example, few people who were asked to estimate the relative number of moles versus cats in their neighborhood would conclude "there must be more cats because I've seen several of them but I've never seen a mole." Nevertheless, as this book documents, people often fail to distinguish between legitimate and superficially similar, but illegitimate, uses of the availability heuristic.

THE REPRESENTATIVENESS HEURISTIC

The second judgmental heuristic to be introduced is one which Kahneman and Tversky (1972, 1973; Tversky & Kahneman 1974) termed the *representativeness* heuristic. This heuristic involves the application of relatively simple resemblance or "goodness of fit" criteria to problems of categorization. In making a judgment, people assess the degree to which the salient features of the object are representative of, or similar to, the features presumed to be characteristic of the category.

In the following sections we try to provide a coherent grouping of examples. It should be emphasized, however, that our classification system is neither exhaustive nor theoretically derived. We also should note that we make no attempt to specify the precise criteria by which individuals calculate the representativeness of one object or event to another. (For the interested reader, a recent but already classic paper by Tversky, 1977, takes a first step in this direction by introducing a formal theory of similarity judgments.)

Judgments of the Degree to Which Outcomes Are Representative of Their Origins

People often are required to predict some outcome or judge the likelihood of some event on the basis of information about the "generating process" that produced it. On such occasions, the judgment is likely to reflect the degree to which the specified outcome represents its origin. Let us consider an example adapted from one used by Kahneman and Tversky (1972):

> Subjects are asked to assess the relative likelihood of three particular sequences of births of boys (B) and girls (G) for the next six babies born in the United States. These sequences are i) BBBBBB, ii) GGGBBB, iii) GBBGGB.

According to the conventional probability calculation, the likelihood of each of these sequences is almost identical. (Actually, the first sequence is slightly more likely than either the second or third sequence, since male births are slightly more common than female births. The latter two sequences are simply different orderings of identical, independent events.) Subjects who rely upon their intuitions and upon the representativeness criteria which guide such intuitions, are apt to regard the GBBGGB sequence as far more likely than either of the other two. In doing so, they are responding to what they know about the population of babies and about the processes of "generation," that is, that each birth is a "random" event in which the probability of "boy" and "girl" are nearly equal. Only the GBBGGB sequence is "representative" of the generating process. The GGGBBB sequence seems too "orderly" to represent a random process. The BBBBBB sequence satisfies the criteria even less: It captures neither the randomness of the birth process nor the equal sex distribution of the population from which the six births were "sampled."

The representativeness heuristic also accounts for the familiar "gamblers' fallacy." After observing a long run of "red" on a roulette wheel, people believe that "black" is now due, because the occurrence of black would make the overall sequence of events more representative of the generating process than would the occurrence of another red. In a similar vein, any researcher who has ever consulted a random number table for an unbiased ordering of events has probably felt that the result was somehow insufficiently "representative" of a chance process, that it contained suspiciously orderly sequences, suspiciously long runs, suspicious overrepresentations or underrepresentations of particular numbers early or late in the sequence, and so forth (cf. Tversky & Kahneman 1971).

Judgments of the Degree to Which Instances Are Representative of Categories

Many everyday judgments require people to estimate the likelihood that some object or event with a given set of characteristics is an instance of some designated category or class. Typically, the judgments are made in relative terms, that is, is Event X more likely to be an instance of Class A or of Class B? Consider the following problem, which is similar in form to those in the empirical work by Kahneman and Tversky described in detail in a later chapter.

> The present authors have a friend who is a professor. He likes to write poetry, is rather shy, and is small in stature. Which of the following is his field: (a) Chinese studies or (b) psychology?

Those readers who quickly and confidently predicted "psychology" probably applied some version, whether sophisticated or crude, of conventional statistical canons. We congratulate these readers. We suspect, however, that many readers guessed "Chinese studies," or at least seriously considered that such a guess might be reasonable. If so, they probably were seduced by the representativeness heuristic. Specifically, they assessed the relative "goodness of fit" between the professor's personality profile and the predominant features of their stereotypes of Sinologists and psychologists. Finding the fit better for the former than for the latter, they guessed the professor's field to be Chinese studies.

In succumbing to the lure of the representativeness heuristic, what the reader likely has overlooked or not appreciated is some relevant category *base-rate* information. Let the reader who guessed "Chinese studies" now reconsider that guess in light of the relative numbers of psychologists and

Sinologists in the population. Then consider the more restricted population of people likely to be friends of the authors, who themselves are psychologists. Surely *no* reader's implicit personality theory of the strength of association between academic discipline and the professor's various characteristics, that is, poetry-writing, shyness, and slightness of stature, warrants overriding such base-rate considerations.

Errors in problems of the Sinologist/psychologist variety may reflect that the judge has been led to answer the wrong question or, more specifically, to ponder the wrong conditional probability. The judge seems to be responding to the question "How likely is it that a psychologist (versus a Sinologist) would resemble the personal profile provided?" when the actual question posed is "How likely is someone resembling the personality profile to be a psychologist (versus a Sinologist)?" The representativeness heuristic leads people to give a similar answer to the two questions, since it entails consideration only of the resemblance of the two occupational stereotypes to the given personality description. The error is the failure to consider the relevant base rates or marginal probabilities, a consideration which is irrelevant to the first question but critical to the second. Although a much higher proportion of Sinologists than of psychologists may fit the profile, there would still be a much greater *absolute* number of psychologists than of Sinologists who fit it, because of the vastly greater number of psychologists than of Sinologists in the population.

We discuss these issues at much greater length in subsequent chapters, especially in chapter 7 in which we discuss the effect of representativeness on a wide variety of prediction problems.

Judgments of the Degree to Which Antecedents Are Representative of Consequences

Earlier we contended that the availability of causal candidates, or of causal scenarios linking outcomes to potential antecedents, influences assessments of causality. We contend that representativeness criteria also may be important to such inferences. That is, a person who is required to account for some observed action or outcome may search the list of *available* antecedents for those that seem to be the most *representative* "causes" of the known "consequences."

Simple resemblance criteria appear to influence causal assessment just as they influence judgments of the representativeness of outcomes to origins or instances to classes. As we see in chapter 6, sometimes the resemblance criterion is used in a crude and unsophisticated way, as it is in primitive medical beliefs attributing a particular illness to an environmental agent with features resembling the illness. Sometimes its influence is less patent, as in the preference for motivational causes in explaining events with strong motivational or affective consequences or the preference for complicated, multifaceted causes for complicated, multifaceted outcomes.

Generally, the use of the representativeness heuristic in causal assessment is more than a simple comparison of the features of effects with those of their potential causes. Normally, people also use *theories* or general *knowledge* of the particular antecedents likely to cause or explain given outcomes and of the specific outcomes likely to follow given antecedents. A person's belief that the cause of Egypt's diplomatic initiative toward Israel was an heroic vision of Egypt's leader rather than economic exigency does not reflect merely a crude assessment of the similarity between historic gestures and heroic visions. Instead, such assessments reflect judgments of the similarity of known effects and potential causes to tacit or explicit models of cause-and-effect relations in international conduct. Application of the representativeness heuristic to the assessment of causality thus ranges from the crude and questionable requirement that potential causes resemble effects, to normatively proper strategies based on a comparison of the similarity of observed effects and potential causes to generalized cause-and-effect models in the given domain.

Appropriate and Inappropriate Applications of the Representativeness Heuristic

Even more than the availability heuristic, the representativeness heuristic is a legitimate, indeed absolutely essential, cognitive tool. Countless inferential tasks, especially those requiring induction or generalization, depend on deciding what class or category of event one is observing; such judgments inevitably hinge upon assessments of resemblance or representativeness (cf. Tversky 1977). Even in our examples, the use of the representativeness heuristic produced errors only because it was overapplied or misapplied while normatively important criteria were overlooked. Let us briefly reconsider each of those examples.

In the case of the representativeness of the outcome to the origin, the problem is clearly one of overapplication. The insight that the features of the sample ought to resemble those of the population or the generating process is generally valid. It leads people to recognize that an all-male or an all-white jury is more likely to reflect a biased selection procedure than will a jury with a more proportionate representation of the overall population. It also leads people to cry foul when a politician's cronies seem to enjoy a disproportionate share of good luck in their transactions with local or state agencies. Unfortunately, when people's understanding of the generating process and its implications is deficient—as when there are misconceptions about randomness—the representativeness heuristic will mislead.

In the second example, the Sinologist/psychologist problem, people are foiled mainly because important information is neglected, that is, the relevant base rates are ignored. In many circumstances, of course, such information is absent, and the representativeness heuristic has no serious contender. In other circumstances, base-rate information may have little practical significance. Sometimes the feature-matching process results in a category determination with a probability near 1.0, and when features are as power-fully diagnostic as that, there is little practical need to consider base rates. For example, in the Sinologist/psychologist problem, if the profile were extended to include the information that the person speaks Chinese, knows no statistics, and has never heard of B. F. Skinner, the relevance of base-rate fre-quencies would dwindle to triviality. There are also occasions when represen-tativeness criteria can be used directly without violating normative standards because the base rates or marginal probabilities are approximately equal. If the Sinologist/psychologist problem were altered to a decision between a sociologist and an historian, the representativeness heuristic would serve the judge quite well, providing that the relevant occupational stereotypes had at least some validity.

KNOWLEDGE STRUCTURES: THEORIES AND SCHEMAS

We have discussed some of the judgmental strategies that people use in a variety of social inference tasks. Often, however, people's understanding of the rapid flow of continuing social events may depend less on such judgmental procedures than on a rich store of general knowledge of objects, people, events, and their characteristic relationships. Some of this knowledge may be represented as beliefs or *theories,* that is, reasonably explicit "propositions" about the characteristics of objects or object classes. (For example: Joe is kind to small animals. Rotarians are public spirited. Adult neuroses have their "origin" in childhood trauma. Decision makers prefer minimax strategies.) People's generic knowledge also seems to be organized by a variety of less "propositional," more *schematic,* cognitive structures (for example, the knowledge underlying one's awareness of what happens in a restaurant, one's understanding of the Good Samaritan parable, or one's conception of what an introvert is like). To describe such knowledge structures, psychologists refer to a growing list of terms, including "frames" (Minsky 1975), "scripts" (Abelson 1976; Schank & Abelson 1977), "nuclear scenes" (Tomkins 1979), and "prototypes" (Cantor & Mischel 1977, in press), in addition to the earlier and more general term "schemas" (Bartlett 1932; Piaget 1936; also Rumelhart 1976).

In the following discussion we largely forsake any attempt at classifying or defining the possible structures. (See Schank & Abelson 1977, Abelson 1978, and Taylor & Crocker 1980.) We do, however, observe the distinction between beliefs or theories that can be summarized in one or more simple propositions, and other more schematic structures. Both types of knowledge structures are important because they provide an interpretative framework for the lay scientist—one that resolves ambiguity and supplements the information "given" with much "assumed" information.

Theories and Their Impact

In the following chapters we emphasize repeatedly the extent to which the intuitive scientist's data are assimilated to preexisting impressions, beliefs, and theories. Chapter 4 describes how theory-based preconceptions guide the initial process of data coding. Chapters 5, 6, and 7 examine respectively, the effect of such preconceptions on biasing estimates of covariation, assessments of causality, and predictions of one variable from knowledge of another. Chapter 8 deals with the processes by which theories survive, and occasionally yield to, various evidential or logical challenges. Chapter 9 discusses the part played by implicit theories in the lay scientist's understanding of his own behavior and mental processes. Our final two chapters expand upon the potential cost and benefits that accrue to the theory user. In this chapter, we restrict ourselves to emphasizing the role of lay psychological theory first in the application of the representativeness heuristic and then in a variety of attributional judgments. The types of theories to be considered vary from the relatively narrow generalizations that people make about particular individuals or groups, to the broadest conceptions of human nature and the determinants of human behavior.

Theory-based Judgments of Representativeness

As we noted earlier, assessments of representativeness often depend less on simple similarity criteria than on more sophisticated "theories" of the types of attributes and events that occur together, or that cause each other. For example, scandal in a parliamentary government is a "representative" cause of an impending election. When a scandal occurs we expect an election and when an election is called we are apt to cite any previous scandal as a contributing cause. The reason for such judgments clearly is not in the relative similarity of the outstanding features of political scandals and parliamentary elections. Rather, the judgment reflects one's adherence to a pair of "theoretical" propositions, first, that scandals weaken governments and second, that weakened governments in parliamentary democracies often must go to the electorate for a vote of confidence. Sometimes, as we shall see, the preconceptions governing causal inferences and likelihood assessments may best be regarded not as a set of propositions but as a schema or "script" (cf. Abelson 1976) in which a succession of "scenes" are linked in a single coherent structure—for example, accusations, denials, fresh accusations, limited acknowledgments of bad judgment and mendacity, resignations, and a final emotional appeal by the political leader for support at the polls.

People rely upon an enormous number of such theories, which are derived from personal experience and from the accumulated wisdom of one's culture, to decide on the representativeness of causes and effects, outcomes and outcome-generating processes, and objects and classes. The costs and benefits of relying upon such specific prior theories, rather than collecting and analyzing further data, for instance, depend both on the accuracy of the theories and on the feasibility of employing other, more empirical procedures.

Global Theories and Situational Versus Dispositional Attribution

Perhaps the most significant and far-reaching of the intuitive scientist's theories are those addressing the general causes of human behavior. These theories determine the meaning we extract from social interaction, and, in large measure, they determine the way we behave in response to the actions of our fellows. For example, the lay scientist, like the professional psychologist, believes that rewards for particular behaviors increase the subsequent likelihood of such behaviors and that punishment decreases their likelihood. The lay scientist, like the professional, believes that people's behavior is guided by plans and goals and believes that people seek to maximize pleasure and minimize pain. Such tacit, "global" theories, as well as many more specific theories, including theories about specific individuals or classes of individuals, govern our understanding of behavior—our causal explanations of past behavior and our predictions of future behavior.

There has been surprisingly little research on those beliefs and theories shared by the mass of people in our culture. Heider (1958) was perhaps the first to emphasize their importance, and Abelson (1968) was the first (and very nearly the only) investigator to attempt to study them empirically. What little research has been done on people's theories has focused on individual differences in the beliefs and theories. Christie and Geis (1970), for example, identified a set of cynical views about human nature that characterizes the highly "Machiavellian" individual and explains his success in manipulating his more trusting peers. Even more relevant to present concerns, Rotter and others (Rotter 1966; Collins 1974; Crandall, Katkovsky, & Crandall 1965;

Lefcourt 1972) investigated general inclinations toward internal versus external explanations (that is, personal effort and ability versus the vicissitudes of chance) in accounting for personal and social outcomes. More recently, Seligman (1975), discussed the part that people's theories of the controllability of outcomes and of the causes of success and failure may have in the clinical syndrome of depression.

The most general and encompassing lay theory of human behavior—so broadly applied that it might more aptly be termed a "metatheory"—is the assumption that behavior is caused primarily by the enduring and consistent dispositions of the actor, as opposed to the particular characteristics of the situation to which the actor responds. Throughout this book we refer to what Ross (1977a, 1978; Ross & Anderson 1980) called the "fundamental attribution error"—the tendency to attribute behavior exclusively to the actor's dispositions and to ignore powerful situational determinants of the behavior. In chapter 6, we argue that such errors are determined partially by perceptual factors. Such errors probably are also prompted partially by domain-specific theories, for example: "Successful people are ambitious and motivated"; "People who hurt others' feelings are rude and not well 'brought up.' " But in large measure the error, we suspect, lies in a very broad proposition about human conduct, to wit, that people behave as they do because of a general disposition to behave in the way that they do.

It is difficult to prove that people adhere to anything like an overarching "general theory" of the relative impact of dispositional versus situational factors. There is reason to suspect, nevertheless, that a rather general, "dispositionalist theory" is shared by almost everyone socialized in our culture. Certainly, it is a part of the world view of the so-called Protestant ethic that one's virtues and successes ultimately reflect one's worthiness and, conversely, that one's vices and failings reflect one's unworthiness. According to this view, good or bad luck, accidents of birth, and situational adversities may forestall matters but one's fate will eventually mirror one's character, and one's personal traits and abilities will ultimately prevail over circumstances. This message is as present in Henry Fielding's novels as it is in Horatio Alger's sentimental doggerel. It is the set of beliefs which Max Weber (1904) long ago identified as a precondition for the rise of capitalism, and it is consistent with the many philosophical positions that have assigned central roles to the concepts of personal responsibility and free will. The "dispositionalist theory," in short, is thoroughly woven into the fabric of our culture. Not surprisingly, therefore, children growing up in our culture come to hold an increasingly dispositional view of the causes of behavior (Ross, Turiel, Josephson, & Lepper 1978).

The opposite view, the "situationalist" position, does not lack advocates. It is espoused by most contemporary experimental social psychologists, behaviorists, and role-theory sociologists. (In a sense, the view is also part of the economic determinism of classical Marxism.) This alternative view, which was perhaps first explicitly articulated by Lewin (1935), maintains that behavior is understood best in terms of states and intentions that are themselves the product of those situational stimuli pertinent to the individual at the moment of action. Such a view garners support, to which we will refer in later chapters, from two sources: One is the failure of researchers to demonstrate anything like the cross-situational consistency in behavior demanded by the dispositionalist view (cf. Hartshorne & May 1928; Newcomb 1929; and more generally Mischel 1968). The second source of support for the situationalist position is in the many studies that demonstrate that seemingly insubstantial manipulations of situational factors can control behavior dramatically and can greatly restrict individual differences. The mass of people may be seen to act in ways that seem either cowardly or brave, honest or dishonest, prejudiced or unprejudiced, or apathetic or concerned, depending on the situational constraints and opportunities present at the time of action.

We do not wish to imply that the evidence massively or unambiguously supports a situationalist view. The recent "metatheory shift" in the social sciences, like all such metatheory shifts or new "paradigms" (Kuhn 1962) is currently quite underdetermined by the available data. Perhaps the chief evidence supporting the situationalist view is the continuing ability of social scientists, even those who subscribe to the situationalist view, to be surprised by evidence both of the lack of individual consistency in dispositional tendencies and of the power of manifestly "weak" situational factors to control behavior.

Whether it is the layperson's metatheory or the social scientist's that is correct (cf. Bem & Allen 1974, Bem & Funder 1978), the metatheory exerts a pronounced influence on people's judgments of the causes and meanings of behavior. Often, as we will demonstrate, this marked dispositional bias can be shown to be incorrect.

Schemas, Scripts, and Personae

To understand the social world, the layperson makes heavy use of a variety of knowledge structures normally not expressed in propositional terms and possibly not stored in a form even analogous to propositional statements. In describing these cognitive structures we shall use the generic designation "schema" and will comment in detail about only two types of schemas—event-schemas, or "scripts," and person-schemas, or "personae."

The most basic type of schema is probably that which underlies the use of common concepts or categories such as *dog, tree,* or *chair,* or concepts of far greater or lesser generality *(animals, flora,* and *furniture,* or *Airedales, Ponderosa*

pines, and *Chippendales*). In recent years there has been an explosion of interest
in and research on people's use of categories, and we cannot digress to summarize this important and ever-expanding literature. Let us note merely that
the "classic" view of a category, one that entails clearly specified boundaries
and a set of defining characteristics necessary to and sufficient for category
membership, has come under increasingly devastating attack (cf. Wittgenstein 1953; Rosch 1978; Tversky 1977). Gradually it has been supplanted by
a more lenient and catholic view—one that allows ambiguous boundaries,
recognizes a variety of differing bases for assessing category membership, and
permits individual members to differ in their prototypicality. What both the
traditional and newer views have in common is the notion that the category
and the concept underlying it form an important basis for inference. That is,
once the criteria for applying the concept have been met, the concept user
readily assigns a number of additional characteristics to the entity. For example, upon deciding on the basis of a particular animal's appearance that it is a
"dog," one makes the inferential leaps that it is trainable, capable of loyalty,
able to bark, and likely to chase cats but is unlikely to climb trees, purr, or
wash its coat.

In principle one could speak of a dog "schema," or even an Airedale
schema or an animal schema. In practice, however, the term "schema" has
come to be differentiated from the term "concept." Since its introduction in
the 1930s by Bartlett (1932) and by Piaget (1936), the term "schema" has
been used more and more to refer to those mental structures having a *dynamic*
or *relational* aspect. For example, Piaget refers to a "thumb-sucking" schema
and a "conservation" schema, both of which, despite the enormous difference in their level of abstractness, have dynamic relationships among the
schema's components. In the former, the schema is a kind of mental summary of the sensory, cognitive, and motor experiences in a sequence of actions involving body parts. In the latter, the schema represents experiential
knowledge of the relationship between mass and volume (or number and position) and the outcomes likely to result from various action sequences involving a fixed mass of material (or a fixed number of objects).

Kelley (1972b) introduced to the attribution literature the notion of a
causal schema. Kelley used the term to refer primarily to a highly abstract,
content-free notion of the formal relations among causes and effects. He
proposed that people possess in very abstract and general form the notions of
sufficiency and necessity in causal relations. This distinction underlies a
number of specific causal schemas, such as the single necessary cause schema
(in which the existence of the effect carries with it the certainty that a particular cause was present) and the multiple sufficient cause schema (in which
the existence of the effect implies the possibility of each of several causes).
There also are more complicated general schemas. For example, people may
have a "discounting" schema: Given an effect capable of being produced by

several causes and certain knowledge of the operation of a particular cause, people reduce their subjective probability that each of the other sufficient causes were operative. People also may possess an inhibitory cause schema: Given knowledge of the existence of a factor operating to block the occurrence of the effect, people infer that one or more facilitative causes were unusually powerful.

Though we are not confident that people actually possess such content-free causal schemas, we will use the term occasionally, to refer primarily to causal-analytic strategies that people do *not* seem to understand or to use in situations in which they would be helpful.

Scripts

The lexicons of cognitive social psychology and artificial intelligence recently were enriched by the introduction of the "script" concept (Abelson 1976, 1978; Schank & Abelson 1977). A script is a type of schema in which the related elements are social objects and events involving the individual as actor or observer. Unlike most schemas, scripts generally are event sequences extended over time, and the relationships have a distinctly causal flavor, that is, early events in the sequence produce or at least "enable" the occurrence of later events. A script can be compared to a cartoon strip with two or more captioned "scenes," each of which summarizes some basic actions that can be executed in a range of possible manners and contexts (for instance, the "restaurant script" with its "entering," "ordering," "eating," and "exiting" scenes). Alternatively, a script can be represented as a computer program with a set of tracks, variables, relationships, operations, subroutines, loops, and the like, which are "instantiated" with particular values for any particular application of the script. Thus, the restaurant script has a coffee shop track, a Chinese restaurant track, a cafeteria track, perhaps even a McDonald's track. The variable representing the decor may take on the value "fancy" or "crummy." The waiter values include "polite," "surly," and "bad enough to prompt a complaint." Exiting entails the operational options "pay waiter" or "pay cashier," and so forth.

Scripts can vary in many ways. They can be highly abstract, culturally pervasive, and may owe their existence only slightly to direct personal experience (for example, the script that links "temptation," "transgression," and "retribution"). Or they may be highly concrete, idiosyncratic, and directly tied to experience (for example, the scripted episode in which Daddy comes home from work, asks Mommy what's for dinner, she gets annoyed and sulks and, depending on what his day has been like, he either apologizes or gets angry too). The importance of scripts to the intuitive scientist lies in the speed and ease with which they make events (or secondhand accounts of events) readily comprehensible and predictable. Their potential cost, as always, is the possibility of erroneous interpretations, inaccurate expectations, and inflexible modes of response.

Personae

Central to any dramatic script is the *dramatis personae,* or cast of characters. Indeed, to specify the characters is often sufficient to convey much of the action of the script (for example, "the prostitute with the heart of gold and the scholarly but naive young man" or "the crusty but benign older physician and the hot-headed, idealistic young surgeon").

Social judgments and expectations often are mediated by a class of schemas which we shall term "personae," that is, cognitive structures representing the personal characteristics and typical behaviors of particular "stock characters." Some personae are the unique products of one's own personal experience (good old Aunt Mary, Coach Whiplasch). Others are shared within the culture or subculture (the sexpot, the earth-mother, the girl-next-door, the redneck, the schlemiel, the rebel-without-a-cause). Many of the shared personae are borrowed from fiction (Shakespeare's tortured Hamlet or television's bigoted Archie Bunker) or even from the popularized professional jargon of psychology and psychiatry (the authoritarian, the "Type A" personality, the anal-compulsive).

Our store of personae is augmented further by metaphors drawn from the animal kingdom and from the many occupational roles in our society. Animal or occupational personae are apt to be very simple and "concept-like," primarily highlighting a limited set of physical or behavioral characteristics. Hence, we readily understand, and are apt to be strongly influenced by, remarks like, "What do you see in that big *ox*," or "I wouldn't trust that *viper* if I were you," or "He wants you to be his Haldeman," or "Surgeon Blochit is a real butcher" (or, alternatively, "Butcher Phelps is a real surgeon").

In each instance the persona constitutes a knowledge structure which, when evoked, influences social judgments and behaviors. Once the principal features or behaviors of a given individual suggest a particular persona, subsequent expectations of and responses to that individual are apt to be dictated in part by the characteristics of the persona.

The concept of a persona is not essentially different from that of a stereotype. We prefer the term persona, however, because it lacks the pejorative implications of the term "stereotype," which has been used to describe culturally shared, indeed hackneyed, notions of particular groups of people. The persona is also similar to the notion of a "person-prototype," proposed and investigated by Cantor and Mischel (1977, in press).

Availability, Representativeness, and the Arousal of Knowledge Structures

The notion that the layperson's experience, understanding, and inferences are structured by a great and varied store of schemas is intuitively satisfying. Indeed, it has become increasingly clear to theorists working in almost all areas of psychology that the schema construct is a cornerstone of psychological theory (Neisser 1976). Workers in social interaction (Berne 1964; Goffman 1959), personality and psychopathology (G. Kelly 1955, 1958), visual perception (Minsky 1975), and especially in language comprehension and artificial intelligence (Abelson 1978; Bobrow & Collins 1976; Bower, Black & Turner in press; Rumelhart, 1976; Rumelhart & Ortony 1976; Schank 1975) all have made essentially the same point—that objects and events in the phenomenal world are almost never approached as if they were *sui generis* configurations but rather are assimilated into preexisting structures in the mind of the perceiver.

Unfortunately, the increasing conviction that schemas exist and are important has not been accompanied by a commensurate increase in our knowledge of them. There still is little evidence that might clarify their properties or define the type of work they perform. Most critical of all, perhaps, is our ignorance of the conditions of their instigation and use. In 1961, De Soto wrote of our "crippling ignorance of the dynamics of schema arousal" (p. 22), and a decade later Kelley (1972b) was obliged to echo De Soto's complaint. Recently, however, matters have begun to improve. For instance, Markus (1977) showed that the speed with which information about the self is processed may be predicted by the presence or absence of schematic self-concepts or "self-schemas." Similarly, Cantor's and Mischel's work (1977, in press) documented the biasing effects of person schemas or "prototypes" on the interpretation of ambiguous information and the recall of specific details about people.

Perhaps the most encouraging development for the question of schema arousal is the theoretical one in Kahneman's and Tversky's work on heuristics. It is obvious that a schema can be aroused only if it exists in the person's long-term repertoire of schemas. What is not so obvious is that the *acute or transient availability* of a schema also may be an important determinant of its application to a particular instance. Two recent experiments support this possibility.

Higgins, Rholes, and Jones (1977) asked subjects to read a brief paragraph describing a young man and then to evaluate him on a number of dimensions. The young man was described as having many risky hobbies, having a high opinion of his abilities, having limited relationships with other people, and being unlikely to change his mind or turn back from a chosen course of action. Before reading about the young man, subjects had par-

36

ticipated in a "learning experiment" in which some were exposed to the words "adventurous," "self-confident," "independent," and "persistent," and some were exposed to the words "reckless," "conceited," "aloof," and "stubborn." Subjects exposed to the positive words later evaluated the young man more highly than did those exposed to the negative words. (Subjects exposed to equally positive or negative but conceptually irrelevant words were uninfluenced.) As Higgins and colleagues suggest, this effect is most likely mediated by the transient availability of different concepts or "personae."

Hornstein, LaKind, Frankel, and Manne (1975) performed an experiment with similar implications. Before playing a prisoner's dilemma game, subjects were left seated in a waiting room listening to what they believed was a piped-in radio program. The music was interrupted for a "human interest" story. In one instance this was a heart-warming account of someone who offered a kidney to someone whom he did not know who was in need of a transplant. In another instance, subjects heard a ghastly account of an urban atrocity. The vignette had pronounced effects on subsequent strategy in the prisoner's dilemma game. Subjects who had heard the heart-warming vignette played the game in a much more cooperative way than did those who had heard the horror. The authors argued persuasively (and with data) against a mood interpretation of the subsequent behavior. Instead, it seems likely that it was an acute manipulation of the availability of different personae or "schemas for the human race" that accounted for the results ("most people are basically decent and kind" versus "it's dog eat dog out there").

It seems equally clear that the representativeness heuristic takes part in the selection of schemas. Indeed, the similarity of the data at hand to some stored representation of objects and events always has been presumed to be the chief determinant of schema arousal and application. But it also seems likely that purely incidental and irrelevant features of the stimulus may prompt the arousal of schemas tagged with similar incidental features. Thus, we have it on the testimony of Colonel House (May 1973) that, on the eve of World War I, President Woodrow Wilson was anguishing over the possibility of war with *Great Britain*. Why? Because, as on the eve of the War of 1812, the British were illegally searching American ships and, as Wilson agonized to House, "Madison and I are the only Princeton men to become President"(!) Apparently, the "search-ships/war with England" schema was a representative one for Wilson in part because of the irrelevant surface detail of the alma mater of the incumbent president.

Availability and representativeness determinants of schema arousal appear to be the probable focal guides of future research in this area. It will be fascinating to see whether these determinants operate in a normatively appropriate way, or whether, as in the Wilson anecdote, they operate so as to leave us at the mercy of arbitrary and incidental features of stimuli and structures.

Appropriate and Inappropriate Utilization
of Knowledge Structures

It would be even more foolish to criticize people's general tendency to employ schemas and other knowledge structures than it would be to criticize their general tendency to rely on the availability and representativeness heuristics. Indeed, the primary reason for the widespread acceptance of the notion of schematic knowledge structures is that it is almost impossible to imagine how mental life could be managed without them. In a world characterized by recurrent stimuli presenting important functional equivalencies, any cognitive system that places a premium on minimizing computing time and effort must take advantage of such redundancy by storing generic concepts, events, event-sequences, and the like.

Despite the important efficiencies that accrue to the schema user, there seems little doubt there often are serious costs as well. Schemas are apt to be overused and misapplied, particularly to the social sphere, and they are apt to be used when other, less rapid and intuitive methods of judgment would fully merit the additional time and effort required.

In the physical world, stimuli categorized in a particular way, or events interpreted in terms of a given schema, may be similar to an extent rarely true in the social domain. In many important respects, it is only a slight overstatement to say that "if you've seen one oak tree, you've seen them all." The number of properties necessary to define uniquely many types of physical objects is highly limited. As a consequence, the number of properties of a particular object that must be perceived in order to place the object in its correct category also is limited. Moreover, once a physical object has been placed in some conceptual category, one can usually disregard much of the information that dictated the categorization (that is, information specifying exactly how, when, and under what observation conditions a particular tree satisfied the requirements for assignment to the "oak" category). Most important of all, classification of a physical object usually permits one to adduce or predict confidently additional properties of the object. Thus, once an object is correctly characterized as an oak tree, it is nearly certain that the tree will provide shade and acorns, that its wood will be hard and burn slowly, that all its leaves will drop in the fall, and so on.

It is quite different in the social domain, in which the observed properties are less diagnostic, in which the number of properties suggestive of a given category are not so sharply delineated, and in which the number of properties that can be inferred confidently, given correct categorization of the object, is very small. To appreciate these differences, let us note how the categorization of a person as a "bigot" differs from the categorization of an object as an oak tree. First, the number of properties that might indicate bigotry is, for all practical purposes, infinite, and information about the circumstances in which a particular person satisfied the "bigot" criterion can be ignored or forgotten only at one's peril. Similarly, the number of properties dictated by the categorization of someone as a bigot is large only in proportion to the naiveté of the perceiver. Few characteristics or behaviors can be confidently assumed about any particular "bigot." Schemas in the social domain rarely are more than rough outlines and tentative guides for perception and behavior. When they are relied on heavily, there are bound to be inferential errors and misguided actions.

E. R. May, in his fascinating book entitled *"Lessons" of the Past* (1973), presented some thought-provoking examples of erroneous political judgments and policies that seem to have originated in the overutilization or misapplication of particular schemas. For example, May describes how a schema, which might be termed the "Munich Conference" script, 'exerted an undue influence on the thinking of politicians (most notably President Lyndon Johnson), who invoked the specter of the infamous "Munich Conference" to defend the aggressiveness of their military policy or the intransigence of their diplomacy. These politicians seem to have been influenced greatly by—or perhaps hoped to influence the public and their potential detractors through—a particularly vivid, historic script. The script has two scenes or vignettes, *"The Political Compromise,"* in which one yields to a power-hungry and unprincipled foe, and *"The Military Consequence,"* in which one's country or that of one's ally is subsequently overrun by the foe. To the extent that politicians rely on such historical scripts, they may be unduly dogmatic and constrained and may be unresponsive to features that ought to distinguish a current political decision from an historical one. They may even be unduly responsive to prominent but superficial considerations of script representativeness, that is, the Munich script may be particularly likely to be evoked if the foreign leader requests the conference in his own country rather than on neutral grounds or if he has a small moustache!

A "persona" can mislead as badly as a script can, as other examples from May's book show. President Harry Truman, a man not given to speaking kindly of all whom he met, demonstrated a peculiar willingness to trust his wartime ally, Joseph Stalin. His personal correspondences reveal a surprising source of this trust. To Truman, Stalin evoked the persona of Tom Pendergast, his former Missouri benefactor. Pendergast was a ruthless and corrupt political kingmaker, but he had always been completely trustworthy in his relations with Truman. Apparently because some of Stalin's characteristics were representative of the Pendergast persona, Truman seemed to feel that other Pendergast characteristics also could be assumed—specifically, trustworthiness in matters relating to Truman.

To May's examples of schema-induced errors in the judgment of politicians, we add one related to us by Dorwin Cartwright. Cartwright told us that spokesmen for the pure sciences, lobbying for financial aid in the postwar period of the late forties and early fifties, effectively argued that the technological innovations of World War II had "depleted the stockpile of basic knowledge." Congressmen, accustomed to arguments about the depletion of stockpiles and the need for replenishing them, apparently accepted the idea that the "basic knowledge stockpile" was one of those depleted. The "stockpile" concept, as applied to basic scientific knowledge, is not entirely invalid, that is, the more knowledge the better, the more money and effort spent, the faster it will grow, and so on. But the "depletion" schema is invalid and highly misleading. For heavy use of basic scientific knowledge, far from exhausting the "stockpile," makes it grow.

Our examples so far have been of the misapplication of particular schemas when more cautious and critical application of the same schemas would have served the intuitive scientist quite well. It is possible, however, to describe particular conceptual categories, scripts, or personae that are so lacking in foundation and predictive value that they almost invariably serve the user badly. Many racial or ethnic stereotypes fit this designation. The Volvo-Saab "thought experiment" described in chapter 1 is another example. The brother-in-law's litany of mechanical woes derives its impact, in part, from its ability to evoke the familiar "lemon" schema that haunts most prospective car buyers. Such a schema invites the assumption that mechanical difficulties are not distributed in a normal curve but that there is instead a distinct "bump" at the high-difficulty end of the continuum. It is doubtful that there is such a bump, and if there is not then it is clearly counterproductive to direct one's efforts toward avoiding a mythical lemon when one's efforts could be better directed toward obtaining a car with the best overall record for trouble-free performance. But even if the lemon schema is true, the anecdote about the brother-in-law's Volvo provides far less evidence about the distribution of lemons across car makes than do drab statistical surveys of repair records.

An example of inappropriate schema usage that may hit even closer to home is the behavior of the typical faculty committee charged to select students for a graduate program. A letter of recommendation for Elsa Doud may note that Ms. Doud was shy in Professor Smith's class at Ohio State. Doud's shyness and "midwesternness" may call to mind Priscilla Frimp, another shy midwestern woman who never made it through the program. The Frimp persona may then be used as a basis to reject Doud. Any reliance on personae in such a situation is utterly without foundation. The only currently valid grounds for predicting graduate performance seem to be the candidate's GRE (Graduate Record Examination) scores, grades, research experience, quality of undergraduate institution, and evaluations in letters of recommendation. Of course, if the anti-Doud professor wishes to construct a shyness measure and can show that it is related to quality of graduate performance, then the professor may administer this measure to the entire pool of applicants and reject those scoring high on it. If an interaction among shyness, sex, and region of the country is found, such that shyness is particularly crippling to the performance of midwestern females, then a lower cutoff point on the shyness scale may be set for midwestern females than for male or female students from other parts of the country. Unless the professor is willing to perform the requisite validation research, however, any persona ruminations should be kept out of the student selection procedure.

INFERENTIAL ADJUSTMENT AND ITS LIMITATIONS

In this chapter we described some inferential strategies on which the lay scientist seems to rely in forming judgments of the social world. There were two common themes in our observations. The first and more obvious—that people's errors and insights are intimately linked together and are typically a matter of appropriate versus inappropriate application of a given heuristic, theory, or schema—was reiterated often enough that we trust it needs no reemphasis. There was a second and less obvious theme that merits some elaboration. At several points we emphasized that it is not only people's eagerness to apply simple heuristics and immediately available knowledge structures that leads to grief; it is also the failure to make necessary *adjustments* of initial judgments. That is, once a simple heuristic or schema has been used, subsequent considerations fail to exert as much impact as common sense or normative considerations might dictate that it should.

Some simple, direct demonstrations of inadequate adjustment or "anchoring" effects were provided in work by Tversky and Kahneman (1974). In one study, for example, subjects were asked to adjust an arbitrary initial estimate of the percentage of African countries in the United Nations. Those starting with "anchors" of 10 percent and 65 percent produced "adjusted" estimates of 25 percent and 45 percent, respectively. The same anchoring effects were demonstrated with initial "estimates" dictated by the subject's own previous spin of a roulette wheel! Even though it would have been obvious to the subjects that these "starting points" were wholly arbitrary and unrelated to the judgment task, they nevertheless had an influence on final estimates.

Our present contention is essentially an extension of Tversky's and Kahneman's point about the effects of a cognitive "anchor." That is, once subjects have made a first pass at a problem, the initial judgment may prove remarkably resistant to further information, alternative modes of reasoning, and even logical or evidential challenges. Attempts to integrate new information may find the individual surprisingly "conservative," that is, willing to yield ground only grudgingly and primed to challenge the relevance, reliability, or authority of subsequent information or logical consideration. As a result, the method of first choice—and we believe heuristics and schemas to be such methods of first choice—may have disproportionate impact, while other methods (notably, methods considering pallid base lines, mitigating situational factors, possible sources of unreliability in the data, and the like) have relatively little impact.

SUMMARY

The chapter describes two of the general tools that people use to "go beyond the information given," judgmental heuristics and knowledge structures.

The availability heuristic is used to judge the frequency and likelihood of events and event-relations. Since the availability of remembered events is sometimes biased at the stage of sampling, sometimes at the stage of encoding and storage, and sometimes at the stage of retrieval, frequency and likelihood estimates often will be biased correspondingly.

The representativeness heuristic is used to estimate the likelihood of some state of affairs given knowledge of some other state of affairs, for example, the likelihood that an object is a member of some category because it has certain characteristics. Such judgments are based on the perceived similarity of the known characteristics of the object to the presumed essential characteristics of the category. The heuristic sometimes misleads because, in some circumstances, notably when diagnosticity is low or category base rates differ widely, mere similarity is an unreliable guide to likelihood.

In addition to heuristics, people use certain knowledge structures in approaching judgment tasks. These include relatively propositional structures such as theories and beliefs, and more schematic structures like scripts and personae. These knowledge structures are invaluable aids to understanding social events, but they may mislead to the extent that they are poor representations of external reality and to the extent that they preclude attention to the details of the actual object at hand.

The judgmental heuristics may prove to be the primary determinants of the arousal and application of the various knowledge structures. Availability of a given structure, including transient, arbitrary increments in its availability, may increase the likelihood of its application. The representativeness of a given structure, including the similarity of quite superficial and incidental features of the stimulus to features of the structure, may be a chief determinant of the arousal and application of a given structure.

It is emphasized that it is not the existence of heuristics and knowledge structures that can be criticized but rather, their overuse, misuse, and use in preference to more appropriate strategies. Even when more appropriate strategies are subsequently employed for a given judgmental task, the undue influence of the simpler, more intuitive strategies may persist.

3

assigning weights to data: the "vividness criterion"

> Popular induction depends upon the emotional interest of the instances, not upon their number.
>
> *Bertrand Russell.*
>
> The death of a single Russian soldier is a tragedy. A million deaths is a statistic.
>
> *Joseph Stalin.*

Social scientists sometimes are inclined to compare their mission with that of the novelist. Both the social scientist and the novelist attempt to discover and to communicate insights into the nature of people and of human society, often with the vague and distant goal of improving the human condition. The social scientist is apt to marvel at the audacity of the writer who undertakes the quest armed with only personal experience, imagination, and literary skill—free of the protection and the burden of statistics, controlled experiments, logical constraints, and the rest of the scientist's arsenal.

The social scientist may be most impressed by (and perhaps jealous of), however, the *impact* of vivid writing on the aspirations and actions of both intellectuals and society at large. Abraham Lincoln is said to have met Harriet Beecher Stowe at the height of the Civil War and to have greeted her with the rueful comment that he was "happy to meet the little lady who started all this." Other books that had a powerful impact on people's perception of themselves and their society include Erich Remarque's *All Quiet on the Western Front,* Upton Sinclair's *The Jungle,* and Aleksandr Solzhenitsyn's *Gulag*

Archipelago. The facts and arguments presented in these works were not completely original. There are more authoritative, better reasoned and more factual writings on each of the topics of these books, but their readers' beliefs and actions were influenced greatly by these books' vivid, concrete, and absorbing writing, as in passages like the following from Sinclair's *Jungle:*

> Some worked at the stamping-machines, and it was very seldom that one could work long there at the pace that was set, and not give out and forget himself, and have a part of his hand chopped off. There were the "hoisters," as they were called, whose task it was to press the lever which lifted the dead cattle off the floor. They ran along upon a rafter, peering down through the damp and the steam; and as old Durham's architects had not built the killing-room for the convenience of the hoisters, at every few feet they would have to stoop under a beam, say four feet above the one they ran on; which got them into the habit of stooping, so that in a few years they would be walking like chimpanzees. Worst of any, however, were the fertilizer-men, and those who served in the cooking-rooms. These people could not be shown to the visitor,—for the odor of a fertilizer-man would scare any ordinary visitor at a hundred yards, and as for the other men, who worked in tank-rooms full of steam, and in some of which there were open vats near the level of the floor, their peculiar trouble was that they fell into the vats; and when they were fished out, there was never enough of them left to be worth exhibiting,—sometimes they would be overlooked for days, till all but the bones of them had gone out to the world as Durham's Pure Leaf Lard (1906, p. 117).

Such powerful writing sometimes is enough to overwhelm the novelist's own less vividly expressed didactic intents. *The Jungle* is a case in point. Sinclair's specific concern was the exploitation and brutal working conditions of the immigrants who labored in Chicago's stockyards; his broader themes were the evils of capitalist monopolies and the brighter promise of socialism in America. It was in this context that Sinclair's opening chapters detailed, with compelling, horrifying realism, the filth and danger of the slaughterhouses and the diseases afflicting both workers and livestock. The social impact of Sinclair's polemic was dramatic but undoubtedly disconcerting to the author himself. The public was indeed moved to anger and to demands for reform, but its demands pertained neither to the maladies of capitalism nor to the exploitation of Chicago's immigrant workers. Instead, the public outcry focused (with considerable success, ultimately) on the need for better sanitation and stricter health standards in the meat-processing industry!

This chapter examines the question of why people's inferences and behavior are so much more influenced by vivid, concrete information than by pallid and abstract propositions of substantially greater probative and evidential value. We argue that part of the reason for the greater inferential impact of vivid information is theoretically trivial but pragmatically very important: *Vivid information is more likely to be stored and remembered than pallid information is.* Information that is easily remembered is by definition more likely to be retrieved at some later date and therefore to affect later inferences.

We also contend that the vividness of information exerts a disproportionate impact on inferences via processes quite separate from memory. First, we analyze the factors that contribute to the vividness of information. Then we explore some of the mechanisms that account for the greater impact on inferences of more vivid information. Next we examine anecdotal and experimental evidence indicating that highly probative but pallid statistical summaries are often ignored by people in favor of much less probative but more tangible and concrete case history information. Finally, we examine the normative questions raised by people's *de facto* assignment of inferential weight to information in proportion to its vividness.

Our discussion necessarily is lacking in empirical evidence. Important as the thesis of this chapter is, it has scarcely been touched by psychologists. This is perhaps partially because of its truistic nature and partially because the factors contributing to vividness and its greater impact on inferences are complex and intertwined. Psychologists are loath to embark on complicated and difficult research projects when the results are likely to surprise no one. Because of the empirical vacuum, we have to rely on speculation and on spotty and indirect evidence. Most embarrassing of all, given the theme of the chapter, we have to rely substantially on anecdotal and case history evidence!

FACTORS CONTRIBUTING TO THE VIVIDNESS OF INFORMATION

Information may be described as vivid, that is, as likely to attract and hold our attention and to excite the imagination to the extent that it is (a) emotionally interesting, (b) concrete and imagery-provoking, and (c) proximate in a sensory, temporal, or spatial way. In practice, these factors are not usually independent, but they are at least conceptually distinct. We will describe these factors and analyze their components, and argue that each of the components may make an independent contribution to the greater inferential impact of more vivid information.

Emotional Interest

A given event may have greater or lesser emotional interest, depending on several factors. One important set of factors is the nature of one's acquaintance with the participants in the event. Normally, events that happen to us personally are more interesting for perhaps no other reason than it is to us that they are happening. But events also are more interesting when they happen to people we know than when they happen to people we do not know, and they are more interesting when they happen to people about whom we have strong feelings than when they happen to people about whom we have neutral feelings. Another important set of factors is the hedonic relevance of the event *to the participants*. Independent of our familiarity with, and affective stance toward, the participants in an event, the emotional interest of the event is influenced by the degree to which it affects the participants' needs, desires, motives, and values.

An extended example may illustrate these points. Consider the information that "Jack skidded on an icy road and demolished a parked car." If the demolished parked car belongs to an individual whom one does not know, the inference is apt to be that Jack was a bit unlucky and that he and other drivers really ought to lower their speed on icy roads. If the car belonged to a close friend or relative, one might regard Jack as a careless driver who ought to be indicted for his offense and/or might regard the authorities as being insufficiently concerned about icy roads as a safety hazard. If it were one's own car that was destroyed, one might well conclude that Jack is a menace who ought to be barred for life from operating any moving vehicle and/or that travel should be forbidden by the authorities when roads become icy. Similarly, the more one likes or dislikes the subject or object of a deed, the greater its impact will be on one's inferences about it. The news that Jack demolished an old Edsel will affect our inferences in proportion to our previous affective involvement both with Jack and with Edsels. Finally, one is apt to make stronger inferences about Jack's carelessness if the accident proves to have great rather than small personal consequences for Jack and for others affected by it. For instance, stronger inferences will be made if one learns that the demolished car was expensive and dearly loved by its owner or that it contained a priceless antique that also was destroyed, than if one learns that it was a heap ready for the junk yard.

Walster (1966) conducted an experiment providing results consistent with the last of these propositions. Walster described an accident to two different groups of subjects. A man had left his car parked on a hill, and after he had gone, the car rolled down the hill. The description of the context, car owner, and sequence of events was identical for the two groups, save in one respect. For one group of subjects the consequence of the accident was that the car struck a fire hydrant. For the other group the consequence was that the car struck and injured a person. Subjects who read about the more severe consequence found the car owner more responsible for the accident than did subjects who read that the consequence was trivial.

Needless to say, the hedonic relevance of the accident, and the nature and degree of one's acquaintance with the participants, are by any normative standards irrelevant to the issues of causality and responsibility raised in situations such as those described in Walster's study and in our example. The fact that Jack skidded out of control on an icy road and hit a parked car with sufficient force to destroy it may or may not imply something about Jack's personal dispositions or about the foresight of highway authorities. Such matters as the kind of the car that was hit and one's relationship to the car's owner are a matter of chance and indicate nothing about Jack's degree of carelessness or the wisdom of the authorities.

Concreteness

Another set of factors that seems to influence informational vividness both directly and indirectly through enhancement of emotional impact, can be summarized under the heading of "concreteness." These include the degree of detail and specificity about actors, actions, and situational context. These factors contribute to the "imaginability" of information, that is, its tendency to prompt sensory imagery.

The information that "Jack was killed by a semitrailer that rolled over on his car and crushed his skull" has more impact than the information that "Jack sustained fatal injuries in an auto accident." This is true quite independently of one's familiarity with, or attitude toward, Jack. The concreteness of the first statement and the resulting involuntary imagery contribute substantially to its emotional impact, and because of that impact, there is an effect on inferences as well. When semitrailers roll over on people and crush their skulls, it is time to take action—whether that is the reinforcement of autos' passenger compartments, a crackdown on speed violators, or at least a resolution always to wear one's seat belt. In contrast, when someone sustains fatal injuries in an auto accident, it seems to be one of those unfortunate things that sometimes happen.

A study by Enzle, Hansen, and Lowe (1975) supports the proposition that information which prompts imagery has a greater impact on inferences. These investigators asked subjects to play a standard, two-person prisoner's dilemma game. The payoff matrix would lead to high payoffs for both subjects, if both made "cooperative" choices, and low payoffs if both made "competitive" choices. If one subject made a cooperative choice and one a competitive choice, the former received no payoff and the latter a high payoff. Subjects did not actually play against each other but instead were taken to separate cubicles where they played against a preprogrammed, 100 percent cooperative-choice pattern or a 100 percent competitive-choice pattern. Enzle and colleagues manipulated the manner in which the subjects learned about their partner's choice. Half of the subjects received the choice information in the form of a light on an impersonal electronic display panel. The other half received a more personal indication of partner choice and one which we presume would be more likely to prompt imagery of a living, breathing person in the other cubicle. An initialed note, ostensibly written by the subject's partner, was slipped through a slot in the wall.

The mode of communicating partners' choice, manipulated in this way, had extreme effects on subjects' perceptions of their partner and on their own behavior. Subjects perceived their partner as having more clearly intended to cooperate, or compete, in the note passing than in the electronic conditions. They similarly perceived a note-passing partner as having had more choice of whether to cooperate or to compete. In addition, subjects trusted a cooperative partner much more and trusted a competitive partner much less, in the note passing than in the electronic conditions. Finally, subjects' own strategies in the game were influenced by the manipulation. Subjects in the note-passing conditions responded in kind to cooperative or competitive partners to a greater extent than subjects in the electronic display conditions did.

The argument that people's inferences are affected by the concreteness or imaginability of information is supported by considering people's reactions to events at the extreme low end of the concreteness continuum. We refer to those *potential* events that do *not* occur. Such "null" information tends to be overlooked and underappreciated. Sherlock Holmes directed our attention to this failing. In "The Silver Blaze" (*The Memoirs of Sherlock Holmes* by Sir Arthur Conan Doyle), the great detective invited Inspector Gregory to consider "the curious incident of the dog in the night-time." Inspector Gregory, a conventional intuitive scientist, remarked correctly that "The dog did nothing in the night-time," to which Holmes replied triumphantly, "That *was* the curious incident" (1974, p. 33). For the premier practitioner of the science of deduction this *nonincident* or *nonoccurrence* furnished the key to the identity of an intruder in the night. Holmes recognized that although a dog barking at an intruder might have furnished little useful evidence, the event of a dog's *failure* to bark proved the intruder to be someone the animal knew.

For us ordinary mortals, events that *do* occur are vastly more real and immediate than the corresponding nonoccurrences of potential events. The greater salience of events that have actually occurred means that they are more available for inference than are events that have not occurred. Thus, Jill may meet a new acquaintance, Jack, and after some personal interaction with him, she may form the vague impression that he does not like her. If Jill looks for specific actions that reveal Jack's dislike, she probably will be frustrated in her search since, under normal circumstances, acquaintances do not express such sentiments in overt words or deeds. If Jill relies upon the sample of events she can recall from memory, she may well conclude that her impression is incorrect and unjustified by the evidence. Alternatively, she may cling to her impression but resort to "intuition" or "sixth sense" to justify it. If the peerless Mr. Holmes were available for consultation, he doubtless could end

Jill's attributional dilemma by focusing her attention on the relatively pallid evidence of what Jack did *not* do. That is, Jack did *not* deliberately prolong encounters, did *not* furnish positive nonverbal feedback, and, in general, did *not* show any of those responses that normally signal attraction or interest.

The difference between an occurrence and a nonoccurrence can sometimes be one of semantics: The absence of eye contact can be coded more positively as the presence of gaze avoidance (for example, Ellsworth & Ross 1975). The absence of sexual responsiveness similarly can be coded and interpreted as the presence of something concrete—for example, frigidity. These seemingly moot semantic distinctions can have substantial consequences for the intuitive psychologist. Indeed, if these speculations are warranted, it should be possible to demonstrate that particular absences of response are more noted, more remembered, and more likely to be deemed relevant when concrete, vivid, and active category labels are applied to such absences.

There is some evidence that indirectly supports these contentions. Both humans and animals have great difficulty learning associations that involve "null" information which lacks concreteness and imaginability. For example, in concept-learning experiments, people have been shown to underutilize negative instances (blue things *are not* "gleeps") compared to their use of positive instances (red things *are* "gleeps") [Wason & Johnson-Laird 1965]. In fact, people sometimes make no use at all of negative instances even in learning situations in which they are logically as informative as positive instances are.

Similar underutilization of negative instances has been found in discrimination-learning tasks, in which an animal is required to distinguish between two stimuli that are identical except for one feature. If it is the "distinctive feature absent" stimulus that is reinforced rather than the "distinctive feature present" stimulus, the animal may never learn the discrimination (Jenkins & Sainsbury 1970). Young humans also may fail to learn when the stimulus that lacks the distinctive feature is the one that is reinforced (Sainsbury 1973) and though adults can learn, at a retarded rate, under such conditions, they appear to do so by making the task conceptually positive. That is, they seem to learn which stimulus has the distinctive cue and then respond to the *other one!*

Temporal, Spatial, and Sensory Proximity of Information

Information seems vivid in proportion to one's temporal, spatial, and sensory proximity to it. The news that a bank in one's neighborhood has been robbed just an hour ago is more vivid than the news that a bank on the other side of town was robbed last week. The former bank robbery, accordingly, is likely to have a greater impact on one's views of the seriousness of the crime problem in one's city or the need for stiffer prison sentences for bank robbers. Such effects may be mediated partially by other factors such as emotional involvement, familiarity, sensory intensity, or informational concreteness. Proximity of information, however, seems to increase vividness and impact even when these other factors are held constant.

There is much anecdotal evidence that information obtained firsthand, through one's own sensory apparatus, is more vivid and more likely to exert an impact on one's judgments and inferences than is information obtained verbally from a secondhand or thirdhand source. This effect of informational directness seems to apply even when the information itself is purely verbal, as in the contrast between reading something oneself and hearing about what someone else read.

The importance of the "proximity" of information may be illustrated by the following anecdote. One of the authors recently was told by a respected colleague that an anthropologist friend of his, whom the colleague greatly respected, recently had been on a field trip to a remote African village. While sitting in the village one day, the anthropologist saw a man with a compound fracture of the shin being helped by two other men into the hut of the village shaman and healer. The seriousness of the injury was obvious. Both ends of the shin bone could be seen protruding from the torn tissue of the leg. Nevertheless, two hours after entering the hut, the man with the fracture emerged with a bandaged leg, walking under his own power.

In a sense, all three parties—the author, the colleague, and the colleague's anthropologist friend—believe this story. The author trusts his colleague's veracity and judgment completely, and the colleague similarly trusts his anthropologist friend. Furthermore, the story, while surprising in some respects, is probably no more or less implausible to any one of the three parties than to the others. Yet, we suspect that by placing each of them in a relevant test situation it could be shown that the three parties have not made the same inferences from the information. Imagine each of them finding themselves in a remote African village with a compound fracture of the shin! The author is confident that he would sooner ask for a revolver to put himself out of his misery than place himself in the hands of a shaman; his colleague no doubt would be terribly frightened but might take faint hope from the story he had heard from his anthropologist friend; and the anthropologist probably would quickly and calmly request that someone fetch the local practitioner of shamanistic medicine.

The principle that information should be weighted more heavily if it is obtained firsthand often is acknowledged explicitly by the layperson. People often say "I was there," or "I saw it myself," in order to enhance the credibility of their assertions. Doubters are urged to go see for themselves. To some extent, this principle reflects a justified sense-impression empiricism, one which protects against incompetent or mendacious informants. But in some contexts the consequence is gullibility, as with scientists taken in by charlatans who demonstrate telepathy and telekinesis "in front of their very eyes." In other contexts, the consequence is unjustified skepticism, as in the reluctance to believe anything implausible that one reads in the newspaper or in the refusal to be influenced by anything containing complicated figures and statistics.

EXPLAINING THE IMPACT OF VIVID INFORMATION

Just as there are many complex and interrelated factors contributing to informational vividness, a similarly great number of intertwined factors probably accounts for the *effects* of informational vividness. The most obvious way in which vividness could affect inferences is through memory. It is clear that information that is more concrete and imaginable is retained more easily in memory. Thus, the more vivid the information is, the greater its impact can be on inferences that occur at *some temporal remove* from the initial exposure to the information. We now will discuss the evidence for this proposition and add our speculations about other, nonmemorial mediators.

Memorial Availability of Information

There is good evidence that informational concreteness and imaginability promote recognition and recall. A number of investigators have shown that memory of pictures is astonishingly good and is markedly better than memory of either words or sentences (Shepard 1967; Standing, Conezio, & Haber 1970; Gehring, Toglia, & Kimble 1976). This superiority of picture retention is shown at every retention interval from a few minutes to several months. In addition, Paivio (1971) has shown that recognition and recall of concrete words (for example, boat) are substantially better than of abstract words (for example, justice). In accounting for this phenomenon, Paivio (1971) and Bower (1972) proposed that concrete words are coded both in images and in verbal forms, whereas abstract words may be coded only in verbal forms.

Imagery also enables better retention of arbitrarily yoked concepts. Bower (1972) showed that simple paired-associate learning is greatly facilitated when subjects are given instructions to link the stimulus word to the response word using images. For example, if subjects are required to learn the stimulus-response pair "dog-bicycle," their learning is aided greatly by creating an image linking the two terms (for example, a mental picture of a dog riding a bicycle). The memorability of linked items of information, like that of individual items, is improved if the link contains sensory images.

Since more memorable information is, by definition, more available for incorporation into inferences, these findings are an empirical foundation for the assumption that firsthand, sensory information, and even secondhand information, if it is concrete and imagery-provoking, will have more effect on inferences that occur at some temporal remove than more pallid and abstract information will have.

This presumption has been tested and supported by Thompson, Reyes, and Bower (1979). These investigators asked subjects to read defense and prosecution testimony allegedly given in a trial of a defendant accused of drunk driving. The defendant was described as having either a generally good or a generally bad character. The vividness of the testimony was manipulated so that half the subjects read pallid prosecution testimony and vivid defense testimony, while the other half read vivid prosecution and pallid defense testimony. For example, one item of prosecution evidence was intended to establish that the defendant was drunk shortly before leaving a party to drive home. The pallid version of the item stated that the defendant staggered against a table, knocking a bowl to the floor. In the vivid version, this action knocked "a bowl of guacamole dip" to the floor "splattering guacamole all over the white shag carpet." An item of defense evidence that was intended to establish that the defendant had not been drunk described the defendant's ability to leap out of the way of an approaching vehicle. In the pallid version, the vehicle in question was "a car." In the vivid version, it was "a bright orange Volkswagen." The items were constructed so that the manipulation of vividness did not logically affect the probative value of the evidence.

After reading ten items each of prosecution and defense testimony, subjects indicated their judgment of the defendant's guilt on a 100-point scale and were asked to return the next day without being told why. The following day, subjects were requested to recall as many items of testimony as they could and to render a new verdict of the defendant's guilt.

The immediate judgment of guilt did not show any effect of the vividness manipulation, suggesting that the investigators had been successful in manipulating vividness without affecting the perceived probative value of the evidence. In contrast, the delayed judgments did show a substantial effect of the vividness manipulation on the judgments of guilt for the good character defendant. Subjects exposed to vivid prosecution testimony shifted toward guilty verdicts, and subjects exposed to vivid defense testimony shifted toward not-guilty verdicts. (Oddly, delayed judgment did not show any effect of the vividness manipulation for the bad character defendant, and there was not even a main effect of the character manipulation on either immediate or delayed verdicts. The authors speculate that the subjects, who reported being suspicious that the bad character manipulation was intended to bias them, may always have made rigidly conservative judgments of the bad character defendant.)

Delayed recall of evidence showed only a slight, but nonsignificant, tendency for vivid evidence to be recalled more than pallid evidence. However, within the "good character" conditions, a significant correlation was found between recall of prosecution testimony versus defense testimony (weighted by subjects' rated subjective importance of the items) and verdict shifts. Differential memorability of the items appeared to mediate differential shifts in judgments of guilt.

REDUNDANCY, RECRUITMENT, AND REHEARSAL

The experiment by Thompson and colleagues is important because it showed that vividness effects sometimes may be due solely to the differential availability of information. Differences between vivid and pallid conditions were not observed immediately; they appeared only after a delay. We believe that vividness effects on inferences are not caused only by availability and that such effects often will be observed immediately after receiving the information. There are several reasons to believe that the effect of vividness on inference is independent of availability. It also seems likely that most of the factors resulting in greater immediate inferential effects of vivid information also would cause greater memorability of the information. Most of the ingredients of vividness should have a dual effect, an immediate effect on initial inferences and a delayed effect, mediated by availability, on subsequent inferences.

Information Quantity and Redundancy

More vivid information is normally more information, at least with respect to the sheer number of units or chunks it presents. Consider the difference in the amount of information in the sentence "Jack sustained fatal injuries in an auto accident" and that in the sentence "Jack was killed by a semitrailer that rolled over on his car and crushed his skull." The amount of codable information in the latter is substantially greater, aside from the additional "information" generated by the involuntary imagery in reading it.

Now contrast the amount of information in the second, concrete sentence with the amount of information that would result from actually viewing a semitrailer rolling over on a car and crushing its occupant. The duration of the event might not exceed the time it takes to read the sentence, yet to describe verbally even a small fraction of the information about the actual event that might be coded could take a very long time. A picture can be worth a thousand words, and real life exposure to the object can be worth many thousands more.

Redundancy, both as the number of units of information that encode the same conceptual fact and as the number of sensory pathways that store the information, should enhance the ability to recall the conceptual facts at any later time. Besides these availability effects, there should be an immediate attentional effect. Attention is limited, and the more time that is spent in attending to and processing more vivid information the less time may be spent attending to and processing less vivid information of equal or greater relevance to the inferential task at hand. This imbalance in attention and processing time could cause greater *de facto* weight to be given to more vivid information.

Recruitment of Additional Memories and Schematic Knowledge Structures

Bower (1972) suggested that the number of locations in which information is coded in one's storage system and the number of pathways from these locations to other stored information are likely to be influenced by factors grouped under our heading of informational vividness. More vivid information, therefore, is more likely to recruit additional information from memory than less vivid information is, because there are more access routes to the additional information. Much of the information added from memory normally would point to the same inferential conclusions as the initial information would, since the laws of association are governed by similarity.

Vivid, concrete, sensory information may recruit not only additional specific memories; such information also may recruit organized, dynamic schemas and scripts. In the previous chapter we illustrated the impact of such scripts on social inferences and judgments. In the Volvo-Saab thought experiment, for example, the vivid account of mechanical woes evoked the familiar "lemon" script for defective cars. Once evoked, this script in turn can elicit a wealth of additional images and stored episodes about other "lemons" one has known. The "lemon" script is particularly rich and potent. With its cast of characters (impassive or evasive service managers, bumbling mechanics, snickering neighbors who told you that you could have had a nice Blatzmobile for half the price), and its stock scenes (waiting for buses in the rain, begging rides, bringing the car home only to hear some ominous new sound as you pull into the driveway), the lemon script is capable of strongly influencing one's inferences and behavior. Mere statistics describing drive-train dependability records or average per-year costs are less likely to call up the rich and evocative lemon script and its various instantiations and are consequently less likely to influence our inferences and behavior.

Rehearsal and Reflection

More vivid information, for the reasons just discussed, is likely to remain "in thought" for a longer time after being received. One might think that time in thought, by itself, might have no particular consequences. But this presumption is apparently wrong. Tesser (1978) showed that the longer an object or proposition remains in thought, the more extreme are the attitudes toward it. For example, subjects asked to ponder a particular football play for a longer time end up with more extreme judgments of its advisability than do subjects allowed to think about the play for a shorter time. It seems likely that more vivid information may generate more extreme inferences partially because it incidentally is likely to remain in thought longer.

A second temporal effect of more vivid information is its influence on availability. Greater time in thought means more rehearsal, and more rehearsal means greater memorial availability. Thus, more vivid information is likely to be more available not merely because it is more interesting and hence likely to be stored. More vivid information normally will prompt more rehearsal and more elaborate and effective encoding processes, both of which should improve later availability.

Finally, a part of the power of more vivid information may be reflexive. To a degree, people may weight evidence more heavily simply because they find themselves thinking about it: "If it weren't important, why would I keep coming back to it in my thoughts?" There is a song with the refrain, "I can't get you out of my head." The presumption is that the singer is using this as evidence of the importance of the person whom she cannot get out of her head. Something like this reflexive weighting may operate in the Volvo-Saab thought experiment. One is likely to find oneself thinking much more about the story of the brother-in-law's Volvo than about the data tables and summary statistics from *Consumer Reports*. If people tacitly assume that what occupies their thoughts must be important, they may add weight to the anecdote and subtract it from the table.

INFERENTIAL EFFECTS OF PALLID DATA SUMMARIES VERSUS VIVID CASES

The most disconcerting implication of the principle that information is weighted in proportion to its vividness is that certain types of highly probative information will have little effect on inferences merely because they are pallid. Aggregated, statistical, data-summary information is often particularly probative, but it is also likely to lack concreteness and emotional interest. Consequently, highly probative data summaries often should be ignored or have little effect on inferences, while more vivid, anecdotal, or case-history information of substantially lesser probative value should have a strong effect on inferences. Nisbett, Borgida, Crandall, and Reed (1976) cited several examples of this effect.

1. In the early 1930s the U.S. government attempted to disseminate information about the enormous production increases that had been made possible through agricultural advances. The initial communication attempt relied upon pamphlets filled with tables, charts, and statistics that were no doubt thrilling to technocratic eyes. The pamphlets had little effect, however. Only when a clever government official set up a demonstration program in which government agricultural agents cultivated the crops on selected farms, working alongside the dubious farmers, were there more positive results. Neighboring farmers watched the harvest and immediately converted to the new techniques whose merits had been illustrated so vividly.

2. The mastectomies performed on Mrs. Ford and Mrs. Rockefeller in the fall of 1974 produced a flood of visits to cancer-detection clinics. Widely disseminated statistics about the lifetime risk for breast cancer (5 percent) had never produced an impact approaching that of these two highly publicized, highly concrete cases.

3. The two decades since publication of the surgeon general's report linking cigarette smoking to cancer have witnessed no per-capita decline in cigarette consumption. One subpopulation, however, has shown a definite decline in smoking—physicians. This exception, however, probably should not be attributed simply to the physician's superior knowledge and intelligence, or the desire to ''set a good example.'' All physicians are aware of the statistical evidence, yet there are clear differences among their specialities in the degree of decline in smoking. The probability that a physician smokes is directly related to the distance of the physician's specialty from the lungs. Physicians who diagnose and treat lung cancer victims are quite unlikely to smoke, and radiologists have the very lowest rate of smoking (Borgida & Nisbett 1977). Informational vividness seems to influence even the most sophisticated people, even when they have been exposed to the most probative data.

4. In his book on the press coverage of the 1972 presidential campaign, Timothy Crouse (1974) reported that, on the eve of the election, the reporters covering Senator George McGovern agreed unanimously that he could not lose the election by more than ten points. The reporters all knew that McGovern was trailing by twenty points in all the polls and that no major poll had been wrong by more than 3 percent in twenty-four years. What information had caused these reporters to disregard both the polls and the base-rate information on the accuracy of the polls? Crouse's guess—and ours—is that it was the concrete evidence of their own experience. The reporters had seen wildly enthusiastic crowds acclaiming McGovern all over the country, and they gave this vivid information, despite the obvious bias in the sample to which they were exposed (see chapter 4), disproportionate weight.

Personal anecdotes and actual accounts of people's responsiveness or indifference to informational sources can be multiplied ad infinitum to illustrate the proposition that data summaries, despite their logically compelling implications, have less impact than does inferior but more vivid evidence. Fortunately, there are some laboratory demonstrations that make the same point and that control for the exposure and attention effects which often could account for the differential impact of data summaries versus actual, vivid case histories and experiences.

A recent experiment (Hamill, Wilson, & Nisbett 1979) demonstrated that a single, vivid instance can influence social attitudes when pallid statistics of far greater evidential value do not. Subjects were given a description of a single welfare case. The description (condensed from an article in the *New Yorker* magazine) painted a vivid picture of social pathology. The central figure was an obese, friendly, emotional, and irresponsible Puerto Rican woman who had been on welfare for many years. Middle-aged now, she had lived with a succession of "husbands," typically also unemployed, and had borne children by each of them. Her home was a nightmare of dirty and delapidated plastic furniture bought on time at outrageous prices, filthy kitchen appliances, and cockroaches walking about in the daylight. Her children showed little promise of rising above their origins. They attended school off and on and had begun to run afoul of the law in their early teens, with the older children now thoroughly enmeshed in a life of heroin, numbers-running, and welfare.

In a second set of conditions, the article was omitted and subjects were given statistics showing that the median stay on welfare for all middle-aged welfare recipients was two years and that only 10 percent of recipients remained on the welfare rolls for four years or longer. These statistics, which actually are approximately correct, stood in sharp contrast to the subjects' beliefs about welfare. (Control subjects believed that the average stay on welfare was about ten years.)

Because they so sharply contradict previous beliefs and because they have clear implications for the character of welfare recipients generally, it might be expected that subjects given the statistics might change substantially and favorably their attitudes toward the character and motivation of welfare recipients. Indeed, refusing to change opinions in a favorable direction after finding out that lengthy stays are much rarer than thought is tantamount to asserting the curious belief that the average length of stay on welfare is irrelevant to an evaluation of the character and motives of the recipients. For the subjects given vivid information about the single welfare family, however, it seems clear that any inferences about recipients in general would be normatively quite suspect, since subjects undoubtedly were already aware that there were cases of marked social pathology among the population of welfare recipients (and, indeed, among the population of nonrecipients!).

The surprising-but-pallid statistical information, however, had no effect on subjects' opinions about welfare recipients. In contrast, the vivid description of one particular welfare family prompted subjects to express more unfavorable attitudes toward recipients than control subjects did. Thus highly probative but dull statistics had no effect on inferences, whereas a vivid but questionably informative case history had a substantial effect on inferences.

Another contest between pallid statistics and vivid, concrete information was posed by Borgida and Nisbett (1977). Introductory psychology students who planned to major in psychology were given one of two forms of information about ten upper-level psychology courses. Subjects were told that the department wished to have tentative preenrollment figures for long-range planning and that the subjects would be given some information about these courses and then would be asked to check off those courses they currently planned to take. Two types of course information were provided. Subjects in a "statistical summary" condition received what was purported to be actual mean evaluations (on five-point, excellent-to-poor scales), based on the reports of the dozens of students who had taken each course the preceding term. Subjects in a "face-to-face" condition were exposed to a panel of ten upper-level psychology students: For each of the courses, two or three students who had actually taken the course rated the course on the five-point scale and then made a few comments about the course, consistent with their evaluations. The mean evaluation for a given course which was given to subjects in the statistical summary condition was fixed so as to coincide with the mean of the evaluations in the face-to-face condition.

Following their exposure to course evaluation information, subjects were asked to specify which upper-level courses they planned to take and to indicate how confident they were about their choices. Subjects proved to be more affected by the face-to-face information than by the statistical summary information: Face-to-face subjects indicated an intention to take more of the highly evaluated courses and fewer of the poorly evaluated courses than did statistical summary subjects. They also expressed greater certainty about their plans.

The study thus indicates that face-to-face recommendations may be more influential than informationally superior data summaries are. It does this, however, only if one can be confident that the statistical summaries are in fact informationally superior. It could be argued that the comments in the face-to-face group might have included important information, such as the difficulty level of the course or its value for professional training, that could not be conveyed by the statistical summaries. In order to rule out the possibility that such extra information was critical, the experiment was replicated, this time giving the statistical summary subjects a written transcript of the comments made in the face-to-face condition *in addition to* the statistical data. This condition, which still denied subjects exposure to actual people, again proved less influential than did the condition which provided face-to-face contact.

One other feature of the Borgida and Nisbett study should be mentioned. The participants in the study all had identified themselves, early in the term during which the study was conducted, as prospective psychology majors. In the interim between the subjects' preliminary declarations of academic major and their participation in the study, a number of subjects had decided *not* to major in psychology. The contrast between these subjects' responses and those of the declared psychology majors is instructive. It was the psychology majors—for whom the course selections were most important and least hypothetical—who revealed the greatest effect of face-to-face evidence and the least effect of the abstract statistics. The nonmajors, by contrast, showed a relatively greater impact of the statistical summaries and a relatively smaller impact of the face-to-face ratings. This pattern of results argues against the possibility that only inconsequential judgments are disproportionately influenced by vivid data. On the contrary, the anecdotal and laboratory evidence alike suggest that personally relevant and important choices may be the most disproportionately influenced by vivid evidence.

A final aspect of the Hamill and colleagues (1979) and Borgida and Nisbett studies that should be emphasized is that both studies avoid the "exposure" confound that may compromise much of the anecdotal evidence. In the real world, people's inferences sometimes may be unaffected by statistical information for the simple reason that they find such information too boring to pay any attention to it. Although this is of practical importance to would-be communicators, it is of little theoretical interest. It is only when people are exposed to such information, learn it, and still fail to make the appropriate inferences that the phenomenon establishes the theoretical contention that pallid information has little impact on inferences. In both the Hamill and colleagues and Borgida and Nisbett studies, subjects were perforce exposed to the pallid, data-summary information, and manipulation checks showed that they learned such information quite well. This information's lack of inferential impact was therefore because of its insufficient weighting and not because of a failure to notice it.

NORMATIVE CONSIDERATIONS

The tendency to assign inferential weight to information in proportion to its vividness has some genuine value for the intuitive scientist. Concrete, sensory data have a certain priority recognized by philosophical and scientific canons of inquiry. When an abstract theory or a secondhand report is flatly contradicted by the evidence provided by the senses, it is the former that must yield under nearly all circumstances. Moreover, vivid experiences and observations can be a source of new insights, can provide "phenomenological reality" (Brickman, 1978) to otherwise poorly understood propositions, and can inspire action in circumstances in which previous knowledge or opinions had not overcome inertia.

In keeping with the strategy of this book, however, we have chosen to emphasize the serious inferential and behavioral costs associated with the disproportionate weighting of vivid information. The problem with the use of the vividness criterion is simply stated: The vividness of information is correlated only modestly, at best, with its evidential value. By accident or by the design of a communicator, vivid information is often misleading, particularly when duller but more probative information is cast aside in its favor. Thus, a vivid case history, unless it is known to be typical, ought to be given very little weight in forming opinions about welfare recipients. It surely ought to receive less weight than should accurate statistics on median and extreme stays on the welfare rolls which flatly contradict prior expectations. Similarly, the mean recommendations of the dozens of students who took a particular course the previous semester more reliably indicate the quality of the course than do face-to-face recommendations by two or three individuals. A judgment of the trustworthiness of an opponent in a prisoner's dilemma game should be influenced only by the opponent's tactics and not by the means of communication chosen by the experimenter. The responsibility assigned to the perpetrator of an accident should be a function of the perpetrator's actions and not of the magnitude of those actions' unforeseeable consequences.

It may be worth speculating that there could be good evolutionary reasons for our tendency to weight more vivid information more heavily. During all but the most recent moments of our evolutionary history, dangers and opportunities have been relatively concrete and vivid. Saber-toothed tigers and food and water resources are highly palpable entities, and responsiveness to thirdhand accounts (let alone abstract statistics and data summaries) might have conferred few advantages. Now, however, our world has come to have pressing dangers which are complex and abstract matters such as the destruction of the distant ozone layer or exposure to invisible carcinogens, dangers best described by abstract and often statistical information. Opportunities often are similarly abstract—stock investment options and home mortgage plans are best understood by data that are pallid compared to the prospects in a primitive subsistence economy.

As human existence has come to rely more and more on the social transmission of information, the likelihood of being deliberately misled by concrete, vivid accounts also has increased dramatically. Social communicators bombard us with concrete instances and vivid incidents carefully selected (or constructed) to influence our inferences and behavior. In some specific domains—in our response to advertisements, for example—we have managed to become wary of the concrete illustration or "testimonial." But these specific skepticisms probably produce little generalized protection. Polls show repeatedly that the U.S. public trusts the evening TV news over all other information sources. This medium comes closest to direct sensory contact with information. Only a sophisticated few understand that it is almost as easy to convey misinformation through sight and sound media as through any other medium. (Readers who might be interested in the nearly limitless possibilities for making filmed "reality" tell whatever story one wants are advised to see the "documentaries" of skilled film makers such as Frederick Wiseman.)

In many if not most contexts, we seem to lack prescriptive rules to protect us from being overly influenced by concrete, sensory data. Oddly, there are many rules for our protection against secondhand data: "Don't believe everything you read," "You can prove anything with statistics," "Seeing is believing," "I'm from Missouri . . .".

In addition, people often engage in a kind of ritualistic offering of the anecdote or case history in order to contradict the implications of abstract reasoning or statistical information. Such single-case presentations might be called "man-who'"statistics, because of the recurrent reference to the "man-who . . ." that one finds in such offerings. Thus abstract or statistical arguments meet responses of the following type:

> "But I know a *man who* smoked three packs of cigarettes a day and lived to be ninety-nine."
> "We once admitted a *man who* had graduated from Farnsworth State, and he dropped out in his first year."
> "I've never been to Turkey but just last month I met a *man who* had, and he found it . . . etc., etc."

Or, to return to our familiar example:

> "I knew a *man who* owned a Volvo and it turned out to be . . . etc., etc."

Needless to say, the presentation of a man-who statistic seldom warrants the inferential weight which the communicator intends for it and which the recipient often grants to it.

Although people seem to be aware that the senses may mislead ("Your eyes can play tricks on you"), there seems to be little recognition that concrete information, even if perceived correctly, still can generate incorrect inferences. What is needed, perhaps, is a new set of prescriptive homilies of the following type: "Just because it's punchy doesn't mean it's important," "Yes, it's interesting, but what does it prove?" or "Don't try to use a 'man-who' statistic on me."

SUMMARY

People give inferential weight to information in proportion to its vividness. Vividness is defined as the emotional interest of information, the concreteness and imaginability of information, and the sensory, spatial, and temporal proximity of information. Though these factors normally covary, they independently influence the inferential impact of information.

The most obvious mediator of the effects of vividness on inference is availability. More vivid information is more likely to be remembered and hence to be disproportionately available for influencing inferences at any time after the information is initially encountered. The inferential impact of more vivid information usually is apparent immediately upon receiving the information, however, as well as after a delay. The factors influencing such impact include (a) the likelihood that more vivid information provides a larger quantity of information and receives more attention and "time in thought"; (b) the greater likelihood that more vivid information will recruit additional information of similar import from memory; and (c) the greater likelihood that more vivid information will be pondered and rehearsed.

Research indicates that highly probative, data-summary information sometimes is ignored while less probative, case-history information has a substantial impact on inferences. Although people's responsiveness to vivid information has a certain justification and confers occasional advantages, the policy of weighting information in proportion to its vividness is risky. At best, vividness is associated imperfectly with probativeness. Consequently, highly probative but pallid information sometimes will be ignored, and conversely, evidentially weak but vivid information sometimes will have an undue impact on inferences.

part II

INFERENTIAL TASKS: NORMATIVE PRINCIPLES AND LAY PRACTICE

4

characterizing
the datum, sample,
and population

It is quite wrong to try founding a theory on observable
magnitudes alone. In reality the very opposite happens.
It is the theory which decides what we can observe.

Albert Einstein

In part 1 we described some of the general strategies of human inference
that broadly and profoundly influence the lay scientists' judgments and
behavior. These strategies include the reliance on preexisting propositional
theories and other, more schematic knowledge structures, the use of the
availability and representativeness heuristics, and the tendency to weight data
in proportion to their vividness. In the five chapters of part 2 we focus on the
specific tasks of the lay scientist, indicating how the performance of each task
is shaped by the influence of the intuitive strategies and by the layperson's
imperfect appreciation of various normative principles of inference.

In this chapter, we deal with three tasks basic to almost all higher order
inferences: First, one must be able to describe or code the individual datum.
Second, one must be able to characterize accurately data aggregates or
samples, including both sampled observations from a population and sampled
attributes of an object. Third, one must be able to generalize from the sample
of observations to make inferences about the population or object from which
they were sampled.

Before embarking on a formal consideration of these topics, let us examine briefly a simple ex.mple of what is entailed in characterizations of social data. Consider, for example, the formal scientist—or the informal counterpart—whose concern is the human smile. Before any higher order inferences can be made about the causes or implications of smiling, the scientist must be able to code the individual datum, that is, to decide which facial expressions are smiles and which are not. Next, it is necessary to characterize accurately a sample of individual observations, such as the proportion of people who smiled when Jane entered the room, or the total amount of time that Jack smiled, or even the mean amount of smiling done by males versus females, by high status versus low status participants, or by Jack in the presence of Jane versus Jack in the presence of Marie. Finally, the scientist must use such data samples to infer general characteristics of the objects or populations in question—for example, the amount of smiling done at parties in general, the degree to which Jack's smiling indicates his friendliness in general, or the extent to which males in general smile in the presence of females.

Conventionally, the first two tasks, characterizing the individual datum and characterizing a sample of observations, are regarded by measurement theorists as *descriptive,* while only the third task, parameter estimation, is regarded as *inferential.* It should be clear that the simplest characterizations still contain an element of inference. As a member of the House Judiciary Committee observed during the impeachment hearings of President Richard Nixon, even the task of deciding that a particular creature is an elephant requires something of an inferential leap, because the beast could be "a mouse with a glandular condition." The congressman's waggish comment was intended as a rebuke to the president's defenders for their reluctance to make the leap from evidence to seemingly clear-cut implications, but it is important to present concerns. It reminds us that at every stage of data characterization there is room for interpretation and hence for bias. It also suggests that some inferential leaps may be more reasonable than others are. Indeed, the contention that inferences about data may be biased raises normative issues more complicated and controversial than might be expected: As we shall see, some sources of "bias" may, overall, contribute far more to accuracy than to error.

CHARACTERIZING THE DATUM:
THE ROLE OF PRECONCEPTIONS

Perhaps the most basic of all undertakings of science—for both intuitive science and formal science—is characterizing the immediately given datum. Unfortunately it is very difficult to attempt even the most tentative assessment of the layperson's overall adequacy in such tasks. Because this assessment is of people's ability to apprehend "reality," it is more an ontological or metaphysical assessment than a scientific one. If this assessment is restricted to narrower questions of judgmental precision and reliability, examples may be found ranging from exquisite accuracy to buzzing confusion to everything in between. It is clear that people are extraordinarily adroit at many types of data description and coding. For instance, Gibson and Pick (1963) reported that people can distinguish direct eye contact from noncontact even when the two differ by only a fraction of a degree of visual angle, a coding capacity that is critical to regulating social exchange and guiding social inferences. On the other hand, no one seems immune to serious coding errors in attempting to distinguish shyness from aloofness, feigned enjoyment from genuine pleasure, or political conviction from political rhetoric.

Although we cannot generalize about people's proficiency in data coding, we can discuss what is one of the most venerable ideas of both traditional epistemology and cognitive psychology: that *preconceptions* can be important to interpreting data and therefore can strongly influence all other tasks that depend on this most basic inferential undertaking. We shall not pause here to demonstrate that prior theories, schemas, perceptual and problem-solving sets, and other preconceptions can powerfully influence subjects' interpretation of ambiguous stimuli. The impact of preconceptions is one of the better demonstrated findings of twentieth-century psychology, from the Gestaltists' "Einstellung" phenomenon to countless demonstrations of the effects of stereotypes on judgments of individuals. In our opinion, the phenomenon has been overdemonstrated and underanalyzed. It seems to us that the literature has scarcely addressed either of the most interesting questions about the phenomenon: (1) When is it appropriate for characterizations of data to be influenced by preconceptions and when is it inappropriate? (2) What are the factors that increase or decrease the likelihood that preconceptions will influence data coding? In discussing these questions we depart somewhat from the standard terminology of statistical treatment of inductive inference in order to clarify the case of social perception.

The Normative Status
of Theory-biased Data Coding

To date, remarkably little attention has been paid to the normative status of knowingly, or even unknowingly, letting one's preconceptions bias one's interpretation of events. Rather, investigators generally have been content merely to demonstrate the existence of the phenomenon. The normative issue, however, is both critically important and particularly complicated. Consider, for a moment, the data-coding decision that Jane must make when someone fails to return a smile that she has offered across a crowded room. If the intended recipient is a close friend, she is likely to code the event as a simple failure of the other person to see her smile. If the recipient were notoriously cold and interpersonally aloof, or if Jane were currently competing with the recipient for some desired goal, she is likely to code the same event as a deliberate rebuff. Is such a biased interpretation of the same physical event unreasonable or counternormative? Surely, the answer is not a definite "yes"!

In attempting to decide exactly what answer to the normative question we will wish to endorse, let us consider the results of an actual experiment, a classic in the "preconception" tradition. In a study reported in 1950, Kelley showed that people's impressions of another person's personality were greatly influenced by a simple manipulation of prior expectations. Subjects in this study, before hearing a guest lecturer in a psychology course, received a seven-adjective description of the lecturer, one that included either the word "warm" or the word "cold" in an otherwise identical list of traits. This simple manipulation consistently influenced the perceptions of the subjects. Those expecting a "warm" instructor perceived him to be relatively sociable, informal, even-tempered, friendly, and so on, and they responded accordingly by participating more actively in the class. In contrast, subjects expecting a cold instructor rated the same person as relatively self-centered, unsociable, and formal, and they showed a corresponding reluctance to participate in the class.

When this study is cited, the implication often conveyed (though never intended by Kelley) is that the subjects were somehow *misled* by their preconceptions and that they incorrectly coded the behavior they witnessed. But let us examine these "errors" more closely. Presumably, what the subjects did was to give the presupposed "warm" instructor every "benefit of the doubt" in interpreting or coding his behavior. When he smiled, for example, it was seen as a response to the class rather than an expression of self-satisfaction. When he hurried his presentation, his haste was attributed to enthusiasm rather than to impatience and when he dwelt on a point it was seen as a symptom of involvement and not condescension. Similarly, when he offered eye contact it was accepted as a friendly and accepting gesture rather than as an icy challenge or expression of disapproval, and so forth. The presupposed "cold" instructor presumably was denied such benefits in the subjects' interpretation of potentially ambiguous behavior.

The evidence for bias is undeniable. Since the same set of actions could not "objectively" reflect both warmth and coldness, subjects in one or both conditions must have coded the data incorrectly. But what exactly was the subjects' collective error? Did it lie in their willingness to select and distort data in the light of their preconceptions? In a sense it did, but an error was committed only because one or both sets of preconceptions was fallacious. Surely it would have been accurate data interpretation for subjects in the "warm" condition to have given an instructor the benefit of the doubt as described if he were, in fact, an unusually "warm" individual. For such an individual, smiles generally *would* reflect approval of the class rather than smug self-congratulation, eye contact generally *would* be friendly rather than hostile, and the pace of presentation generally would reflect a benign, accommodating intent. Thus, as in our description of Jane's interpretation of an unreturned smile, there is nothing unwise per se about the use of a coding system that gives substantial weight to preconceptions.

We do not wish to deny that the preconceptions used in data-coding often are quite erroneous. Consider, for example, the reviewer who must characterize the worth of a journal article submitted for publication, but whose preconceptions of credibility and originality are dominated by sexist stereotypes. Such a reviewer is bound to let his or her stereotypes and expectations influence the evaluation; for example, by giving or withholding benefit of the doubt about procedural ambiguities, by labeling opaque passages as "difficult" rather than as "confused," and by reflecting on potential implications rather than by ferreting out seeming inconsistencies in data or logic. Such a strategy not only would be unjust, it also would fail in its goal of accepting superior manuscripts and rejecting inferior ones. But this is true only because an author's sex is probably a very *poor* predictor of the value of an ambiguously worthy intellectual product. Had one used a different basis for forming preconceptions, for instance a prior receipt of the Nobel Prize versus a prior denunciation for incompetence or fraud by a group of scientific peers, the use of this "biased strategy" would have been quite appropriate.

It is intriguing to speculate on why scientists who have demonstrated the influence of preconceptions on data-coding usually have taken such a disapproving position on the practice. We suspect that they have done so because the practice is indeed the cardinal sin for the formal, pure scientist. The first rule that a formal scientist learns is that a theory should never be allowed to influence the coding of the data testing that theory. Thus, if the investigator's hypothesis is that women have more "fear of success" than men do, even the scientific ingenue knows that the investigator must be blind to the sex of the subject when coding free-response protocols for expressions of fear of success. To allow one's knowledge of the subject's sex to bias one's interpretation of whether a given utterance was indicative of "fear of success" versus "uncertainty about ability" would be to permit the possibility that any positive findings might reflect only the influence of the theory on the coder.

We have no desire to take issue with this time-honored methodological principle. It seems clear, however, that it would be unwise to bind the lay scientist to it. Indeed, we would not even wish to bind the *applied scientist* or practitioner to the principle. On the contrary, for the "non-pure" scientist, it is often normatively correct for theories and other preconceptions to influence the characterization of the data. Consider a medical practitioner who must decide whether to order a painful and somewhat risky biopsy for a patient with an ambiguous-appearing, chronic sore on the back of his neck. The practitioner probably *should* characterize the sore as "potentially cancerous" and order the biopsy if the patient is a fair-skinned cowboy with a family history of skin cancer, who rides the range in the sun-bleached desert of New Mexico. The practitioner probably should *not* so characterize the sore and should not order the biopsy if the patient is a swarthy accountant living in Seattle.

The practitioner and the layperson normally are concerned with characterizing as accurately as possible the *individual case*. That purpose is best served by allowing valid preconceptions and theories to influence the characterization of the individual case to the extent that the data themselves are ambiguous. In contrast, the pure scientist typically cares little about the individual case, except as an exemplar of a class. Slight preconception-induced errors in characterizing individual cases therefore can subvert the scientist's purpose of correctly characterizing the class or differentiating it from other classes. In measurement theory terms, the practitioner and the layperson need to reduce measurement error of all types, and "systematic" error, of the sort that a theory could produce, is not more damaging than "random" error is. In contrast, the pure scientist often can tolerate substantial random error, but "systematic" error, even when small in absolute terms, must be avoided at all costs.

Our conclusion about the appropriateness of allowing one's preconceptions about an object to influence one's characterization of the object is thus consistent with the conclusion we reached in chapter 2 about the general appropriateness of assimilating information into preexisting knowledge structures. The practice cannot be criticized per se. On the contrary, the practice will produce, in general, more accurate interpretation of experience than would the practice of ignoring such preconceptions entirely. It is not the practice per se which is wrong, but the particular circumstances in which it is followed. It seems to us that there are three broad sets of circumstances in which the practice of allowing preconceptions to influence the characterization of data is normatively questionable.

(1) *When the theory is held on poor grounds.* If an individual applies a theory to the data at hand with inadequate justification for that theory, or inadequate justification for believing it relevant to the immediate data, then the practice is open to criticism.

(2) *When the theory is applied unconsciously in the belief that the data are being interpreted without the aid of the theory.* It is a well known social-psychological theory that people hold many erroneous stereotypes, for example, of racial and ethnic groups and of the differences between the sexes. Social psychologists have rejected people's protestations that their interpretations of the behavior of particular blacks or whites, or women or men, are direct "read-outs" of the data. Instead, they have argued that such interpretations may be the dis-

torted products of "unconscious ideologies." If this is true, it is a very serious accusation indeed. If people apply theories to data in the belief that their interpretations are unaided by theory, then the practice is clearly dangerous and self-deluded.

(3) *When the theory preempts examination of the data.* One of the best established phenomena in the "biased coding" literature is the set or primacy effect. Once people have formed a strong theory or expectation of what the data will look like, they sometimes fail to examine the particulars of the case. For example, Jones, Rock, Shaver, Goethals, & Ward (1968) showed that people characterize target individuals as having more ability when they solve many problems early in a series and few late in the series, than when they solve few problems early in the series and many late in the series. The belief formed early in the series seems to persist, possibly because, as both Jones and Goethals (1972) and Anderson and Jacobson (1965) suggested, once a belief is formed less weight is given to subsequent information. Such a tendency, it should be noted, is not itself counternormative. The tendency becomes unwise only to the extent that the economy of rapid impression formation is offset by errors arising because of the variability or changeable nature of the object.

In summary, theory-biased coding of data seems to be normatively allowable, even appropriate, in principle. In practice, however, such biases often are questionable, and it is both possible and necessary to distinguish between appropriate and inappropriate instances of theory-biased coding of data.

Factors Promoting Theory-biased Coding of Data

Just as there has been little attention paid by investigators to the normative appropriateness of biased coding, there also has been insufficient consideration of the factors that increase or decrease the likelihood of such bias. We may speculate that there are several factors that make bias more or less likely.

1. *Confidence in the theory.* Subjective certainty about a given theory or belief is likely to be one important determinant of its capacity to foster biased processing, and this certainty is likely to reflect the extent to which the theory seems congruent both with one's past experiences and with one's general ideas about the world. Confidence in a theory, of course, may be well founded or ill founded. If one's characterization of an event is influenced by a theory of which one is confident on solid epistemic grounds, then such an influence is apt to be appropriate and to lead to accurate characterization. Any effect that *emotional commitment* may have on strengthening one's certainty about one's theories is less reasonable.

2. *Chronic and transient availability of the theory.* The likelihood that a theory will influence data coding is necessarily a function of its availability, that is, its likelihood of being triggered by the data at hand. The determinants of theory availability were discussed in chapter 2. They include both the nature of one's past experiences and the tenor of one's current preoccupations. Thus, for the disciple of Freud, psychodynamic concepts and relationships are likely to be highly available and readily triggered whenever a slip of the tongue or a momentary lapse of memory is observed. For more eclectic observers of the human scene, such psychodynamic conceptions are likely to be evoked only when the event seems to demand such interpretations—for example, when the content or context of the parapraxis is explicitly sexual, or the setting is a psychology lecture, or a bust of Freud overlooks the proceedings.

3. *Presumed clarity versus ambiguity of the data.* The *ambiguity* presumed to characterize a particular type of data probably is important to determining its malleability by a prior theory or belief. Although one is unlikely to distort one's recording of the temperature on a particular day in the light of some theory of weather patterns, one is considerably more likely to adjust one's perception of the warmth of a social gathering in the light of theories of the character of the participants or of the nature of the occasion. One's beliefs about apparent perceptibility of a given type of data seem to affect the weight one gives to preconceptions. These beliefs, however, are sometimes accurate and sometimes not. The layperson normally believes, for example, that color is a property of objects that can be known independently of any background knowledge of the object or the conditions under which it is viewed. This belief is incorrect, since apparent hue is influenced by a number of factors including, for example, the intensity and wavelength of ambient illumination. Similarly, in the social domain, people probably overestimate the perceptibility of an individual's attributes on the basis of brief exposure to them. Thus, the one-hour personal interview has virtually no validity for predicting job performance, yet people often feel convinced after such interviews that they have a good idea of the candidate's attributes and how well the candidate would perform in the job. Indeed, such an inflated belief in the certainty of knowledge obtained in the interview may cause people to overturn completely (and wrongly) preconceptions of the candidate based on job recommendations that probably *do* have some validity. As this example and similar examples in chapter 3 make clear, preconceptions do not always overwhelm data. Sometimes it is quite the reverse; the immediate implications of the data overwhelm the preconceptions. Psychologists' concern with the capacity of preconceptions to distort data interpretation has blinded them to the equally obvious and potentially equally dangerous fact that data sometimes can completely override preconceptions. The normative considerations of the wisdom of the latter tendency are identical to those we already have discussed. On the

one hand, it is highly adaptive to be able to recognize that one's preconceptions may be wrong and to accept the implications of current evidence. On the other hand, the openminded empiricist who accepts all evidence at face value will pay a high price for such malleability. In chapter 3 we discussed some of the costs incurred by overweighting immediately available data as a function of their vividness. In chapter 7, on prediction, we discuss some of the costs of underweighting certain types of valid and useful preconceptions, for example, population base rates.

CHARACTERIZING THE DATA SAMPLE: AVAILABILITY BIASES

The characterization of a particular datum is sometimes influenced heavily, rightly or wrongly, by preexisting theories and other knowledge structures. Concrete or vivid data often may be taken at face value and may escape—again, rightly or wrongly—the biasing influence of prior theories. It should be clear that preconceptions have the same possibilities to influence unduly or insufficiently characterizations of *samples* and *populations*. We will not dwell on these issues, however, since they are essentially the same as those in the characterization of the individual datum. We will focus instead on quite a different set of issues, concerning the *accuracy* of people's characterizations of samples and populations.

The Lay Scientist's Computational Abilities

Everyday experience demonstrates that people are often quite proficient at estimating frequencies, proportions, and averages, even when actual counting and computational procedures are difficult or impossible. We also expect people's errors to be reasonably random, so that a large number of individuals estimating anything from their hamburger consumption to their sexual activities should produce mean estimates that approximate the true figures. Indeed, this expectation is the article of faith upon which much of the survey-researchers' trade rests.

Until recently, the psychological literature offered little reason to doubt people's ability to estimate descriptive statistics such as means or proportions and even more complex statistics such as variance. As recently as 1967, Peterson and Beach were able to conclude a survey of the literature with a very favorable assessment of the layperson's computational capacities. Less than a decade later, however, further studies of the *failings* of the "intuitive statistician" had dramatically altered this assessment.

As subsequent surveyors (Slovic, Fischhoff, & Lichtenstein 1976) noted, anyone "who had dozed off after reading Peterson and Beach and roused himself only recently would be startled by the widespread change . . . " (p. 20). What happened in the intervening years to change the flattering characterization of the layperson's capacities?

To answer this question and to begin to appreciate people's limitations in characterizing samples, it is instructive to consider the studies that initially prompted Peterson's and Beach's conclusions. Most striking is the degree to which early investigators had relied on highly impoverished stimuli. Almost without exception, subjects' judgments were of numbers, letters, lights, tones, and other simple, barren stimuli unlikely to trigger complex, potentially erroneous cognitive responses. Furthermore, the boundaries of the relevant stimulus set were carefully marked for the subject. For example, in a typical study, subjects might be asked to estimate the ratio of low cycle tones to total tones in a rapidly presented series. There is no doubt that a subject's accuracy can be good under such circumstances, even when stimuli are so numerous and are presented so rapidly that actual counting and computation are precluded. Indeed, although the optimistic conclusions reached by Peterson and Beach can no longer be accepted, the studies themselves remain quite important. They show that if large and systematic errors occur in the estimation of sample statistics or population values, they do not reflect any inherent inability to perform the judgmental equivalents of counting or computation.

The remainder of this chapter explores some of the sources of error that arise when the intuitive statistician's task is changed—that is, when stimuli are more interesting and more complex, when the boundaries of the relevant stimulus domains are less clear, and when recall, imagination, or inference provide the basis for the subject's estimates.

Extremity, Salience, and Availability

Perhaps the most important influence distorting people's characterization of data samples is that of event *salience* and of consequent availability biases. In one study, for example, Kahneman and Tversky (1972) showed that subjects asked to read lists of well known personalities of both sexes subsequently overestimated the proportional representation of that sex whose members on the list had been more famous. If the list contained the names of very famous women (for example, Elizabeth Taylor), and less famous men (for example, Alan Ladd), subjects recalled the list as a whole as containing proportionally more women's names than it actually did. A study reported by Rothbart and others (1978) examined a related availability bias. Subjects were asked to estimate the proportion of individuals over six feet tall in two samples in which members' heights were specified individually. In both samples the actual percentage of six-footers was 20 percent. When those in the subset meeting this criterion were only moderately tall (6′1″ to 6′4″), the subjects' estimates, on the average, came quite close to the correct percentage. However, when the subset contained extremely tall individuals (6′5″ to 6′11″), the mean estimate was 30 percent. Very similar results were obtained when the judgments were on the proportion of criminals in two samples and when the *severity* of the criminal offenses within a sample was manipulated. The sample as a whole was recalled as having more criminals if the nature of the individual offenses had been particularly heinous than if the offenses had been relatively slight.

The criterion used by subjects to guide their estimates in the studies by Kahneman and Tversky and by Rothbart and others may have been the absolute number of cases they could recall, or it may have been the subjective *difficulty* they experienced in recalling such cases. Either criterion would constitute a use of the availability heuristic in a context in which availability did not faithfully reflect relative frequency.

Availability effects, it should be noted, can be dictated by factors that operate *before* the perceiver has had any chance to store or recall data. In everyday experience, for instance, media reporters and other communicators may overexpose us to some events and underexpose us to others, ensuring that our later ease of recalling or imagining the relevant events will produce a distorted estimate. Slovic, Fischhoff, and Lichtenstein (1976) presented what appeared to be intriguing examples of this phenomenon in their findings on people's beliefs about causes of death. For instance, people erroneously regard death from fire to be more likely than death from drowning, and they believe accidental death to be more likely than death from "stroke," despite strikingly conflicting mortality figures for both cases. Slovic and colleagues argued persuasively that such erroneous estimates, which could have serious consequences for one's decisions on health care and risk reduction, arise because fires and accidents typically dominate local news coverage, while drownings and strokes are more difficult to cover and are generally less interesting to readers or viewers.

In a similar vein, veterans of the huge antiwar marches of the Vietnam era will recall the frustration of seeing the media devote almost as much film to the hundred counterprotestors as to the 100,000 marchers. The marchers' concern, of course, was that the media made both protesters and counterprotesters equally available to the viewers who might, in turn, reach inaccurate conclusions about the relative size of the opposing activist groups. In a sense, the media prevented the protesters from enjoying the fruits of their efforts to make their antiwar sentiments disproportionately available and influential relative to the more muted sentiments of the so-called silent majority.

Thus far we have emphasized the availability advantage enjoyed by actions, events, and personal characteristics that are particularly vivid, extreme, or newsworthy. Ross, Greene, and House (1977) conducted a series of studies that suggest a rather different availability-mediated influence on people's estimates of samples or populations. Ross and colleagues showed that subjects are prone to regard the behavior of other people as relatively uncommon (and therefore relatively revealing of their personal dispositions) to the extent that their behavior differs from the subjects' own responses in the same situation. People presume that a larger fraction of others behave as they themselves behave and hold opinions that they themselves hold, than is actually the case. In accounting for this "false consensus" effect, the investigators suggested that availability may be important, for two reasons. First, we tend to know and associate with people who share our own personal background, experiences, interests, values, and outlooks. Such people *do*, in disproportionate numbers, respond much as we would in a wide variety of situations. Indeed, our association with them is apt to be determined precisely by such consensus. Second, the responses that we have chosen, or believe that we would choose, are probably easier for us to recall or imagine. We are apt to have superior "scripts" for generating instances of responses that correspond to our own, and this ease of generation may influence our estimates of the probable responses of others.

A possibly related "egocentric bias" was explored by M. Ross and his colleagues (M. Ross & Sicoly 1979), who asked subjects to estimate the proportion of actions contributed to joint enterprises by themselves and by coparticipants in the enterprises. Across a wide range of activities, from simple informal discussions and household tasks to scientific collaborations, subjects seemed prone to exaggerate their own contributions compared to those of their peers. Although the subjects' characterizations seemed superficially to be self-serving, simple availability effects, rather than any motivational bias, may have been largely responsible. In general, one's own efforts and actions may be disproportionately available and hence their frequency compared to those of one's peers may be overestimated. If this interpretation is correct, two predictions follow: First, one's own "contributions" may be *underestimated* relative to others', if others' contributions happen to enjoy the availability advantage. For example, people may underestimate the relative frequency of their own nonverbal behaviors (hand gestures, nods, smiles, frowns, etc.) or any other behaviors that are poorly monitored by the actor but well monitored by the observer. Second, people may overestimate their own behaviors even when they are unattractive, as long as they are disproportionately available. For example, people might overestimate the number of occasions, compared to other people, when they daydream on the job, break dishes, or become depressed after receiving criticism. Indeed, this is the theoretical concept underlying the notion of "pluralistic ignorance," in which individuals all believe they are more often guilty of certain socially undesirable behaviors than their neighbors are.

GENERALIZING FROM INSTANCES TO POPULATIONS: REPRESENTATIVENESS VERSUS SAMPLING THEORY

Many important social judgments of everyday life force the intuitive scientist to take a step beyond characterizing individual observations or data samples. That step is using the data at hand to make inferences about the general characteristics or "parameters" of the *population* from which those data were drawn. In some cases the inferences are generalizations about a class of people, objects, or events, that are made on the basis of one's knowledge of one or more members of the class. For example, one arrives at impressions about Russians, female psychologists, Volvos, Italian movies, or Rubinstein concerts based on the particular sample of that class that one encounters. In other cases, the generalizations are about an entity, based on a limited sample of its attributes. Thus, one decides what Joe is like from a sample of his actions and opinions or what Albania is like from a sample of its people and institutions.

Besides the various factors already discussed that influence such judgments through their impact on the coding of data or on the characterization of data samples, there are two other influential shortcomings of the intuitive scientist. The first is insensitivity to considerations of sample *size;* the second is insensitivity to considerations of sample *bias.* In a sense, peoples' erroneous inferences about populations again can be traced to a theory but, in this case, to a theory they *do not* know.

Insensitivity to Sample Size

Kahneman and Tversky (1972) showed that, in making judgments, people have little appreciation of the statistical principle summarized in the "law of large numbers." It is this law which describes the consistency with which large-sample statistics approach corresponding population values. The larger the sample, the more likely it is that its properties will faithfully reflect the properties of the population. Conversely, small samples often provide population estimates far wide of the mark.

In a typical demonstration of people's failure to understand the relevance of sample size, Kahneman and Tversky asked subjects, all of whom were untutored in statistics, to guess which of two hospitals in a given town had more days on which 60 percent or more of the babies born were boys: (i) a large hospital with an average of forty-five births per day, or (ii) a small hospital with an average of fifteen births per day. Most subjects thought that the two hospitals would have about an equal number of days with 60 percent male births, and just as many subjects thought it would be the larger hospital as thought it would be the smaller that would have more such days. Such insensitivity to the importance of sample size, it should now be apparent, reflects people's reliance on the representativeness heuristic in judgments to which other considerations are crucial. Small samples with 60 percent males are not less representative of a population known to have 50 percent males than are larger samples with 60 percent males. Despite representativeness criteria, the two samples are very different in their likelihood of occurrence. The actual probability of 60 percent male births on a given day is roughly twice as great for the smaller hospital sample as for the larger one.

This problem is an extremely elementary one for the statistics student. In fact, the authors' own informal studies suggest that a standard introductory statistics course is sufficient to enable most undergraduates to provide the correct answer. A knowledge of elementary statistics, however, is not enough to prevent errors when the problem becomes somewhat more complicated. Kahneman and Tversky posed the following problem to University of Michigan students, all of whom had completed at least one course in statistics:

> The average heights of adult males and females in the U.S. are, respectively, 5 ft. 10 in. and 5 ft. 4 in. Both distributions are approximately normal with a standard deviation of about 2.5 in. An investigator has selected one population by chance and has drawn from it a random sample. What do you think are the odds that he has selected the male population if:
> (i) The sample consists of a single person whose height is 5 ft. 10 in.?
> (ii) The sample consists of 6 persons whose average height is 5 ft. 8 in? (1972, p. 449)

As expected, a substantial majority of subjects estimated the odds favoring the male population to be greater in the first case than in the second. The median odds favoring the male population, as rated by the subjects, were 8:1 for the single individual case and 2.5:1 for the six-person case. The *correct* odds, in contrast, are 16:1 and 29:1, respectively. Thus, it seems clear that even these relatively sophisticated subjects were overly influenced by the representativeness heuristic. A height of 5 ft. 10 in. clearly is more representative of the male population mean and less representative of the female population mean than is a height of 5 ft. 8 in.. What the subjects were *insufficiently* influenced by was the greater variability or sampling error that can be expected for a sample of one observation than for one of six observations.

Tversky and Kahneman (1971) argued that even a high degree of knowledge of statistical matters is insufficient to appreciate fully the influence of sample size on the stability of sample means. In fact, in an ingenious series of demonstrations, they were able to show that even professional mathematical psychologists can be overly influenced by the representativeness heuristic and insufficiently influenced by considerations of sample size. For example, when making estimates of the appropriate N to use for a replication study, these scientists tended to recommend sample sizes that gave little better than a fifty-fifty chance of rejecting an incorrect null hypothesis. As Tversky and Kahneman explained, people "expect any two samples drawn from a particular population to be more similar to one another and to the population than sampling theory predicts, at least for small samples" (p. 105).

It is easy to see how people could be led to make erroneous inferences in their daily lives by failing to appreciate the stability of population estimates based on large samples and the unreliability of estimates based on small samples. Consider again Borgida's and Nisbett's (1977) demonstration (discussed in chapter 3) of people's susceptibility to small amounts of vivid, concrete information. In one condition, introductory psychology students were given mean course evaluations (indicated on typical five-point rating scales) and were told that the relevant means summarized the opinions of "dozens of previous students." In a second condition, subjects saw and heard two or three students first evaluate the courses on a similar scale and then make a few brief comments consistent with their evaluations. The results showed that the abstract, large-sample means had much less impact on the students' tentative course selections than did the very small samples of concrete, personal recommendations. Because these manipulations were compound, it was difficult to assess the specific effect of the sample-size factor. It seems clear, however, that the subjects would have been protected from the normatively questionable pattern they showed if they had appreciated fully the low reliability of the small, face-to-face samples and the very high reliability of the large samples summarized by the statistics.

The "interview illusion" discussed earlier, in which employers or other gatekeepers are confident of the validity of their assessments of various candidates based on one-hour interviews, can also be understood as a failure to appreciate the law of large numbers. The recommendations of other people, based often on literally hundreds of times as much information as can be extracted from the one-hour interview, can be blithely set aside in favor of one's own impressions only by people who are functionally oblivious to the implications of the law of large numbers or who are convinced that any possible limitations of their own data are much less important than possible biases in the past observations or current reports of those writing recommendations.

Not only informal social judgments and personal decisions are undermined by insensitivity to considerations of sample size. Even society's most important decision makers, when discussing policy matters in institutional settings, are not immune. An acquaintance of the authors, who often testifies at congressional committees on behalf of the Environmental Protection Agency, conveyed the following frustration to us. She reported that the bane of her professional existence is the frequency with which she reports test data such as EPA mileage estimates based on samples of ten or more cars, only to be contradicted by a congressman who retorts with information about a single case: "What do you mean, the Blatzmobile gets twenty miles per gallon on the road?" he says. "My neighbor has one, and he gets only fifteen." His fellow legislators then usually respond as if matters were at a standoff—one EPA estimate versus one colleague's estimate obtained from his neighbor.

Even in the U.S. Supreme Court, the lawyer who presents data on the efficacy of capital punishment as a deterrent (or, more usually, on its lack of efficacy) is apt to find statistics "rebutted" by a small number of case histories. Analyses comparing overall murder rates in states that have abolished capital punishment with those that have not, or analyses comparing crime rates before and after abolition, are countered with case histories of a few felons whose solemn affidavits claim that they personally were deterred or undeterred by the threat of a death penalty.

Thus far, we have dealt with social judgment errors that conceptually are estimates of population values. But the failure to recognize the importance of sample size also can result in errors in judgments of a single entity. We offer two anecdotes to illustrate this point, while piously recognizing that they are a poor substitute for more formal evidence based on large-sample investigations.

Our first anecdote concerns the cousin of one of the authors who expressed astonishment when the author happened to remark that Chicago was one of his favorite cities and that he visited it every chance he got. "I don't see how you could like Chicago," the cousin said. "Oh, you don't like it," the author asked. "No," said the cousin, "I saw all those ugly tenements and factories from the freeway when I was driving here to visit you."

The reader undoubtedly knows enough both about sampling theory and about the variegated nature of American cities to be immune to any tendency to judge a city on so small a sample of its attributes. But we invite the reader to share with us the experience of the noted psychologist Irving Janis, a clever man by any standards and as knowledgeable about inferential rules as the most astute of us.

Janis told us that he was recently on the island of Hawaii and decided to go to see an active volcano there. After a rather lengthy hike, he reached the rim, looked over, and saw a large pit filled with clouds of smoke. "Oh," mused Janis, "so that's what the volcano is like." He reports that he continued looking into the crater rather longer than seemed justified by the interest of the spectacle and then, just as he was about to turn away and hike back down the mountain, he saw a fountain of red lava burst through the smoke. The sight was very impressive, and he stayed to watch as, every few minutes, a column of fiery liquid would split the clouds. In fact, he remained at the spectacle for several hours, congratulating himself on having had the patience to discover what the volcano was *really* like. During periods of quiescence, he spent his time explaining to tourists who were about to start back down the mountain after "seeing the volcano" that there was more to be seen.

So impressed was Janis with the spectacle, in fact, that he went back the next day. This time, when he looked over the rim, he gasped in astonishment. There was no smoke at all. Instead, he could see to the bottom of the crater where he beheld a heaving sea of molten lava. The fountains of lava he had seen occasionally the day before turned out to be not the discrete, infrequent events he had supposed, but instead a continuous process. They had seemed isolated and rare the day before, only because most of them had been obscured by the clouds of smoke.

Janis, incidentally, insisted that he cannot be excused for his initial willingness to assume that he had found out "what the volcano was like" on the grounds that he had never been told what to expect. He had seen many pictures of active volcanos and knew that some of them, at least, had precisely those exciting properties that he nearly missed seeing for himself. His accurate preconceptions, however, had had little influence when pitted against a single, short-lived (but concrete and first hand) observation of a sample of its attributes.

An inevitable consequence of the willingness to make strong inferences based on small amounts of data is that people often will find themselves in sharp *disagreement* about the objects and events they encounter. Thus it is common for two people to come away from a social gathering with very different impressions about a third person whom they both have met or for two tourists to disagree on the courtesy of Parisian taxicab drivers. The two individuals may politely acknowledge that they "just had different experiences" or even that they "really did not have a good basis for definitive judgments." We suspect, however, that in such cases each individual harbors private suspicions that the peer is a "poor judge of people," or at least that that person just happened to see an atypical sample of the particular person or population. One is likely to believe that, if properly interpreted, it is one's own sample that holds the key to what the person (place, institution, or event) is "really" like. People are likely to do this, moreover, even though they are fully aware that any small sample of their *own* behavior (or of their spouse's or children's behavior) might well be misleading.

In the cases covered thus far, consideration of sample size has been pitted against the potent representativeness heuristic, and in each instance the former has been vanquished by the latter. This evidence makes it clear that people have only a very limited, general appreciation of the law of large numbers, or, as Kahneman and Tversky (1973) pointedly suggested, that people believe that the law of large numbers applies also to small numbers. Such a generalization should not be taken to mean that all problems of sample size will be treated incorrectly. Indeed, it is quite possible to specify problems for which the use of the representativeness heuristic is helpful. When entities or populations tend to be consistent or invariant, it may be safe to assume the representativeness of small samples, and when statistical summaries are prepared by those who would deceive us, it may be well to trust one's own experiences or those of trusted informants. In addition, problems that are logically parallel to those which expose people's weaknesses frequently are handled quite well. Consider, for example, what would happen if people were asked whether it was more likely that it would rain three days out of the next four or thirty days out of the next forty. Most people surely would answer that the first possibility is the more likely one and this answer would be correct. Such an insight, however, would not be based on the recognition that extremely divergent proportions are less probable for samples of large size than for samples of small size. Instead, the answer probably would be based on the application of the representativeness heuristic: "Rain three days out of four" is a recognizable, fairly representative weather pattern, but "rain thirty days out of forty" is a rarely experienced and highly unrepresentative weather pattern.

Insensitivity to Sample Bias

If one wishes to estimate population values from sample characteristics, discern the nature of an entity from a sample of its attributes, or judge the dispositions of an actor from a sample of the actor's behavior, there is one concern even more important than sample size. That is sample *bias*. Accurate judgments of population or entity values can be made under only two circumstances: (1) when the relevant sample is truly random or unbiased or (2) when the observer can identify the biases in the available sample and then make adequate allowances for them. The existing evidence suggests that in many important contexts people may have no more intuitive sensitivity to the implications of sample bias than to the implications of inadequate sample size.

An early indication of people's insensitivity to considerations of randomness versus bias in sample selection came from a study by Nisbett and Borgida (1975). They asked subjects to make predictions of the behavior of participants in psychology experiments. Some subjects were shown brief videotaped interviews with two participants who, subjects were assured, had been drawn at random from the population of original participants. Subjects were told that both participants had behaved in an extreme, intuitively unlikely way (based on control subjects' predictions of how participants would behave). A second group of subjects was shown the same videotapes and also was told that the participants had behaved in an extreme, intuitively unlikely way. These subjects, however, were told nothing whatever about how the two participants were selected. Indeed, for all these subjects knew, the two participants they saw were the *only* ones who had behaved in the extreme way and might even have been selected precisely for this reason.

Predictions of the two groups were, despite sampling considerations, nearly identical. Both the group assured of random selection and the group given no sampling information whatever shifted their predictions of population values markedly in the direction of the behavior of the two participants whom they viewed.

It might be argued that this result merely revealed what every social scientist already strongly suspected, namely, that the layperson has little conception of the statistical meaning of "randomness." Indeed, a "random" selection procedure is often regarded by the layperson as if it were a slapdash, haphazard procedure, as in Tversky's and Kahneman's (1971) joke about the cabinet officer who dismissed the results of a poll he did not like by saying that they were based on people chosen "completely at random."

A failure to appreciate the meaning of randomness is no mere foible, however. It can be argued that the failure to understand the inferential advantages of a random selection procedure automatically betokens an insensitivity to the *disadvantages* of a *biased* sampling procedure. The concept of randomness and the concept of bias are intimately linked. Any sampling procedure that fails to yield values identical on the average to those produced by a random procedure is biased, by definition. Despite Nisbett's and Borgida's results, though, one still might hope that people would be somewhat reluctant to generalize when they have reason to be *certain* about the existence of a sampling bias. Ross, Amabile, and Steinmetz (1977) provided evidence that addresses this question.

Ross and colleagues asked two subjects to play a question-and-answer game of general knowledge. The subjects were assigned randomly to the roles of "questioner" and "contestant." Both subjects then heard a description of their own role and that of their coparticipant. The questioner's duties consisted of preparing ten "challenging but not impossible" questions from his own store of general knowledge which he was to pose to the contestant. The contestant was to give his answers aloud. After each answer, the questioner was to state either "correct" or "incorrect" and then supply the correct answer. As the session proceeded, the substantial advantage of the questioner's role in self-presentation asserted itself. Again and again, the questioner displayed esoteric knowledge in the questions he posed (for example, "What is the world's longest glacier?") and in the answers he supplied when the contestant failed to respond correctly. Finally, at the conclusion of the session, both of the participants, and, in a subsequent reenactment, observers as well, were required to rate the questioner's and the contestant's general knowledge.

It should be emphasized that the source of the bias in the respective "samples" of general knowledge displayed by questioner and contestant could hardly have been more blatant. The questioner's role guaranteed that he would reveal no area of ignorance. The contestant's role, by contrast, gave no opportunity for such selective, self-serving displays. Instead, it made displays of ignorance virtually inevitable. (In fact, contestants on the average correctly answered only about 40 percent of the questions posed by the questioners.)

What were the effects of these biased displays of knowledge? It may be seen in Figure 4.1 that, despite the explicit specification of the "privileges" and "disadvantages" of each role, the contestants judged themselves substantially inferior in general knowledge to their questioners. Observers also judged that the contestants had less knowledge than did the questioners. These erroneous inferences about general knowledge level formally reflect the failure to make adequate allowance for the biased nature of the questioner's own sample of knowledge compared to that of the contestant. That is, the questioner's sample consisted entirely of facts known to him but sufficiently recondite to be unknown to most of his peers, while the contestant's sample inevitably included many instances of ignorance.

The overall pattern of ratings by the two participants and by the observers emphasizes this interpretation. It is particularly important to note that the *questioners* did *not* show any systematic distortion in rating their own or their partner's general knowledge. Presumably these correct estimates occur-

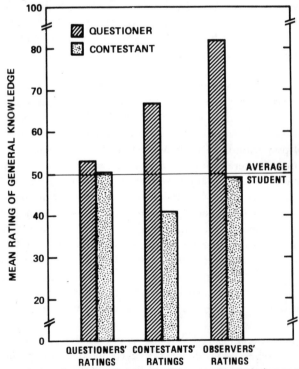

Fig. 4.1 Ratings of questioners' and contestants' general knowledge as a function of status as questioner, contestant or observer. (From Ross, Amabile, & Steinmetz 1977.)

red because the questioners did, in a sense, have a random sample of the contestants' knowledge (that is, of their ability to answer a set of very difficult questions). Furthermore, they were aware of the many gaps in their own knowledge not revealed in their encounter with the contestant. Observers, on the other hand, were restricted to the same *biased* sample of the questioner's knowledge possessed by the contestants and to the same *unbiased* sample of the contestant's knowledge enjoyed by the questioner. In addition, observers had one other clue to help them decide whether the questioner was unusually knowledgeable or whether the contestant was unusually ignorant. They knew that they *shared* the contestant's inability to match the questioner's knowledge. Accordingly, observers rated questioners even more positively than the contestants has rated them, but they rated the contestants less negatively than the latter had rated themselves.

"Role-conferred" advantages and disadvantages, with resulting biases in the behavior samples presented by the coactants, are common features of many social situations, and inaccurate social inferences are frequently the result. Ross and colleagues called our attention to the ordeal of the oral Ph.D. examination as a possible real-life counterpart of their demonstration. The candidate is required to field questions from the particular, and occasionally esoteric, areas of the examiners' interest and expertise. In contrast to the examiners, the candidate has relatively little time for reflection and relatively little power to define the domain of inquiry. In light of the experiment just described, it might be predicted that the typical candidate would leave the ordeal feeling more relief than pride, while the examiners depart with increased respect for each other's insight and scholarship. In the authors' experience, at least, this prediction generally has been confirmed.

The evidence reviewed thus far indicates that people are not sufficiently concerned about the possibility that the available data may be biased. A more direct and even more surprising demonstration of people's insensitivity to sample bias recently was provided by Hamill, Wilson, and Nisbett (1979). In the first study we shall consider, Hamill and colleagues presented their subjects with one of two videotaped "interviews" in which a person alleged to be a guard at a state prison discussed his job. In one condition the guard was a model of decency who exuded compassion and concern for rehabilitation. In the other, he was a veritable brute, scoffing at the idea of rehabilitation and characterizing the prisoners as "animals" responsive only to coercion. Crosscutting this manipulation was another, systematic manipulation of the information available to subjects about the guard's "typicality." Some subjects were given no information about typicality, some were told before seeing the videotape that the guard was quite typical of those at the prison, and the remainder were forewarned that his humaneness (or inhumaneness) was quite *atypical*—that he was "one of the three or four most humane (inhumane) of the sixty guards at the prison."

All subjects later were presented with a questionnaire on the criminal justice system. Included on the questionnaire were four items that measured the subjects' current views of the characteristics of American prison guards, their interest in rehabilitation, their concern for the welfare of prisoners, and so forth. Before describing the effects of the manipulations on these measures, it is important to consider what degree of attitude change toward prison guards might be logically defensible in each of the three "sampling information" conditions. Subjects who saw either the humane guard or the inhumane guard and who were assured that his humaneness was typical would be justified in making an inference about the humaneness of prison guards in general based on what they saw. They would be justified in doing so, at least to the extent that they would be willing also to make the somewhat risky assumption that guards at the nearby state prison were reasonably representative of American prison guards in general. Subjects who were told nothing about the typicality or atypicality of the guard would be far less justified in making inferences either about the guards at the state prison in question or about prison guards in general. Finally, subjects who were told that the guard was highly atypical were warned explicitly that any inference about the overall population of prison guards would be totally unwarranted.

Despite these logical considerations, subjects in all three sampling conditions made essentially the same inferences about "prison guards in general." Subjects who saw the humane guard reported that they believed prison guards in general to be more humane, and subjects who saw the inhumane guard reported that they believed prison guards to be less humane than did control subjects who saw no interview with a guard. In fact, as may be seen in Figure 4.2, the difference between the humane and inhumane guard conditions was virtually identical under all three sampling instructions.

A second experiment by Hamill, Wilson, and Nisbett (1979) was introduced in chapter 3. In that experiment, subjects were asked to read an article about a middle-aged welfare recipient in New York. The article painted a factual and lifelike portrait of social pathology. In chapter 3 we compared the impact of this article on subjects' attitudes toward welfare recipients with that of abstract summary data on tenure on welfare. In the full study, however, different subjects were given different sets of instructions about the *typicality* of the case described in the article.

In one condition, the woman's very long stay on welfare was characterized as *typical:* "The average length of time on welfare for recipients between the ages of forty and fifty-five is fifteen years. Furthermore, 90 percent of these people are on the welfare rolls for at least eight years." In the second condition, the woman's length of time on welfare was made to seem atypically high: "The average length of time on welfare for recipients between the ages of forty and fifty-five is two years. Furthermore, 90 percent of these people are off the welfare rolls by the end of four years." After reading the article,

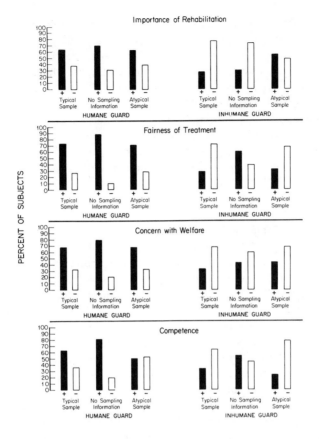

Fig. 4.2 Percent of subjects with favorable vs. unfavorable opinions about guards in general as a function of exposure to humane guard or inhumane guard and as a function of sampling information. From Hamill, Wilson, & Nisbett (1979).

subjects were asked to express their attitudes toward a number of questions about welfare recipients (for example, "People on welfare are as willing to work as anyone else is").

Unlike the prison guard study, it is not clear that the subjects in either of the experimental conditions could logically have made unfavorable inferences about welfare recipients on the basis of what they had read. Even when subjects were assured that the woman was typical of welfare recipients with regard to the length of time she had been on welfare, this did not mean she was typical in other respects. It was possible that other long-time recipients led lives of quiet respectability and responsibility. Thus it is not clear that the subjects even in the "typical" condition should have been permitted any unfavorable inferences about welfare recipients in general. Subjects in the "atypical" condition were warned in the most explicit terms about unfavorable generalizations. In fact, since they had been told (accurately, as it happens) that lengthy stays on welfare were rare, they would have been justified in holding more *favorable* beliefs about recipients than control subjects would have been, who had never read the article but who believed lengthy stays to be the rule rather than the exception.

Once again, however, subjects did not respond in anything like a normatively appropriate fashion. Subjects who had read the article expressed more unfavorable attitudes toward welfare recipients than did control subjects and did so to nearly the same degree whether they had been told that the target was typical in terms of length of time on welfare or were told that she was atypical.

Consequences of Sampling Theory Ignorance

The intuitive scientist seems to lack a full appreciation of the perils in attempting to make generalizations about entities and populations on the basis of limited, often biased, samples of attributes or cases. In many social judgment contexts, the layperson's problems may be compounded by a circumstance that we have not yet considered—the availability of data samples that are highly biased despite being compellingly large. Consider, for example, the high school disciplinary officer who is convinced that the school is filled with drug users or the choral director who marvels at the musicality of the students in the school. Often one is handicapped by one's location in a social system, or one's lifestyle, or personal preferences, or even one's mode of interacting with one's peers, which can mislead by producing large and compellingly consistent samples of evidence nonetheless hopelessly tainted by biased selection.

People's failure to appreciate sampling theory will not leave them defenseless against *all* biased data samples. Indeed, most people are armed with a variety of scripts, schemas, theories, and maxims that make them appropriately wary of small and/or biased samples in at least some judgmental domains. Thus, the experienced shopper knows that the quality of a box of strawberries cannot be judged simply by looking at the ones the grocer has placed on top of the pile. Most used-car buyers know the folly of accepting the freshness of the paint job and the cleanliness of the interior as infallible indicators of the automobile's overall condition. But a person's sophistication in one domain does not guarantee similar sophistication in other, even similar domains. The American who has traveled widely in the United States might scoff at the idea that one can tell what a city is like by traveling from the airport to a hotel but nevertheless might be heavily swayed by a peer's report, based perhaps on no better evidence, that "Bulgaria is dull" or "Bermuda isn't safe anymore." The problem is that, lacking a general appreciation of sampling theory, the layperson is doomed to frequent inferential errors in unfamiliar domains and in familiar domains in which there are no prescriptive homilies consistent with sampling theory.

SUMMARY

People's characterization of data is heavily influenced by theory and by other preexisting knowledge structures. Under many if not most circumstances, this influence is normatively appropriate. Theory-biased coding is inappropriate, however, if (a) belief in the theory is without foundation; (b) the theory is applied unconsciously, in the belief that the data are speaking for themselves; or (c) adherence to the theory preempts observation of blatantly contradictory data.

The conditions affecting the likelihood that theories or other preconceptions will influence the characterization of the datum include (a) one's certainty of the accuracy and applicability of the theory or preconception; (b) the availability of the theory or preconception at the time the datum is encountered; and (c) one's belief about the clarity versus the ambiguity of the data, that is, the degree to which the data can speak for themselves unaided by theory.

People have difficulty accurately characterizing parameters of data samples. This is not because of any computational deficit but rather because of the difficulty of specifying the boundaries of the sampling domain and, more importantly, because of the influence of availability biases. More available instances influence the characterization of the sample unduly—a problem whenever differential availability is not associated with differences in actual frequency.

People make errors when characterizing objects and populations based on samples of attributes or instances. This is because people have little appreciation of the unreliability of small samples or of the damage done by bias in sampling procedures. Consequently, people often make erroneous generalizations about objects and populations.

5

assessment of covariation

> It is evident that when the instances on one side of a question are more likely to be remembered and recorded than those on the other; especially if there be any strong motive to preserve the memory of the first, but not of the latter, these last are likely to be overlooked, and escape the observations of the mass of mankind.
>
> *John Stuart Mill.*

Kelley's (1973) "covariation principle," which is perhaps the most fundamental assumption of contemporary attribution theory and of that theory's characterization of people as generally adequate intuitive scientists, is essentially an assertion that the layperson can recognize and make appropriate inferential use of covariation between events. Common sense also suggests that the ability to detect covariation would seem necessary for understanding, predicting, and controlling social experience. The assessment of covariation between early symptoms and later manifestations of problems, of covariation between particular behavioral strategies and subsequent environmental outcomes, and of covariation between potential causes and observed effects seems critical to people's success in responding adaptively to the opportunities and dilemmas of social life. Indeed, one might well be tempted to regard harmonious social interchange and the general effectiveness of personal functioning as *evidence* of people's capacity to recognize covariation between events.

Most research that has dealt explicitly with people's abilities to recognize and estimate covariation has not been flattering to the layperson's abilities. Even Peterson and Beach (1967), in their generally positive evaluation of "man as an intuitive statistician" were not very optimistic about people's capacity to appreciate relationships between variables. In this chapter we first review evidence of these shortcomings and then attempt to reconcile the apparent contradiction between peoples' failures in the laboratory and their successes in meeting the demands of everyday social judgment and interaction.

JUDGING COVARIATION
FROM FOURFOLD TABLES

Most of the research available at the time of the Peterson and Beach review was on people's ability to estimate association correctly from fourfold, presence-absence tables of the type presented below, in which the task is simply to determine whether symptom X is associated with disease A.

		DISEASE A	
		Present	Absent
	Present	20	10
SYMPTOM X			
	Absent	80	40

This task would seem superficially to be the least demanding covariation-detection problem that one could pose. The data are dichotomous rather than continuous. There are no problems of prior data collection, estimation, or recall; there are no prior, potentially misleading notions of the relationship; and the data are conveniently arrayed in a summary form that should promote accurate assessments of covariation. Nevertheless, the evidence (for example, Smedslund 1963; Ward & Jenkins 1965) shows that people generally perform such tasks quite poorly.

Almost exclusive reliance upon the "present/present" cell seems to be a particularly common failing. Many subjects say that symptom X is associated with disease A simply because many of the people with the disease do in fact have the symptom. Other subjects pay attention only to two cells. Some of these will conclude that the relationship is positive because more people who have the disease have the symptom than do people who do not have the disease. Others conclude that the relationship is negative because more people with the disease do not have symptom A than have it.

Without formal statistical training, very few people intuitively understand that no judgment of association can be made legitimately without simultaneously considering *all four* cells. The appropriate method compares the ratio of the two cells in the "present" column to that of the two cells in the "absent" column.

One might be tempted to dismiss this research as simply a demonstration that laypeople cannot "read" contingency tables and that the errors and biases shown are artifacts of the unusual format of the judgmental task. The incapacity, however, resembles shortcomings that have been observed in circumstances that do not require "table reading." In chapter 3 we reviewed the literature on the ability of people (and animals) to learn from negative or null instances. It should be recalled that learning is greatly retarded or prevented altogether when the instances are conceptually negative ("blue things are *not* gleeps"). The finding that subjects are preoccupied with the present/present cell in contingency tables is reminiscent of people's inability to learn readily from negative instances.

The logic exhibited by subjects in the fourfold table experiments is suspiciously similar to the logic shown by poorly educated laypeople in discussing a proposition such as "does God answer prayers?" "Yes," such a person may say, "because many times I've asked God for something, and He's given it to me." Such a person is accepting the data from the present/present cell as conclusive evidence for the covariation proposition. A more sophisticated layperson may counter this logic by asking for the data from the (prayers) present/(positive outcome) absent cell: "Have you ever asked God for something and not gotten it?" Very few people understand that even these two cells are inadequate to assess the covariation proposition (unless the proposition is that covariation is perfect, that *all* prayers are answered). Indeed, even the reader's intuition may balk at the assertion that data from the absent/absent cell—favorable outcomes that were not prayed for and that did not occur—are fully as relevant to the proposition that prayers are answered as are data from the present/present cell—favorable outcomes that were prayed for and that did occur.

There is further reason to regard people's failure in judging relationships in the fourfold table as evidence that difficulties will be experienced in everyday estimates of association. As we mentioned earlier, the fourfold table task is probably easier and freer of major sources of distortion and error than almost any covariation assessment that people face in everyday experience. Consider, for the sake of contrast, the task of the individual who seeks to test empirically the popular stereotype that "red-haired people are hot tempered," that is, that red-haired people are disproportionately likely to have a hot temper. Note first the many problems that arise in sampling, coding, retrieving, and arranging the relevant data, problems that the layperson was spared in the simpler laboratory task. How shall the data sample be chosen? Should one attempt to sample instances of hot-tempered red-haired people, or sample red-haired people to see if they are hot tempered, or hot-tempered people to see if they are red haired? People probably would adopt some such strategy or combination of strategies. Unfortunately the proposition to be tested contains no hint that "even-tempered brunettes" might be relevant. This contrasts with the fourfold table task which at least makes all four cells available to the subject.

Suppose that the person attempts to follow something like the social scientist's method, first sampling individuals and then assigning them to appropriate cells. But how does one draw an appropriate sample? Should one consider the first twenty persons that come to mind or should one consider all of the people in some restricted class (for instance, the members of one's family or circle of friends or the tenants in one's apartment building)? There are many potential sources of error in such sampling procedures. Availability biases undoubtedly are pertinent, but even more obvious and mundane sources of bias can be identified. Using a sample of one's friends or family members to assess covariation clearly violates important independence and randomness assumptions of sampling theory. That is, one's family or one's friends are apt to share important behavioral characteristics such as displays of temper, and even physical characteristics such as hair color.

When we consider problems of coding, storage, and retrieval, many other factors must be dealt with. What may prove to be the most serious intrusion into the task is the biasing properties of the hypothesis itself. The hypothesis under test, that redheads are hot tempered, may bias the decision about who is or is not hot tempered and whose hair is or is not red. Our discussion of clinical judgments in the next section of this chapter and our more general discussion of theory testing in chapter 8 consider this problem in some detail. For now, let us merely note that the knowledge that an individual is red haired may produce a tendency to code ambiguous behavior as hot tempered. One may even code someone's reddish auburn hair as red or auburn based on the hot headedness or even temperedness of the person's behavior.

Surely we do not need to belabor the point. In everyday experience, covariation-estimation tasks pose enormous difficulties in sampling, coding, and arraying the relevant data. The possibilities for bias are many. These obstacles to accurate assessment are apt to be more significant than any problems arising from the unfamiliar and abstract character of the fourfold presence/absence table. These considerations suggest that everyday covariation assessments of bivariate distributions will prove at least as difficult as the fourfold table research indicates that they will.

ILLUSORY CORRELATION

The most thorough and provocative work on people's ability to detect covariation was conducted by the Chapmans (Chapman 1967; Chapman & Chapman 1967, 1969). These researchers started from a seemingly narrow problem in clinical psychology: How could practicing clinicians, bright and scientifically sophisticated as most of them are, persist in reporting observed associations between certain projective test responses and particular clinical symptoms, when innumerable validation studies have found those presumed associations to be devoid of any empirical basis? For example, objective assessments of the Draw-a-Person test (DAP) reveal that the test has virtually no validity. Nevertheless, many clinicians still insist that the DAP has been a valuable diagnostic tool in their private practice—that paranoid patients tend to emphasize the eyes in their drawings, that dependent patients exaggerate the mouth, and so on. Objective assessment of the Rorschach test similarly reveals that the great majority (although not all) of the sign-symptom associations frequently reported by clinicians in summarizing their case-study experience are not supported by validation data.

The Chapmans proposed that such "illusory correlations" were the product not of clinicians' singular obtuseness, but of a more widespread human failing. Specifically, the Chapmans hypothesized that (a) beliefs about the covariation between events frequently are based on semantic associations (and the "a priori theories" these associations may reflect or may produce), rather than on any accurate observation of the events in question, and that (b) such beliefs survive actual experience with the relevant data even when those data contradict the expected covariation; indeed, from the perceiver's perspective such contradictory data may appear to support the covariation hypothesis. Let us consider the progression of their research.

In the first of their studies, the Chapmans (1967) wrote to practicing clinicians who used the DAP test in diagnosis to ask them what test responses (signs) they had found to be associated with symptoms such as "suspiciousness of other people," "concern with being fed and taken care of by other people," and "impotence." The clinicians' reports showed considerable reliability, that is to say, they mostly agreed with one another about the sorts of signs that they personally had found to be associated with the six symptoms tested.

In the next stage, the Chapmans obtained forty-five DAP drawings made by patients at a state hospital and *randomly* paired the drawings with each of the six symptoms previously considered by the clinicians. These pairs of drawings and symptoms were then presented to introductory psychology students who were given thirty seconds to examine each pair. Following their perusal of the series of paired drawings and symptoms, subjects were asked to state which signs in the drawings most frequently had been associated with each symptom. They were asked, in other words, to report their judgments of the covariation of symptoms with signs in "clinical data" that contained no systematic relationships. As the Chapmans had expected, the reports produced by these naive subjects virtually duplicated those of the experienced clinicians. As did the clinicians, the naive subjects reported that patients who were suspicious of other people tended to emphasize, deemphasize, or otherwise distort their drawings of eyes. They reported that dependent patients tended to emphasize the mouth and to make feminine or childlike drawings. They discerned that impotent patients tended to draw figures that were broad shouldered or muscular and manly in other ways, and so forth.

The implication seems clear. Naive subjects had "seen" the same covariations in random data that clinicians had claimed to see in their own practices (which, if the objective studies of the DAP are indicative, offered equally random data). Therefore, it could reasonably be postulated that shared sources of bias underlay the shared misconceptions of the naive and the sophisticated clinical judges. It seemed likely that the verbal connotations or associations linking particular signs and symptoms were the culprits. Thus, dependent people were presumed to have emphasized mouths in their drawings because of the verbal connotations of "mouth" for "dependency" and vice versa. In order to show this more conclusively, the Chapmans asked still another group of subjects simply to rate the tendency of a given symptom to "call to mind" a given body part. As expected, the ratings were highly predictive of the illusory associations reported. Almost without exception, the body part that was most frequently "called to mind" by the symptom was the same that both clinical and lay judges had reported to be associated empirically with the symptom.

In a still more elegant and conclusive series of studies, the Chapmans (1969) turned their attention to Rorschach responses. The Rorschach test, unlike the DAP test, does have some validity. For example, two categories of percepts in the Rorschach have been shown to differentiate successfully male homosexuals from male heterosexuals. Homosexuals more frequently report seeing monsters on Card IV and seeing a figure that appears to be "part animal" and "part human" on Card V. In addition to these actual predictors, there are many other, more "face valid" signs that have been examined and that have *failed* to differentiate significantly between homosexuals and heterosexuals. These include human or animal anal content, feminine clothing, male or female genitalia, humans with sex confused, and humans with sex uncertain. This pattern of validity and invalidity permitted a further test of the Chapmans' "illusory correlation" hypothesis, one that revealed more sharply the limitations shared by the naive and the sophisticated clinician.

In the first phase of these studies, the Chapmans obtained reports from thirty-two practicing clinicians who stated that they had analyzed the Rorschach protocols of a number of homosexual men. The five most common responses listed by these clinicians as characteristic of homosexuals were the five "face valid" but *empirically invalid* responses just listed. Indeed, only two of the thirty-two clinicians ever listed one of the empirically *valid* signs. The second phase of this research once again was to ask laypeople to rate the tendency of homosexuality to "call to mind" each of the valid and invalid signs treated in the study of clinicians' ratings. Not surprisingly, the tendency of homosexuality to call to mind each of the invalid but plausible signs was "moderately strong," while its tendency to evoke the two valid but implausible signs was "very slight."

In the third and crucial phase of the research, naive subjects again were given a set of purported clinical data. The materials were a series of

Rorschach cards with homosexual symptoms (for example, "has sexual feelings toward other men") or neutral symptoms (for example, "feels sad and depressed much of the time") written on one part of the card and responses to the Rorschach image on another part of the card. The Rorschach responses included valid homosexual signs, invalid (but face valid) signs, and "filler" signs such as geographic responses or food responses. The series was constructed so that there was no relationship whatever between the symptoms and the response categories presented. The naive observers were given sixty seconds to examine each of the thirty cards and, having done so, they were requested to indicate which responses had been associated with the homosexual symptoms.

As in the research with the DAP test, the naive subjects reported seeing the same pattern of correlations that the clinicians had reported in summarizing their experiences with actual patients. That is, invalid signs were reported to have accompanied the homosexuality symptoms very frequently, while neither the valid signs nor the filler signs were reported to have been associated with homosexuality.

The Chapmans were careful to note that, in contrast to their previous research with DAP materials, the pattern of sign-symptom associations presented to the naive observers probably differed from those encountered by the clinicians in their practices. For the DAP materials, there had likely been no true associations in the data available to clinicians. For the Rorschach materials, the clinicians were probably being exposed to a series that did include some valid signs, that is, some true associations between homosexuality symptoms and Rorschach signs. For their next variation, the Chapmans created some true covariations for their naive subjects. They manipulated the degree of covariation between valid signs and the homosexuality symptom, while holding constant the degree of association between symptoms and both the invalid and the filler signs. In all conditions, all symptoms were associated 50 percent of the time with each of several invalid and filler signs. In one condition, the homosexuality symptom also was associated 50 percent of the time with the valid signs. For the other conditions, homosexuality was associated with one of the two valid signs 67 percent, 83 percent, or 100 percent of the time. The results showed that the naive observers, like the clinicians, failed to recognize the presence of true covariation. Increasing levels of true covariation were not accompanied by increasing levels of perceived covariation.

It would be tempting to conclude that the Chapmans (and those who have replicated and extended their research; for example, Hamilton 1979; Golding & Rorer 1972) demonstrated that people's reports of covariation, at least in the clinical domain on which they focused, are totally theory-driven and are unaffected by actual levels of covariation. Such a summary would be slightly overstated, however. In one study with the Rorschach materials, the Chapmans (1969) found that, if all of the invalid signs were deleted, then subjects would be at least slightly sensitive to the true covariation of the valid signs with homosexuality. For example, when the misleading invalid signs were deleted, somewhat more subjects reported that the valid signs were associated with homosexuality when the covariation held 83 percent of the time than when it held 50 percent of the time. Furthermore, in a study with DAP materials, the Chapmans found that when they built in massive *negative* covariations between symptoms and illusory covariates, the reported covariation, though still perceived as positive, was at least somewhat reduced in magnitude.

Perhaps the most accurate summary of the Chapmans' work is that reported covariation was shown to reflect true covariation far *less* than it reflected theories or preconceptions of the nature of the associations that "ought" to exist. Unexpected, true covariations can sometimes be detected, but they will be underestimated and are likely to be noticed only when the covariation is very strong, and the relevant data set excludes "decoy features" that bring into play popular but incorrect theories.

Comparing the task of the Chapmans' naive subjects with the demands of everyday covariation detection is both instructive and depressing. The subjects' task in the laboratory was in every discernible way much easier than that undertaken by practicing clinicians or by most people in their everyday experience. Instead of encountering sign at one time and symptom at another (cf. Golding & Rorer 1972) and instead of encountering information about a given patient at sporadic and infrequent intervals, the Chapmans' subjects received the relevant data in a form that made the most modest demands upon their memories. In addition, the descriptions of both potential covariates (signs and symptoms) were far less ambiguous than those that normally would be provided in everyday clinical or social judgments. It seems clear that if the Chapmans' subjects could not detect covariation accurately under such nearly optimal conditions, there is even less reason to expect people to do so in their daily lives with equally complex or more complex stimuli. Consistent with these considerations, the Chapmans found that the clinicians were more prone than the naive observers were to report the relevant illusory correlations. This finding may reflect not only the greater difficulty of the clinicians' tasks in processing information, but also the clinicians' greater confidence in their incorrect theories and expectations.

DATA-DRIVEN AND THEORY-DRIVEN JUDGMENTS OF COVARIATION

The Chapmans' research posed a contest between expectations and evidence, or theory and data, in clinical judgment. Their findings strongly suggest that the contest generally proves to be an unequal one, that expectations based on a priori theories or on semantic connotations overwhelm the influence of data that do not coincide with expectations or even refute them. Two separate questions are posed by the Chapmans' findings. First, how capable are people of assessing covariation when allowed to view data about which they have no strong theories or expectations? In a sense, this first question is a "psychophysical one." It pertains to the relationship between purely "data-driven," subjective judgments of covariation and objective measures of that covariation. The second question concerns accuracy of covariation estimates in the opposite case, in which the available data are spotty and imprecise but in which the person holds or readily can generate theories about the degree of covariation in the data. For example, what degree of covariation do people estimate for political attitudes and social attitudes, or between different behaviors tapping the same personality trait, for example, a disposition toward honesty or the ability to delay gratification? Everyone possesses what might be called "data" on the degree of covariation between various socially relevant attitude dimensions and behavior dimensions, but the data are usually skimpy, hit-or-miss, vague, and subject to bias and distortion in both encoding and recall. We thus would expect such judgments to be primarily "theory driven." As with the Chapmans' psychopathology dimensions, theory and verbal connotations should be rich enough to be a strong basis for expectations of the degree of association to be found among such dimensions.

In a series of studies, one of the authors and his colleagues pursued these two issues (Jennings, Amabile, & Ross 1980). The procedure followed by these investigators was to present subjects with various types of covariation estimation tasks. Some of these tasks were based on materials for which previous theoretical expectations were anticipated to be weak, and some were based on materials for which such expectations were anticipated to be strong.

Three of the tasks required subjects to make covariation estimates for relatively "theory-free" bivariate distributions for which the degree of true association ranged from 0 to 1. The three tasks differed in their information-processing demands on subjects. The materials for one task consisted of ten number-pairs. Subjects were allowed to study the ten pairs briefly and then were asked to indicate whether the relationship was positive or negative and finally to choose a number from 0 (no relationship) to 100 (perfect relationship) to describe their subjective impressions of the strength of the linear relationship in the distribution. This task required neither magnitude estimation nor commitment of information to memory. The data were presented in parametric form and remained available while subjects made their covariation estimates.

The second type of materials portrayed a set of ten men holding walking sticks. The subjects were required to estimate the relationship between the heights of men and the heights of their walking sticks, using the same simple 100-point rating scale described earlier. This task required that the subjects themselves estimate the relevant magnitudes (that is, heights of men and walking sticks), but, as in the simple number-pairs task, it placed minimal demands on memory. The stimulus materials in each distribution remained available to subjects while they considered each of their estimates for that distribution.

The third type of "theory-free" materials made still greater demands on the subject's information processing capacities. Subjects heard a tape recording in which each of ten people first enunciated a letter of the alphabet (purportedly the initial letter of that person's surname) and then sang a musical note of variable duration. Subjects were asked to estimate the strength of the relationship between alphabetical order and note duration, again using the same 100-point scale used for the other two types of stimulus materials. In this task subjects were forced not only to estimate a magnitude (that is, the durations of the notes) but also to *remember* the ten data pairs they had heard.

The results of the "theory-free" covariation estimates are presented graphically in Figure 5.1. It should be noted first that, regardless of which type of materials were used, the task proved to be very difficult, and the standard errors associated with each point in the figure were very large. Second, it is clear that the function relating subjective covariation estimates to objective covariation measures was sharply accelerated. Relationships in the range most frequently treated by psychologists concerned with traits or other individual dispositions (that is, $r = .2$ to $r = .4$) were barely detectable. Even relationships in the range considered very strong by most social scientists (that is, $r = .6$ to $r = .8$) prompted estimates that fell, on the average, in the bottom third of the subjective 100-point scale. Only when the correlations began to approach the $r = .8$ to $r = 1.0$ range did subjects seem certain to detect covariations and to venture to the upper half of the scale. Finally, it should be noted that the three types of stimulus materials, although differing greatly in their information-processing demands on participants, produced very similar power functions relating subjective to objective covariation. That is why the three were combined in Figure 5.1. For all three sets of materials, the subjects' judgments were represented best not by a simple linear function of r, or even of r^2, but rather by the function $1 - \sqrt{1 - r^2}$, a statistic which some readers may recognize as the "coefficient of alienation," a measure of the reduction in the standard error in predictions of one variable resulting from knowledge of the second, associated variable.

So far, the data could be suggesting merely that the layperson's subjective metric is a very cautious one compared to that used by the formal statistician. When we turn to the results of the second major covariation estimation task, however, such a notion is quickly dispelled. For this relatively "theory-driven" task, pairs of variables were specified, and the subject was asked simply to estimate the degree of relationship between each pair. Some of these pairs dealt with behavioral measures of personal dispositions (for example, two measures of honesty used by Hartshorne & May 1928 in their classic

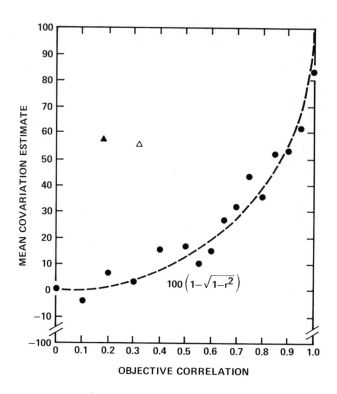

Fig. 5.1. ("Theory-Driven" vs. "Data-Driven" estimates of covariation. (From Jennings, Amabile, & Ross 1980.)

Key

● *Data-Driven Estimates:* (Mean of covariation estimates for 3 bivariate domains)

Theory-Driven Estimates:

▲ Covariation estimate for divergent measures of dishonesty (based on Hartshorne & May 1928)

△ Covariation estimate for ability to delay gratification and ability to resist temptation to cheat (based on Mischel & Gilligan 1964)

study). Others dealt with personal attitudes, habits, and preferences. In each case, the experimenters could compare the subjects' covariation estimate (made using the same 100-point scale introduced in the previous tasks) with an empirically based correlation coefficient.

An examination of two of these estimates (Figure 5.1) shows that when subjects were asked to characterize relationships based on their intuitive theories and personal experience, they were not necessarily conservative. They willingly ventured to the middle and even to the upper region of their subjective 100-point scale. Subjects' estimates of the covariation between two measures of "honesty" or two measures of "ability to delay gratification" were in the 55 to 60 range on the 100-point scale. When we consider the function relating subjective estimates to product-moment correlations for the *theory-free materials,* the meaning of such estimates becomes apparent: Covariations in the range of $r = .85$ to $r = .90$ had been required to coax subjective ratings of this magnitude from the subjects!

The implications of these data seem clear. Subjects' "theory-based" estimates of associations are far higher than any data derived from firsthand experience could possibly justify. If our subjects' views of the relationship between different measures of honesty (or many other traits, attitudes, and behavior) have any empirical basis, that basis cannot be an objectively observed and recalled sample of bivariate observations. More importantly, these assumptions about bivariate relationships must have survived the subjects' exposure to real-world data which, viewed in the absence of a theory, would have led them to estimate that there was very little if any relationship. People's views of covariation in the social world, it must be concluded, are not formed primarily on the basis of some computational process analogous to the statistician's procedures. Rather, the layperson's views of the data are greatly influenced by theories and expectations.

We are not claiming that all covariations will be overestimated. If a particular relationship is not readily derived from a theory, or if the individual holds a theory which incorrectly presumes a weak or null relationship, there are apt to be *under*estimates. Furthermore, we are not claiming that there are *no* data that can affect theories about the degree of association between classes of events. Our point is simply that such an impact of actual data does not depend on the covariation criteria used by the formal scientist.

CONDITIONING AND COVARIATION DETECTION

Our bleak portrait of the layperson's ability to assess covariation may seem at first to be incongruent with the huge body of evidence on classical and operant conditioning. Every rat that has ever learned to press a lever for a food pellet, every child who has ever learned to stay away from electrical outlets and appliances, and every mother who has ever shown a lactation reflex in response to the cry of a child, proves that organisms sometimes can do a superb job of recognizing covariation among events.

Does the work of the Chapmans and of Jennings and colleagues examine some artificial or very narrow class of covariation assessment in which the layperson is peculiarly deficient? We believe not. On the contrary, we maintain that it is the standard laboratory conditioning paradigm which is the exception and that the phenomena shown by the Chapmans and others is the rule. We argue that conditioning is very fragile and that there may be relatively few stimulus contingencies in social life that match the extremely stiff requirements that have been demonstrated to be essential in order for conditioning to occur in the laboratory. These requirements, as it turns out, are well understood in terms of people's (and other organisms') reliance on the availability and representativeness heuristics.

Availability of Stimuli
and of Stimulus-Response Linkages

As everyone who has ever been required to condition a rat in an experimental psychology course knows, both classical and operant conditioning are obtainable only under sharply constrained circumstances. Unless the stimuli and stimulus linkages are highly available, perceptually and memorially, learning will not occur. We will examine some of the constraints on the conditioning process and show how they are related to the availability construct.

1. *S–S and O–R intervals.* Perhaps the sharpest constraint on the possibility of conditioning is the short interval required between critical events. In classical conditioning, the optimum interval between the conditioned stimulus (CS—for example, bell) and the unconditioned stimulus (UCS—for example, meat powder) is 0 to 5 seconds. Longer intervals, even intervals of less than a minute, are usually unsuccessful in producing conditioning. Similarly, in instrumental conditioning, the interval between the occurrence of an operant response (0) and the provision of the reinforcement (R) should be very short if conditioning is to occur. 0–R intervals of more than a few seconds normally will not result in learning. Contrast these intervals with the typical intervals to be expected in the social domain, for example, the interval between finding that a patient has responded to Card IV of the Rorschach by seeing a monster and the discovery that the patient has homosexual tendencies, or the interval between finding out that someone is a Rotarian and finding out that he is public spirited.

2. *Interval between event pairings.* In conditioning studies, brief intervals between the event-pair occurrences are typically used. In classical conditioning, a CS–UCS pairing is typically followed within a few seconds by another CS–UCS pairing. In instrumental conditioning, O–R pairings usually are arranged so that they can succeed one another as rapidly as the organism can emit an operant and can avail itself of the reinforcement. To our knowledge, the outer limits of the allowable intervals between event pairings have not been explored, but it seems highly improbable that conditioning with typical stimuli and response would ever occur if the event pairings were separated by

a matter of days or weeks. In the social domain, such intervals are common. Usually there are long intervals between displays of hot temper by different individuals, occurrences of dishonest behavior by different schoolchildren, or reports of seeing monsters on Card IV of the Rorschach by different patients.

3. *Stimulus salience and distinctiveness.* In classical conditioning, both the CS and the UCS should be prominent in order for conditioning to take place. Weak stimuli, that is, stimuli that are not highly noticeable, are not likely to result in learning. Stimulus salience is probably an even more important organismic consideration than environmental consideration. Neither classical conditioning nor instrumental conditioning is likely for an organism that is less than highly motivated to attend to environmental stimuli. In fact, it is customary in conditioning studies using rats to starve them down to 80 percent of their normal body weight. This apparently is helpful in gaining the rat's complete attention! It is also important that stimuli be distinctive in order for either classical or operant conditioning to take place. It would be difficult, for example, to condition a rat to the sounds of its neighbor's nest-building or drinking activities. Such happenings might be apparent, but they would not be very distinctive. Conditioning is aided by the unusual and distinctive qualities of the stimuli—tone, light flash, and so on—that are typically used by investigators. Relatively few events in the human social arena are as distinctive or as motivationally relevant as the stimuli used in the animal conditioning studies.

4. *Strength of covariation (reinforcement schedule).* Conditioning is not normally attempted with low covariation between CS and UCS or between O and R. Typically, investigators use 100-percent covariation; that is, the CS or O is invariably followed by the UCS or R. (So-called "partial reinforcement" studies use 100-percent reinforcement at the outset and then work down gradually to some lower level.) When the covariation is less than perfect, conditioning is problematic. The lower limits of covariation possible for conditioning have not, to our knowledge, been explored, but it would be extremely interesting to find out whether either animals or humans would show conditioning if covariation were within the relatively low range typical for dichotomous events of social relevance (for example, the relationship between gender and views on abortion, or that between willingness to lie in one situation and willingness to cheat in another situation).

The work on conditioning cannot be invoked to support a view of people (or other organisms) as universally accurate covariation detectors. When every possible precaution is taken to ensure that stimuli and stimulus linkages are highly available—when intervals between the pairings of stimuli are extremely brief, when stimuli are highly salient, distinctive and motivationally relevant, and when covariation between stimuli is perfect—conditioning normally takes place. If any of these factors is less than optimal, then conditioning is, at the very least, retarded. If *all* of these factors are *substantially* less than optimal, conditioning seems quite out of the question. In the human social domain, most of these factors normally are substantially below optimal levels.

Theory versus Data in Conditioning:
Rats and Representativeness

We have argued in this chapter that people's theories exert a stronger influence on their estimates of covariation than do the data themselves. A consideration of the conditioning literature suggests that the same generalization may apply to animals. Much evidence, some old and some new, supports this speculation.

One of the great virtues of the behaviorist tradition was that investigators usually stated their hypotheses so clearly that they were capable of clear refutation. In 1924, Watson asserted: "The importance of stimulus substitution or stimulus conditioning cannot be overrated. . . . So far as we now know . . . we can take any stimulus calling out a standard reaction and substitute another stimulus for it" (p. 24).

Few hypotheses in psychology ever have been so amply disconfirmed as this one was, although it took nearly four decades of research for investigators to realize it. Watson himself was among the first to provide evidence contradicting the hypothesis, though he probably did not recognize it as such. It is well known that Watson and Raynor produced an enduring fear of rabbits in poor little Albert by pairing the appearance of a rabbit with the onset of loud noise. Less well known are the experiments that failed. A student of Watson's tried pairing a block of wood with the noise and also paired a cloth curtain with the noise. Happily for little Albert, but unhappily for Watson's hypothesis of the ability of stimuli to be substituted limitlessly, the experiments failed, and Albert began life encumbered only with a rabbit phobia and not with wood block or cloth curtain phobias.

The findings of Watson and colleagues somehow are not very surprising. It seems much more plausible that a phobia of an animate object, a center of self-initiated action and movement, could be established, than that a fear of a wood block or curtain could be produced. A rabbit or other animal is a more *representative* cause of noxious events than is wood or cloth.

Similar representativeness or plausibility effects have been found for infrahuman subjects. Animals, like humans, behave in many conditioning experiments as if they entered the study with prior "theories" about the likelihood of certain event linkages. The most impressive demonstration was performed by Garcia and his co-workers (Garcia, McGowan, Ervin, & Koelling 1968; Garcia, McGowan, & Green (1972). They found that the minimal CS–UCS interval necessary for classical conditioning can be raised to twelve or more hours, and that conditioning will occur with only one trial, if the CS is a distinctive, new-tasting food and the UCS is gastrointestinal illness. If a rat is allowed to eat a new-tasting food and then many hours later is made ill (by massive X-irradiation or by some other technique) it will avoid the new food thereafter. It is not because the illness cue is somehow generally exempt from the 0-5-second interval requirement, however. If the animal is made ill several hours after eating a food of *familiar taste but unfamiliar shape,* it does not show subsequent avoidance of the new-shaped food. Conversely, if the animal eats food of a new shape and then is shocked immediately afterward, it will learn to avoid eating food of that shape even though it will *not* learn to avoid eating food having a *new taste* that is followed immediately by electric shock. The rat thus may be described as possessing two "theories" useful in its ecology: (1) Distinctive gustatory cues, when followed by delayed gastric distress, should be considered suspect. (2) Distinctive spatial cues, when followed by immediate somatic pain, should be considered suspect. These expectations are powerful enough to prevent the animal from learning certain kinds of covariation and to ensure that it will "discover" other covariations which do not, in fact, exist.

These generalizations are by no means restricted to the special case of gustatory/gastrointestinal covariations. Seligman (1970) showed that it is impossible to understand the conditioning literature without assuming that animals enter the laboratory with strong prior expectations about the causal relationships between their behavior and events in the environment and the causal relationships among environmental events. Cats can learn to escape from a puzzle box by pulling strings or pressing levers but learn only with very great difficulty to escape by licking or scratching themselves, and this is true although the "operant level" of these latter responses is much higher than that of the former. Similarly, it is nearly impossible for dogs to learn to yawn to get food reinforcement. Just as it is extremely difficult to teach animals to perform some kinds of operants to obtain reinforcement, it is nearly impossible to teach them *not* to perform certain other operants. Pigeons will peck at a lighted key to obtain food even when there is no contingency whatever between pecking and food. Indeed, pigeons will persist in pecking even when the pecking *costs* them reinforcements.

To Seligman's examples of what he calls "preparedness" to learn certain operant-reinforcement associations, Testa (1974) added many examples of differential preparedness to learn certain associations among environmental events. For example, rats show more fear of a gradual light onset followed by a gradual shock onset than of a gradual light onset followed by a sudden shock onset, and they show more fear of a sudden light onset followed by a sudden shock onset than of a sudden light onset followed by a gradual shock onset. Apparently rats are primed to expect that sudden things are signaled (caused?) by sudden things and gradual things by gradual things. Similarly, a rat can be taught in one trial to avoid shock from a grid floor if it can escape to a compartment with a smooth black floor. But if the compartment to which it must escape has a grid floor continuous with that of the shock compartment, it takes closer to ten trials to learn the avoidance response. The rat apparently is primed to assume (quite reasonably) that the grid floor is the cause of its pain and does not readily form the hypothesis that a mere change in compartments would be efficacious.

It has become clear that not all S-S or O-R pairings can be learned equally easily. Such pairings can be learned by an organism to the extent that its prior "theories" make such pairings plausible. Some pairings will be "learned" even when they do not exist, if the organism has a powerful enough theory. Other pairings will never be learned if the organism does not have a theory suggesting the possibility of their joint occurrence, and especially if the organism has a theory indicating that such pairings are implausible. Thus, detection of covariation for animals, like that for humans, is influenced strongly by preconceptions of covariation and is sometimes relatively unresponsive or even impervious to actual data on covariation.

A consideration of the conditioning literature bolsters rather than ameliorates the present bleak view of people's ability to detect covariation in their social environments. If even animals, who are surely less fecund theorists than people, can fail to see perfectly covarying relationships that happen not to fit their preconceived notions and can persist in seeing a relationship where none or the perfect opposite exists, then this state of affairs argues against human detection of covariation outside the laboratory.

COVARIATION DETECTION
AND THE PERCEPTION OF PERSONAL CONSISTENCY

Our discussion of the struggle between theory and data in assessing covariation is relevant to the domain of "person perception" in which a controversy has raged since the publication of Mischel's (1968) book *Personality and Assessment*. In that book, Mischel reviewed the large amount of evidence indicating that cross-situation consistencies are generally quite low for behaviors expressing such classic "traits" as honesty, dependency, and aggressiveness. That is, the ambitious attempt to apply to socially relevant traits the measurement techniques that had so effectively assessed individual differences in ability, achievement, or aptitude, had failed. Paper-and-pencil measures of social dispositions seldom correlate beyond .30 with the overt behaviors they were designed to predict. Behavior/behavior correlations (for example, between honesty manifested by reluctance to lie in situation *A* and honesty manifested by reluctance to cheat in situation B) seldom exceed .20. Thus, the evidence indicates that a person's behavior in a given situation cannot be predicted well either by personality test scores or by a simple extrapolation from the person's behavior in another, similar situation.

Mischel's literature review and summary, however, did not initiate the controversy. Several classic papers (for example, Newcomb 1929; Hartshorne & May 1928) had previously called attention to the fact that cross-situational measures of traits such as dominance, talkativeness, or honesty were poorly correlated. What disturbed the personality theorists was Mischel's insistence that these poor correlations reflected not the inadequacies in the relevant measures, definitions, sampling procedures, or any other technical problem, but rather reflected the actual amount of variance accounted for by personality traits. That is, Mischel asserted that there was a solid empirical basis for denying the existence of stable, usefully predictive, individual differences in social traits. He went on to argue, essentially, that the "problem" to be explained was not the empirical failures to verify the existence of social traits but the persistent *illusion* that such traits are more powerful predictors of behavior than the data show them to be.

To this end Mischel (1968, 1969, 1973) and Jones and Nisbett (1972) listed a number of reasons why laypeople (and, no doubt, sophisticated personality theorists) might expect and perceive more consistency among traits than actually exists. These included: (a) We tend to see most people in a limited number of roles and situations and thus are exposed to a more consistent sample of behavior than we would obtain from a truly random sample of the person's behavioral repertoire. (b) Perceived refutations of presumed consistencies will be rare, given our sophisticated linguistic abilities and elaborate psychological theories which could render any apparent discrepancy into an irrelevancy or even a confirmation of consistency (c) Our subjective feelings of control will be heightened by a conviction that (other) people are consistent in their traits and thus predictable. Most importantly, these authors, as well as D'Andrade (1974), stressed the importance of theories to expectations of consistency. Our theories of human behavior contain the strong assumption that people behave in trait-consistent ways: Honest people behave honestly and dishonest people dishonestly; people who are aggressive in one situation are apt to be aggressive in another. It was this assumption to which we referred in chapter 2 as the "dispositional theory of behavior." Human behavior is understood by the layperson primarily as the expression of stable traits and dispositions instead of being understood as the result of situational forces operating at the time of action.

Amazingly, the response of Mischel's colleagues to his devastating critique was a period of stony silence. Goaded by social psychologists, personality assessment specialists finally came forth with a barrage of generally questionable technical criticisms coupled with accusations that Mischel's review was selective and nihilistic. Not until 1974, with the publication of Bem's and Allen's paper, "On Predicting Some of the People Some of the Time," was there an empirical study that addressed itself seriously to the strengths and limitations of Mischel's argument. Basically, these investigators followed Allport's idiographic/nomothetic distinction by stressing the importance of first identifying the subset of individuals to whom the relevant trait "applies," that is, those individuals who *are* consistent in the behavior under consideration. Within the more restricted samples identified in this way, Bem and Allen produced correlation coefficients in the .50s and .60s for measures of friendliness and for measures of conscientiousness. (More recently the use of "aggregate measures" has been heralded as a solution to the problem of low cross-situational consistencies, though such a tactic is not, it should be noted, a challenge to Mischel's basic contention that people who are honest, aggressive, and so on, in one particular situation are not particularly likely to be the ones who show such dispositions in some other related situation.)

Given the evidence on people's covariation-detection capacities, Mischel's once heretical views seem quite moderate. In a sense, Mischel's contentions represent a special case of the very general propositions that, (a) covariation theories typically overwhelm data when the two are in conflict and (b) covariation data processed through the filter of a theory may be perceived as consistent with the theory, even when the relevant data objectively offer no such support.

It is premature, perhaps, to offer any final conclusion about the debate between Mischel and his critics. It may be that Mischel's attack is more appropriately directed at the professionals' utilization and defense of nomothetic "personality scales" to measure all people on particular dimensions than at the layperson's conviction that many people can be usefully categorized by a trait label. Certainly, Bem's and Allen's work suggests that more idiographic labeling—for example, George is honest, Janet is aggressive—may have considerable predictive value. Better methods for defining the domains within which personal consistency is to be expected (Bem & Funder 1978) may boost the personologists' success even further. Regardless of the final outcome of the debate between Mischel and the personologists, and regardless of the ultimate reconciliation between Mischel's data and the layperson's intuitions, one conclusion seems sure. Whether accurate or inaccurate, the layperson's perceptions of social traits (whether in the nomothetic sense of the personality assessment psychologists or in the idiographic sense emphasized by Bem and Allen) are not simple products of data observation. The layperson's theories influence perceptions of covariation much more than do the data themselves, and the accuracy of these perceptions therefore depends less on the layperson's covariation detection capacities than on the accuracy of the theories.

COVARIATION DETECTION AND SOCIAL ADAPTATION

The existing evidence suggests that people's ability to detect even fairly powerful covariation, among even those events that are quite important and distinctive, may be seriously limited. When the covariation is less than massive, when the events are of less than pressing importance, when the stimuli are not highly distinctive, or when any of several factors that make data processing difficult intervene, covariation-detection capacities diminish still further. Work by the Chapmans, Jennings and others, Golding and Roher, Hamilton, and D'Andrade (1965, 1974) and unwitting evidence provided by countless personality psychologists shows how objectively low or nonexistent covariations can be parlayed into massive *perceived* covariations through a priori theories and assumptions.

The immediate implications of such work seem extremely dire and therefore seem, in a sense, to be contradicted by the evidence that people *do* manage to understand, predict, and control most facets of their lives and of their societies. People do seem to diagnose many personal problems quite well from their symptoms. They do seem to share interpretations of events and to coordinate their plans well, and they do seem to plan effectively for a wide variety of events. How can we reconcile the layperson's failures at covariation detection in the laboratory with such overwhelming evidence of social adaptation in contexts that demand considerable accuracy about covariation? Essentially, we believe that the laboratory demonstrations are valid but that their most serious implications for everyday life are mitigated to some extent by factors that now can be outlined in some detail.

1. *Many of the most important covariations that we must learn are observed in those limited sets of circumstances that do permit accurate recognition of covariation and adaptive conditioning*—for example, covariations that approach unity, stimuli that are distinctive, salient, and motivationally relevant, short interstimulus and interpairing intervals, and, perhaps most importantly, opportunities for decisively testing the particular covariation hypotheses that one forms.

Thus, we learn that flames, glowing filaments, and objects that have recently been in contact with them, burn. We learn that switches turn on lights, television sets, and other devices capable of producing sharp and immediate stimulus changes. We discover that slight rightward pulls on bicycle handlebars and, later on, on automobile steering wheels, turn vehicles in rightward arcs. In the social domain, we learn that serious disobedience to parents results in punishment, and that soft answers turneth away wrath.

By the same token, many extremely important and useful covariations will *not* be learned because one or more of the conditions for learning are not propitious. Mere importance of the covariation, even if the covariation is quite large, will not be sufficient if other factors essential to conditioning are absent. For instance, few insomniacs are aware of how much more difficult their sleep is made by an overheated room, by the presence of an odd smell, by having smoked a cigarette, or by having engaged in physical exercise or intense mental concentration just before retiring. Indeed, research by Freedman and Papsdorf (1976) showed that insomniacs whose sleep onset has been delayed *objectively* by a prebedtime exercise program nevertheless *subjectively* report that the exercise program has reduced their insomnia. In the case of insomnia, the O-R interval and the intervals between O-R trials probably are too long to allow for detection of covariation. In addition, prior theories (for example, exercise makes you tired, tiredness makes you sleep) interfere with accurate detection.

2. *Beliefs about covariation may be formed through strategies which do not meet conventional logical or statistical criteria but which provide reasonably accurate estimates under some circumstances.* People may achieve reasonably good results relying upon very small amounts of data. For instance, they may consult the most representative case of category *A* or the most extreme observation on dimension *A* and then simply observe the associated value on category *B* or dimension *B*. The relationship between academic performance and career success may be assessed by recalling a couple of the most (or least) proficient students one has encountered and then noting their subsequent success. It should be apparent that this method essentially constitutes a use of the representativeness heuristic and will work quite well in a limited set of circumstances. Specifically, if the covariation is very strong, a single "extreme" or "prototypic" case generally will convey an accurate picture of an overall relationship. (Perfect covariation implies that every data point will accurately reflect association between the dimensions.)

The use of extreme cases and representativeness criteria are subject to obvious and severe limitations. Although it is useful for detecting the existence of strong relationships, it is far less useful for revealing the *absence* of a relationship: A small sample of points will not necessarily be "representative" of a zero correlation. Indeed, if the number of data points examined is small enough, the likelihood of falsely "discovering" a relatively high correlation is quite great. An equally serious limitation is that a number of information processing biases may influence the selection of the "representative" cases to be examined. Most notably, the covariation theory being tested is apt to have a biasing influence. Consider, for instance, the covariation hypothesis "Southerners are bigots" (that is, membership in the category "Southerner" and in the category "bigot" are not statistically independent). Given such a prior hypothesis, the prototypic bigot one samples is apt to be a Southerner and the prototypic Southerner one samples is apt to be a bigot. That is, the criteria for being selected as a "prototypic Southerner" are a "red-neck" stereotype which *includes* bigotry or, at the very least, all those personal characteristics likely to be associated with bigotry.

3. *Perhaps the most basic reason for our successful social adaptation is that the individual is not usually required to detect covariation anew.* Each culture has experts, people of unusual acumen or specialized knowledge, who detect covariations and report them to the culture at large. Thus, most (though not by any means all) cultures recognize the covariation between intercourse and pregnancy. This is a covariation detection task of enormous difficulty, given the interval between the two types of events and the rarity of pregnancy relative to the frequency of intercourse, not to mention the occasional unreliability of the data ("Honest, I never did it"). We are inclined to suspect, in fact, that few cultures would have detected the covariation were it not for a priori theoretical considerations of the enormous emotional significance of both events and the mutual locus of, as it were, input and output. Nevertheless, once a covariation is detected and the new hypothesis seems to be confirmed by perusing available data, the entire culture is the beneficiary and may take action in accordance with the knowledge. Such a cultural transmission principle applies to almost all human affairs, from farming ("Plant corn when the oak leaf is as big as a mouse's ear") to tourism ("The German restaurants in Minnesota are generally quite good") to urban survival ("The South Side is unsafe").

Experts and cultural transmission are scarcely infallible, and we do not wish to imply anything more optimistic than the principle that a culture's competence can approach, as a limit, the covariation-detection capacities of its most expert members. Thus the Emperor Justinian, for all his enlightenment, believed that sodomy was a chief cause of earthquakes, and President Dwight Eisenhower was persuaded that Scandinavian-style socialism was a chief cause of suicide.

SUMMARY

The evidence shows that people are poor at detecting many sorts of covariation. The layperson apparently does not understand intuitively the basic logic of covariation assessment underlying the 2 x 2 contingency table. Perception of covariation in the social domain is largely a function of preexisting theories and only very secondarily a function of true covariation. In the absence of theories, people's covariation detection capacities are extremely limited. Though the conditioning literature shows that both animals and humans are extremely accurate covariation detectors under some circumstances, these circumstances are very limited and constrained. The existing literature provides no reason to believe that either animals or humans would be able to detect relatively weak covariations among stimuli that are relatively indistinctive, subtle, and irrelevant motivationally and, most importantly, among stimuli when the presentation interval is very large. Like humans, animals seem to be greatly influenced by their "preparedness" to expect certain covariations and not others.

The evidence on covariation detection capacities gives strong empirical support to Mischel's assertion that socially relevant "traits" are as weak predictors of behavior as the data show them to be. The personality theorist's (and the layperson's) conviction that there are strong cross-situational consistencies in behavior may be seen as merely another instance of theory-driven covariation assessments operating in the face of contrary evidence.

People probably suffer less than might be expected from their covariation-detection shortcomings. (1) Many of the most important covariations, particularly those in the physical world, fall within the domain of the detectable with respect to their relevant parameters. (2) Other strong associations can be assessed with fair validity by using the representativeness heuristic. (3) We fortunately are not left to our own devices to detect all or even most of the covariations important to us.

6

causal analysis

The attribution theorists, who contributed much to psychologists' current interest in the "intuitive scientist's" activities, have been guided in their research by a normative model of causal analysis. The central organizing device of this model is Kelley's (1967) analysis of variance (ANOVA) cube which systematized Mill's "method of difference" for ascertaining the nature and magnitude of causal influence in the social domain. The three dimensions of Kelley's ANOVA cube are "distinctiveness," the degree to which the effect occurs primarily in the presence of one particular causal candidate and not in the presence of others; "consistency," the degree to which the effect is observed reliably when a particular causal candidate is present; and "consensus," the degree to which people other than the target actor show the effect. The normative model requires that people respond to each of these in assessing causal influence. Effects should be attributed to those stimulus conditions with which they covary reliably.

Because this normative approach guided most of the early attribution work, a relatively flattering portrait of the layperson's capacity to use normatively correct principles of causal inference emerged. It is not necessary for us to review the earlier attribution research in any detail, since it is often reviewed. Suffice it to say that Kelley's initial papers (1967, 1972a, 1972b, 1973), supported by other major studies (for example, McArthur 1972; Orvis, Cunningham, & Kelley 1975: Weiner, Frieze, Kukla, Reed, Rest, & Rosenbaum 1972), provided ample evidence that subjects' causal inferences often are at least directionally responsive to the variables that normatively "ought" to influence them. These variables include presence versus absence of a given causal candidate, the strength of a given causal candidate, the existence of one versus more than one causal candidate, and Kelley's ANOVA dimensions of distinctiveness, consistency, and consensus. Thus, when subjects are told that John is enthralled by a particular painting, that he is enthralled by few other paintings, that he always has been enthralled in the past by this particular painting, and that almost all other people are enthralled by the painting, subjects attribute John's positive response more to the painting than to some disposition of John to be enthralled by paintings (McArthur 1972). Similarly, if subjects are told that Jane succeeded at a task, that most people do not succeed at that task, and that Jane did not try hard to succeed at the task, subjects are more likely to attribute Jane's success to ability than to luck, effort, or the easiness of the task (Weiner and colleagues 1972).

It is important to note that most of the studies showing normatively justified causal inferences used quite impoverished stimulus materials, presented to the subject in a streamlined and well organized form. Usually, the subject is not asked to decide which data might be relevant to the problem and is spared the tasks of data collection, storage, and retrieval. Most importantly, the subject is not required to observe, estimate, or summarize *covariations* between potential causes and apparent effects. This research strategy may be perfectly reasonable for the investigator who wishes to determine people's ability to perform adequate causal analyses per se, uncontaminated by previous errors in data collection or data summary. This strategy, however, seems certain to give an inflated estimate of people's capacities for causal analysis in everyday experience. In their daily lives, people deal with data that are biased, insufficient, or of questionable relevance to the inferential task at hand and, as we showed in chapter 5, people's ability to make the covariation estimates critical to causal inference is seriously limited.

Much of the research to date showing normatively adequate causal analysis can be generalized only to the ecologically infrequent case in which the subject is presented with data that are relevant, sufficient, and unbiased, and with covariations among the data that are specified in advance. As will be seen, people are imperfect causal analysts even under these pristine conditions. The intuitive scientist is prone to several major sources of error in causal analysis, including the following: (a) overreliance on the representativeness heuristic and on a priori theories of doubtful validity, (b) over-reliance on the availability heuristic, (c) use of simplistic and "overly parsimonious" criteria for causal attribution, (d) absence or weakness of certain normatively appropriate causal-analytic schemas, and (e) intrusion of causal theories applicable to one domain into other domains to which they are inapplicable and misleading. These sources of error are collectively sufficient to impair causal inferences even when prior biases in "data processing" have not already preempted the possibility of correct analysis.

CAUSAL ANALYSIS AND THE REPRESENTATIVENESS HEURISTIC

As we indicated in chapter 2, there are two distinct ways in which some form of the representativeness heuristic may be said to underlie causal analysis. If the individual looks for causes whose principle features match those of the effect, then he may be said to be using what may be called the "resemblance criterion," that is, searching for causes resembling the effects. If the individual looks for a causal factor resembling the general type of causal factor specified in one of his causal models for effects of the general type he is trying to explain, then he may be said to be applying a "causal theory" to the particular case at hand. For the most part, the two practices have a completely different normative status, with the former being primitive, simplistic, and likely to lead to erroneous conclusions and the latter being a generally appropriate, indeed essential, strategy of causal analysis. Nevertheless, as we hope to show, the two practices blend imperceptibly with each other, and the latter, generally appropriate, practice is subject to substantial abuse.

The Resemblance Criterion

Mill (1843/1974) proposed that the most deeply rooted fallacy in causal reasoning may well be the "prejudice that the conditions of a phenomenon must *resemble* the phenomenon" (p. 765). This fallacy, Mill observed, "not only reigned supreme in the ancient world, but still possesses almost undisputed dominion over many of the most cultivated minds" (p. 765). Nisbett and Wilson (1977a), in considering the intuitive psychologist's lack of ability to analyze correctly the causes of his own behavior, essentially restated Mill's proposal. They suggested that causal explanations are influenced by a primitive version of the representativeness heuristic. People have strong a priori notions of the types of causes that ought to be linked to particular types of effects, and the simple "resemblance criterion" often figures heavily in such notions. Thus, people believe that great events ought to have great causes, complex events ought to have complex causes, and emotionally relevant events ought to have emotionally relevant causes (cf. Rothbart & Fulero 1978). Such explanatory biases, as we shall see, have been noted by scholars in a number of disciplines.

The resemblance criterion is transparently operative in the magical thinking of prescientific cultures. The anthropologist Evans-Pritchard (1937), in his treatment of magical thinking in the Azande culture, reported such Azande beliefs as the theory that fowl excrement was a cure for ringworm and the theory that burnt skull of red bush-monkey was an effective treatment for epilepsy. Westerners unacquainted with Azande ecology might be tempted to guess that such treatments were the product of trial and error or laboriously accumulated folk wisdom. Unfortunately, the truth is probably less flattering to Azande medical science. Fowl excrement resembles ringworm infection; the jerky, frenetic movements of the bush monkey resemble the convulsive movements that occur during an epileptic seizure. As Evans-Pritchard observed:

> Generally the logic of therapeutic treatment consists in the selection of the most prominent external symptoms, the naming of the disease after some object in nature it resembles, and the utilization of the object as the principal ingredient in the drug administered to cure the disease. The circle may even be completed by belief that the external symptoms not only yield to treatment by the object which resembles them but are caused by it as well. (p. 487)

In the early stages of Western medicine, the therapeutic version of the representativeness heuristic became enshrined in a general medical theory called the "doctrine of signatures," which, in the words of the nineteenth-century physician John Paris, was "no less than a belief that every natural substance which possesses any medicinal virtue indicates by an obvious and well-marked external character the disease for which it is a remedy, or the object for which it should be employed" (cited in Mill 1974, p. 766).

> The lungs of a fox must be a specific remedy for asthma, because that animal is remarkable for its strong powers of respiration. Turmeric has a brilliant yellow color, which indicates that it has the power of curing the jaundice . . . the polished surface and strong hardness which so eminently characterize the seeds of the Lithospermum officinale (common gromwell) were deemed a certain indication of their efficacy in calculous and gravelly disorders . . . (cited in Mill 1974, p. 767).

In prescientific analysis, curative agents may resemble either the properties of the disease or the properties *opposite* to those of the disease. Thus, epilepsy is cured by a drug made from a monkey whose movements appear epileptic (the animal's movements resemble the *illness*), and respiratory weakness is cured by a drug made from the lungs of a fox (the animal's powers of respiration resemble the desired state of *health*). The notion that an effect may resemble either its causes or the opposite of its causes is thus well established in prescientific modes of thought. These notions perhaps facilitated many useful discoveries ranging from the prophylactic effects of vaccination to the capacity of cold compacts to relieve burns. The insight that seems absent in prescientific thinking guided by the resemblance criterion is that the salient features of the effect may not be reflected in any of the features of the actual cause.

Much of the causal reasoning characteristic of the psychoanalytic tradition, as we emphasize in chapter 10, shares with prescientific thought a heavy reliance on this crudest form of the representativeness heuristic. Thus, the psychoanalyst proceeds from the conviction that symptoms and causes will seldom prove unrelated in their distinctive external features and from its corollary that overt symptoms may have features either identical or opposite to their psychic causes. To the analyst, one patient's excessive interest in a topic of discourse and another's marked unwillingness to explore the same topic both may reflect the influence of similar pathologies. An ostensibly generous action may reflect either kindness or hostility. A given distortion in a patient's drawing or a certain preoccupation in that patient's interpretation of projective materials may reflect an "obsession" which is either consistent with or totally opposite to its underlying psychic cause.

Our point is not that the analyst is necessarily wrong in all such interpretations. Rather, it is that the specific interpretations, and the broader theories that underlie them, are strongly biased by the resemblance criterion—so much so that the analyst may remain blind to valid but less representative cause and effect covariations and may continue to believe in and even "detect" the invalid associations in everyday exposure to clients. As in prescientific medical thought, the insight that seems absent is that causes and effects may bear little or no resemblance to one another.

Psychoanalytic thought is far from unique in its assumption that the features of causes and the features of effects ought to resemble each other. As Nisbett and Wilson demonstrated, and as Mill noted long ago, the layperson and scientist alike are far more confident than is warranted in their ability to judge the plausibility of a specific cause-effect relationship based on superficial resemblance of features. It is only very recently that educated laypeople have become wary of jeering at scientific explanations on the grounds that the proposed causes are insufficiently representative of the effects in question. As late as the early twentieth century, for example, an editorial in a Washington newspaper complained about all the money that the government was spending on hare-brained ideas about the cause of yellow fever. The newspaper singled out for special ridicule the preposterous suggestion by one Walter

Reed that yellow fever might be caused by the *Aedes aegypti* mosquito. The resemblance criterion still has not been completely abandoned by critics of science. At the time of this writing, a U.S. Senator continues to award a "Golden Fleece" award periodically to a scientist who, in his opinion, is studying a problem too small to affect larger world problems. Work on the reproductive processes of sea urchins or on weather conditions during the Ice Age in Africa are damned, while research proposals promising to deal directly with representative causes and effects of social evils such as cancer, crime in the streets, or reading problems among the educationally disadvantaged are praised and rewarded.

If the relatively formal efforts of scientists (and their critics) often seem to rely on the simple resemblance criterion, then it is scarcely surprising that the layperson uses it so often. "Old wives' tales," for example, emphasize the causal relationship between the prenatal experiences of the mother and the characteristics of the offspring ("His mother was frightened by a dog."). Similarly, future causal import is often attached to the conditions of birth for a child. A child born with a "veil" (part of the amniotic sac over the face) or under unusual celestial conditions was considered to be marked for eminence. Such superstitions have largely disappeared, undoubtedly because they conflict with widely disseminated causal theories. But it seems to us that the logic of such superstitions has a certain continuity with contemporary lay views of the relationship between childhood experience and adult character (cf. Shweder 1977). Thus, political radicalism and nonconformity are attributed to the "permissiveness" in child rearing practiced by a generation of parents tutored by Dr. Spock; sex crimes are attributed to the accessibility of pornography to youths; and adult maladjustment is attributed to childhood trauma. By the same token, faithful pursuit of a paper route is deemed an early indicator of adult responsibility and entrepreneurial ambition. Such causal views do not conflict with well-established scientific laws of causality in the way that old wives' tales and superstitions do. Indeed, many such views may contain more than a germ of truth. But it is hard to avoid the suspicion that the resemblance criterion is an important part of their appeal.

The Use and Abuse of Causal Theories

Everyday causal analysis is not restricted to the use of causal theories based on the simple resemblance criterion. Sometimes people search for a general causal model for effects of the general type for which an explanation is sought. If there is a model which posits a causal factor similar to one known or presumed to be present in the case at hand, then that causal factor may be adduced as being probably operative. Stated in this abstract fashion, such a practice is beyond reproach. How else could one explain political unrest, economic recession, insomnia, backache, or a rash of tantrums by one's child? The problem is not with the theory of theory use but with its practice. It is possible to distinguish two circumstances which render the practice suspect. These circumstances pertain to the origin of the causal theory or model and the degree of confidence in the analysis based on it.

ORIGIN OF THE THEORY. If a cause seems representative of a given effect because it is similar to the causal factors specified in a well-justified causal model, then it is often proper to infer that the cause may have been operative. It is beyond the scope of this book to specify when use of a particular causal model is justified. This is one of the most difficult and the most hotly debated current topics in epistemology. It is much easier to specify when use of a causal model is *not* well justified. It seems obvious that many causal theories originate not from summaries of scientific theories or informed expert opinion, or from close and systematic observation, or even from reasoned armchair analysis, but rather originate from much more haphazard and uncertain sources. Many causal theories seem to have come from maxims, parables, myths, fables, epigrams, allegories, well-known songs or novels, and anecdotes about famous people or personal acquaintances. One could scarcely expect sources so numerous and diverse, and so unconstrained by inferential canons, to yield a unified and consistent set of causal insights. Culturally shared maxims often contradict each other, and there are few rules specifying how often each maxim applies or what situations favor one over the other. For example, consider the two cultural maxims regarding the effects of separation on affection: "Absence makes the heart grow fonder" and "Out of sight, out of mind." In a sense, the contradiction is superficial. One could maintain that absence has variable effects on relationships and that both maxims probably have some sphere of applicability that could be determined through careful scientific investigation designed to specify the relevant moderator variables. But for the lay social analyst, these qualifications are not apt to be specified when an event occurs that is consistent with one of these maxims. Instances of cooled ardor will lead the observer to cite the representative cause "separation," while heightened romantic interest following separation also will be attributed to the separation. The informal store of haphazardly generated causal theory that each of us inherits is too facile and imprecise. An explanation of any given effect or its opposite usually are readily found by a little rummaging around in this bloated system.

OVERCONFIDENCE. Philosophers have long noted that people are often much too confident of their "knowledge" and the accuracy of their judgments. Empirical research has provided evidence of this overconfidence and of the alarming extent to which confidence may often be completely unrelated to accuracy (Goldberg 1959; Oskamp 1965; Einhorn and Hogarth 1978; Fischhoff, Slovic, & Lichtenstein 1977). This seems especially true of causal explanation. The lay scientist seems to search only until a plausible antecedent is discovered that can be linked to the outcome through some theory in the repertoire. Given the richness and diversity of that repertoire, such a search generally will be concluded quickly and easily. A kind of vicious cycle results. The subjective ease of explanation encourages confidence, and confidence makes the lay scientist stop searching as soon as a plausible explanation is adduced, so that the complexities of the task, and the possibilities for "alternative explanations" no less plausible than the first, are never allowed to shake the lay scientist's confidence. In this way, an insomniac may adopt the quite reasonable explanation of "emotional problems" as *the* cause of insomnia but then overlook less representative (and more controllable) causes such as an overheated room or smoking, working, or exercising before going to bed.

Even when practicing that version of causal analysis that can be least criticized in the abstract, people are prone to the errors of relying on causal theories of questionable origin and validity and of applying all theories, whether well founded or poorly founded, with undue confidence. When relying on the the cruder version of the representativeness heuristic, demanding that cause and effect resemble one another in their outward features, errors are still more likely: Cause and effect are rarely as similar in scientific laws as they are in the causal lore they replace.

Representativeness
and the Fundamental Attribution Error

In part, the "fundamental attribution error" can be traced to people's reliance upon the representativeness heuristic. This error, it will be recalled, is the tendency to attribute overt behaviors to corresponding personal dispositions, thereby underestimating the causal role of environmental influences relative to such dispositions and overestimating the degree of cross-situational consistency in individuals' behaviors.

In chapters 2 and 5, we referred to some of the evidence indicating that people's theories of the causes of human behavior may give excessive weight to personal, dispositional causes. The evidence for the inaccuracy of the dispositional theories, or metatheory, is of two types. First, research indicates that individual differences in behavior, though often marked in any given situation, are not very consistent across situations. That is, people who behave in a particularly "X-like" fashion (honest, dependent, aggressive) in one situation are not very likely to be those who behave in a particularly "X-like" fashion in another situation. Second, slight differences in situations often produce large differences in the behavior of most people in those situations.

To these types of evidence, we can add some further illustrations of people's erroneous attributional tendencies. As Kelley (1967) noted, the attitude change manifested by subjects in many classic "dissonance" experiments can be traced to the subjects' erroneous conviction that their behavior was "dispositionally" rather than "situationally" caused. In one typical dissonance paradigm, for example, subjects are induced by the experimenter to give a talk or write an essay that is inconsistent with their private beliefs. In "sufficient justification" conditions, subjects are given large monetary incentives for such behavior and consequently attribute their compliance to the incentive rather than to any corresponding private belief. In "insufficient justification" conditions, by contrast, subjects are paid little or nothing for their counterattitudinal action and, noting no salient external factors sufficient to account for their actions, and wrongly assuming that those actions must therefore reflect corresponding private beliefs, they change their attitudes so as to bring them in line with their behavior. These subjects thus commit the fundamental attribution error. Had they correctly identified the *situational* cause of their behavior, that is, the subtle social pressures to comply exerted by the experimenter and the experimental context, they would have had no reason to change, or even to reassess, their private beliefs.

Another demonstration of people's overwillingness to ascribe behavior to enduring dispositions was provided by Jones and Harris (1967) and by follow-up investigations by Jones and others (see especially Jones 1979). Jones and Harris showed that observers who read an essay advocating or opposing legalization of marijuana or Castro's leadership of Cuba strongly inferred that the author held the view espoused in the essay, even when it was made clear to the observer that the substance of the essay had been dictated by a political science instructor, debate coach, or psychology experimenter. The overwhelming situational constraints, in other words, were discounted by observers in favor of a tendency to assume that the views were congruent with the dispositions of the author.

Perhaps the most direct evidence of the layperson's tendency to underestimate the role of situational factors in controlling behavior is Bierbrauer's (1973) investigation of lay impressions of the forces operating in the classic Milgram (1963) obedience study. In Bierbrauer's study, observers were exposed to a verbatim reenactment of one subject's obedience to the point of delivering the maximum shock to the supposed victim, and then were asked to predict how other subjects would behave. Bierbrauer's observers consistently and dramatically underestimated the degree to which subjects generally would yield to the situational forces that they had viewed at first hand. The observers did so, moreover, even in a set of conditions in which *they themselves* played the role of a subject in a vivid reenactment of Milgram's experiment. In other words, they assumed that the obedience of the particular subject whom they had "observed" reflected his distinguishing personal dispositions rather than the potency of the situational pressures and constraints that acted upon *all* subjects.

In the next section, we emphasize perceptual reasons for the fundamental attribution error. We would like to suggest here that considerations of representativeness, both conceptual and linguistic, may be significant. Actors (and their dispositions) may be a more representative cause of behavior than are situations, because it is, after all, the actor who does the acting. The fact that different actors behave differently in seemingly similar situations, or at least in situations that the *observer* has coded as similar, may make the observer regard situational attributions as less plausible than dispositional ones. As several theorists have noted, linguistic factors also may be pertinent to the fundamental attribution error. It is usually possible to describe both the action and the actor using identical or synonymous terms (generous action, generous actor; hostile action, hostile actor), but the language only seldom allows labeling situations using synonyms for the action, or indeed, using any economical terms at all. (What is the word to describe situations which typically elicit generous behavior?) Linguistically mediated judgments of similarity are apt to favor a causal linkage between action and actor and to slight any potential linkage between action and situation.

CAUSAL ANALYSIS AND THE AVAILABILITY HEURISTIC

It is axiomatic that particular causal factors can be adduced in explaining an effect only if these factors are perceptually or memorially available. But availability is more than a boundary condition. It appears that the *degree* of availability influences the acceptability of causal candidates. That is, the relative salience of potential causal factors or the ease of their retrieval from memory seems to influence the explanation process greatly. Just as the relative frequency of highly available events is overestimated, so the causal significance of highly available antecedents is overestimated. Several sources of evidence support this contention.

Availability and the Fundamental Attribution Error

The fundamental attribution error, as perhaps befits an error labeled "fundamental," may be derived as readily from the availability heuristic as from the representativeness heuristic. The actor is an easily "available" explanation of his action because of his perceptual proximity to his action. The actor, moreover, is dynamic and interesting, while situations more commonly are static and pallid. As Heider explained, "behavior . . . has such salient properties it tends to engulf the total field", (1958, p. 54). The actor and his action, in other words, are "figural" against the "ground" of the situation. Situational cues are therefore likely to be less apparent than the actor himself and consequently are likely to be slighted in causal attribution.

Divergent Causal Attributions of Actors and Observers

An important consequence of deriving the fundamental attribution error from the availability heuristic is that one then may advance the corollary that actors themselves should be less prone to the fundamental attribution error than should observers of their actions. The actor cannot see himself when he acts. On the contrary, as Jones and Nisbett (1972) emphasized, it is the situation that commands the actor's attention, because it is the situation which contains the opportunities and constraints that guide the actor's behavior. It is the situation, and not the actor, which normally will be figural for the actor. Accordingly, the actor should be more inclined than the observer is to attribute his behavior to situational factors and less inclined to attribute his behavior to underlying personal dispositions. This proposal has received substantial empirical support. For a wide variety of behaviors and across a wide variety of situations, actors have been found to attribute their behavior relatively more to situational factors, and observers relatively more to dispositions of the actor. (See Jones 1976, for a review.)

The first persuasive demonstration that these differing attributional tendencies of actor and observer might in part reflect differing attentional perspectives and consequent differences in the availability of causal candidates, was provided by Storms (1973). Storms asked two subjects to have a brief conversation in which they were to "get acquainted with one another" in the presence of two observers who were seated at a table in a position such that each of the observers could easily view one of the actors (who was seated across the table from him) but not the other (who was seated close beside him). The conversations were videotaped. Following the conversation, the actors were asked to explain causally the degree of nervousness, friendliness, talkativeness, and dominance they believed they had displayed in the conversation, and each observer was asked the same questions about the actor whom he viewed during the conversation.

In the control condition, no events intervened between the conversation and the causal analysis task. In the experimental conditions, a videotape of the conversation showing only one of the actors was presented to all subjects before asking the attribution questions. For one of the actors and for one of the observers, this videotape presented no new information: One actor simply again saw his conversation partner, and one observer again saw the actor he originally had watched. For the other actor and observer, the videotape provided a new perspective: The actor on the tape saw himself, and the observer of the other actor now could see the situation confronting the actor he originally had watched, that is, the behavior of the actor's conversational partner.

Figure 6.1 shows that, in the control (no videotape) condition, actors and observers exhibited the traditional differences in causal perceptions, with the observers attributing the actors' behavior more to dispositional factors than the actors did. A similar, indeed slightly exaggerated, pattern of attributions was found for the actors and observers who watched a replay of the event. For the actors and observers who had had their original perspectives reversed by the videotape, causal attributions also were reversed. The actors who viewed themselves on videotape attributed their behavior fully as much to dispositional factors as had the observers who had viewed them in the initial conversation or in the initial conversation plus the videotape replay. The observers who viewed a new actor on the videotape, that is, saw the situation that had confronted their target actor, attributed the target actor's behavior to the situation more than the other observers did and as much as the actors themselves did in the control condition.

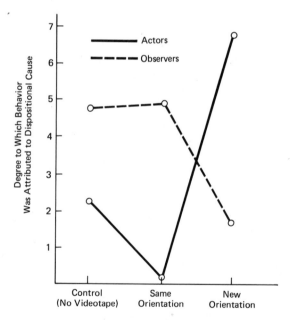

Fig. 6.1 Actors' and observers' attributions of cause of actors' behavior. Same information condition actors saw on videotape the actor they spoke to in the actual conversation and same information condition observers saw their target actor again. New information condition actors saw themselves on videotape and new information condition observers saw the actor their target actor spoke to. (From Storms 1973.)

Storms' work established that the visual salience of actor versus situation is an important determinant of causal attribution and strongly suggested that the differing availability of these causal candidates is important to the differing causal attributions usually found for actors and observers.

Person Salience and Person Perception

The implications of Storms' work extend far beyond the issue of actor-observer differences in causal attribution. His work strongly indicated that, generally, the more visually salient a potential causal agent is, the greater the causal role observers will assign to that agent in accounting for particular outcomes or events. This suggestion has been pursued in a series of studies by Taylor and her colleagues. In this section we draw heavily on their work, especially on an important theoretical paper by Taylor and Fiske (1978).

In their first study, Taylor and Fiske (1975) showed that a participant in a discussion is seen as causally influential in the outcome of the discussion to the extent that the participant is visually prominent. Observers were placed away from each of the four sides of a table at which two actors were seated. The actors then engaged in a brief "get-acquainted" conversation while the observers watched. The seating arrangement guaranteed that one observer could see one of the actors well but could see only the back of the other actor. A second observer had a clear view of only the opposite actor. The remaining two observers were seated so that they could see both actors equally well. At the end of the conversation, all observers were asked which actor was more influential in the discussion. The two observers who could see one actor well and the other poorly believed that the actor whom they could see had set the tone of the conversation, had determined what information would be exchanged, and had caused the other actor to behave as he did. Observers who could see both actors equally well felt that each had contributed equally to all of these outcomes.

In another study, Taylor, Fiske, Close, Anderson, and Ruderman (1979) manipulated the salience of an actor by manipulating the uniqueness of the actor's race or sex. In their first study subjects listened to a tape recording of a discussion among six males. While each spoke, a slide allegedly portraying the speaker was projected on a screen. By varying the race of the individuals portrayed in the slides, but holding constant the discussion tape, the investigators were able to compare the observers' perceptions of a given individual when he occupied a "solo" status (was the only black in the group) with their perceptions when he occupied a "non-solo" status (was one of three blacks in the group). The solo black was perceived as having been more prominent and influential than his co-participants. The same participant (that is, same picture, same tape recording) as a "non-solo" was not perceived as a more potent causal agent than his black or white peers. Similar effects were found for the perceived causal influence of a solo vs. non-solo female in a group of males and for that of a solo vs. non-solo male in a group of females. Thus, arbitrary facts of group composition, like arbitrary manipulations of visual perspective, can influence the salience and therefore the perceived causal influence of particular individuals.

Work by other investigators suggests that almost any circumstance that affects the salience of an actor will affect causal attributions. McArthur and Post (1977) manipulated the prominence of actors by illumination or by having the actor move. The actor's behavior was attributed less to his situation when he was brightly illuminated or moving than it was when he was poorly illuminated or stationary. Conversely, Arkin and Duval (1975) showed that an actor's behavior was attributed less to his environment when the environment was stable than it was when it was in motion.

Studies by Duval and Wicklund (1972), like Storms's (1973), indicates that salience or availability effects are found for actors' perceptions of their own behavior. When actors were made "self-conscious" by viewing themselves in a mirror or by placing videotape equipment in the room, they attributed their behavior more to themselves and less to their environment than they did without such equipment.

The results of the work on salience by Taylor and other investigators have far-reaching implications. Salience manipulations of an everyday, ecologically common sort may have effects, often very pronounced effects, on causal attributions. Accidental features of the environment and one's own location in it therefore can be important in determining causal interpretations and consequent assignments of credit and blame.

Linguistic Influences
on Availability of Causal Candidates

A causal candidate can be made salient by verbal means as well as by visual ones, and there is evidence that verbal manipulations of availability, like visual ones, can influence causal attribution. Kiesler, Nisbett, and Zanna (1969) demonstrated this through a verbal salience manipulation in the context of an attitude change study. Kiesler and colleagues induced subjects to agree to speak about the importance of combating air pollution to passers-by on a street corner. A confederate, in the presence of the subject, agreed to make similar arguments on a different issue, the importance of improving automobile safety. In so doing, the confederate voiced one of two reasons for his compliance. In one condition the confederate attributed his own compliance to his belief in the value of the experiment. In the other condition he attributed his compliance to his strong belief in the importance of improving auto safety. Subjects who heard the confederate cite his underlying beliefs as the reason for his compliance apparently adopted a similar explanation for their own behavior. They asserted that they were more concerned about combating air pollution and were more willing to proselytize than were subjects who heard the confederate cite the value of the experiment as his reason for complying.

Other, more subtle linguistic manipulations also can affect the salience of causal candidates. Salancik (1974, 1976; Salancik & Conway 1975) asked people to complete sentences giving reasons for their own behavior (for example, doing extra course work). The "stem" lead-in to the explanation was manipulated. Some subjects were asked to complete the statement "I (engaged in the behavior) *because* I . . ." while other subjects were asked to complete the statement "I (engaged in the behavior) *in order to* . . . ." The former stem tends to elicit intrinsically motivated reasons for engaging in a given behavior (*because* I like the material in the course), while the latter stem tends to elicit extrinsically motivated reasons (*in order* to do well in the course). The different causal explanations elicited by this manipulation influenced the subjects' subsequent perceptions both of the desirability of the behavior (how much they enjoyed doing the course work) and the desirability of the goals subserved by the behavior (how important it was to do well in the course).

Pryor and Kriss (1977) manipulated the availability of a possible causal agent simply by varying its location in a sentence describing an event. They found that a given causal candidate is more likely to be preferred if it is the subject of a sentence than if it is the object. Thus, Sue is more likely to be identified as the causal agent in her preference for a restaurant if subjects are told that Sue likes the restaurant than if they are told that the restaurant is liked by Sue!

In summary, it appears that both perceptual and verbal manipulations of the availability of potential causal factors substantially influence causal inferences. This susceptibility depends in part on yet another shortcoming in everyday causal inferences, one which we examine next.

MISGUIDED PARSIMONY:
THE "HYDRAULIC" MODEL OF CAUSATION

In his analysis of the limitations of human understanding, Mill described a bias he called "the prejudice that a phenomenon cannot have more than one cause" (1843/1974, p. 763). Kanouse elaborated on the implications of this tendency:

. . . individuals may be primarily motivated to seek a single sufficient explanation for any event, rather than one that is the best of all possible explanations. That is, individuals may exert more cognitive effort in seeking an adequate explanation when none has yet come to mind than they do in seeking for further (and possibly better) explanations when an adequate one is already available. This bias may reflect a tendency to think of unitary events and actions as having unitary (rather than multiple) causes; individuals may assume, in effect, that no more than one sufficient explanation is likely to exist for a single phenomenon. Thus, when more than one satisfactory explanation is potentially available to an individual, which one he adopts may depend primarily on which of the various possible explanations is most *salient*. (1972, p. 131)

As we have seen, there is now good evidence for Kanouse's "salience" hypothesis. We wish now to consider Kanouse's "misguided parsimony" hypothesis and to underscore the link between the two hypotheses. The pronounced availability effects on causal attribution would appear to *depend on* the individual's willingness to be content when a single sufficient cause has been adduced and to forego exhaustive searches for further, potentially influential antecedents. That is, by manipulating the causal factors that the person will notice or ponder first, one can manipulate the person's ultimately preferred explanation for the event in question. Availability would not have such an important influence on causal attributions if people continued to search vigorously for additional sufficient explanations, even after finding a first sufficient explanation.

It would almost certainly be an overstatement to say that people *believe* that most events have unitary causes. Indeed, there is evidence that people often recognize and even cite multiple causes for their own behavior or for that of their peers. For instance, Wilson and Nisbett (1978) found that subjects usually listed several factors when accounting for a given behavior. Moreover, politicians, historians, urbanologists, and sometimes even students explaining the lateness of a term paper, show no unwillingness to cite multiple causes for a given event. The contradiction between such evidence and the "parsimony" contention may be more apparent than real. In explaining or justifying an action, the individual may continue to search for and to cite as many causal factors as are necessary to satisfy subjective criteria for sufficiency. It may be only when there are several causal candidates, *any one of which* would be deemed sufficient for the explanation, that a predilection for parsimony misleads the intuitive causal analyst.

Although people sometimes acknowledge the existence of multiple causes, it is clear that they frequently *act* in ways far more consistent with beliefs in unitary causation. In a sense, they behave as if causation were "hydraulic" or as if causal candidates competed with one another in a zero-sum game.

Evidence for such hydraulic assumptions and for resultant inferential errors comes primarily from work on perceived intrinsic versus extrinsic motivation (for example, Deci 1971; Lepper, Greene, & Nisbett 1973; Kruglanski 1978). The basic paradigm introduces an obvious, extrinsic, causal factor, such as reward or surveillance, in a context in which subjects perform some activity that they would and normally do happily perform in the *absence* of the extrinsic factor. The result is an "undermining" of intrinsic interest. The subject acts as if the activity were caused by the extrinsic factor rather than by the intrinsic interest or enjoyment of the activity itself.

In one study Lepper, Greene, and Nisbett (1973) presented nursery school children with the opportunity to play with magic markers, a new and very attractive activity for the children. Children in an extrinsic motivation condition were told that by drawing with the magic markers they would have an opportunity to win a "good player award," an impressive certificate with a blue ribbon and a gold seal. Other children were given no such extrinsic justification for their activity. All children then drew with the magic markers for an appreciative experimenter. Children in the extrinsic motive condition were thanked for drawing so nicely and then were given the award they had anticipated receiving for good performance. Other children were simply thanked for drawing so nicely and then were taken back to the classroom. The remaining children also were thanked for drawing so nicely and also were given a "good player award" about which they had not previously been told. Two weeks later, the drawing materials again were placed on a table in the classroom as one of the play options for the day and the amount of time each child spent drawing with the materials was recorded. It was expected that children in the extrinsic motivation condition would infer that drawing with magic markers was something they did in order to win awards and thus would be less inclined to draw with them in the classroom where there was no opportunity to win such an award. In fact, children in that condition drew only half as much with the magic markers as did children who received no award or as did children who received the award but had not "contracted" for it.

The phenomenon has been demonstrated repeatedly in a wide variety of contexts by a number of different investigators using a variety of extrinsic factors and intrinsic interests (see Lepper & Greene 1978, for a comprehensive review). The work strongly supports the conclusion that when subjects are induced to believe that there is an extrinsic motive for engaging in a particular activity, they proceed to behave as if they had little or no intrinsic motive to engage in the activity. The phenomenon would appear to depend on an erroneous "hydraulic" or unitary cause theory: Behavior has only one sufficient cause; therefore, when one sufficient causal factor is known to be present, any other potential causal factors must be weak or inoperative.

A similar hydraulic assumption may operate in social perception contexts as well. Work by Strickland (1958) suggested that surveillance leads people to distrust those whom they have been assigned to oversee. Conscientious behavior by the overseen individual is attributed by the overseer to his own surveillance, and apparently the overseer comes to regard such surveillance as necessary to ensure conscientious performance.

Perceptions of political behavior often appear to be influenced by the assumption that, if a factor is both present and known to be a sufficient cause of some action, then other factors must be nonexistent or relatively uninfluential. For instance, President Richard Nixon's trip to China was seen widely as an attempt to achieve domestic political gain, and the alternative possibility that it reflected some deep conviction, even the possibility that it *also* reflected such a conviction, was largely discounted. (Many sophisticated political observers, incidentally, would categorize domestic political considerations as an inhibitory factor rather than as a cause of Nixon's decision. Before the trip, Nixon and his advisors were quite apprehensive of the possibility of adverse political reaction.) The notion that political gain constituted a sufficient cause blinded observers to the fact that the trip could have reflected *several* causes. Indeed, the sophisticated observer should have recognized the need to consider multiple causes when reflecting on the particular action Nixon chose to undertake "for political gain," since many other actions that might have been equally advantageous in political terms were *not* undertaken. Skepticism about the motives of politicians may have a healthy effect on democratic freedoms, but it rests on an unreasonably simple, hydraulic view of human motivation.

MISSING CAUSAL SCHEMAS

An important shortcoming of everyday causal analysis is that people lack, or possess in only a rudimentary form, certain normatively essential causal-analytic schemas. Perhaps the most thoroughly researched example of an underutilized schema is the one prescribing the causal implications of consensus information. In Kelley's (1967) analysis, he proposed that when observers know that most actors respond to an entity in the same way, the observers infer that the entity exerts a strong force on actors to elicit that particular response. Observers then hesitate to infer dispositional causes for the response of any particular actor. Since Kelley's proposal of this normatively correct attribution principle, however, substantial evidence has been collected showing that informal causal inferences are surprisingly *unaffected* by consensus information.

In McArthur's (1972, 1978) important studies of the effects of consensus, distinctiveness, and consistency information, she found that consensus information had little impact on causal attributions. For example, when subjects were asked to infer why "Ralph tripped on Joan's feet while dancing," their causal attributions were little affected by the knowledge that either "almost everyone" or "hardly anyone" was in the habit of tripping over Joan's feet. In contrast, both distinctiveness information ("Ralph trips over almost everyone else's/hardly anyone else's feet") and consistency information ("In the past, Ralph has almost always/hardly ever tripped on Joan's feet") had much more impact on causal attribution. In a follow-up study, Ruble and Feldman (1976) did find substantially more utilization of consensus information than reported by McArthur, but only when such information appeared *after* the distinctiveness and consistency information and immediately before the attribution questions were asked. It was notable that neither distinctiveness information nor consistency information was similarly vulnerable to position effects. In another study using children as subjects and using concrete, visual materials, McArthur (1978) found some slight utilization of consensus information, but its utilization was developmentally delayed as compared to utilization of both distinctiveness and consistency information. The latter two types of information were used by children of all ages studied, but only the older children also used consensus information.

In a remarkable demonstration of the failure of consensus information to affect causal attribution, Miller, Gillen, Schenker, and Radlove (1973) showed that consensus information about the behavior of subjects in Milgram's (1963) obedience study had little effect on judgments about a particular subject who delivered the highest possible amount of shock to a confederate. All subjects in Miller's and colleagues' experiment were told about Milgram's procedures, including that his subject sample was a cross-section of the community in which the study was conducted. Some subjects also were shown the results, notably that 65 percent of the subjects delivered the maximum possible shock. All subjects were then told about two people who had delivered the maximum shock and were asked to rate these people on a number of trait scales, including warmth, likeableness, dependency, aggressiveness, and attractiveness. The consensus information had an effect on only one of eleven such trait ratings. That is, the knowledge that giving the maximum shock was actually the *modal* response did not reduce subjects' tendency to make strong negative dispositional inferences about a particular person who showed that response.

Consensus information is probably underutilized at least as much in self-perception as it is in the perception of others. Nisbett, Borgida, Crandall, and Reed (1976) performed three experiments in which they attempted to externalize the perceived cause of depression by a consensus-information manipulation. Depressive states studied ranged from the "Sunday Blues" that many college students feel to the "first-year faculty syndrome" of anxiety and depression experienced by many new faculty members. Nisbett and colleagues attempted to convince their subjects that feeling depressed was a very common response for people in their situation. The investigators reasoned that, if subjects could be persuaded by this consensus information to attribute their depression to the situation in which they found themselves, they would be less inclined to wrongly attribute their psychological malfunctioning to personal inadequacy and weakness, and hence would be less depressed. No such therapeutic effect of consensus information was found. Neither mood nor behavior was much influenced by subjects' knowledge that their feelings and responses were the rule rather than the exception for people in their situation.

Nisbett and colleagues also studied the effect of consensus information on psychological states that would seem to be less intransigent than depression. Subjects in a "cracker-tasting experiment" were asked to sip a "neutralizing solution" (a tepid mix of lemon juice, sugar, and water) after each bite of cracker in order to wash away its taste before taking the next bite. After completing the cracker tasting, subjects were led to believe that they had drunk either much more or much less of the neutralizing solution than other subjects had drunk. They then were asked how much they had liked the neutralizing solution, how thirsty the crackers had made them, and how thirsty they had been before they started tasting the crackers. These questions would seem to exhaust the possible causal explanations for drinking either a particularly large or a particularly small amount of the neutralizing solution. Nevertheless, subjects' answers to these questions were virtually unaffected by the manipulation of consensus information.

It should be noted that in the "depression" and "neutralizing solution" studies, the subjects' behavior was not necessarily counternormative. If a subject does not choose to feel better after being told that everyone in his situation is miserable, then we can scarcely fault him for being illogical. We can say only that sensitivity to the personal implications of consensus information *might* have led people to hold less unfavorable views of themselves and therefore to be less unhappy. The fact that subjects did not respond in this way suggests merely that they gave little weight to consensus information, and not that they were illogical in ignoring it. Similarly, subjects in the "neutralizing solution" experiment were not logically obligated to change their views of the factors that could have resulted in their drinking more or less than other subjects did. The study merely suggests that people are not sufficiently sensitive to consensus information to change their views in logically permissible ways in response to such information. The studies are presented because they shed light on the possible reasons, discussed next, for people's failure to be affected by consensus information.

Information Vividness and Causal Attribution

Why are people so unresponsive to the information provided by consensus data? One possibility is the nature of consensus information, or perhaps more accurately, the character of consensus manipulations used in most research conducted to date. Consensus information generally has been quite pallid and abstract, especially as compared to competing information about the stimulus or the actor. In the study by Miller and colleagues (1973), in which subjects were told of the Milgram demonstration, a table of data (of the percentage of subjects who administered various levels of shock) was required to compete with more concrete and vivid information about the behavior of a particular person (whose photo the subject was allowed to see). Similarly, statistical information about the reactions of other people to "Sundays" or "the first year of teaching" may have little chance to affect the depressed individual who is responding to vivid, unpleasant, and all too real stimuli. Clearly a more concrete and compelling presentation of consensus data and consensus information—perhaps something akin to a "buddy" support system—would provide a better test of the therapeutic possibilities of consensus information.

Some support for the proposition that the relative pallor of consensus information is responsible for its failure to be utilized comes from work by Hansen and Donoghue (1977). These investigators, using a "neutralizing solution" procedure similar to that used by Nisbett and colleagues, found that *observers* of the experiment, in contrast to the actors themselves, *were* influenced by consensus information. They attributed the actor's drinking behavior to the actor's personal qualities more when he drank an unusual quantity of the neutralizing solution than when he drank a typical amount of the neutralizing solution. Actors would have available to them the sensory qualities of their own experience, including the taste of the solution. For them, information about the behavior of other people would seem comparatively pallid and remote, and, accordingly, it would be given little weight compared to that of their own sensory experiences. To observers, in contrast, no such vivid, competing information was available.

Information Directness and Causal Attribution

The vividness interpretation of the failure of consensus information to affect attributions is not applicable to the McArthur (1972) study and its follow-ups. All of the information provided to subjects in such studies was relatively pallid, and the consensus information ("Almost everyone/hardly anyone trips over Joan's feet") would seem to be neither more nor less pallid than the distinctiveness information ("Ralph trips over almost everyone else's/hardly anyone else's feet") or consistency information ("In the past, Ralph had almost always/hardly ever tripped over Joan's feet"). Yet consensus information had a comparatively small effect in these studies, was vulnerable to position effects, and was utilized at a later point developmentally than the other types of information were.

McArthur (1978) recently proposed that the explanation of the weakness of consensus information in these "equal-concreteness" studies may be the relative directness of the three kinds of information vis-à-vis the actor. In all of the research, the attribution questions concern the actor—"Why did A behave in X fashion?" Both distinctiveness and consistency information refer directly to the actor's behavior. Actor A behaves either in X fashion toward most stimuli of the general type or he does not; actor A behaves either in X fashion toward the particular stimulus most of the time or he does not. In contrast, consensus information informs us only about people other than the actor. Learning anything about the actor from such information requires an inference of a rather roundabout sort—from knowledge of (a) the behavior of other people to inferences about (b) the X-evoking properties of the stimulus to inferences about (c) the effects of the X-evoking properties of the stimulus on the particular actor. McArthur proposed that the power of information to influence attributions is a function of the number of inferential steps necessary to make use of it (cf. Nisbett & Borgida 1975). This notion provides a highly plausible alternative account of the relative weakness of consensus information.

Consensus Information and Ability Attributions

Though we have two, quite satisfactory, theoretical explanations of the general failure of consensus information to exert sufficient influence on attributions, there is one domain in which it is clear that consensus information is utilized quite well. This is the domain of ability attributions (see, for example, Weiner and colleagues 1972). When people are told that the target actor succeeded at a particular task and that most other people failed, they infer that the actor is unusually able. When they are told that the actor failed but that the majority of other people failed as well, they attribute the actor's failure to task difficulty rather than to ability.

It is interesting to speculate about why abilities should provide so striking an exception to the general rule. Our guess is that it may be partially because abilities, uniquely among personal dispositions, usually are *defined* consensually. The statement that an individual is a good typist or tennis player is primarily a comparison of that individual to other typists or tennis players in situations which are relatively fixed and constant across actors. Accordingly, the primary evidence that speaks to an individual's typing ability consists of data that directly compare the individual's accuracy and speed with the accuracy and speed of other typists under the same circumstances.

In contrast, the statement that an individual is kind, easygoing, or honest is not so direct a comparative assessment. Judgments of traits such as these are likely to rest mainly on the number of instances and counterinstances of behavior consistent with the particular trait appellation, and a broad variety of acts, in a wide range of situations, may be consistent with such labels. People are regarded as kind or unkind mainly because of the number of "kind" or "unkind" acts we have seen them perform, not because of how kind they are relative to other people in the same situation.

That abilities, unlike other traits, can be defined consensually, may be a consequence of the clear and universally accepted criteria providing a basis for assessment. Typing ability is measured exclusively by performance with a typewriter and tennis playing ability is measured by one's success on a tennis court. Everyone must test his or her mettle in the same way, in the same situation, and under the same ground rules. The condition of situational constancy facilitates the cross-individual comparisons necessary for consensual definition. Without it, ordinal ranking and consensual assessment would be difficult if not impossible.

For our purposes, what is interesting about the fact that consensus information is utilized well in ability attributions is the illustration it provides that a given causal schema (or a special-purpose rule consistent with such a schema) may be operative in one domain but not in another to which, logically, it is just as applicable. In other words, there may be substantial compartmentalization of causal analysis strategies. Healthy development of a given strategy in one arena may not ensure its use in others to which it is equally applicable. Often the pertinent principles may be appreciated in the form of popular maxims or as dynamic scripts limited to particular domains of experience. The "unfair exam" followed by a plethora of failing grades (and probably by protests and regrading on a curve) is an easily available script for college students, just as the "pitcher you can't touch when his knuckle ball is working" is an easily available script for ball players and sports fans. But in both cases the correct "situational" attributions probably are made without resort to any abstract consensus schema. What we find then is limited or domain-specific appreciation of particular inferential or statistical principles. Similar domain-specific utilization of inferential rules are explored in more detail in the following chapter.

INTRUSION OF CAUSAL THEORIES
INTO INAPPROPRIATE DOMAINS

Just as people may fail to apply a causal schema to situations to which it is appropriate, they also may apply a causal schema or theory to situations to which it is inappropriate. Work by Langer (1975, 1977; Langer & Roth 1975) provided specific examples of such intrusion. Langer showed that in situations in which the outcome is determined purely by chance, people often behave as if the outcome were in large part skill determined. In one study

(Langer 1975), subjects drew cards from a deck in competition with another person. They were willing to bet larger amounts of money on the outcome of the draw if the other person presented a "schnook persona" than if the person presented a competent, self-confident impression. In another study, Langer (1975) sold one dollar lottery tickets to employees of an insurance agency and of a manufacturing company. Some of the subjects, upon paying, were simply handed one the lottery tickets, while others were allowed to *choose* their own ticket from several. On the morning of the lottery, the experimenter approached each of the subjects and attempted to buy back the ticket. No-choice subjects sold their tickets back for an average of $1.96. Choice subjects, who had personally selected their tickets, held out for an average of $8.67!

The principle at work in both these studies seems to be that the presence of elements that might be influential in the outcome of a skill-determined task affects people's judgments in a purely chance-determined situation. In true skill-determined situations, the apparent competence or incompetence of an opponent, or the ability to exercise some control, might appropriately affect one's confidence in the outcome. The fact that people's confidence is affected by the presence of the same elements in circumstances to which only luck or chance is relevant suggests the ease with which causal theories appropriate to some situations can intrude into others to which they are inappropriate.

As Langer noted, the "intrusion" notion also may underlie Lerner's "just world" findings. Lerner showed that people often derogate the victims of totally chance-determined misfortune. In a typical demonstration, Lerner and Matthews (1967) asked pairs of subjects to draw lots to determine which subject would receive electric shocks in a learning experiment. Subjects devalued the unlucky member of the pair only when they were "responsible " for determining the other subject's fate—that is, when they selected their own lot first, leaving the other subject "holding the bag," as it were. Subjects did not devalue the unlucky member if he chose his unfortunate lot first, thereby "sealing his own fate."

The intrusion of theories of skill and personal responsibility into the domain of chance events undoubtedly occurs partially because people's grasp of the concept of chance is very tenuous. Even in gambling, in which people know that the laws of chance are operative and have at least some rudimentary theories for dealing with likelihoods, people can show remarkable blindnesses and biases. The very notion of chance determination of other sorts of events was a very late development in our culture. Only people with special training in probability theory are likely to have a truly adequate and general appreciation of the meaning of randomness. For other people, that is to say almost everyone else, the hazy conception of chance readily permits the intrusion of other causal theories into the understanding of random events.

This point may be generalized by saying that when the appropriate schema for analysis of a given situation is weak, then obvious and powerful theories used habitually in other domains will likely intrude. Langer's (1975, 1977) explanation of the circumstances that promote such intrusion into the domain of chance also may be generalized. Langer observed that when the salient features of a chance situation strongly resemble the salient features of a situation in which skill operates or in which there is personal responsibility for outcomes, then intrusion of theories from these latter domains is to be expected. In general we would expect that intrusion of a given inappropriate causal theory is determined largely by representativeness criteria, that is, by surface features of the situation resembling surface features of the situations to which the theory is applied appropriately.

SUMMARY

Although there is evidence that causal attributions sometimes are responsive, at least directionally, to the factors that normatively "ought" to influence them, this evidence comes primarily from research in which the relevant data, including covariation information, have been summarized for subjects in advance by the investigator. Thus, generalization of such research to real-world conditions, especially those which require people to assess covariation for themselves, may be hazardous.

Causal analysis is influenced strongly by two versions of the representativeness heuristic. One of these is a primitive requirement that the features of any putative cause resemble the features of the effect to be explained. The other, more normatively appropriate version, is the requirement that a putative cause resemble a causal factor in a theory explaining effects of the type in question. People often rely on poorly justified causal theories of questionable origin and place too much confidence in even those explanations prompted by causal theories held with good justification.

Causal analysis is also overly influenced by the availability of various causal candidates. People's explanations for events are therefore at the mercy of arbitrary shifts in the perceptual, verbal, or memorial salience of potential explanatory factors. This tendency, in turn, rests on an overly simplistic or "hydraulic" view of causality. People often seem to believe that a given event can have only one sufficient cause.

Despite evidence that people use Kelley's normative ANOVA strategy at least under ideal data conditions, there is evidence that, even under ideal conditions, people infrequently use one of Kelley's most important principles of causal analysis—the "consensus" rule. There are two explanations for people's failure to utilize consensus information sufficiently: (a) the relative pallor of consensus information as compared to more vivid information about the stimulus and the actor, and (b) the relative indirectness of consensus information, which seems remote from an understanding of the particular actor and his action. An exception to the general rule that people underutilize consensus information is found in the case of abilities, in which people seem to respond quite appropriately to such information. This exception probably occurs because most abilities, unlike other dispositions, generally are defined consensually, by direct comparison of different people's behavior in fixed and stable situations.

Just as people seem unable to use certain causal schemas and theories in domains in which they would be helpful, they seem to use certain other causal schemas and theories in domains in which they are inappropriate and lead to error. Such intrusion is abetted by the lack of adequate tools for understanding causality in a given domain and by the degree to which stimuli in the domain have features similar to those in the intrusive theory.

7

prediction

> Probability is like the cane that the blind man uses to
> feel his way. If he could see, he would not need the cane,
> and if I knew which horse was the fastest, I would not
> need probability theory.
>
> *Stanislaw Lem (reviewing*
> *"De Impossibilitatae Vitae" and*
> *"De Impossibilitatae Prognoscendi"*
> *by Professor Cezar Kouska).*

Intuitive predictions interest the social scientist because they mediate social behavior. Consider the plight of John, a law school graduate about to take the state bar exams. Much of his behavior will be affected by his subjective assessment of the likelihood of passing those exams. But what will be his subjective estimate of his chances of passing the exam, given that his friend Sam failed last year while his sister-in-law Beth passed, that he knows he scored at the eighty-fifth percentile on his law school entrance exams and has studied diligently, that he generally performs poorly under pressure, that the test features essay questions, and that his horoscope shows Venus rising? Consider also Jane, a promising young executive in the breakfast-cereal industry, whose company has just concocted a new product. A dozen business decisions depend on her prediction of the fate of that new product. What will she predict about national sales, given her knowledge that 70 percent of the five year olds surveyed like the package design, that her own five year old said the product tasted "mushy," that Kellog has a similar but more costly product which now occupies 26 percent of the market, and that her own track record as a prognosticator reveals that she usually has been too conservative?

As these examples illustrate, problems of predictions often are both consequential and exceedingly difficult in their cognitive demands. The accuracy of predictions is influenced by the adequacy of one's knowledge and theories, by the selection of relevant facts, by one's assessment of the strength of covariation between variables whose values are known and variables whose values one wishes to predict, and by one's beliefs about the causal factors operative in the situational context of the prediction. In addition to these cognitive tasks, which have been discussed in previous chapters, prediction carries a special set of requirements concerning knowledge of statistical and probabilistic principles which are sufficiently complicated and counterintuitive that many of the most important have been established only within the past century.

It will come as no surprise then to learn that people perform many prediction tasks very poorly. Some of the most recent evidence, however, suggests that people may sometimes do a better job of prediction than would be expected, given their intuitive failings. Sometimes, predictions may be guided by inferential strategies that reflect only imperfectly or not at all the normatively appropriate criteria; yet these strategies may prove fairly adequate rules of thumb in some contexts.

HUMAN INTUITIONS VERSUS ACTUARIAL FORMULAS

One of the general strategies of this book—the criticism of intuitive judgments with respect to normative, statistical standards—was pursued a generation ago by psychologists concerned with clinical predictions. By 1955, when Paul Meehl wrote his classic *Clinical vs. Statistical Prediction*, there already were a score of studies in which clinical psychologists' predictions of patient outcomes (for example, recidivism versus continued health) had been compared to predictions made by actuarial formulas, usually simple regression equations applying empirically derived weights to the available diagnostic information. At the time of Meehl's book, virtually all the available studies showed the actuarial method to be at the least the equal of, and usually quite superior to, the clinical judge.

The intervening years have supported, extended, and refined this generalization. Not only clinicians, but human judges in general, make predictions inferior to those of actuarial formulas. This result has been obtained under almost all conditions studied in which the information employed by the human judges and statistical formulas is at all diagnostic of the outcomes. (See Slovic & Lichtenstein 1971, and Dawes & Corrigan 1974, for excellent summaries of the evidence on this point.) Stockbrokers predicting the growth of corporations, admissions officers predicting the performance of college students, and personnel managers choosing employees are nearly always outperformed by actuarial formulas, which use only the scores on a few attributes known to be empirically associated with outcomes. Human judges make less accurate predictions than formulas do, whether they have more information than is fed into the formula or precisely the same amount of information. Human predictions are worse than actuarial ones even if the judges are informed of the weights used by the formula and are worse even if the judges are informed of the specific predictions generated by the formula for the cases in question.

Human judges are not merely worse than *optimal* regression equations; they are worse than almost any regression equation. Even if the weights in the equation are *arbitrary,* as long as they are nonzero, positive, and linear, the equation generally will outperform human judges (Dawes & Corrigan 1974). Human judges do not merely apply invalid weights; they apply their invalid weights unreliably: A computational model of an individual judge, one which calculates the weights applied by the judge to the first N cases, will outperform the judge on the next batch of cases because of improved reliability alone.

To this already humbling picture of human predictive frailty, we must add that research in this tradition has studied human judges at something approximating their best advantage. The judges typically are not amateurs, but professionals, making predictions in domains of which they have special knowledge and often years of training, and in which they commonly have had repeated opportunities for feedback on the accuracy of their predictions. In most of the studies, the judges also were allowed all the time they wished to make their predictions, as well as the opportunity to perform systematic calculations. And, in many of the studies, the judges have had not merely expertise in the particular judgmental domain, but also formal training in the statistical procedures necessary for prediction.

In the next sections, we discuss research on subjects who, for the most part, lack such advantages. As might be expected, the findings are even more unsettling.

BASE RATES VERSUS THE REPRESENTATIVENESS CRITERION

Over the past few years much experimental evidence has accumulated which indicates that people underutilize an important source of information in making predictions. That source is base-rate data, that is, prior probabilities, population proportions, or information about central tendencies in the outcome domain. The same evidence shows that intuitive predictions usually overutilize information about the target case, that is, the particular object or person about which predictions are made. People are thus insufficiently concerned with the relative frequencies of the various outcome possibilities and are overly concerned with the degree to which the features of the target are similar to the features of some particular outcome. We alluded to these tendencies in our introduction to the "representativeness heuristic" in chapter 2, and now we pursue them in greater detail.

Assessed Base Rates versus Assessed Similarity

Let us begin by reviewing the first of a series of demonstration experiments conducted by Kahneman and Tversky (1973). Groups of subjects were given one of three tasks. The first group of subjects was asked simply to estimate the percentage of graduate students enrolled in each of nine specified academic fields. These estimates allowed the investigators to establish subjects' beliefs about the base rate for various fields of graduate specialization (outcomes).

The second group was asked to indicate how similar a person named "Tom W." was to the typical graduate student in each of these fields. This group was given the following brief personality sketch:

> Tom W. is of high intelligence, although lacking in true creativity. He has a need for order and clarity, and for neat and tidy systems in which every detail finds its appropriate place. His writing is rather dull and mechanical, occasionally enlivened by somewhat corny puns and by flashes of imagination of the sci-fi type. He has a strong drive for competence. He seems to have little feel and little sympathy for other people and does not enjoy interacting with others. Self-centered, he nonetheless has a deep moral sense. (1973, p. 238)

The third and final group was given the same sketch and was told that it was compiled on the basis of projective tests taken by Tom W. when he was in high school. This group was then asked to predict the likelihood that each of the nine academic fields was Tom's current field of graduate study.

By normative Bayesian standards, the likelihood estimates of the third group ought to have been influenced by (a) the relative frequencies of the various occupations and (b) the similarity of Tom W's characteristics to the presumed characteristics of the members of the various occupations. The relative "weight" given to each factor, moreover, ought to have been determined by the raters' beliefs about the "diagnosticity" of Tom's characteristics vis-à-vis occupation. Kahneman's and Tversky's results showed that a far simpler prediction strategy was employed. Likelihood estimates by the third group were almost perfectly correlated with the similarity ratings that had been offered by the second group. That is, fields of specialization were judged likely for Tom precisely to the extent that his personality profile corresponded to the raters' stereotypes of the members of those fields. By contrast, the awareness that the fields differed markedly in the size of their memberships (as shown by the first group's estimates) seemed to have virtually no impact on likelihood ratings. For instance, 95 percent of the group assigned to rate likelihoods rated computer science as a more likely field for Tom than humanities or education was, although the "base rate" group estimated computer science to be only one-third as common as humanities and education.

This heavy use of information about the target case, while overlooking base rate probabilities, might have been reasonable in terms of conventional Bayesian rules if the subjects had firmly believed that the personality sketches, purportedly made on the basis of high school projective test results, were both accurate and diagnostic of later career choices. As Kahneman and Tversky took pains to demonstrate, their subjects actually held projective tests in quite low esteem and did not believe that such tests would be very helpful in predicting later career choice. Subjects thus relied greatly on specific information about the target case that they recognized to be relatively invalid and only weakly diagnostic while ignoring base rates or prior odds which, according to Bayesian dictates, could be "overcome" only by very strong diagnostic information.

**Manipulated Base Rates
versus the Representativeness Criterion**

Kahneman's and Tversky's perhaps most stringent test of the hypothesis that intuitive predictions are sensitive to representativeness or similarity criteria rather than to prior probabilities was an experiment which *manipulated* the base-rate information available to subjects at the time that they made likelihood estimates. Half the subjects received the following instructions designed to manipulate "prior odds" in a simple and explicit fashion.

A panel of psychologists has interviewed and administered personality tests to 30 engineers and 70 lawyers, all successful in their respective fields. On the basis of this information, thumbnail descriptions of the 30 engineers and 70 lawyers have been written. You will find on your forms five descriptions, chosen at random from the 100 available descriptions. For each description, please indicate your probability that the person described is an engineer, on a scale from 0 to 100 (Kahneman & Tversky 1973, p. 241)

For the remaining subjects, the base rates were reversed—that is, the five personality sketches were purported to have been drawn at random from a sample of seventy engineers and thirty lawyers. In both conditions subjects were urged to be as accurate as possible and, in fact, were promised a "bonus" if their estimates corresponded to those of an "expert panel."

The five personality descriptions were quite brief but were designed to differ in their representativeness vis-à-vis subjects' stereotypes of engineers versus lawyers. One description designed to be compatible with the subjects' engineer stereotype and incompatible with their lawyer stereotype read as follows:

> Jack is a 45-year-old man. He is married and has four children. He is generally conservative, careful, and ambitious. He shows no interest in political and social issues and spends most of his free time on his many hobbies which include home carpentry, sailing, and mathematical puzzles. (p. 241)

After each such description, subjects were asked to make a likelihood estimate in a simple format that reiterated the base-rate information. For instance, subjects in the low base-rate condition for engineers were asked to estimate "the probability that Jack is one of the 30 engineers in the sample of 100" (p. 241).

The results showed that subjects seriously violated Bayesian standards for prediction. Subjects responded to personality portraits that seemed "engineerlike" by estimating the probability of engineer to be high and to "lawyerlike" portraits by guessing the probability of lawyer to be high. The difference in prior odds, which, according to Bayes' rule should have had a potent influence on the relevant probability estimates, had practically none. Subjects estimated the likelihood of a given target's being an engineer to be virtually the same whether the target came from a group composed largely of engineers or one composed largely of lawyers.

Figure 7.1 illustrates the findings. The five data points indicate the two probability estimates of "engineer" made for each of the five personality sketches under the 70 percent engineer instruction and the 30 percent engineer instruction. For example, the personality sketch which produced a probability estimate of .05 in the "low" base-rate condition also produced an estimate of .05 in the "high" base-rate condition; the sketch that produced an estimate of .31 in the low base-rate condition produced an estimate of about .39 in the high base-rate condition, and so forth. The curved line displays the correct relation according to Baye's rule. That is, a sketch that yielded a probability estimate of only .10 in the "low" base-rate condition, "ought" (according to Bayes's rule) to have yielded an estimate of .35 in the high base-rate condition; one sufficiently diagnostic to yield an estimate of .5 in the low base-rate condition ought to have yielded an estimate of over .8 in the high base-rate condition.

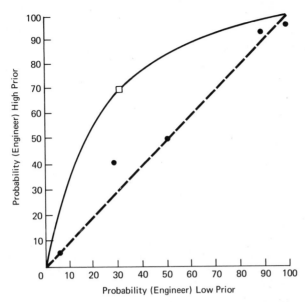

Fig. 7.1 Median judged probability (engineer) for five descriptions and for the null description (square symbol) under high and low prior probabilities. (The curved line displays the correct relation according to Bayes's rule. (From Kahneman & Tversky 1973.)

One other finding from this study should be emphasized. Subjects in one condition were asked to estimate likelihoods for target cases in the *absence* of any personality information. They were asked to estimate the probability that "an individual chosen at random from the sample," about whom you have "no information whatsoever" was an engineer. In this "null" condition, subjects consistently made appropriate use of the base-rate data. They estimated likelihoods to be either 70 percent or 30 percent, depending on the base-rate information provided. However, when subjects were given any information at all about the target case, *even totally nondiagnostic* information, they ignored the base rate. For example, consider subjects' response to the following description:

> Dick is a 30-year-old man. He is married with no children. A man of high ability and high motivation, he promises to be quite successful in his field. He is well liked by his colleagues. (p. 242)

Whether the subjects were given the 30 percent base rate or 70 base rate, those who read this description typically rated the engineer and lawyer likelihoods to be equal, that is, 50 percent. The implications of this contrast between the "no information" and "totally nondiagnostic information" conditions seems clear. When *no* specific evidence about the target case is provided, prior probabilities are utilized appropriately; when *worthless* specific evidence is given, prior probabilities may be largely ignored, and people respond as if there were no basis for assuming differences in relative likelihoods. People's grasp of the relevance of base-rate information must be very weak if they could be distracted from using it by exposure to useless target case information.

Representativeness and Compound Probabilities

Among the most striking demonstrations of the layperson's overuse of the representativeness criterion are those of likelihood estimates for "compound" versus "simple" events. The most basic probability axioms (and, on reflection, common sense as well) imply that compound events cannot be more likely than the least probable of the simpler events that constitute the compound. A randomly selected person cannot be more likely to be both a gentleman *and* a scholar than just a gentleman or just a scholar. Similarly, the likelihood that I will stub my toe *and* burn my toast tomorrow morning approaches, as an upper limit, the likelihood of the less probable of these two events.

Kahneman & Tversky (in press) showed that people violate this obvious normative requirement when they rely too much on the representativeness heuristic. In one experimental condition the subjects were given personality profiles for various target persons and then were asked to rate the compound likelihood that particular persons both belonged to a particular political party *and* held a particular job. In another condition, simple probability estimates were separately made of political affiliation and of occupation. As the investigators expected, subjects based their estimates on the *average similarity* of the personality profiles to stereotypes of members of the political parties and occupations in question. An individual who closely matched the stereotype for the specified political party but poorly matched the stereotype for the specified occupation, was judged to be moderately likely to belong to *both* the party and the occupation specified. Translating their Israeli example into American terms, an individual judged *very* likely to be a Republican but rather *unlikely* to be a *lawyer* would be judged *moderately* likely to be a *Republican lawyer*. Reliance on representativeness or similarity criteria would produce such a result because a set of features which closely resembles a stereotypical Republican but poorly resembles a stereotypical lawyer might well be expected to moderately resemble a stereotypical Republican lawyer. Conventional probability axioms, by contrast, obviously demand that the likelihood estimate of Republican lawyer be somewhat less than that of lawyer alone: If it is unlikely that the target is a lawyer (of *any* political party), it will be still less likely that the target is a Republican lawyer.

A similar demonstration by Slovic, Fischhoff, and Lichtenstein (1977) further illustrated people's difficulties with compound probabilities. These investigators studied subjective likelihood estimates of event sequences. Subjects were given personality descriptions of particular targets and then were asked to rate the likelihood either of simple events (for example, John chooses an engineering major) or of a compound sequence of events (for example, John first becomes an engineering major and then switches to journalism). As in the Kahneman and Tversky study just described, subjects violated the most fundamental probability axioms by judging certain event sequences to be more likely than the least likely of their simpler constituents. For example, if the target sounded quite gregarious and literary in his interests, subjects would judge the event "chooses an engineering major" as extremely unlikely but would judge the event sequence "chooses engineering and then switches to journalism" as moderately likely! Subjects apparently judged the plausibility or representativeness of the entire "script" as suggested by the compound event. Such judgments, in turn, probably reflected the *average* representativeness of the events in the sequence ("I guess it's pretty *unlikely,* given the personality description, that John would become an engineering major, but if he did, it's pretty *likely* that he would switch to something like journalism"). The fact that the upper limit in likelihood logically is dictated by the *least* likely event in the script was essentially ignored.

These laboratory studies have far reaching, although as yet untested, implications for everyday social judgments. For example, a string of accusations, some very plausible but only slightly damaging and others only slightly plausible but very damaging, may be given far greater credence than would the serious but implausible accusations alone. Similarly, rumors may be more likely to be believed and spread if their critical but implausible details are embedded in a vivid and "scriptal" sequence that includes many plausible, concrete details, even if these are essentially irrelevant to the rumor.

Behavioral Consensus versus Concrete Target Cases

The importance of Kahneman's and Tversky's work to one of the general concerns of attribution theory soon became apparent to social psychologists. As we noted in the previous chapter, many studies of causal attribution showed that, in judging why a particular actor behaved as he did, observers seemed surprisingly uninfluenced by information about how many or how few actors had behaved similarly in the same situation. Normatively, observers should infer that words or deeds reflect corresponding personal dispositions of the actor when such responses are relatively uncommon, but should eschew such inferences when the actor's behavior is typical. For example, when subjects are told that most people acceded to a particular request, they should infer little about the personality of any particular person who acceded to the request. Empirically, however, this consensus information seems to have relatively little impact on subjects' causal inferences.

Nisbett and Borgida (1975) suggested that the weak effects of consensus information on attributional judgments might be analogous to the weak effects of base-rate information on category prediction. Pursuing this parallel, these investigators examined intuitive behavioral predictions. Would behavioral predictions, like category membership predictions, prove to be indifferent to consensus or behavioral base-rate data? The procedure they followed was simple. Two previously conducted experiments from which surprising, nonobvious results had been obtained were described to subjects. In one of these experiments, a majority of participants had willingly received very high levels of electric shock in a purported shock tolerance study; in the other, a majority of participants had failed to come quickly to the aid of the victim of an apparent epileptic seizure. Following descriptions of each of these experiments, subjects in one set of conditions were told about the actual results, that is, they were given accurate information about the distribution of responses shown by the participants. For subjects in a second set of conditions this base-rate information was omitted.

The subjects in both conditions then were asked to predict (or rather to postdict) the behavior of various target cases who supposedly had participated in the original experiment. Specific, although relatively undiagnostic, information also was provided about these target cases in a written description or in a videotaped interview. For example, one description read, in part, as follows:

> Physically, he was short and somewhat stocky, with reddish brown hair and a wide face with small, distinct features. He was quiet and a bit aloof in manner, though not shy. . . . The personality tests indicated that he had a good sense of humor, was prone to anxiety and fears of rejection, and that, although he would not be an easy person to get to know, he was probably loyal and intense in relationships with his closest friends. (p. 937)

Nisbett's and Borgida's results showed that base-rate or consensus information had minimal impact on their subjects' predictions. When informed about the surprisingly high levels of shock tolerance or surprisingly low levels of altruistic response shown by the overall sample of participants in the original experiments, subjects made predictions for specific participants that were nearly indistinguishable from those made by other subjects who had never received such behavioral consensus data. Subjects given consensus data and subjects not given such data both predicted that particular, unremarkable individuals such as those described would tolerate only mild shock levels or would come quickly to the aid of a peer in the throes of an epileptic attack. Similarly, consensus information failed to influence subjects' attributions concerning the relative importance of situational versus dispositional factors in determining the behavior of particular participants in the two studies and failed to influence their predictions of what their *own* behavior might be.

It may be recalled from our discussion in chapter 4 that Nisbett's and Borgida's research design also included the *opposite* prediction task, that of predicting overall base rates for behavior based on knowledge of the responses of two target individuals. The results were dramatic. Subjects readily made predictions of the behavior of "participants in general" based on knowledge

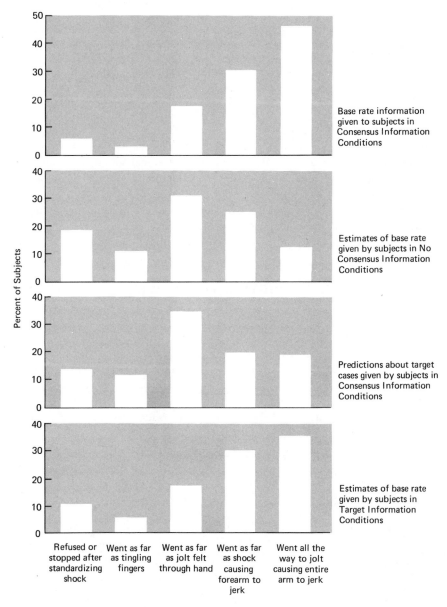

Base rate estimates and target case predictions. (From Nisbett & Borgida, 1972).

of the behavior of only two specific individuals. Subjects who learned, to their surprise, that two specific, but seemingly nondescript, participants had tolerated the maximum shock or never had helped the victim, were subsequently willing to ignore their prior, quite contradictory expectations and to predict that similar behavior would be *modal* for participants as a whole.

Figure 7.2 presents these predictions for the shock experiment, along with the base-rate predictions of uninformed subjects and the predictions about target cases by subjects informed of the base rate.

Both of the normatively inappropriate tendencies in social prediction shown in Figure 7.2 can be summarized. People seem unwilling to believe that a particular, seemingly typical person will behave as others have behaved when that behavior contradicts prior expectations. But, one or two cases in which an apparently typical person's behavior violates expectations can overturn prior theories and lead to the expectation that people in general will behave as the target cases do. This result recalls our earlier discussion (in chapter 3) of the capacity of vivid, concrete data to make a greater impact on inferences than that made by data that are evidentially superior but dull and abstract in quality. The implications for predictions of social events are quite unnerving: Logically required deductions from group tendencies to individual cases are stubbornly resisted; and normatively dubious inductions from individual cases to group tendencies are willingly embraced.

NONREGRESSIVE PREDICTION TENDENCIES

Many everyday predictions are about continuous variables or dimensions rather than discrete categories: A salesperson needs to predict how much money a particular shopper or class of shoppers will spend; a teacher is required to predict how well a student will perform relative to her peers; a suitor wishes to predict how amorous his partner feels on the basis of her body language. In such problems, the person must decide how heavily to weight specific information about the target case relative to beliefs about the central tendencies of the population of which that target case is a member. In category prediction, normative principles and common sense alike dictate that the intuitive statistician ought to guess the most frequent outcome category unless the specific information about the target case is highly diagnostic. In numerical prediction, the same considerations demand that the intuitive statistician *regress* estimates toward the mean (or, depending on the specific "payoffs" associated with particular types of accuracy and error, toward the median or mode). The appropriate amount of regression, according to conventional statistical criteria for minimizing error, depends on the degree of covariation between the available predictor variables and the outcome variable.

Correlation, Regression and Prediction

The conventional linear regression equation, in z-score (standard deviation units) form, is simply: $\tilde{Z}_y = r_{xy}Z_x$. That is, the best prediction of variable y ($\tilde{Z}_y$), in terms of maximizing accuracy or minimizing error, is the *product* of the correlation coefficient (r) and the z-score for the predictor variable (Z_x). The two limiting cases, correlation coefficients of zero and unity, both have common sense implications. In the case of a totally nondiagnostic predictor variable ($r_{xy} = 0$), one ought to disregard completely the target's score on variable x and simply guess that the outcome value will be equal to the mean (0, in z-score form) of the distribution from which it is sampled. In the case of a perfectly diagnostic predictor variable ($r_{xy} = 1.0$), one ought to estimate that the variable to be predicted will be as far from its mean (in standard deviation terms) as the score on the variable from which it is predicted ($\tilde{Z}_y = Z_x$). Thus, if $r_{xy} = 1.0$, the best guess about a target which is two standard deviations from the mean on the x variable is that it also will be two standard deviations from the mean of the y variable. Correlations between 0 and 1 require that predictions give weight both to the score on the predictor variable and to the mean of the variable to be predicted, with the weight given to the predictor variable being a direct function of the correlation between the two variables. One important consequence of these normative statistical principles is that, with decreasing diagnosticity of one's predictors, the range of one's predictions ought to "shrink" until, in the limiting case of totally worthless predictor information, one's predictions ought to be the same no matter what the score on the predictor variable. That is, with a totally nondiagnostic predictor one ought simply to predict that every score will be equal to the mean of the outcome distribution.

This elementary review of regression theory will be familiar to most readers, if not to most laypeople. But why ought one to "regress" to the mean in making predictions? Essentially, one ought to do so because the mean is the point in the distribution closest to the largest number of observations. In other words, the mean is a base line from which one should deviate only to the extent that the risks or costs of such deviations are likely to be compensated by the diagnosticity of the other information one has about the target. The numerical prediction and the category prediction cases thus are equivalent, and the tendency to be insufficiently regressive in numerical prediction closely corresponds, logically, to the tendency to ignore base rates in category prediction.

Laboratory Demonstrations
of Nonregressive Prediction Strategies

The layperson's inability to recognize regression phenomena (and the frequent inability of the sophisticated social scientist as well) is so familiar that we need not document it at length. We will focus on one of Kahneman's and Tversky's (1973) more dramatic illustrations of the extent of this failing. In this study, subjects were asked to predict the grade point average (GPA) of students based on one of three types of information which had widely varying predictive validity. The information presented to some subjects was the target's GPA expressed in percentile form, a virtually perfect predictor of numerical GPA. The information presented to a second group of subjects was the target's score on a mental concentration task, a fairly good but imperfect predictor. The information presented to a third group was a measure of sense of humor, a very poor predictor of GPA. Lest subjects be under any illusion, the experimenter specified that the relevant predictors were, respectively, perfect, good, or virtually valueless as predictors of GPA. Subjects' predictions showed only the slightest hint of regressiveness. Subjects tended to predict GPA scores that were as divergent from the mean GPA as the predictor score was from its mean, regardless of whether the predictor score was a perfect indicator, was merely a good one, or was the nearly valueless sense of humor score.

Follow-up experiments by Amabile (1975) and Ross, Amabile and Jennings (1976) somewhat extended and clarified Kahneman's and Tversky's findings. Ross and colleagues explored the prediction strategies of individual subjects by collecting a large number of predictions from each participant (in contrast to Kahneman's and Tversky's (1973) procedure which used one prediction per subject). The investigators also used "authentic" data distributions—derived from previous research reports, student records, self report questionnaires, and so on—thus permitting direct assessment of the degree of accuracy and direction of error in the subjects' estimates. There was little difficulty in replicating the basic phenomenon described by Kahneman and Tversky. For bivariate distributions in which population or large sample correlations were in the range of $r = 0$ to $r = +.30$, the subjects made predictions that would have been justified only by correlations in the range of $r = +.60$ to $r = +1.00$. Very few individuals systematically applied anything like a simple linear "prediction equation." When subjects believed the relationship between variables to be strong, their individual predictions were often well matched by a simple linear function, but when they believed the relationship to be weak, their predictions varied widely around any potential regression line. Specifically, when subjects believed the relationship between X and Y to be relatively weak, they did not respond to extreme values of X with predictions of Y that were consistently moderately close to the mean. Instead, they responded by *varying* the extremity of their predictions (for example, by predicting one very extreme value of Y and one value of Y close to the mean when given two identical values of the predictor variable X).

The data on accuracy also were revealing. The great majority of individual subjects would have decreased the magnitude of their errors by simply repeating their *average* prediction for Y and never varying it on the basis of their knowledge of the target's scores on X. This result, in some respects, is reminiscent of the tendency reported earlier for useless diagnostic information to dissuade subjects from using base rates in category prediction. It is difficult to resist concluding that, when it comes to predictions, a little knowledge (that is, knowledge of the target's score on a weakly related predictor variable) is a dangerous thing.

These studies indicated that the tendency to be insufficiently regressive can be traced to two distinct sources. First, as we observed in chapter 5, people typically overestimate the degree of covariation between events in the social domain. They do so, at least, when such events can be linked by plausible causal theories, scripts, or stereotypes. In this chapter, we have noted that people fail to make regressive predictions even when they recognize that the available predictor variables are poorly correlated with the outcome variable. Thus, the failure to make appropriately conservative predictions is overdetermined. Incorrect theories of the strength of relationships in the social domain lead to exaggerated beliefs about the utility of various predictor variables, while intuitive prediction strategies result in nonregressive predictions even when the weakness of the relationships is recognized.

A Conservative Self-image for the Radical Predictor?

We should note that although the intuitive scientist's nonregressive prediction strategies may be labeled "nonconservative," this label may be misleading with regard to the intuitive scientist's own view of the strategy. Indeed, nonregressive predictions may result from a chain of inferences that seem impeccably "conservative." Consider, for example, a request to predict Jane's percentile score on a mathematics test, given only the information that she scored at the ninetieth percentile in a reading test. The intuitive statistician may begin by recognizing that academic abilities tend to be positively correlated and by reasoning that Jane's math score is likely to be better than average. These correct assumptions may then flow readily, but treacherously, into the quite incorrect assumption that, having no information about Jane's math score, there is no basis for predicting whether it will be higher or lower than her reading score. Given such an assumption it may thus seem conservative to guess that the math score will be equal to the reading score (a judgment that would be justified, in conventional statistical terms, only by a perfect correlation), for such a guess seemingly represents the "middle course" between guessing either that Y is higher than X or that Y is lower than X.

THE DILUTION EFFECT:
PRODUCING "REGRESSIVE" PREDICTIONS
BY EXPOSURE TO NONDIAGNOSTIC INFORMATION

The research to date indicates that people's predictions often will be very wide of the mark. Under the conditions typified by the research, it seems clear that people combine information poorly for purposes of prediction and usually fail to make predictions that reflect outcome base rates and regression considerations. It is important to be specific about what those conditions are. Almost all research on prediction has been characterized by a paradigm in which subjects are given a *small* amount of information, all or most of which the subjects believe to be *diagnostic*. Typically, subjects are given information about a target case in the form of values on one or more dimensions. Sometimes these values are numerical values, as in much of the work in the Meehl tradition, and sometimes the "values" are verbal statements that may be regarded as tacit "scores" on some outcome-related dimension.

Many predictions in everyday life are conceptually identical to this research paradigm, from college student admission procedures to casual conversations in which one person summarizes a few "diagnostic" tidbits for another and then asks that person to make a prediction. Many prediction tasks, however, are importantly different in that the individual has much more information about the target, including much information of no diagnostic value whatever. It would be interesting to know how people respond to a mixture of diagnostic and nondiagnostic information in such information-rich, complex, prediction tasks. Nisbett and his colleagues (Nisbett & Zukier 1979; Zukier 1979; Nisbett & Lemley 1979) recently have begun to study predictions of this sort. It might well be expected that such predictions would be even more inaccurate than simpler ones. Surprisingly, this appears not to be the case.

In an initial experiment, Nisbett and Zukier (1979) asked subjects to make predictions about the behavior of particular male undergraduates in two different psychological studies, a shock tolerance study and a survey of movie attendance. Subjects were given various items of information about these "target" individuals, items that had been rated (by pretest subjects) either as highly "diagnostic" of probable behavior in the study or as totally "nondiagnostic." Some subjects were presented only with a single diagnostic item—the target individual's major field of study. Other subjects were presented with both the diagnostic item and a series of nondiagnostic items, such as the target individual's home town, religion, and so forth. As the reader should now be able to anticipate, the presentation of a single "diagnostic" item led subjects to make extreme (and wrong) predictions. Science majors were predicted to tolerate about twice as much shock as humanities majors and to go to only about half as many movies. When the diagnostic item was accompanied by a set of nondiagnostic items the result was quite different. The predictions for humanities majors and science majors converged sharply. In other words, items judged by pretest subjects to be *worthless* for purposes of prediction nevertheless served to "dilute" dramatically the effects of an item judged to be highly diagnostic.

In a follow-up study, Nisbett and Lemley (1979) found that as few as two worthless items of information can dilute the effect of one "diagnostic" item. The subjects were social work graduate students who were instructed to estimate the likelihood that several social work clients, described by a small amount of "background information," were child abusers. "Diagnostic" information, for example, that the client was known to have "sadomasochistic sexual fantasies", served to produce a strong presumption that the client might be a child abuser. But that damning presumption was sharply reduced by the inclusion of the "nondiagnostic" information that the client "fixes up old cars in his spare time" and "once ran away from home as a boy."

Work by Zukier (1979) indicated that the dilution effect in no way reflects a general understanding of the principles of regression. Zukier asked subjects to predict the grade point average of undergraduate targets. When subjects had only "diagnostic" information, that is, an extreme value on a dimension believed to be correlated with GPA, subjects made extreme, nonregressive predictions. When they were given average values on each of several other dimensions, they "regressed" their predictions almost back to the mean. But they did so to precisely the same extent whether they believed that each of the "diluting dimensions" was *highly* correlated with GPA or believed that each of the dimensions was *uncorrelated* with GPA. (The regressive predictions would have been quite justified in the former case of high correlation but quite unjustified in the latter case since the low correlation of the dimension with GPA made these values, whether average or otherwise, irrelevant to predictions.)

In interpreting the "dilution effect" Nisbett and Zukier (1979) relied on Tversky's (1977) analysis of similarity judgment. They argued that nondiagnostic information about the target person, though logically irrelevant to the prediction task, has the capacity to render the target person less "similar" to that hypothetical individual who might be most likely to exhibit extreme and atypical responses. It is these simple similarity or "representativeness" judgments, rather than more normatively appropriate strategies, that underlie the subject's predictions. This argument (which hinges upon Tversky's theoretical assertions about the role of "common" and "noncommon" features in similarity judgment) is rather complex and need not concern us further here. What does concern us, however, are the implications of the dilution effect for everyday accuracy in prediction.

The dilution effect findings are, in one sense, hopeful in that they suggest that predictions in many everyday life situations may be more "regressive" than past research has implied. They would be more hopeful if they provided any indication that such relatively accurate predictions reflected any understanding of the normatively correct approach to prediction. The findings provide no such indication, nor does any other research that we can report. There is some research, however, which, like the dilution effect findings, indicates that predictions will sometimes be regressive in form, if not in spirit. The circumstances that may occasion such relatively accurate strategies are discussed next.

CIRCUMSTANCES PROMPTING THE UTILIZATION OF BASE RATES IN PREDICTION

There are several kinds of evidence suggesting that people do sometimes give prior probabilities or base rates considerable, even adequate, weight in category prediction. There is even evidence suggesting that people occasionally appreciate the wisdom of regressive predictions in problems involving continuous variables. As research in this area has expanded, it has become clear that there are at least three circumstances that promote the use of prediction strategies that conform reasonably well to normative dictates.

Lack of Alternative Prediction Strategies

It is obvious from both laboratory research and everyday experience that when means, base rates, or prior probabilities are the *only* information available, people seem quite able to recognize the significance of such information and to make appropriate use of it. Thus, subjects asked to guess the height, IQ, or hair length of an individual about whom nothing else is known are apt to rely on their guesses of relevant population means. Similarly, subjects told only that an individual has been randomly sampled from a population consisting of 70 percent engineers and 30 percent lawyers recognize that the sampled individual will, in fact, be an engineer 70 percent of the time. We also have no doubt that people would predict that a randomly selected citizen is more likely to be a Mr. Taylor than a Mr. Shoemaker, is more likely to be a native of California than of Nevada, and is more likely to be a Presbyterian than a Druid. In fact, there can be little doubt that the layperson possesses and uses the general predictive schema that, other things equal, more numerous outcomes are more likely to occur or to be sampled than less numerous outcomes.

At the same time, it is also important to reiterate the layperson's demonstrated willingness to disregard base-rate information when there is the slightest opportunity to utilize any *other* strategy. In fact, once the form of a prediction problem invites the layperson even to *consider* potentially diagnostic information about the target, utilization of the base rate does not seem to serve even as a strategy of "last resort" should the target information prove valueless. Recall that the subject in the Kahneman and Tversky (1973) studies who was given both base-rate information and valueless target-case information was apt to ignore both types of information and act as if there were no basis whatever for making a prediction. Indeed, the subject asked to predict the behavior of "a college sophomore named Joe" in a particular psychological experiment, may largely ignore base-rate information about the overall distribution of responses shown by participants in the experiment. The subject may rely instead upon (erroneous) intuitions about how a "typical" participant ought to act. Having decided that neither the status "sophomore" nor the name "Joe" are sufficiently diagnostic, the subject responds as if intuitions about typical college student behavior are more useful for making predictions than base-rate information that happens to contradict those intuitions. Data showing that subjects make minimal use of the behavioral base rate when given such scant and worthless target-case information may be found in a study conducted in 1977 by Wells and Harvey (though the authors chose to emphasize the fact that such information was used at all).

The Use of Causally Relevant Base Rates

There is a second and far more significant class of problems in which base rates are appropriately utilized. Consider the behavior of a person asked to assess the likelihood that the next card dealt will be an ace or that the next roll of a single die will produce a six. We have very little doubt that, on the average, people's estimates will be quite close to the "correct" probabilities of one-thirteenth and one-sixth, respectively. We suspect that the additional information that the dealer is named Tom, has five children, wears argyle socks, and subscribes to *Readers' Digest,* will not preempt reliance on these familiar base rates.

Why are such base rates utilized so faithfully? There may be several reasons. The base rates are well rehearsed and are not counterintuitive. The domains, furthermore, are ones in which popular scripts and maxims describe the folly of "disregarding the odds." Most important of all may be that the relevant base rates seem consistent with a *causal theory*. That is, people can appreciate the generating function producing the outcomes and hence the probabilities under consideration. Recent studies by Ajzen (1977) and Tversky and Kahneman (1978) have illustrated the importance of such causal theories in determining people's willingness to use base-rate information.

In Ajzen's study, subjects were asked to assess the probability that a given student, whose level of effort, intelligence, and motivation were described in a brief sketch, had passed a particular scholastic examination. All subjects were provided with base-rate data on the percentage of passes and failures in the sample from which that student allegedly was selected. Specifically, all subjects were told that 75%, or only 25%, of the students in the relevant sample had passed the course. In one condition, the "non-causal" base-rate condition, the subjects were told that percentage of passes vs. failures in the sample reflected the investigators' deliberate decision to sample primarily successes (or primarily failures) because that was the outcome in which he was most interested. Subjects in this condition gave very little weight to the base-rate information in making their estimates; instead, they estimated the probability that the student had passed the course to be high or low almost entirely on the basis of the information provided in the personal description. In a second condition (the "causal" base-rate condition) the subjects were told simply that 75%, or only 25%, of the students enrolled had passed the course, thereby suggesting that the specified base rate reflected the ease or difficulty of the test. In this condition, by contrast, subjects made very substantial use of the base rate, and their probability estimates about the student's outcome in the course gave only moderate weight to the information provided about his intelligence, effort and motivation. In summary, the subjects' willingness to utilize a base rate was determined by the presence or absence of a clear indication of the cause of that base rate. If the base rate could be interpreted as reflecting causal influence, for example that of test difficulty, it was utilized very heavily; if the base rate reflected only "arbitrary" group composition, it was utilized only slightly.

An equally impressive demonstration of the same phenomenon, one offering striking evidence of a normative violation on the part of subjects, was reported by Tversky and Kahneman (1978). These investigators told their subjects that in a particular town there were two cab companies, the Blue Company and the Green Company. There had been an accident involving a cab, and subjects were to judge the likelihood that the cab had been blue, as opposed to green. They were to do so on the bases of an imperfect eye witness identification, coupled with some information about base rates. The relevant base rate was manipulated in one of two ways. Some subjects were told that 85 percent of the town's cabs were blue and 15 percent were green. These subjects largely ignored the base rates provided, and instead based their judgments primarily on the reliability of the eye witnesses' color identifications. Other subjects were told that though the town had an equal number of blue and green cabs, 85 percent of the cab-related accidents involved blue cabs whereas only 15 percent involved a green cab. These subjects relied heavily on the base rate. Normatively, the relevance of the base rate would seem to be the same in the two conditions; yet it was only when the base rate could be given a causal interpretation, pertaining to careless versus careful driving tendencies, that it was utilized substantially.

It appears that when base rates can be given a causal interpretation, they will be reflected in predictions. Though people's use of causally interpretable base rates is based on a normatively questionable distinction, they do at least possess a strategy that will generate reasonably accurate predictions in some instances.

Concretizing the Base Rate

Another cure for people's base-rate blindness is implicit in Nisbett's and Borgida's (1975) analysis of one of the chief causes for the blindness, the fact that base-rate data usually are dull and uninteresting. If the base rate were presented in a more concrete and vivid way than has been done in most of the research, it seems likely that it would have more influence on judgments.

Anecdotes and thought experiments suggest that concretized base rates do have some influence. A fledgling auto mechanic, informed that only about 70 percent of the repair shop's efforts are successful on the first attempt, nevertheless may send his first dozen cars out of the shop convinced that the problem has been solved in every case. As the contrary evidence mounts up, it seems likely that the mechanic's confidence in each individual repair job will decline. Similarly, young couples may assume that the divorce rates have little relevance to people like themselves and their friends. As reality intrudes, with its concrete evidence that divorces occur also among their set, they may become less convinced of the durability of their friends' marriages, and even of their own.

Work by Manis and Dovalina (1979) indicated that these suppositions are well founded. These investigators asked subjects to make predictions of the attitudes (for example, toward marijuana legalization) of college students whose photographs they were shown. Subjects in feedback conditions were told, after each guess, what was the "actual" attitude of the student. For some subjects, the feedback indicated an 80 percent-pro/20 percent-anti pattern, while for other subjects the pattern was reversed. This concrete, experiential manipulation of base rate was highly influential. Subject predictions came to match the base rate. Such a "probability-matching" approach does not maximize "hits," but it does result in much more utilization of base rate than commonly results from dull, one-shot, data summaries.

The evidence suggests that, although people lack an intuitive understanding of Bayesian principles of prediction, there are several circumstances in which predictions will be much less impaired than might be implied by such a failure. If no other information except base rate can be invoked, if the base rate has a causal interpretation, or if the base rate is correctly experienced, predictions are likely to be much more accurate than they are under other judgment conditions.

REGRESSION PHENOMENA: OCCASIONAL RECOGNITION AND CHRONIC MISCONSTRUAL

Just as people recognize and use base rates in some specific contexts, they often are able to recognize specific regression phenomena. As we shall see, such insights do not seem to be the product of any *general* understanding of the nature of regression. That is, people fail to appreciate that regressiveness in the overall relationship of the future to the present, the whole to the part, or the unknown to the known, occurs because (and to the extent that) the two measures under consideration are imperfectly correlated with each other. This lack of insight, it should be emphasized, applies not only to formal mathematical statements or to regression equations, but to their everyday verbal equivalents as well. Thus, the layperson does not seem able to articulate or utilize, and may even disagree with, propositions of the following sort:

> —Events that are extreme on some dimension will, on the average, be less extreme when they recur, when they are reassessed, or when they are assessed on any other dimension.
> —Events or objects that appear to be extreme on some dimension on the basis of preliminary information or on the basis of a limited sample of evidence, will, on the average, prove to be less extreme when all of the relevant evidence becomes available.

It is true that there are some general cultural maxims that seem to reflect a recognition of regression phenomena. ("A bird in the hand is worth two in the bush;" "This too shall pass;" "You can't tell a book from its cover.") These maxims, however, are not stated in terms that help the layperson recognize their general applicability in *all* circumstances in which covariation is imperfect. The maxims also lack any hint that predictions should give weight to the "central tendencies" of the outcome dimension and certainly do not convey instructions to be regressive as a function of the strength of the relationship between target indicators and outcome values. Furthermore, they are contradicted by other maxims that we suspect are far more common, that may appear equally wise and that tend to undermine comprehension of regression phenomena. ("As the twig is bent, so grows the tree," "As ye sow, so shall ye reap," "A chip off the old block," "Birds of a feather flock together.")

Although a general appreciation of regression phenomena is rare among lay observers, there are many instances in which the individual's experience, or collective wisdom culled from the experience of many individuals, does lead to predictions that appear regressive. In such cases, however, unparsimonious theories and inappropriate scripts often are invoked both to "explain" individual cases of regressiveness and to account for regression phenomena within particular domains of experience. Indeed, as will be clear from some examples, even statistical sophistication bestows an imperfect protection from such failings.

Assessments of Professional Potential

Almost all academicians recognize, or soon come to realize on the basis of painful experience, that the most talented graduate students will only seldom prove to be equally outstanding professionals. The academician usually can offer a host of theories or scripts to account for such disappointments.

> He was good at executing research but didn't really have any ideas of his own.
> She had all the ability in the world but lacked the necessary drive and aggressiveness.
> He let himself get bogged down in administrative responsibilities.
> She settled for the gratifications of being a popular lecturer.
> He just didn't get the necessary moral support and guidance from his colleagues.

What such an academician fails to recognize is that this domain is simply one in which the predictor variables (accomplishment and talent shown in graduate school) are imperfectly correlated with the outcome variable (professional achievements). Thus, the unspectacular performance of many highly touted new professionals is simply another regression phenomenon. *Ad hoc* explanatory theories, like those described, obscure the fact that such disappointments are the rule and not the exception. Indeed, most such "explanations" are probably best regarded simply as an account of some of the sources of the imperfect relationship that exists between predictors and outcome. Like postgame analyses by coaches whose teams have lost, they are accounts of "how" and not "why" a statistically likely event has occurred.

The mirror image of this misunderstanding of regression phenomena is that the very best professionals are often a "pleasant surprise;" they have proved to be relatively *more* successful as professionals than they had been as graduate students, surpassing peers who once had seemed better prospects. Again, explanations for these pleasant surprises are easy.

State U. turned out to be very good for her.
What he really needed was the competition he got at Ivy U.
When you think about it, she always was a slow starter.
All he needed to take off was independence from his advisor.

The readiness with which the "anomalies" are explained preempts the possibility of recognizing that the entire array of outcomes, including both pleasant and the unpleasant surprises, are inevitable under conditions of imperfect predictability.

What are the consequences of misconstruing predictable regression effects in academic accomplishment as causally explicable exceptions? Sometimes, the only cost is an unnecessary expenditure of intellectual energy and the risk that a colleague will smile and ask "have you ever heard of regression effects?" Sometimes the costs are far more substantial. One search committee with which we are familiar reasoned that since the best graduate students are usually disappointments and since the best professionals are often dark horses, the department should largely ignore the letters of recommendation and publication records that currently serve as our predictors and simply search for congenial people with interesting or offbeat research interests. Another committee is plagued by suggestions to use "persona matching" as a search strategy; for example, "Let's find someone who looks the way Jane Shimmer, our rising departmental star, did as a graduate student" (that is, cautious letters of recommendation, two or three publications, but a high energy level and a smashing "job talk").

Correctly labeling the relevant phenomena as instances of predictable regression should help to prevent such folly. While it is appropriate to be conservative in one's predictions or expectations of outstanding prospects, such conservatism hardly justifies ignoring predictor variables or settling for moderately positive values of these variables when extremely positive values are available. This is particularly important when one's concern is maximizing the likelihood of selecting exceptionally able candidates. Consider, for instance, a case in which one's set of predictor variables correlates with the relevant outcome variable at a modest level (for example, $r = .33$). An exceptional candidate (for example, one who is three standard deviations above the mean on the set of predictors) is, on the average, apt to be only a moderately successful professional (one standard deviation above the mean). Nevertheless, if Smith is three standard deviations above the mean on the set of predictors while Jones is only one standard deviation above, Smith is an order of magnitude more likely to prove an exceptional professional than Jones is. Specifically, using conventional linear regression computational formulas, Smith is more than *seven times* as likely as Jones to be three standard deviations above the mean in professional accomplishment.

In summary, the misunderstanding of regression phenomena can result in unrealistic expectations and ill-advised policies, both of which could be prevented simply by recognizing the everyday relevance of the regression principles taught in introductory statistics courses.

Assessing the Effects of Personal and Social Interventions

The failure to label regression phenomena correctly can have important consequences whenever the observer notes the apparent covariation between changes in personal or social outcomes and the introduction, by accident or design, of factors that might plausibly influence such outcomes. Kahneman and Tversky (1973) provided a paradigmatic illustration of the superstitious beliefs that can result from failure to recognize simple regression phenomena. Israeli flight instructors had been urged to use positive reinforcement and to avoid negative reinforcement in shaping the performance of pilots attempting to master difficult flight patterns and maneuvers. After following this practice for a while, the instructors expressed skepticism about the wisdom of such a strategy. In their personal experience, they argued, praise of exceptionally good performance typically led to diminished performance on the next trial, while criticism of an exceptionally poor performance typically produced an immediate improvement. The instructors were so impressed with this phenomenon that they even challenged the more general psychological doctrine that had been presented to them. Punishment, they concluded, was more effective than reward in shaping desired behavior.

We suspect that such mislabeling of simple regression phenomena (whereby extremely good or bad performances will, on the average, be followed by less extreme performances whenever there is an element of chance in such performances) is common in everyday experience. One disconcerting implication of such mislabeling is that measures designed to stem a "crisis" (a sudden increase in crime, disease, or bankruptcies, or a sudden decrease in sales, rainfall, or Olympic gold medal winners) will, on the average, seem to have greater impact than there actually has been. Illusions of personal or social control are likely to result, particularly when a causal influence of the various interventions or incidents can be inferred on the basis of plausible theories.

Explaining the "Sophomore Slump"

There are some domains in which, we suspect, even the most sophisticated scientist is guilty of developing causal explanations for simple regression phenomena. Consider, for example, the oft-cited "sophomore slump" familiar to baseball fans, even fans who happen also to be scientists familiar with the use and interpretation of statistics. A sensational rookie hits home runs or pitches shutouts at such a rate that everyone is convinced that he is bound to be a superstar for the next decade. In the next year, however, the young sensation suffers a serious "slump" in performance. The phenomenon is familiar to all who watch the sport, and the explanations for the phenomenon are equally familiar. ("Success and fame spoiled him"; "The pitchers/hitters made the necessary adjustments"; "He pressed too hard, stopped working as hard, gained weight, lost weight, got married in the off-season, got divorced in the off-season.") Indeed, the veteran sports fan may simply cite the sophomore slump as cause enough!

What is seldom recognized is that simple regression principles guarantee that, by chance alone, some mediocre athletes will perform exceptionally well in their first year but perform less well in subsequent years. Since the relevant outcomes (homeruns, strikeouts, and so on) are statistically relatively unreliable phenomena, these regression effects are bound to occur. In other words, the best explanation for a sophomore slump is that the first year was atypical for the performer in question while the second year showed regression toward his "true" ability level or performance base line.

If the reader doubts this interpretation we invite consideration of the following two facts: First, so-called sophomore slumps seem to be far more common in athletic events in which there is unreliability and instability in performance than in events in which there is great reliability. For example, weightlifters and runners seem to show dramatic slumps far less often than baseball players do. Second, an examination of star ballplayers (for example, those who were ultimately inducted into the Hall of Fame) shows no sign of sophomore slumps. For these performers, strong first-year-performances reflected the athletes' long-term ability, rather than "chance," so there should have been no regression.

We need not belabor the point. The sophomore slump is simply (or, at least, largely) a specific instance of the general regression principle that, on the average, extreme first observations of an unstable phenomenon are typically more extreme than subsequent ones. While careful data collection and analysis would be required to prove the point, we suspect that equivalent "slump" phenomena occur in other domains and are equally likely to be mislabeled. For instance, the theory that academic tenure (or, for that matter, the Nobel Prize) reduces subsequent productivity either in specific cases or "in general," is likely to be offered to explain a simple regression phenomenon. Similarly, superstitions about what one must change to end a "bad streak" of outcomes, or must *not* change for fear of ending a "good streak," will arise from the observation of simple regression phenomena.

People's failure to recognize regression phenomena for what they are appears to be inevitable, given that intuitive strategies of prediction utilize principles that resemble only tangentially the appropriate statistical strategies. While predictions may often be passably accurate in daily life, they often will be quite inaccurate. Equally serious is the fact that people often will think that they can explain and control events that are largely chance determined and conversely will ascribe to caprice many events which really are modestly predictable.

SUMMARY

People perform many prediction tasks quite poorly both in the laboratory and in everyday life. This is true in part because people do not understand fundamental statistical principles, notably the principles of regression, essential to normatively appropriate prediction strategies.

People do not seem to utilize population base rates in many prediction tasks and instead greatly overutilize the representativeness heuristic; that is, they match the features of the target with those of the outcome and predict that the target will have the outcome to the extent that the target resembles the outcome. Similarly, people make generally nonregressive predictions for continuous variables. They tend to predict that the target will be as extreme on the outcome dimension as it is on the predictor dimension.

The representativeness heuristic paradoxically may produce relatively accurate, "regressive" predictions if people possess nondiagnostic information in addition to diagnostic information. In that case, the nondiagnostic information appears to "dilute" the implications of the diagnostic information, with the result that predictions are less extreme than they would have been if based on diagnostic information alone.

In addition, though people do not understand the basic probabilistic principles of prediction, they do sometimes utilize base rates. They seem to do so when: (a) No target information is available which can encourage utilization of the reprsentativeness heuristic; (b) base rates may be given a causal interpretation; or (c) base rates are "concretized" through feedback about particular members of the population.

Though people have a rudimentary understanding of regression effects in some particular domains, their lack of generalized appreciation of the regression concept exposes them to serious misunderstanding of the nature of other domains. Thus, people offer special-purpose causal explanations of events that are more properly understood as a simple consequence of regression. Such *ad hoc* explanations leave their illusions of near-perfect predictability intact and set them up for further, continual surprises. Similarly, illusions of control are sustained because improvements in temporarily malfunctioning social systems or processes, which are actually due to regression, are attributed instead to purposeful interventions.

8

theory maintenance
and theory change

> The human understanding when it has once adopted an opinion draws all things else to support and agree with it. And though there be a greater number and weight of instances to be found on the other side, yet these it either neglects and despises, or else by some distinction sets aside and rejects, in order that by this great and pernicious predetermination the authority of its former conclusion may remain inviolate.
>
> *Francis Bacon.*

Few critiques of human judgmental failings ring as true as Bacon's (1620) attack on people's tendency to adhere to a preconceived belief in the face of evidence that ought, rationally, to weaken or even reverse the belief. Each of us is confronted almost daily with the perversity of those who persist in their misguided political, social, and scientific beliefs even after we have informed them of the facts. People's readiness to cling to discredited beliefs is a constant, depressing reminder that most people are less intelligent, less objective, and less committed to the truth than we ourselves are!

Empirical research and philosophical analysis since the time of Bacon have tended to support Bacon's critique. Work by Luchins (1942, 1957) and by the Hovland group (for example, Hovland, Janis, & Kelly 1953) showed that opinions, once formed, are slow to change in response to new evidence. Other investigators have demonstrated the rigidity of theories and beliefs in their studies of attitude formation (Asch 1946; Edwards 1968), post decisional judgments and attitudes (Festinger 1957; Janis 1968), and the maintenance of

167

racial, ethnic, religious, and sex-role stereotypes (Allport 1954; Taynor & Deaux 1973; Goldberg 1968; J. Jones 1972; Katz 1960). Scientists themselves have been a chief target of such criticism. The tendency of professional scientists to persist in adhering to theories well past the point at which such adherence can be justified by the evidence has been observed by many (for example, Barber 1952; Kuhn 1962; Mahoney 1976, 1977; Mahoney & DeMonbreun 1977; McGuigan 1963).

Unbridled empiricism in the doctrinaire positivist tradition, on the other hand, also has had its critics (for example, Polanyi 1958, 1964). These authors, like Kurt Lewin, have emphasized the practicality of theories. Theories are useful because they structure knowledge into coherent wholes, organize experience, and facilitate supplementation of the data given with information that can be retrieved readily from memory. The implication of this position is that conservatism with respect to theories is often advisable. Neither the layperson nor the scientist should readily dispose of a well-established theory because it happens to conflict with some new evidence. It is often proper to look askance at, or even to totally ignore, reports of virgin births or new cancer cures. It may even be proper to dismiss evidence collected by reputable scientists if it conflicts with some powerful, parsimonious and integrative theory (Polanyi 1958).

The central question of this chapter directly parallels one discussed in chapter 4. In that chapter, we discussed the extent to which people's theories influence their characterization of data. In this chapter we discuss the extent to which data forces the revision of theories. Our conclusion about the former question, in chapter 4, was that characterizations of data are very heavily influenced by theories but that this is normatively appropriate, at least for most inferential tasks encountered by the practitioner and the layperson.

We now must qualify that conclusion by pointing out that *assimilation* of data into preexisting theory is normatively appropriate only if it is accompanied by adequate *accommodation* of the theory to the implications of the new data to preexisting theory is normatively appropriate only if it is accomto force their revision, then this is dangerous precisely because it would make a mockery of the practice of perceiving new data through the filter of a theory. The picture that would emerge, if Bacon and company are correct, is that of an intellectual Bourbon—a person whose understanding of the world, no matter how erroneous, cannot change, because relatively ambiguous data are interpreted in light of a theory while relatively unambiguous data contradicting the theory force little or no revision of the theory.

The question thus is of critical importance: Do our theories change in response to new data as much as normative standards require? We already presented some evidence on this question in chapter 5, when we dealt with the degree to which people's theories about covariation responded to actual data on covariation. We concluded that such theories generally were almost impervious to data and that people who subscribe to a given covariation theory before encountering evidence that should have served to overturn the theory, often emerge from such encounters with the theory unblemished and unscathed. It could be argued that this occurs merely because people have little ability to perceive covariation accurately and that the picture might be different for other kinds of theories.

Unfortunately, we cannot be so optimistic. We believe that the lesson of chapter 5 is a general one and that Bacon is correct: People seem to persist in adhering to their theories to a point that far exceeds any normatively justifiable criterion of "conservatism." Ross and Lepper and their colleagues have given this tendency the pejorative label "belief perseverance." Their work, together with some older work in the literature on impression formation, supports three hypotheses about perseverance of belief.

1. When people already have a theory, before encountering any genuinely probative evidence, exposure to such evidence (whether it supports the theory, opposes the theory, or is mixed), will tend to result in more belief in the correctness of the original theory than normative dictates allow.

2. When people approach a set of evidence without a theory and then form a theory based on initial evidence, the theory will be resistant to subsequent evidence. More formally, people's response to two sets of evidence with opposite implications does not adhere to the commutativity rule which demands that the net effect of evidence A followed by evidence B must be the same as for evidence B followed by evidence A.

3. When people formulate a theory based on some putatively probative evidence and later discover that the evidence is false, the theory often survives such total discrediting.

OLD THEORIES AND NEW EVIDENCE

Everyday experience demonstrates that people often do not believe evidence that opposes some theory they hold. If the evidence cannot be discredited outright, it may nevertheless be given little weight and treated as if it were of little consequence. Thus, the theory often survives intact new data which ought, superficially, to force revision of confidence in the theory or perhaps even to reverse the theory. As many analysts have noted however, such conservatism often may be well advised. Even if one cannot recall the evidence from which the theory was originally derived or the more general beliefs from which the theory was deduced, this does not mean that the evidence does not exist or that there is not a well-justified argument leading from more general propositions to the current specific one. It may mean only that we cannot currently recall such evidence or the logic from which we inferred the view we now hold.

Though a certain hesitancy in approaching new evidence may be justified, it is difficult to rationalize certain types of response to new evidence. An experiment by Lord, Ross, and Lepper (1979) shows that people's response to new evidence sometimes may be quite inappropriate. They presented two purportedly authentic studies on the deterrent effects of capital punishment to Stanford University students who had indicated previously either that they strongly believed capital punishment to be a deterrent to potential murderers or strongly believed it to be worthless as a deterrent. In a counterbalanced design, each subject read first about the results and method of an empirical study that supported their own position and then about the results and method of a study that opposed it, or they read first about an opposing study and then about a supporting one. For all subjects, one of the studies had a "panel" design, comparing murder rates for states before and after adoption of capital punishment, and the other study had a "concurrent" design, comparing murder rates during the same time period for states with versus those without capital punishment. For half of the subjects, it was the panel design study that supported their position and the concurrent design study that opposed it, and for the other half of the subjects it was the reverse.

Was the symmetry in probativeness and implications of the evidence reflected in a comparable symmetry of beliefs about the deterrent effect of capital punishment? It was not.

1. Subjects found whichever study supported their own position to be significantly "more convincing" and "better conducted" than the study opposing their position. If it was the panel study that supported their position and the concurrent one that opposed it, the subjects could see clearly the superiority of a panel design, in which a state was compared with itself before and after introduction of capital punishment, over the sloppy technique of the concurrent study which compared, say, bucolic North Dakota with urbanized New Jersey. If it was the concurrent study that supported their position, the subjects could readily appreciate the wisdom of a design that held time period constant, and found no trouble in exposing the flaws in a design that compared one state with itself, to be sure, but allowed everything else to vary without control, including temporal changes in the demographic composition of the state, changes in conviction rates and parole procedures, and the like. The subjects thus treated the evidence in a highly asymmetric way: Supportive evidence was handled with kid gloves; opposing evidence was mauled.[1]

2. The design of the study made it possible to evaluate attitude change at

[1] Any resemblance between the behavior of subjects in this experiment and that of any professional scientist, living or dead, is purely coincidental.

several points. Subjects were asked about their beliefs after reading about only one study, which either supported or opposed their view. Whether the study had a panel design or a concurrent design, belief in initial position was strengthened if the study supported the subject's initial position. But, again regardless of design, belief in initial position was affected relatively little if the study opposed the subject's initial position.

Neither of these first two responses, it should be noted, is clearly counternormative. If one were to assume that subjects already had good evidence supporting their beliefs (an assumption the authors regard as dubious), then their responses could be considered appropriate. It can be proper to criticize evidence that contradicts one's (well justified) belief more harshly than one criticizes evidence that supports it, and consequently it can be proper to change belief more in response to supporting evidence than in response to contradictory evidence.

3. The third result was an inevitable consequence of the reasoning that produced the previous results and this result was clearly counternormative. After reading about *both* studies—one that supported their initial position and one that opposed their initial position (and with normatively identical probative status on the average because of the counterbalancing of study design with study outcome)—the subjects were more convinced of the correctness of their initial position than they were before reading about *any* evidence.

The work by Lord and colleagues suggests that people's response to new evidence addressing a previous belief may sometimes be quite inappropriate. (a) Different standards are used for criticizing opposing evidence than are used for criticizing supportive evidence. (b) Evidence generated by a method that does not much affect belief when it is opposed to the belief, strengthens belief substantially when it is supportive. (c) Most importantly, mixed evidence, which gives equal support to each of two opposing views, does not reduce confidence for holders of either view but instead reinforces confidence for holders of both views.

The study is disturbing on many grounds, but we wish to highlight a particularly upsetting implication of the last finding. Before the advent of modern social science, many questions, like the issue of the deterrent value of capital punishment, were ones for which there really was no empirical evidence one way or the other. It was nevertheless possible to appeal to logical or theoretical considerations in support of one's views, and it was possible to justify such views on epistemic grounds. One might expect, though, that once genuine empirical evidence for such questions became available, that evidence would sway opinion to whichever side it supported or, if the evidence were mixed, that it would serve to moderate opposing views. Instead, the effect of introducing mixed evidence may be to *polarize* public opinion, with proponents of each side picking and choosing from the evidence so as to bolster their initial opinions. At any rate, this is the dreary possibility suggested both by Bacon's suppositions and by the data of Lord and colleagues.

SEQUENTIAL PROCESSING OF EVIDENCE: THE PRIMACY EFFECT

Well schooled children are told, almost as their earliest principle of social inference, that "first impressions are important." The implication is that one should take special care with one's self-presentation when meeting someone for the first time. This rule is so widely taught, and contrary principles so seldom find expression in the folk wisdom, that one would have to suspect that it expresses some fundamental truth about social judgment and impression-formation.

In this case psychological research reinforces rather than questions the social-psychological lore. First impressions *are* important, and the primacy effect in impression formation, in which early-presented information has an undue influence on final judgment, is found almost as universally as would be suggested by its predominance in lay psychological theorizing. To be sure, recency effects, in which later-presented information has undue influence on final judgment, are sometimes found, but these are rare and appear to depend on the existence of one or more potently manipulated factors. These include (a) special memorial constraints favoring the recall of later-presented information, (b) circumstances producing strong contrast effects, and (c) presentation of information about an object or process which can be presumed to be capable of changing over time, so that later information, if it has implications different from those of early information, can be presumed to be more valid (Jones & Goethals 1972). Although order of presentation of information sometimes has no net effect on final judgment, and recency effects sometimes are found, these are the exception; several decades of psychological research have shown that primacy effects are overwhelmingly more probable.

We would like to argue, following Jones and Goethals (1972), that primacy effects in information processing are the rule because people are "theorists" in their approach to information about the social and physical world. Early-encountered information serves as the raw material for inferences about what the object is like. These inferences, or theories about the nature of the object, in turn bias the interpretation of later-encountered information. In line with the chief contention of this chapter, then, theories about the nature of the object are revised insufficiently in response to discrepancies in the later-presented information.

We will make no attempt to review even partially the literature on order effects in impression formation. Instead, we will briefly describe a few exemplary experiments in order to highlight the issues central to our concerns.

Solomon Asch, in his classic (1946) investigation, began a research tradition and a set of controversies which have continued until the present day. In the paradigmatic Asch experiments, his subjects were presented with a series of adjectives allegedly describing a person and then were asked to evaluate the person. For example, subjects were asked to evaluate a person who was: intelligent-industrious-impulsive-critical-stubborn-envious. This person was evaluated more positively than if the subject were exposed to the identical adjectives presented in the opposite order. The favorable impression created by the early-presented adjectives in the first sequence, and the unfavorable impression created by the early-presented adjectives in the second sequence tended to persist, with the consequence that early-presented information was more influential in the final judgment than later-presented information was.

Asch's interpretation of the results was essentially an extreme version of the "early-hypothesis" argument outlined earlier. Asch held that early information was processed "holistically" and that the resulting Gestalt colored the *meaning* of later-presented information. In our example, the early-presented information that the target was intelligent, industrious, and impulsive created not only a favorable impression but a particular *kind* of favorable impression which actually altered the meaning of the later, less favorable adjectives so as to render them affectively consistent with the early-formed "Gestalt" of a bright, energetic person, who, now, can be forgiven for his "critical" nature (hard to avoid if you're smarter than your peers) and his "stubbornness' (a consequence perhaps of being *right* because you're on your toes and do your homework). This left "envious," but let him who is without sin . . . . In contrast, the opposite sequence also created a particular kind of *unfavorable* impression. "Envious," "stubborn," and "critical" created a recognizable persona of someone who was hostile and pig headed. "Impulsive" now made such a person doubly dangerous, out of control. "Industrious" was also scary—all that venom put to work. "Intelligent" amplified the threat—at least if he were stupid, you'd have a chance.

Asch's contention that the words had a different meaning when encountered in one order than in the other has been challenged by a number of investigators, including Osgood, Suci, and Tannenbaum (1957), Bruner, Shapiro, and Tagiuri (1958), and, most notably and effectively, by Anderson (1965, 1971, 1974). These authors all argued that there is no direct evidence for any such change in meaning and that final evaluations are easily predicted by a simple formula which assumes constant weights for each of the adjectives modified only by the position of the adjective in the list. Final evaluation is a function of the valence of the adjective taken by itself and the position of the adjective in the series . . . period. There is no change in meaning because of the "Gestalt" created by preceding adjectives.

The change-in-meaning hypothesis still has many vociferous adherents, it should be noted, including Rokeach and Rothman (1965), Wyer and Watson (1969), Hamilton and Zanna (1974), and Higgins and Rholes (1976) who hold a similar, "change-in-referent" hypothesis, and the issue is far from resolved.

For our concerns, however, it does not much matter whether the change-in-meaning account or the differential weighting account is correct, as long as the primacy effect can be interpreted as occurring because early-formed impressions predominate over the implications of later information. It seems that most parties to the debate agree on this interpretation. The interpretation is central to the change-in-meaning view, but it is also implicit in the view of Anderson and his colleagues, who appear to prefer a "discounting" explanation of the phenomenon. That is, later-presented information, if it is inconsistent with the affective implications of early-presented information, is "discounted" or given a lower weight by the subject. The discounting explanation can account for the primacy effect only if one presumes that it is the early information that produces the impression or belief against which the later information is discounted. If the discounting of inconsistent information were purely symmetric temporally, then there could be no primacy effect.

Anderson and others have suggested another possible explanation for the primacy effect, however, which assigns no role at all to processes of early theorizing and insufficient theory revision. This is the possibility that some primacy effects may be caused solely by "attention decrement" or simple failure to notice or properly encode later-presented information.

Fortunately, a series of experiments by Jones and his colleagues effectively ruled out this possibility as the sole explanation for primacy effects. In the best known of these experiments (Jones, Rock, Shaver, Goethals, & Ward 1968), subjects were asked to watch as a target person attempted to solve thirty multiple-choice analogy problems. The problems were described as being of equal difficulty. The target person always solved fifteen of the problems. In one (descending) condition he solved disproportionately many problems early in the series and disproportionately few problems late in the series, but in the other (ascending) condition the pattern was the reverse. Strong primacy effects were observed such that early performance received undue weight. If the target person solved many problems early in the series, subjects predicted that he would perform better on a second series of similar problems, rated his intelligence as higher, and recalled that he had solved more problems in the first series than they did if he solved few problems early in the series.

These results, especially the distorted recall results, would appear superficially to be readily explained as due to attention decrement. Subjects, having "got the point" about the target person early in the series, might well have let their attention wander later in the series, having better things to do with their time than to pay close attention to what must have been, after all, a rather boring stimulus situation.

Jones and colleagues, however, explicitly manipulated attention by requiring subjects, in one set of conditions, to make probability judgments of success before each trial. The target's success or failure then served as immediate feedback on the accuracy of the subjects' predictions. Subjects, as it happens, tracked changes in objective probability quite well and thus were highly responsive to the feedback. This manipulation of attention, contrary to what would be expected on the basis of the attention decrement hypothesis, did not reduce primacy effects. On the contrary, the attention manipulation resulted in a slight *increase* in primacy effects.

Other experiments by Jones and his colleagues shed further doubt on the view that primacy effects are wholly or even partially due to attention decrement. They supported instead the view advocated by Jones and Goethals and the present writers that primacy effects are due to theories that are formed early and which are insufficiently sensitive to the implications of subsequent data.

The mechanisms of premature commitment and insufficient revision are probably aided and abetted in most real life contexts by people's adherence to what we have called the dispositionalist metatheory. This metatheory produces what Heider called "the false idea of the invariance of the behavior of the other person" (1958, p. 55). If we regard people's behavior as invariant, then this gives license to the mechanisms underlying the primacy effect. (1) Theoretical commitment at an early stage is justified because the individual's characteristics are invariant and a small amount of information is quite sufficient to allow one to know what a person's dispositions are. (2) Theory revision is rarely necessary because, again, characteristics are invariant, and later information seldom will be truly inconsistent with earlier information.

BELIEF PERSEVERANCE AFTER EVIDENTIAL DISCREDITING

The third class of perseverance phenomena is the individual's response, not to new evidence, but rather to challenges of the evidence that initially led to the belief's formulation. At an anecdotal level it is easy to cite circumstances in which such challenges occur. Jack believes that he dislikes abalone because of his first and only exposure to that food and then is assured by an abalone connoisseur that he sampled an inferior frozen product prepared in a notoriously dreadful restaurant. Jane is heartened by a correspondence school's enthusiastic appraisal of her potential as a commercial artist and then finds that three of her peers who answered the same advertisement received equally glowing assessments. A scientist is told by a colleague about an experiment showing some surprising effect and then is later told by the sheepish colleague that the experiment was only a "thought-experiment" described in a popular psychology magazine.

Normatively, it is clear what the effects of such evidential discrediting should be. Jack's belief about his dislike for abalone, Jane's belief about her artistic potential, and the scientist's belief about the surprising phenomenon ought to return to something close to their "preevidential" levels.

The perseverance hypothesis, as developed by Ross and Lepper and their colleagues, suggests that people such as those described would persist in their initial assessments to an unwarranted degree. This hypothesis presupposes that we can determine when the person is "inappropriately" persisting in an impression or belief whose basis has been undermined. Though it can often be difficult to make such a determination, it is not impossible in principle. To explore the perseverance hypothesis experimentally, a paradigm is required which permits us to specify precisely how much perseverance and how much change might be "warranted" by some acceptable normative standard.

One response to this strategic dilemma has been the adoption of the *total discrediting* or "debriefing" paradigm. There is one challenge to the evidence underlying an initial impression that does suggest a decisive test of the perseverance hypothesis, and it occurs when a person discovers that the entire evidence base for the initial judgment is not merely biased or tainted but is completely without value. This situation should be familiar to all social psychologists who have ever used deception in their research, for postdeception "debriefing" procedures are designed to discredit totally the previous deceptive information and thereby to eliminate any effects that such information originally may have had on the subjects' feelings or beliefs.

It is noteworthy that informal accounts of the difficulty of debriefing are common. While the vast majority of deception studies involve manipulations of relatively innocuous impressions, many professionals nevertheless have expressed concern that experimental deceptions may sometimes do harm that conventional debriefing procedures fail to completely undo (Kelman 1972; Miller 1972; Orne 1972; Silverman 1965). Later in this chapter we will return to both the practical problem of improving debriefing procedures and to the far more general issue of overcoming discredited personal and social impressions. For now, let us merely observe that it was partially this professional concern (along with a provocative hint from an earlier study by Walster, Berscheid, Abrahams, & Aronson 1967) that led Ross and Lepper and their colleagues to adopt the "debriefing" paradigm to explore the theoretical problem of belief perseverance.

In the first such study (Ross, Lepper, & Hubbard 1975), subjects were recruited for a study allegedly concerned with the effects of problem-solving feedback on various physiological responses. Subjects were presented with a novel task, distinguishing between authentic suicide notes and unauthentic ones. As the subjects worked, they were provided with false feedback after each trial, which indicated that, overall, they had performed at close to an average level, at a level much above average (success condition), or at a level much below average (failure condition). Following this outcome manipulation, subjects were thoroughly debriefed concerning the predetermined and random nature of their task outcome. They not only were told that their feedback had been false but also were shown the experimenter's instruction sheet assigning them to the success, failure, or average performance condition and specifying the feedback to be presented. Subsequent to this debriefing, subjects were asked to fill out a postexperimental questionnaire (ostensibly to help the experimenter interpret their physiological records) on which they were required to estimate their actual performance at the task, to predict their probable success on related future tasks, and to rate their ability both at the suicide discrimination task and at other related tasks involving social sensitivity.

The results revealed a remarkable degree of postdebriefing perseverance. Even after debriefing, subjects who had initially been assigned to the "success" condition continued to rate their performance and abilities far more favorably than did subjects whose initial feedback had indicated average performance, while subjects initially assigned to the failure condition showed the opposite pattern of results, continuing to rate themselves as unsuccessful and lacking ability for the experimental task and for other, similar ones.

To replicate this perseverance phenomenon and extend it from the domain of self perception to that of social perception, a second experiment was undertaken. This time, actor subjects distinguished real from fictitious suicide notes while yoked observer subjects (from behind a one-way mirror) witnessed the initial false feedback presentations and the later debriefing given by the experimenter. Several additional experimental conditions were incorporated into the experimental design of this follow-up study. First, "no-debriefing" conditions were included to assess the initial impact of the false feedback. Second, a set of "process" debriefing conditions was included in which actors, overseen by observers, received not only the information about the random assignment and false feedback presented in the standard "outcome" debriefing conditions but also an extensive discussion of the perseverance phenomenon, the processes that might contribute to it, and the potential personal relevance and costs of erroneous impression perseverance.

The results, presented in Figure 8.1, revealed that there was substantial perseverance of the initial impressions for both actors and observers after standard "outcome" debriefing procedures. Approximately half of the predebriefing difference in self-perceptions and social perceptions remained despite the thorough discrediting of the basis for these initial impressions. Most of these differences were successfully eliminated when actors were exposed to the considerably more pointed and extended "process" debriefing. For observer subjects, the perseverance effect seemed even stronger. Even after process debriefing, the observers continued to view the actor's ability as consistent with the actor's discredited initial experience of success or failure.

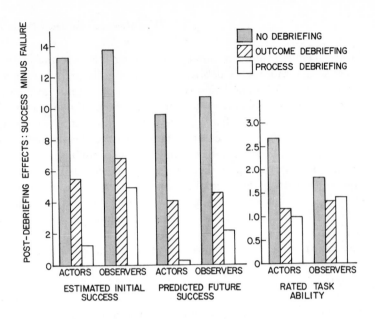

Fig. 8.1 Post-debriefing differences between success and failure groups in beliefs about performance and ability, for actors and for observers. From Ross, Lepper, & Hubbard 1975.

The data from the process debriefing conditions are important from a practical and ethical standpoint as well as from a theoretical one. Actors, who had personally received the pointed description of mechanisms that might lead their erroneous self perception to persevere, showed very little residual effect of the discredited outcome manipulations. Observers, who merely had witnessed the actors' process debriefing, continued to show considerable perseverance in their beliefs about those actors. It seems probable that a process debriefing directed specifically at the social perceptions of the observers might have been more effective, although this remains to be demonstrated empirically. In any case, the advisability of buttressing debriefing procedures with a discussion of possible perseverance mechanisms seems clear. Equally clear is the researchers' ethical responsibility to evaluate, rather than merely assume, the sufficiency of any debriefing procedures, at least in those studies where the manipulated impressions are relevant to self esteem or to perceptions or attitudes of social consequence.

Demonstrations of postdebriefing perseverance now have been extended to a variety of impressions and beliefs (for example, Anderson, Ross & Lepper 1979; Jennings, Lepper and Ross 1979; Ross & Anderson 1979). Two experiments were conducted outside the laboratory setting (Lepper, Ross & Lau 1978). High-school students were led to form erroneous impressions of their abilities to solve "logical-reasoning" problems. Half the subjects received a clear, coherent lecture that promoted subsequent success by illustrating the use of a simple matrix to solve one of the seemingly difficult and complex puzzles. The remaining subjects, by contrast, witnessed the solution of the same puzzle accompanied by a rambling and unhelpful series of exhortations. The subjects then attempted to solve a series of puzzles on their own. As planned, "tutored" subjects performed extremely well on the task, while "placebo-treated" subjects performed poorly.

Following the instructional sessions and tests, half the subjects in each condition were fully "debriefed" on the likely cause of their test performance. The experimenter explained in detail the superior or inferior nature of the instruction they had received. (In fact, in one of the studies, subjects actually were allowed to view the same videotaped lecture that had been shown to subjects in the opposite condition.) "Debriefed" subjects also were allowed to solve a new problem using the subsequently revealed technique. The other half of the subjects were given no such debriefing experience. All participants then rated their abilities for the task, their liking for the task, and their probable future performance both at the experimental task and at other related tasks. A delayed posttest, dissociated from the experimental setting, also was given. Students were asked, in their regular classrooms, to respond to a survey allegedly conducted by the school's mathematics department which solicited student reactions to various potential additions to the department's curriculum, including one which involved problem-solving tasks of the sort subjects had worked on during the experimental session several weeks before.

Although "debriefed" subjects were aware of the differential effectiveness of the two teaching procedures (that is, they accurately predicted the extent of performance difficulties for peers exposed to the two procedures), they continued to judge their *own* ability according to their initial experience of success or failure. Particularly dramatic were the results of the delayed follow-up measures which indicated that "debriefed" subjects' self-appraisals and task preferences continued to be quite influenced by their original success or failure. In fact, the debriefed subjects were virtually indistinguishable on most of these measures from the subjects who were never debriefed.

MECHANISMS UNDERLYING PERSEVERANCE PHENOMENA

The evidence suggests that Bacon was correct in his assertion that "the human understanding when it has once adopted an opinion draws all things to support and agree with it" (1620/1960, p. 50). Conflicting evidence is treated as if it were supportive of beliefs, impressions formed on the basis of early evidence survive exposure to inconsistent evidence presented later, and beliefs survive the total discrediting of their evidence base. Why do people persevere in adhering to beliefs and theories? Or, to ask a more easily answered question, how do they persevere?

One obvious answer is that they persevere because they want to. Many beliefs are cherished because they embody strongly held values. When such beliefs are challenged, people then put into operation whatever cognitive machinery will suffice to discredit uncongenial evidence and to bolster supportive evidence. Though such an answer is not a sufficient explanation, because it does not specify precisely what the relevant cognitive machinery might be, it is a satisfactory "first-cause" explanation for many belief perseverance phenomena. To the extent that a person is emotionally committed to a given belief, it certainly seems likely that that person would cling to that belief by whatever cognitive tricks are necessary. Such a motive surely is present in the reactions of religious fundamentalists to historical evidence of Biblical matters, in the reactions of scientists to research discrediting their life work, and perhaps even to the reactions of subjects in some of the experiments we have discussed. It seems entirely likely, for example, that the extreme counternormative reaction to new evidence by subjects in the experiment by Lord and colleagues (1979) was at least partially because of the relative importance and value centrality of beliefs about capital punishment. It is doubtful that such extreme reactions would have been elicited to evidence concerning subjects' beliefs about the advisability of an annual chest X-ray or about the financial advantages of the Common Market to its participants.

Emotional commitment, however, seems to us to be generally neither a necessary nor a sufficient explanation of belief perseverance phenomena. Emotional commitment is scarcely likely to be an important component of subjects' initial impressions of a target person described by Asch's adjective strings or to initial impressions of the problem-solving ability of a target person in the experiments by Jones and others (1968), or, still less, to the discredited belief of a subject in the Lepper, Ross, and Lau (1978) experiment that he has little ability to solve mathematical puzzles. The notion of emotional commitment also tells us nothing about the precise cognitive means by which commitment could serve the goal of belief perseverance.

We prefer several other, more purely information-processing explanations for perseverance phenomena, while acknowledging that these often may be triggered or strengthened by purely motivational considerations. (See Katz 1960.) We already have discussed some of these cognitive mechanisms. We now add three more, the first two of which are particularly appropriate to understanding belief perseverance following total discrediting of the evidence base, and the last of which seems to augment all three types of belief perseverance phenomena we have discussed.

Biased Recollection and Interpretation of Evidence

Why is it that Jane, a subject in the Ross, Lepper and Hubbard (1975) experiment, who learns that her excellent "performance" on the suicide note discrimination was determined by a random number table, clings to the hypothesis that she is actually rather talented at such discriminations? Even more perplexing, upon learning that her *abysmal* "performance" was randomly determined, why does Jane not breathe a sigh of relief and revert to her initial opinion of this ability and related ones involving social sensitivity? It seems to us that these questions are puzzling only if one assumes that the only mental events transpiring in Jane's head as she pursues the task are bland and passive registrations of the feedback given by the experimenter. That assumption is unjustified, and it seems much more likely that the impression of her ability that is created by the feedback prompts a search for additional information pertinent to the impression.

Suppose Jane receives feedback suggesting that she is uncannily successful at the task. It seems likely that she will have no trouble generating additional "evidence" that seems consistent with her apparent social sensitivity. Her reasonably good performance in her abnormal psychology course, her ability to make new friends easily, and her increasing sense of confidence and assurance as she progressed in the suicide note task, all might be seen as "further evidence" of such powers. Suppose, on the other hand, that Jane receives feedback suggesting that she is particularly poor at the task. Again, supporting "evidence" probably can be generated with ease. Jane might note her difficulty in imagining herself as lonesome or alienated, her mediocre performance in her social problems course, and her increasing sense of confusion and hesitation as she progressed in the suicide note task. Needless to say, even an objectively neutral set of evidence, if processed in accord with such a "confirmation bias," could bolster the implications of either the success or the failure outcome.

We have no direct evidence that subjects in the experiment by Ross and colleagues (1975) engaged in such confirmation-biased processing of evidence stored in memory. But there is a rich research literature that shows the operation of a variety of encoding and decoding biases that favor confirmation of prior hypotheses or beliefs over disconfirmation. There is good evidence, for instance, that people tend to recognize the *relevance* of confirming cases more readily than that of disconfirming ones, and therefore tend to *search for* such cases in evaluating their hypotheses (Wason and Johnson-Laird 1965). As philosophers of science (Popper 1959) have long maintained, this strategy is not merely inefficient, it is bound to make even the most dubious of hypotheses appear to enjoy empirical support.

Snyder and Swann (1978) examined confirmation tendencies in the domain of social inference. When subjects were asked to determine in an interview with another, "target" subject, whether or not the target was an "extrovert," they tended to ask primarily those questions to which a positive answer would have provided "evidence" for the target's extroversion, but a negative answer would have provided, at most, weak evidence that the person was not an extrovert. When asked to determine whether the target was an "introvert," subjects used the complementary strategy of asking primarily those questions to which the answer, if positive, would have provided "evidence" for the target's introversion but, if negative, would have provided only weak evidence that the person was not an introvert. Such strategies would tend to establish that almost anyone is an extrovert if one starts with an "extrovert hypothesis," and to establish that almost anyone is an introvert if one starts with an "introvert hypothesis." And, in fact, in one of Snyder's and Swann's experiments, observers listened to the target subjects' answers to the interviewer subjects' probes and concluded that the target was an extrovert if the interviewer was testing the "extrovert hypothesis" and concluded that the target was an introvert if the interviewer was testing the "introvert hypothesis."

We should emphasize that it is not always the case that confirming instances are more available to the theory holder than disconfirming ones. As Hastie and Kumar (1979) noted, surprising or incongruent events may be attended to and even stored in memory more than expected or "hypothesis-confirming" events. The literature is not uniform on this point, however, and there is also evidence that congruent information is sometimes stored more readily than incongruent information. The literature is quite consistent, however, in showing the advantage that confirmations enjoy over disconfirmations in the *retrieval* or output stage.

A study by Snyder and Cantor (1979), closely paralleling the Snyder and Swann study, shows that memory searches favor hypothesis-confirming evidence even when the hypothesis is merely a tentative one. Subjects read a lengthy story about a young woman who behaved in a number of ways that could be characterized either as "extroverted" or as "introverted." Two days later, some of the subjects were asked to assess the woman's suitability for an "extroverted" occupation, namely, real estate sales, and other subjects were asked to assess the woman's suitability for an "introverted" occupation, namely, research librarian. The subjects had to consult their memories for evidence pertinent to the "hypothesis" of extroversion or introversion. The results showed that there was a strong confirmation bias in the retrieval process. Subjects testing an extrovert hypothesis recalled more extrovert items than did controls or subjects testing an introvert hypothesis, while the subjects testing an introvert hypothesis recalled more introvert items than did controls or subjects testing an extrovert hypothesis.

People's hypothesis-testing strategies are reminiscent of their tendency to utilize only conceptually positive information in concept formation tasks (chapter 3) and reminiscent also of their tendency to pay attention primarily to the present/present cell of 2 x 2 contingency tables (chapter 5). All such strategies indicate people's failure to appreciate intuitively the great power of the scientific strategy of disconfirmation or hypothesis invalidation. If they are ignorant of this strategy, this would help to explain why subjects in the studies by Ross, Lepper, and their colleagues are left so much at the mercy of hypotheses suggested to them by the false "data" they encounter, even when those hypotheses are uncongenial and unflattering. The tendency to search for additional, confirmatory evidence usually will be "rewarded." The person is then left with this additional "evidence" even after the false nature of the experimental feedback is revealed.

Tendency to Search for Causal Explanations

It seems likely that subjects in the experiments by Ross, Lepper, and their colleagues would not have restricted their "extracurricular" mental activity to a search for confirmatory evidence. Like the professional scientist, the lay scientist tends to look for causal explanations of observed data. Returning to Jane, our hypothetical subject in the Ross, Lepper, and Hubbard (1975) experiment, suppose that she has received feedback indicating that she is quite good at distinguishing between authentic and false suicide notes. Would she experience much difficulty in explaining why she might have this particular talent? It seems likely that she would not and that the same storehouse that provided her with additional "evidence" of her ability also could provide her with satisfactory "causal explanations." Her familiarity with the writings of a famous novelist who recently committed suicide, her part-time job as a paramedical assistant, and her generally "open" relationship with her parents and friends all might serve to explain her high level of ability at a task requiring social sensitivity. On the other hand, suppose Jane receives feedback indicating that she is poor at the task. Again, her storehouse of personal information can probably be counted upon to suggest causal explanations. Her lack of personal acquaintance with anyone who is seriously depressed (let alone suicidal), even her lack of secondhand familiarity with such people (save through the writings of one author who recently committed suicide), might help to account for her relative lack of ability to distinguish between authentic and fake suicide notes.

These speculations about Jane's introspections would be plausible if it could be presumed that (a) subjects are indeed inclined to generate causal explanations for events such as successful or unsuccessful performance at the suicide note discrimination task, (b) people generate such explanations with relative ease, and (c) once such explanations are generated, they are reasonably convincing. There is both direct and indirect evidence for each of these suppositions.

Much research on causal attribution shows that people readily generate causal explanations of events when they are asked to do so by an experimenter. Investigators who approach subjects with causal analysis protocols, probing them for explanations of events, are seldom disappointed in their yield. When asked, people are remarkably facile at inventing explanations which they appear to find plausible and presentable even to outsiders as prestigious as scientific investigators. This generalization has been shown to hold even under circumstances in which it can be shown that such causal explanations have no empirical foundation (Nisbett & Wilson 1977b; Wilson & Nisbett 1978).

This sort of research does not suffice to show that people spontaneously engage in much causal explanation in the absence of prompting by an attribution researcher. Unpublished work by Nisbett, Harvey, and J. Wilson (1979), however, suggested that such spontaneous causal analysis may be remarkably common. These investigators "bugged" a total of thirteen haphazardly selected conversations ranging from graduate student bull sessions, to singles bar conversations, to a picnic for lower socioeconomic status senior citizens. The "epistemic" category of each statement uttered, and each of the requests eliciting a statement, were coded. Categories included "gives information," "gives evaluation," "gives advice or suggestion," "makes prediction," and "gives causal analysis." Statements expressing or requesting causal analysis were remarkably frequent, accounting for 15 percent, on the average, of all utterances. Even for the conversation in which causal analysis was the least frequent (the senior citizens' picnic), causal analysis accounted for 5 percent of all utterances.

Thus, people engage in causal analysis frequently, and they do it with facility both in the laboratory and in their everyday lives (judging from the rarity with which conversationalists in Nisbett's and colleagues' study appeared stumped by one another's requests for causal explanations). Do they find such explanations convincing, once generated? A series of experiments by Ross, Lepper, and their colleagues suggested that they do and that once people have generated causal explanations for events and relationships between events, they find those events and relationships to be plausible even when the evidence for them is shown, through the debriefing paradigm, to be nonexistent.

In the first of these studies, by Ross, Lepper, Strack, and Steinmetz (1977), subjects were asked to place themselves in the position of a clinical psychologist attempting to understand and predict a patient's behavior on the basis of background information. To this end, they were given an authentic clinical case history which detailed the early experiences in the life of either an unhappy and somewhat neurotic young woman or a chronically unemployed and depressed middle-aged bachelor. In various experimental conditions subjects were asked to use this case history to *explain* some "critical event" in the patient's later life (for example, a suicide, a hit-and-run accident, joining the Peace Corps, a candidacy for public office). Control subjects were not asked to explain any such events. Following the explanation task, the experimental subjects were carefully informed that the events they had been asked to explain were purely hypothetical and that, in fact, there was no available information about the later life of the patient whose history they had read. Then each subject was asked to assess the likelihood of a number of possible events in the patient's later life, including the critical events that had been explained in the various experimental conditions. As expected, the subjects' likelihood estimates revealed a marked effect of the explanation task. Having initially explained an event, subjects rated the event as more probable after "debriefing" than did subjects who had not explained that event or than did subjects who had explained an alternative event.

The process of causal explanation influences plausibility or subjective likelihood even when there is no previous induction of belief in the event. Ross and colleagues (1977) found that subjects who engaged in purely "hypothetical" explanation—explaining events that they knew from the outset to have been *arbitrarily chosen* and not to have been based on any knowledge about patients' later lives—similarly showed a strong tendency to rate the explained event as relatively likely.

An analysis of the actual explanations written by subjects was instructive. The facility with which subjects could pass from almost any real event in the past history of the client to almost any hypothetical event was positively alarming. For example, one patient's youthful decision to join the Navy was cited as very significant both by subjects asked to explain a subsequent candidacy for political office and by subjects asked to explain a subsequent suicide! In the former case, however, service in the Navy was seen as symptomatic of the "gregariousness" and the "desire to serve" that might characterize a potential politician, while in the latter case it was seen as a symptom of the patient's predisposition to "punish others by running away," thus foreshadowing his suicide.[2]

In another study, Anderson, Ross, and Lepper (1979) explored the role of causal explanations in reinforcing and maintaining more abstract and general theories. In one key condition of the study, subjects were first led, on the basis of only two concrete cases, to hypothesize a positive or negative relationship between a particular occupational outcome (success versus failure as a firefighter) and a prognostic variable (risk preference on a paper-and-pencil test that the firefighters had taken as trainees). They then were asked to write an explanation of that relationship, only to learn later that the relevant data were totally fictitious and that other participants had been exposed to an opposite pattern of results. The degree of belief perseverance among these subjects was substantial. In fact, subjects' belief in whichever relationship they had been encouraged to explain was almost as great as for those subjects who had seen the "data" but neither had explained it nor had been told that it was fictitious! Interviews with subjects who had explained the "data" and then had been debriefed were unsettling. Typically, such subjects justified their views by insisting that, despite the discrediting of the data, it was *obvious* that the particular relationship they had explained was the correct one. Indeed, several expressed surprise that subjects in the other condition had been gullible enough to form the opposite hypothesis.

The evidence suggests that a little causal analysis is a dangerous thing.

[2] Any resemblance between the behavior of subjects in this experiment and that of any clinician, living or dead, is purely coincidental.

People's facility in forming causal explanations is so great that they usually will be able to explain most events and relationships they observe. These explanations may often prove so convincing that they survive even the total discrediting of the ''evidence'' that prompted their invention in the first place.

It is worth focusing on the normative problem here, because it is subtle. There is nothing wrong with continuing to believe in the plausibility of events and relationships when one has a powerful causal model which ineluctably dictates their existence. Consider a student who is told of experiments showing that light rays are deflected when they pass through the gravitational field of the sun and then recognizes, because of his accurate understanding of relativity theory, that such a result is demanded by the theory. Such a student would be justified in maintaining his belief in the hypothesis that light rays bend when passing through the sun's gravitational field, even if he were subsequently told on the best authority that the experiments he had heard about were totally valueless artifacts. It seems to us that the difference between this hypothetical student and the subjects in the experiments by Ross, Lepper, and their colleagues is just as great as the difference between a causal theory as powerful and well-supported as relativity theory and the flimsy, *ad hoc* ''causal theories'' invented by the subjects. It is the misplaced confidence in their facile causal theories which trips up the subjects in these experiments, not their willingness to speculate about them at the request of the experimenter.

Behavioral Confirmation Biases:
The Self-fulfilling Prophecy

The experiments by Ross, Lepper, and their colleagues capture many of the elements of everyday-life situations in which beliefs are seen to persevere beyond the point at which the evidence can sustain them. They lack, however, an element that is often present in everyday life, namely, the ability to intervene and test hypotheses by generating new data. Such intervention provides great opportunities, but it also carries commensurate risks. If hypotheses are tested effectively, for example, if disconfirmatory data are sought as eagerly as confirmatory data are, then belief perseverance can be avoided. If, on the other hand, primarily or exclusively confirmatory data are sought, or worse, if such confirmatory data are manufactured, merely because the person holds a certain hypothesis, then perseverance of incorrect beliefs is made doubly likely.

It is not hard to think of anecdotal evidence suggesting that biased data generation may be as common as biased data retrieval. Consider Jill, a fourteen year old who is positive that she cannot do mathematics (perhaps because she has been assured that "girls are just no good at that kind of thing"). She is likely to select academic courses and activities that promise to spare her from frustration and seemingly certain failure. In so doing, she fulfills her negative self-appraisal by the time she enters college. Or consider Jack, the would-be suitor who "knows" that he is doomed to be rejected. He is not likely to behave in a manner that permits his hypothesis to be overturned by experience. Indeed, if he does summon the courage to approach the object of his affections, his appeal is apt to be so strained, so tentative, and so defensive that rejection becomes highly probable.

Such stories need not have unhappy endings. For instance, consider a person who is convinced that a particular location is "just right for a small grocery store" and invests his life savings to back the "theory." Such an individual is apt to exploit his own time and energies mercilessly and thereby succeed in "proving" that his gamble and the beliefs that prompted it were well advised. Or consider the company that commits its resources to developing motor X rather than motor Y on the basis of a feasibility study and then succeeds in proving its choice was correct by overcoming all of the engineering obstacles necessary to produce motor X.

Like our anecdotes, the literature on self-fulfilling prophecies shows that people often do proceed in such a manner as to alter reality in the direction suggested by the initial hypothesis. The famous (but controversial) "Pygmalion" studies by Rosenthal and Jacobson (1968) are a case in point. Those investigators randomly selected certain elementary school pupils and informed their teachers that psychological tests had shown that the pupils were due for a learning sprint and rapid advance in intellectual ability that year. The teachers apparently behaved toward the children in just such a way as to elicit intellectual growth in these children, since they did gain more in objectively measured intellectual ability during the subsequent year than their peers did.

Particularly persuasive evidence of people's tendency to elicit behavior from others according to their initial hypotheses has been collected by Snyder and his colleagues. We have already mentioned the study by Snyder and Swann (1978), in which it was shown that subjects who were interviewing someone to determine whether or not the person was an extrovert tended to ask questions which primarily elicited "data" indicating that the person was indeed an extrovert. In an even more provocative experiment, Snyder, Tanke, and Berscheid (1977) showed that "hypotheses" may guide behavior toward the target in such a way as to be self-confirming even when the situation is less formal and the person is not given the somewhat artificial task of "testing" the hypothesis. Male subjects were asked to engage in a conversation via intercom with an unseen female partner whom they believed to be either unusually attractive or unattractive in appearance. The female subject's side of the conversation was recorded and then played for a second male subject who subsequently estimated her attractiveness. The second male's beliefs agreed with the hypotheses of the first male subject. The first male subject apparently had elicited verbal behavior from the female that provided the second male with "evidence" of her probable attractiveness.

Work by Kelley and Stahelski (1970) suggests that not merely specific beliefs about particular individuals, but also much more general theories and even what might be called world views, may receive "support" from the behavior of others in response to one's own theory-guided behavior. Kelley and Stahelski presented subjects with a standard prisoner's dilemma game and explained the payoffs associated with various moves and countermoves. They then asked subjects to describe their understanding of the game and the appropriate strategy. Some subjects spontaneously expressed the view that the point of the game was to encourage the other player to adopt a cooperative strategy, so as to maximize the likelihood that the outcome would be a slow, steady payoff for both players. Other subjects thought that the point of the game was to *compete* with the other player. These subjects said that the appropriate strategy was to lure the other player into making the "cooperative" move as often as possible and then to make the "competitive" move so as to get the high payoff for themselves that would result from this pattern (and, incidentally, resulting in a large loss on that move for the other player).

The experience of the cooperative players, when they actually came to play the game, was quite variable. If they were paired with a "cooperator," they quickly settled into a mutually cooperative pattern. If they were paired with a "competitor," they were forced into a competitive strategy in order to avoid consistent, large losses. The experience of competitors, on the other hand, was uniform. If paired with another competitor, they settled quickly into the consistently competitive and ultimately mutually self-defeating strategy. If paired with a cooperator, their own behavior sooner or later forced the cooperator into a defensive competitive strategy also.

The intriguing point of the Kelley and Stahelski demonstration is that cooperators will learn, correctly, that the world contains both cooperators and competitors. Competitors, on the other hand, will learn, incorrectly, that everyone out there is a competitor. This is because competitors' own view of correct strategy will bias the behavior of others so as to produce evidence indicating that everyone shares their own strategy.

WHEN THEORIES AND BELIEFS DO CHANGE

We have been able to present a substantial amount of evidence showing that beliefs tend to persist under circumstances in which they have ceased to be an accurate characterization of the world, and we also have been able to provide some evidence on the mechanisms that foster belief perseverance. But have we committed the same error that our subjects did? Have we selected and generated evidence in such a way as to confirm our own hypothesis of belief perseverance? We believe not. We can find no literature showing that people pursue, even in limited domains, hypothesis-testing strategies that would facilitate the rejection of inaccurate beliefs. The experiments we reported were constructed in such a way that they could have shown evidence for belief perseverance, for its opposite, or for something in between.

We welcome investigations that are guided by the opposite of the hypothesis that produced most of the research we have discussed. We believe, moreover, that an effort in that direction would be rewarded both with instances in which people occasionally revise their theories suitably in accordance with new evidence and even instances in which they behave in the very opposite of the counternormative way we believe to be characteristic; that is, instances would be found in which people reject a well-founded theory on the basis of evidence that is not normatively sufficient to force its revision.

Children do eventually renounce their faith in Santa Claus; once popular political leaders do fall into disfavor, and a generation of feminists somehow has managed to overturn popular views of women and society. Even scientists sometimes change their views!

In part, the issue may simply be one of brute force. No one, certainly not the authors, would argue that new evidence or attacks on old evidence can never produce change. Our contention has simply been that generally there will be less change than would be demanded by logical or normative standards or that changes will occur more slowly than would result from an unbiased view of the accumulated evidence.

It also seems clear that the mechanisms which prompt belief perseverance sometimes are overcome without the brute force of massive amounts of probative, disconfirming data. Dramatic religious and political conversions, for example, typically are accomplished by quite different means. Generally the subject is pressured to reject entire belief networks and to renounce the social, political, or philosophical systems that produced them. He is also induced to adopt a new, very biased, interpretive schema for any new information. Insight therapies similarly attempt to overcome beliefs through combining general assaults on belief systems with the introduction of new explanatory or inferential schemas.

The question of when and why beliefs yield to evidence has been one of abiding interest to the legions of psychologists who have studied persuasive communication and attitude change. We cannot pause even to summarize the major findings that have emerged from this area (for comprehensive reviews, see McGuire 1966; Kiesler, Collins, & Miller 1969). It should be noted that the normative issue has been all but ignored by the attitude change researchers. While we have learned a great deal about which kinds of communicators, messages, audiences, and settings are conducive to attitude change, we have learned very little about the appropriateness of the degree of change produced by such techniques. Indeed, there is even a paucity of speculation on such issues. It is possible, however, to outline two sets of factors that may promote adequate weighting, or even "overweighting," of challenges to one's existing beliefs. As the reader will readily note, our speculations about the factors that determine one's readiness to change beliefs are closely related to our previous speculations (chapters 2 and 3) about the factors affecting belief formation in the first place.

Extra-evidential Features of Information

In previous chapters we maintained that vivid information, that is, concrete, sensory, and personally relevant information, may have a disproportionate impact on beliefs and inferences. These same factors may well influence our responsiveness to particular logical or empirical challenges to prior beliefs. Thus, the published consensus of diners that "the fare at Chez Françoise has declined" may have less impact on our judgments and subsequent behavior than a single personal experience of an overdone entrée or a vivid, secondhand account of one disastrous meal. Similarly, public opinion polls show that a few outstanding and important instances of wrongdoing by people holding high office have dramatically altered the public's willingness to trust the entire class of political leaders. It is worth noting in this regard that participants in the "debriefing" studies typically received discrediting information that was relatively dull and abstract compared to the concrete information that originally induced their beliefs. More vivid debriefing procedures—for example, a videotape replay of the past experimental deception, accompanied by a voice-over account of the key points in the deception—might have proved more successful.

The Role of Causal Explanations and Scripts: Substitution of a Theory by a Better Theory

It seems probable that attempts to discredit beliefs may have relatively greater impact when they prompt the use of plausible theories or "scripts" that encompass both the initial information and the subsequent challenge to that information. Just as people can use otherwise unutilized base-rate information when they have a causal theory explaining differences in base rate, people are probably much more likely to revise theories in response to new evidence when they possess a theory that could account both for initial impressions and for the new, discrepant data. A mere "script" accounting for changes in the nature of information may serve the same purpose. The sequence of events comprising a "false accusation" script, for instance, is surely familiar to almost all adult subjects, whether the origins of the script lie in TV melodramas or in historic frame-ups (for example, the Dreyfus case). Accordingly, the discrediting of evidence might be more successful in overcoming otherwise powerful perseverance mechanisms when it occurs in a setting that recruits such a false accusation script. It is notable that one failure to obtain a perseverance effect (reported by Hatvany, Strack & Ross 1979) occurred in a context in which a "key witness" in a videotaped simulation of a courtroom trial recanted her testimony against the defendant. To the investigator's surprise (but not that of trial lawyers whom they belatedly consulted) an *overcorrection* occurred, with the defendant faring better than he would have in conditions in which no key witness testified against him at all.

The effectiveness of a variety of procedures for discrediting information also may depend on their capacity to make subjects aware of some of the processes underlying the perseverance of their beliefs. As noted in our discussion of the Ross, Lepper, and Hubbard (1975) study, the self-perceptions of subjects who were merely told of the deceptive nature of their previous success or failure feedback continued to be influenced by that discredited information. By contrast, that tendency was almost totally eliminated among subjects who also received an explicit theoretical account of the processes that *cause* perseverance.

BELIEF PERSEVERANCE:
THE NORMATIVE QUESTION

Even more than usual, this chapter touched upon profound and difficult normative issues. Our criticism of subjects' behavior in the experiments we have discussed closely follows conventional epistemological considerations. (See Sklar 1975, for a discussion of the boundary conditions for a rational belief-conservatism in the face of new evidence.) But the perseverance tendencies of subjects in these experiments were so extreme as to force consideration of the possibility that the traditional scientific standards may not apply.

In particular, it seems possible that the behavior of subjects, inappropriate as it is from the standpoint of rationality in the inferential contexts studied, may arise from pursuit of important, higher order epistemic goals. Two such possible superordinate goals are (a) the importance of stability to beliefs and belief-systems, even despite occasional logical inconsistency and (b) real-world constraints on time, which may prohibit the careful and dispassionate perusal and integration of all new evidence pertinent to any particular belief (Goldman 1978). The possibility that subjects were acting in accordance with such higher order goals should make us reluctant to assume that their behavior is as inappropriate as would be implied by narrower considerations of the justification for a particular belief, in a particular context, at a particular time.

On the other hand, we think it would be a mistake to whitewash our subjects' behavior, or to presume that it can be understood wholly in terms of such worthy higher order goals. People's confirmation biases in their approach to the recall and generation of data and their facile and overconfident approach to causal analysis are too well documented to justify such tolerance.

Fortunately, the normative questions here admit at least partial resolution by (admittedly arduous) empirical means: Would people be so inclined to persevere in their beliefs if they knew about their confirmation biases and overconfident causal analyses? And if they did not persevere as much, once they had a full understanding of these tendencies, would such higher order goals as belief-system stability suffer for it?

SUMMARY

People tend to persevere in their beliefs well beyond the point at which logical and evidential considerations can sustain them.

1. When people encounter probative evidence pertinent to prior beliefs they tend to apply asymmetric critical standards to supportive and opposing evidence and tend to become more confident of a belief in response to a set of mixed evidence which normatively should serve to lower confidence.

2. People do not observe the "commutativity" rule in response to sequentially presented evidence. Instead, early-presented evidence seems to create theories which are not revised sufficiently in response to later-presented, conflicting evidence.

3. Beliefs tend to sustain themselves even despite the total discrediting of the evidence that produced the beliefs initially.

Belief perseverance sometimes seems to occur because people have an emotional commitment to the belief. Perseverance is likely even when there is no such investment, however, because (a) people tend to seek out, recall, and interpret evidence in a manner that sustains beliefs, (b) they readily invent causal explanations of initial evidence in which they then place too much confidence, and (c) they act upon their beliefs in a way that makes them self-confirming.

People's tendencies to persevere in their beliefs are so striking as to raise the possibility that such perseverance serves goals that may be more fundamental and important than holding correct views of particular issues.

part III

INFERENTIAL ERRORS: THEIR CAUSES, CONSEQUENCES, AND CURES

9

the lay scientist
self-examined

> The mental, like the physical, is not necessarily in reality
> just what it appears to us to be.
>
> *Sigmund Freud.*

Our primary focus has been on the lay scientist's view of his peers and his environment. Now it is time to consider what happens when the lay scientist turns his attention inward to make judgments of himself—of the nature of his personal dispositions, his feelings and attitudes, and, most importantly, of the determinants of his own behavior.

The general thesis offered in this chapter is a simple one and is largely anticipated by Bem's (1965, 1967, 1972) self-perception theory. We maintain that knowledge of the self is produced by the same strategies as knowledge of other social objects, and is thus prone to essentially the same sorts of bias and error. We do not deny that the actor and the observer sometimes differ in their beliefs about the actor. Our contention, rather, is that accurate perceptions of self and accurate perceptions of others ultimately depend on the successful performance of the same "scientific" tasks—that is, collecting, coding, and recalling data, assessing covariations, inferring causal relationships, and testing hypotheses.

195

Actors seem to have one sort of data available to them that observers do not, namely their own private thoughts and experiences. A key issue is the extent to which people have access to a private source of data. To what sorts of mental events do people have genuine privileged access? What advantage does such access give them in characterizing themselves and explaining their actions? In keeping with the overall organization of this book, we begin by considering people's success in performing relatively elementary tasks involving self-characterization and then turn our attention to the question of people's accuracy in assessing the mediators or causes of their own behavior.

CHARACTERIZING ONE'S OWN BEHAVIORAL DISPOSITIONS

When we considered in chapter 4 the question of how accurately the layperson can characterize objects generally, we said that some characterizations were extremely accurate when judged against objective criteria, others were clearly inaccurate when judged by such criteria, and still others—perhaps the majority of characterizations—simply did not have available objective criteria for comparison. These problems seem even more acute for the characterization of the self. Zimbardo (1977) found, for example, that most people believe that they are "shy." How could one assess the accuracy of such claims, either for the majority taken as a whole or for any given member of the self-described "shy" majority? "Shyness" would seem to have both experiential and behavioral referents. Suppose the proverbial back-slapping extrovert, the sort found swinging from chandeliers at a party, asserts that he is "shy." Are there reasonable grounds on which to contest his right to assert that he experiences emotions that could be described as "shyness"—even when (perhaps especially when) he is found swinging from the chandelier? Suppose he characterizes himself as *behaviorally* shy? Can we safely contradict him even then? What if he asserts that he avoids blind dates, cannot reveal himself even to intimates, and would sooner die than try to give a speech?

The problem is a general one. Neither "objective" behavioral measures nor the assessments of peers or experts offer a satisfactory "criterion" that can be used to evaluate a person's self-assessments. This is not to deny that the amount of *agreement* among the various sources can be explored, and that demonstrations of convergence, or divergence, can be interesting and revealing from many standpoints. Such demonstrations can offer clues about similarities or differences in the data, methods of analysis, perspectives, and theories employed by the various evaluators. (See, for example, Block 1961; Dornsbusch, Hastorf, Richardson, Muzzy, and Vreeland 1965; Goldberg

1978; Norman and Goldberg 1966; Nisbett, Caputo, Legant and Maracek 1973.) But the issue of relative or absolute *accuracy,* or in other words, the "validity" issue, remains refractory.

While we cannot comment authoritatively about the overall accuracy of the layperson's self-characterizations, we can say something about the *determinants* of such characterizations. People's characterizations of themselves, like their characterizations of the objects and events that comprise their environment, are heavily based on prior theories and socially transmitted preconceptions. And as we have documented more formally in chapter 8, the individual's impressions and judgments can survive seemingly potent empirical challenges.

There is much anecdotal evidence for this generalization. One of the authors, in his first years of teaching, was amazed and disturbed by the tendency of many of his female undergraduate students to maintain negative stereotypes of their mathematical abilities even though their successes belied such stereotypes. Often, a student would succeed admirably in a statistics course that, on the first day of class, she had tearfully predicted she would fail. Such a student usually proved capable of readily assimilating her unanticipated success to her previous view of herself, assigning credit to the lucidity and patience of the instructor, to her strenuous efforts, or to the "easiness" of the course. It was quite difficult to get such a student to entertain the possibility that her previous theory about herself was simply wrong, that it had been based upon a combination of insufficient data and sex-role stereotypes that her academic choices heretofore had left largely unchallenged.

Very recently a number of studies have begun to deal explicitly with possible effects on the processing of information about the self produced by one's theories or schemas about the self. For example, Markus (1977) used several criteria to distinguish subjects who had formed or had not formed "self-schemas," (the investigator's term for domain-specific cognitive generalizations about the self, presumably derived from past experience). She then demonstrated that the subjects who possessed self-schemas for a particular domain (for example, who viewed themselves as either "dependent" or "independent") more rapidly processed relevant information about themselves, more readily retrieved relevant behavioral evidence, more confidently predicted new responses in the domain, and showed greater resistance to information that ostensibly contradicted their self-characterizations. Such "economies" arising from the possession of schemas do have a cost, as we have noted in earlier chapters. That cost is the schema-holder's penchant to overassimilate new information to the preexisting schema, thereby sustaining and even strengthening that schema with information that would offer no such support if it were processed without prejudice.

Beyond their impact on the coding of ambiguous information, schemas about the self, like schemas about other people, objects, or events, can be shown to produce distortions in memory. Rogers, Rogers, and Kuiper (1978) were able to observe the same kinds of biases and distortions in recall of self-relevant information that Cantor and Mischel (1977, in press) and others (for example, Tsujimoto 1979; Tsujimoto, Wilde, & Robertson 1979) were able to demonstrate for recall of information about "prototypic" *others*. Rogers and colleagues tested subjects' recall of adjectives and found that the incidence of "false positives" (that is, instances in which adjectives were "recalled" that had not been presented initially) tended to increase progressively as the adjectives in question became more and more self-descriptive.

In a related vein, Mischel, Ebbesen, and Zeiss (1976) demonstrated that experimentally manipulated expectations about the self can produce similar memory biases. Their subjects first received an initial experience of either success or failure on a test of mental abilities, coupled with a set of instructions that led them to expect either future success, future failure, or no subsequent testing. All subjects next were exposed to an equal amount of new positive and negative information about their personalities and then were given a memory test on that information. As predicted, subjects who expected to succeed rather than to fail were inclined to remember their purported personal assets better than their alleged liabilities. Indeed, the effects of *expectancy* overshadowed those of actual experience; only when subjects had no expectation of future success or failure did their past experience have any influence at all on their recall of assets versus liabilities.

The clinical literature, as one might expect, also has many accounts of the capacity of people's preconceptions of themselves to bias their memories or interpretations of event and thereby to influence their expectations and subsequent behavior. Particularly interesting are findings on the phenomenon of depression. Various investigators have suggested that depressed individuals may be less interpersonally or socially skillful than "nondepressed" persons (for example, Libet & Lewinsohn 1973). Others have suggested that depressed individuals may be inclined to perceive their attributes and skills in an "unrealistically negative" manner (cf. Beck 1967). To disentangle possible misperceptions from actual deficiencies, Lewinsohn, Mischel, Chaplin, and Barton (1980) compared self-ratings and peer ratings for three types of people: depressed individuals, individuals with psychiatric problems other than depression, and normal controls. Ratings were made after group interactions. As expected, the depressed individuals rated themselves, and also were rated by others, as less socially competent than the two control groups. Surprisingly, however it was not the depressed group that who showed a tendency to misperceive the actual state of affairs; self-assessments by that group corresponded well with the perceptions of them offered by others. Rather, it was the two control groups who were prone to err, with both groups seeing themselves more positively than they were seen by others.

It is thus possible that unrealistically positive self-schemas or other illusions about the self, together with the processing biases they can engender, may be more socially adaptive than are totally accurate self-perceptions. This possibility is fascinating, and it is beginning to receive the attention it deserves (for example, Seligman 1978). For now, however, we need only reemphasize that self-characterizations, like social characterizations, appear to be heavily influenced by preconceptions or theories about the self.

ASSESSING ONE'S OWN EMOTIONS AND ATTITUDES

Perhaps the most energetically researched aspect of self-knowledge in recent years has been the ability of people to "know," that is, to label or to evaluate, their own emotions, attitudes, and other internal states. In two increasingly convergent and now very familiar areas of investigation, Stanley Schachter (1966, 1970, 1971; Schachter & Singer 1962), studying emotions and Daryl Bem (1965, 1967, 1972), studying attitudes, arrived at essentially the same radical conclusion. Both investigators, in defiance of both existing psychological theory and intuition, questioned the extent to which self-assessments of emotions and attitudes are the product of direct introspection. Both theorists stressed instead the role played by causal inference in such assessments.

Emotional Labeling and Causal Attribution

Schachter's research on the effects of cognitive or situational cues on the labeling of artificially produced states of emotion (Schachter & Singer 1962; Schachter & Wheeler 1962) and scores of follow-up studies utilizing naturally occurring emotional states (for example, Nisbett & Schachter 1966; Ross, Rodin, & Zimbardo 1969; etc.) all illustrated the extent to which the self-assessment of emotion may be an *attributional* process. Once the individual becomes aware of his own state of physiological arousal, the labeling of that state—and the subjective experiences, self-reports, and emotionally relevant behavior that accompany such labeling—is the result of a search for a plausible cause of the arousal. Potential arousal sources might include external events (a growling dog, a come-hither stare, a mendacious politician) or spontaneous cognitions (the thought of an upcoming job interview, the memory of an embarrassing incident) or a combination of the two sorts of stimuli. In both cases, the attribution is made on the basis of the availability and plausibility of the arousal sources under consideration. The result is a high degree of emotional "plasticity"; if the *actual* source of one's arousal is not readily available and reasonably plausible, the individual is apt to label his emotional state in terms of whatever sources *are* easily available and plausible.

This account of emotional labeling has several important implications. When the actual source of the lay scientist's arousal is unambiguous, he is apt to label his state correctly and to respond accordingly. But when chance, clever experimenters, or the complexities of one's emotional life contrive situations in which the actual sources of the lay scientist's arousal are disguised, so that incorrect alternatives are more available or plausible than the correct ones, he is likely to mislabel his state. By holding constant subjects' emotional arousal but manipulating the source to which it may be plausibly attributed, experimenters have been able to produce either a heightening or lessening of many states, including fearfulness, aggressiveness, playfulness, and sexuality.

To take just one example of many, Cantor, Zillman and Bryant (1975) have shown that the rated attractiveness of nudes can be influenced by the degree of arousal produced by an extraneous source and by the degree to which the arousal is incorrectly attributed to the nudes rather than correctly attributed to the extraneous arousal source. Male subjects were required to ride an exercycle with sufficient vigor to induce a high degree of physiological arousal. The fact of the arousal and its source were apparent to the subjects immediately after the exercise. After a few minutes, however, subjects were no longer able to report arousal even though, as measured by physiological indicators, they were still aroused. Nudes examined during this period were rated as more attractive than those examined immediately after exercise (when subjects knew that they were still aroused from their exertions) or than those examined at a still later period (when there was no extraneous arousal to be misattributed).

Schachter's essential insight was that emotional experience and behavior reflect a considerable amount of what can only be termed "causal inference" and that the role of any more direct awareness of the nature or antecedents of that state is at best limited. People's labeling of their emotional states, in other words, depends on an analysis of evidence conducted in the light of preconceived theories about which antecedents produce which states and which states are the product of which antecedents.

Inferences about One's Own Attitudes

Bem's work on the processes by which individuals come to know their own attitudes had a very different starting point. He was influenced by the Skinnerian analysis (1953, 1957) of self-reference behavior (and by philosophical treatments of the same problem by Wittgenstein and Ryle). Bem was concerned at first with self-ascriptions of attitude (cf. Bem 1964, 1965, 1967), but he soon made the connection between his own research and the emerging Schachterian literature—so that in his statement of self-perception theory (1972) Bem explicitly chose to embrace "attitudes, emotions, and other internal states" within the same conceptual framework. Such states, Bem argued, are known to the individual "partially by inferring them from observations of his own overt behavior and/or the circumstances in which this behavior occurs" (1972, p. 2). An important derivation is that "to the extent that internal cues are weak, ambiguous, or uninterpretable, the individual is functionally in the same position as an outside observer who must necessarily rely upon those same external cues to infer the individual's inner states" (p. 2). He then proceeded to demonstrate, in a variety of contexts, how much such "external cues"—and how little any "internal cues"—contribute to actors' self-reports of their attitudes.

The initial research context for Bem's theory was the dissonance or insufficient justification paradigm. In these experiments, it will be recalled from Chapter 6, experimental subjects are required to perform some action that is incongruent with their prior beliefs. When subjects are adequately compensated for their counterattitudinal behavior, for example, when they are offered large monetary payments, their attitudes toward the object to which the behavior was directed typically undergo no change. When subjects are not adequately compensated for their counterattitudinal behavior, their attitudes toward the object typically change in a congruent direction, so as to make attitudes "consonant" with behavior.

Bem found that in "interpersonal replications" of such experiments, in which protocols describing the various experimental conditions were presented to "observer" subjects, these observers made the same judgments of actors' attitudes as did the actors themselves. Observers who read about the behavior of adequately compensated actors inferred that actors' beliefs were less congruent with their actions than did observers who read about the behavior of inadequately compensated actors. Bem argued that this result indicates that actors assess their own underlying attitudes in a manner very similar to observers who have witnessed (or simply read about) the actors' behavior and the context in which it occurred. Thus, when attending pressures and constraints seem sufficient to induce the actor to behave in a particular manner (for example, to present a particular unpopular viewpoint in a speech or essay, or even to endure electric shock), neither the actors themselves nor observers presume that the actors' private views correspond to their overt actions. On the other hand, when pressures and constraints do not seem sufficient to produce the actors' behavior (even when the situational pressures *are*, in fact, powerful enough to control the behavior of the vast majority of subjects), actors and observers both make the same inferences about the actors' beliefs. Both actors and observers overestimate the degree of congruence between the actor's private attitudes and his overt behavior.

Subsequent research has provided abundant evidence for the influence of such causal analyses on actors' assessments of their own attitudes. Some of this research was discussed in chapter 6. For example, the nursery school children in the Lepper, Greene, and Nisbett (1973) experiment, who were given an extrinsic inducement to play with magic markers, showed less interest in playing with magic markers on later occasions than did children who had never been given such an inducement. Offering a Bemian analysis, Lepper and colleagues argued that the children who received the extrinsic inducement to play with the magic markers inferred that they had done so because of the inducement and not because of their intrinsic interest in the activity. Having inferred that they had relatively little intrinsic interest in playing with magic markers, they were less inclined to do so when a subsequent opportunity arose.

It is not necessary for us to spend more time on the very large amount of controversial literature initiated by Bem's self-perception theory. It will suffice to state two relatively uncontroversial conclusions: (1) People's private, introspective access to their attitudes is not so direct and unerring as to preempt the consideration of such public events as one's own behavior toward the object and the pressures and constraints in the situation in which the behavior occurred. (2) It has proved extremely difficult for critics to demonstrate convincingly that the process by which actors assess their attitudes is fundamentally different from that employed by observers. (This is true even if one accepts the dissonance theorists' claim that, for actors, the process is triggered by a painful motivational state [see Zanna & Cooper 1976]).

Our discussion of Schachter's and Bem's contributions anticipates the remainder of this chapter in which we will examine the lay scientist's assessment of the causes of his own behavior. Both Schachter and Bem began by considering people's ability to assess their feelings or beliefs but ended by examining their ability to make causal inferences. The question "What emotion am I feeling?" became "What stimulus is causing me to feel aroused?" Similarly the question "What is my attitude toward X?" became "What forces and constraints are influencing my behavior toward X, and are they sufficient to account for my behavior?" It is clear that people's ability to assess their feelings and attitudes will turn out to be largely dependent on their ability to perform such causal analyses.

CAUSAL EXPLANATIONS OF ONE'S OWN BEHAVIOR

Why were you so depressed last week? Why did you hire Ms. Davis when Ms. Peters seemed so much better qualified for the position? Why didn't you help the old man lying on the sidewalk? Why did you buy a Porsche instead of a Pontiac? Why did you refuse the attractive job offer from Kansas? People answer such queries every day, sometimes with a concession of uncertainty, sometimes with confidence that they are revealing a simple truth.

The Raw Data for Causal Explanations

Why do we often feel convinced of the accuracy of such accounts, and why are we so tolerant of other people's similar accounts? The answer appears to be that we believe, quite correctly, that each of us is privy to a wealth of data pertinent to the generation of such accounts. We know many personal historical facts; we often know what thoughts occupied our attention at the time the behavior occurred; we know of which facts in the external world we were cognizant and of which we were not cognizant; and we know about the plans and goals that we believed the behavior would serve.

But how well founded is the assumption that access to such data guarantees the accuracy of the actor's causal explanations for his behavior. Access to large amounts of data does not prevent us from making errors in our causal explanations of external physical and social events, as chapter 6 illustrated. It seems reasonable to suspect that our confidence in the causal explanations we offer about our behavior may simply be a special case of our largely unfounded confidence in the accuracy of our causal explanations in general. Knowing that an event has occurred, and having some data about antecedent events, our fertile imaginations seize on one or two of the antecedent events, and link them in a causal chain to the effect. Having little recognition of the facility with which we generate such explanations, and having little notion of the size of the set of causal explanations that we would find equally satisfactory, we are content with the explanation.

It might be protested that matters are different for explanations of our own behavior because we have much more knowledge of the antecedent events than we do for other people's behavior. But should such knowledge be regarded as literally complete, or nearly so? There is good reason to believe that it is not, and that regardless of the level at which a "mental event" is defined, access to such events is spotty and imperfect.

The events underlying judgment and behavior, virtually all theorists would agree, are ultimately reducible to physiological occurrences in the central nervous system. The notion of direct access to these events is surely as peculiar as would be the assertion that we have "direct access" to the workings of the eyeball or the adrenal gland—both of which do ultimately produce conscious experiences.

At a somewhat higher level of analysis, there are a large number of mental states and events which clearly influence beliefs and behavior but to which no one would maintain that we have direct access. The philosopher Steven Stich (1979) labeled these "subdoxastic states," that is, states which influence and underlie beliefs but which are not themselves beliefs. For example, our ability to judge the relative distance of objects is dependent on a great many external factors, but many of these are not generally accompanied by any phenomenal representation. These factors include perspective, surface texture, the perception of edges and corners, occlusion, illumination gradients, and stereopsis. It was not until the Renaissance that many of these factors were recognized as influencing our perceptions of depth. As another example, consider the rules of grammar that underlie our ability to produce and comprehend speech. These rules are an enormously complicated and largely inaccessible network. Though people use the network constantly and with near-perfect accuracy, and though educated speakers may have independently stored, verbally represented knowledge of some of the rules, even the most educated people do not have anything like complete knowledge of this network. The question of just what the rules of grammar might be is currently a matter of intense debate among people who have spent a lifetime studying those rules.

Suppose we restrict ourselves to mental events at a still higher level of analysis, to events that many theorists would regard as the most crucial ones mediating behavior—the percepts and meanings, however reached. It seems likely that we have access only to some of these and that some percepts and meanings are not represented phenomenally. (See Jaynes 1976 for a comprehensive discussion.) Research on subliminal perception, reviewed by Erdelyi (1974) and Dixon (1971), has made a number of theoretical and methodological advances. It now seems entirely likely that we are capable of "perceiving" a stimulus, which then influences our behavior, while at the same time showing no ability to report any phenomenal representation of the stimulus, even at the very moment that it is presented. A single illustration of the "unperceived percept" should suffice. After spending some time in a room with a loudly ticking grandfather clock, there will be no phenomenal representation and no awareness of the ticking. The percept is nonetheless present at a subphenomenal level. This can be shown by the simple experiment of stopping the clock. Normally, there will be an immediate orienting response. Thus the set of mental events for which we do not have any phenomenal representation includes many events that may properly be called percepts. To the extent that such subconscious percepts influence our behavior, it is clear that causal accounts may be incomplete.

At least some "meanings" of stimuli and events are accessible, but it seems clear that it is normally the case that not *all* meanings of a particular stimulus are represented phenomenally. If we are asked whether a specific stimulus has a given meaning for us, an answer sometimes requires some thought. Some stimuli are very rich in their associative networks, and these networks and all they encompass are not normally spontaneously available to consciousness. To the extent that some of these subtle meanings influence behavior, then our causal accounts may be partially incorrect.

If we are unaware of so many mental *events*, then a causal account of the mental *process* underlying a behavior must be, at the very least, incomplete. But there is more to be said of our access to mental processes. Mandler has argued that a "process" is by definition a theoretical construct, and that, on logical grounds, there can be no direct conscious access to a mental process.

As Mandler explained:

> "Thinking" or cognition or information processing for the psychologist is a term that refers to theoretical processes, complex transformations on internal and external objects, events, and relations. These processes are not conscious; they are, in the first instance, constructions generated by the psychological theorist. By definition the conscious individual cannot be conscious—in any acceptable sense of the term—of theoretical processes invoked to explain his actions. (1975   p. 231)

For readers reluctant to agree with Mandler that logically there can be no direct conscious access to mental processes, the following argument may be persuasive. It is not controversial that causal accounts for all *nonmental* processes are theoretically guided inferences and not direct observations. Even so simple a causal account as an explanation of the event of a stone's dropping to earth when unsupported is a strictly theoretical enterprise and is one for which accuracy is chiefly a function of the quality of one's theories rather than of the quality of one's observations. Thus a primitive person or a child might say that the stone dropped because it "wanted to." A scientist in Aristotle's time might have said the stone dropped because it had the property of gravity. A Newtonian scientist would have said that the stone dropped because it existed in a field of forces of which the most relevant were the mass of the stone, the earth's gravitational pull, and the relative insubstantiality of the intervening medium, namely, air. None of the accounts is an observation of a causal process, since causal processes cannot be observed; instead they are theory-guided inferences. In Mandler's view and in ours, the same is true for reports of mental processes. A mental process, that is, the means by which one mental event influences another, cannot be observed but only inferred, and the quality of the inference is at least as dependent on the quality of one's psychological theories as on the quantity of data observed.

There are strong theoretical and logical grounds for doubting the extent to which our reports of the causes of our own behavior could be expected to be universally accurate. We lack phenomenal representations of many potentially influential mental events, and such phenomenal givens as exist do not suffice to reveal, but allow us only to infer, the nature of the processes underlying behavior. There also are, as will be seen, empirical grounds for doubting the accuracy of our causal accounts.

The Accuracy of Causal Explanations

As it happens, the self-perception research discussed earlier provides a great deal of evidence on the question of accuracy. Both Schachter's work on emotions and the dissonance or insufficient justification work offered compelling evidence of inaccuracy. Subjects can be made to misattribute wrongly exogenously induced arousal to salient environmental stimuli, and can be made to misattribute arousal produced by environmental stimuli to alleged exogenous sources (for example, a sugar-pill placebo which the subject is told is a physiological stimulant). Insufficient justification studies "work," as we noted in chapter 6, only because of an incorrect causal attribution. The subject is virtually forced, by social pressure from an experimenter, to perform some behavior (for example, giving a counterattitudinal speech) which he would rather not perform. The subject then falls into the trap of attributing the behavior to his own prior beliefs because he does not understand that the real cause of his behavior is the subtle but powerful social pressure generated by the experimenter.

As Nisbett and Wilson (1977a) pointed out, informal, unpublished evidence from both of the above research traditions showed that subjects' causal explanations following their participation in such studies failed completely to take account of the factors that actually prompted their behavior. Subjects did not refer in any way to the stimulus conditions that produced the dramatic effects on their behavior, let alone construct a coherent causal account incorporating such stimuli.

This evidence has limited value, however, for questions about the degree of accuracy to be expected of causal accounts generally. Investigators in the emotional labeling and insufficient justification studies go to unusual lengths to confuse subjects about the true causes of their behavior. In the former, the experimenter cleverly arranges contingencies so that a subject will find himself inexplicably aroused, or aroused under circumstances where the real explanation for his arousal is less plausible than others which the experimenter has suggested. In the latter, the combined wisdom of the high-pressure salesman and the lore of experimental social psychology are put to work to create an illusion that behavior is chosen when in fact it has been coerced. These studies make the important point that people can be bamboozled about the true causes of their behavior, but they say little about the degree of accuracy to be expected under less stage-managed conditions.

To answer the more general question, Nisbett and Wilson (1977a, 1977b; Wilson & Nisbett 1978) conducted a series of studies assessing the accuracy of causal explanations. A wide range of responses was examined, including evaluations, judgments, and choices. Each of the behaviors and behavior settings studied was a routine type encountered frequently in daily life. Deception of any sort was used in only a few of the studies and was limited to "cover stories." In addition, care was taken to minimize ego-involvement of the sort that might prompt subjects to disguise from themselves or others the true causes of their behavior. Despite these precautions, subjects proved to be remarkably inaccurate in their causal reports. Stimulus factors that had a pronounced effect on behavior were denied to have had any effect on behavior, and stimulus factors that had no detectable effect were asserted to have been influential. Because the experiments have been described in general by Nisbett and Wilson (1977a) and in detail by Wilson and Nisbett (1978), we will only sketch them here.

Before we do so, we should point out that Nisbett and Wilson did not select haphazardly the behaviors and settings studied. Instead, they deliberately tried to manipulate some causal factors which they believed their subjects incorrectly would regard as noninfluential, and others which would in fact be noninfluential but which subjects would be apt to regard as effective. Nisbett and Wilson were notably unsuccessful in their attempt. They turned out to be no better than their subjects at estimating which stimuli actually would influence, or fail to influence, the subjects' behavior. In fact, consistent with our later arguments about the basis of subjects' reports, Nisbett's and Wilson's predictions of the effects of the stimuli they manipulated were much closer to subjects' erroneous reports about their effects than to the actual effects revealed by statistical analysis.

Failure to Report Influential Factors

FAILURE TO RECOGNIZE SEMANTIC CUING EFFECTS. In one study, subjects memorized a series of word pairs (for example, "ocean-moon"), some of which were intended to increase the likelihood of certain semantic associates in a later word association task (for example, "Tide" in response to the category "detergent"). Eight such semantic cues were studied, and all eight served to enhance the likelihood of the target association. On the average, the effect of the semantic cue was to double the likelihood of the target word being given as an associate, from 10 percent for control words to 20 percent for cued words. Despite this pronounced effect of the semantic cues, subjects almost never referred spontaneously to the initial word pair when later asked why they had given the target as an association to the category stimulus. In both cued and uncued conditions, subjects tended to cite their familiarity with the target, their liking or disliking for the target, or some other personal reaction to it, as the reason for its coming to mind. When specifically asked about the effects of the word pairs, most subjects denied such an effect. In addition, frequency of reported effects was unrelated to actual strength of the effects. Thus, for most targets, fewer subjects reported an effect of the word pair than were actually influenced by it, while for other targets, more subjects reported an effect than were actually influenced by it.

FAILURE TO RECOGNIZE POSITION EFFECTS. In a second series of studies, passers-by in a shopping mall were invited to examine an array of consumer goods (four nightgowns in one study, four identical nylon pantyhose in another) and to rate their quality. There was a pronounced position effect on evaluations, such that the right-most garments were heavily preferred to the left-most garments. When questioned about the effect of the garments' position on their choices, virtually all subjects denied such an influence (usually with a tone of annoyance or of concern for the experimenter's sanity).

FAILURE TO RECOGNIZE "ANCHORING" EFFECTS. In a third series of studies, subjects were asked to guess what the average behavior of University of Michigan students would be in several different experiments. Some subjects were given an "anchor" in the form of knowledge of the behavior of one particular "randomly chosen subject." Anchoring effects on predicted mean values ranged, across the various experiments, from very large, that is, a pronounced "pull" on subjects' predictions in the direction of the anchor value to slight "antianchoring" effects, that is, movement away from the anchor value. Immediately after making their estimates, subjects were asked about the extent to which they had relied on knowledge of the particular individual's behavior in making these estimates. Subjects reported moderate utilization of the anchor value in all conditions. They reported the same degree of utilization of the anchor value for experiments in which it had not been used at all as they did for experiments in which it had heavily influenced their estimates.

FAILURE TO RECOGNIZE THE EFFECTS OF AN INDIVIDUAL'S PERSONALITY ON REACTIONS TO HIS PHYSICAL CHARACTERISTICS. One experiment by Nisbett and Wilson (1977b) suggested that people may not merely fail to recognize an important causal influence on their behavior but actually may invert the true causal direction in their accounts. Their subjects participated in a demonstration of the familiar "halo effect" in interpersonal perception. Subjects watched a videotaped interview with a Belgian psychology instructor who spoke English with a moderately heavy accent. Half of the subjects saw the instructor answering questions about his teaching practices and philosophy of education in a pleasant, agreeable, and enthusiastic manner (warm condition), while the other half saw him acting like an autocratic martinet who seemed rigid, intolerant, and distrustful of his students (cold condition). Subjects then rated the instructor's likableness and also evaluated three attributes that were invariant across the two experimental conditions: his physical appearance, his mannerisms, and his accent. Not surprisingly, subjects who saw the warm version of the interview liked the instructor much better than those who saw the cold version did. Furthermore, their ratings of his attributes showed a very marked "halo effect." The "warm" instructor's appearance, mannerisms, and accent were rated as attractive, but when the same objectively invariant features were manifested by the "cold teacher," they were rated as irritating.

Some of the subjects in each experimental condition were asked whether their liking for the teacher had influenced their ratings of the three attributes, while the remainder were asked the opposite question, that is, whether their liking for each of the three attributes had influenced their liking for the teacher. The results showed a pattern of reports that, while highly reasonable and plausible, were clearly at odds with the facts about the actual direction of influence. Subjects in both warm and cold conditions strongly denied that their overall liking for the instructor had influenced their ratings of the three attributes. Subjects who saw the warm version also denied that their liking of those attributes had influenced their overall liking of the instructor. Only subjects who saw the cold version consistently reported a causal influence. They claimed that their dislike of the instructor's attributes had lowered their overall liking of him. In short, it would appear these subjects inverted the true causal relationship. Their dislike for the "cold" teacher had made *irritating* the appearance, mannerisms, and accent that had seemed *attractive* in the same teacher behaving warmly. Instead of recognizing this nonobvious but actual causal relationship, they typically offered the more plausible causal hypothesis that their dislike of the attributes had made them dislike the possessor of the attributes.

Erroneous Reporting Of Noninfluential Factors

Subjects not only failed to report some influential factors, also they sometimes reported that particular factors had influenced their behavior when the experimental evidence suggested they had had no such effects. These erroneous reports were found in several studies.

ERRONEOUS REPORTS OF THE EMOTIONAL IMPACT OF LITERARY PASSAGES. In one experiment, subjects were asked to read a selection from the novel *Rabbit Run* by John Updike. The selection describes an alcoholic housewife who accidentally drowns her baby while bathing it. Even when read out of the context of the rest of the novel, the selection has a substantial emotional impact on readers. Some of the subjects read the selection as it had been written, while others read a version which had one or both of two particular passages deleted. (It had been wrongly expected by the investigators that one of the two passages was central to the impact of the selection as a whole.) The resulting two-by-two design made it possible to assess the effect of inclusion or deletion of both passages on the subjects' ratings of the emotional impact of the selection. As it turned out, neither passage had any detectable influence on the rated impact of the selection. When the subjects who had been exposed to the passages were asked about their effect on the impact of the selection as a whole, they insisted that both passages had substantially influenced their reactions. For one of the passages, in fact, 86 percent of the subjects asserted that the passage had increased the impact of the selection.

ERRONEOUS REPORTS ABOUT THE EFFECTS OF DISTRACTION ON REACTION TO A FILM. Subjects in one study were asked to view a documentary on the plight of the Jewish poor in large cities. Some subjects viewed the film while a distracting noise (produced by a power saw) occurred in the hall outside. Other subjects viewed the film while the focus was poorly adjusted on the projector. Control subjects viewed the film with no distractions. After viewing the film, subjects rated it on three dimensions—how interesting they thought it was, how much they thought other people would be affected by it, and how sympathetic they found the main character to be. Then, in the experimental conditions, the experimenter apologized for the poor viewing conditions and asked subjects to indicate next to each rating whether it had been influenced by the noise or poor focus. Neither the noise nor the poor focus actually had any detectable effect on any of the three ratings. (Ratings were in general trivially higher for distraction subjects.) In the only demonstration of reasonably good accuracy in subject report of stimulus effects found by Nisbett and Wilson, most of the subjects in the poor focus condition actually reported that the focus had not affected their ratings. A majority of subjects in the noise condition, however, erroneously reported that the noise had affected their ratings. Fifty-five percent of these subjects reported that the noise had lowered at least one of their ratings.

ERRONEOUS REPORTS ABOUT THE EFFECTS OF REASSURANCE ON WILLINGNESS TO TAKE ELECTRIC SHOCKS. In a third study, subjects were asked to predict how much shock they would take in an experiment on the effects of intense electric shocks. One version of the procedural protocol describing the experiment included a "reassurance" that the shocks would do "no permanent damage." The other version did not include this "reassurance." Subjects who had received the first version were asked if the phrase about permanent damage had affected their predictions of the amount of shock they would take, and subjects who had received the second version were asked if the phrase would have affected their predictions, had it been included. Inclusion of the phrase, in fact, had no effect on predicted shock taking, but a majority of subjects reported that it did. Of those reporting an effect, more than 80 percent reported that the phrase had increased their predictions. Subjects who had not received the phrase were similarly, and erroneously, inclined to say that it would have increased their willingness to take shock had it been included.

Taken together, the Nisbett and Wilson studies show that, across a wide variety of behaviors and behavioral contexts, subjects' reports of the causal influences on their behavior can be very inaccurate indeed. The findings cast considerable doubt on the correctness of similar causal reports in daily life. More importantly, the studies raise a question about the basis of such reports. How do subjects go about inventing (we use the term advisedly, since the subjects were certainly not *detecting*) causal explanations for behavior? It is to this question that we next turn our attention.

THE BASIS OF CAUSAL ACCOUNTS

For several of their studies, Nisbett and Wilson used Bem's technique of asking the same questions of observer subjects as were asked of the actual subjects themselves. Sometimes these observers were the subjects in control conditions who did not receive the critical manipulations, and sometimes they were people who did not participate in the experiments at all but who simply read abbreviated protocols describing one or more experimental conditions and then made predictions of how the real subjects would have responded. Data from both types of observer subjects tell the same story: Observer predictions were essentially identical to the causal reports of the actual subjects who had really been exposed to the experimental setting and the manipulations.

Such a finding for observers raises a central question: How important was the subjects' own privileged access to the mental events triggered by the manipulations? If observers' guesses were essentially the same as the subjects' "reports," this would strongly suggest that both evaluators had been based on something that was as readily available to observers as to subjects. Nisbett and Wilson argued that the "something" obviously could not be a memory of the process by which the manipulations influenced the behavior, since observers had no such memory. The observers could base their predictions only on their theories of the ways in which the particular manipulations would influence the particular responses. Nisbett and Wilson argued that the basis of the actual subjects' causal accounts was the same as their theories, shared with observers, of the ways in which the manipulations would be expected to influence their responses. The only difference between observers and subjects is that observers knew that they were basing their predictions on their theories while subjects presumably thought that they were basing their accounts on their memories of mental data.

This view of the origins of people's causal accounts does not apply merely to cases in which such accounts are inaccurate. It applies also to cases in which such accounts are accurate. Indeed, it allows us to predict precisely when such accounts will be accurate. They will be accurate if, and only if, the theories about the behavior in question are also accurate. Empirically, this means that under most circumstances subjects will be right in their causal accounts if and only if observers, working with similar externally available information, also are right.

People are, despite Nisbett's and Wilson's demonstrations, often right in their accounts of the reasons for their behavior. A person who answers a telephone and asserts that he did so "because it was ringing" is surely right. A person who solves a problem by applying an appropriate algorithm and then asserts that he solved the problem by applying the algorithm, is right. A person who asserts that he opened the refrigerator door because he was hungry is usually right. But we have theories about why we answer telephones, how we solve problems, and why we open refrigerators, and these theories are usually correct. Because these theories are so manifestly correct, however, it would require some ingenuity to find cases in which the knowledgeable observer was not also correct.

The notion that actors' causal accounts are based primarily on theories which they share with observers has strong implications for the behavioral domains in which accuracy is to be expected. For those domains in which people have received explicit training in the use of an algorithm or judgmental strategy, then theories of process would be expected to be correct, and, therefore, causal accounts should be correct as well. Thus, when stockbrokers are asked why they recommended the purchase of a given stock, they can easily report the algorithm they were using for stock recommendations and can report how the features of the particular stock match the features of the algorithm. The same is true of clinicians who are trained in the use of test-score profiles to diagnose mental illness. The clinician knows the structure of the algorithm he was taught and knows how the features of the profile correspond to the features of the algorithm. We would expect reports of such judgments to have at least some accuracy, and they do (Slovic & Lichtenstein 1971). But there is every reason to assume that *observers,* who also are trained in the use of the algorithm, would give equally accurate reports of the influences on the actor's judgment. Sharing the theory, they should be able to duplicate the account.

Many everyday life judgments also are guided by "algorithms" of a sort. A judgment of another person's intelligence is one that we are all "trained" to make, using certain sorts of data in certain ways and ignoring other sorts of data. For other social judgments, however, we receive no special "theoretical" training and little if any feedback from others on the way we make the judgment.

Nisbett and Bellows (1977) studied the effects of a number of factors on judgments of the "algorithm" type versus judgments for which people receive little training. These investigators asked a group of subjects to make a series of four judgments of an applicant for a counseling position. Subjects rated their "liking" for the applicant and assessed her "sympathy," "flexibility," and "intelligence." It was presumed that only for the judgment of intelligence would subjects explicitly follow an "algorithm" against which their judgments could be self-consciously monitored.

Five stimulus factors were manipulated factorially. Four of these factors were the inclusion, or omission, of particular items in the applicant's portfolio: (a) that she was unusually attractive, (b) that she possessed superb academic credentials, (c) that she had suffered a "pratfall" during her job interview (spilling coffee on the interviewer's desk), (d) that she had been the victim of a serious auto accident that still caused her considerable pain. The fifth factor (e) was the rater's expectation that she would later meet the applicant whose folder she had examined or would meet some other applicant. Besides rating the applicant, the subjects were asked to assess how each of the five or fewer factors they were exposed to in their particular experimental condition had influenced their ratings of the applicant on each of the four dimensions.

A second group of subjects was never exposed to the portfolio or presented with any task of rating of job applicants. Instead, they simply were asked hypothetical questions about the impact that the various factors (described to them only in brief summaries) would have had on each of the judgments in question. For example, they were asked: "Suppose you knew that someone was quite physically attractive. How would that influence how much you would like that person?"

Comparisons of actors' and observers' causal assessments strongly supported the hypotheses: (1) that the actors' reports and the observers' predictions would be very similar; (2) that the actors' reports would be more accurate for the "algorithm-guided" judgment of intelligence than for the other judgments; and most importantly, (3) that the accuracy of the actors' reports would not exceed the accuracy of the observer's predictions, for any of the judgments.

The actors' mean assessment of the influence of the various factors on their rating for a given dimension and the observers' mean assessments of the influence of such factors correlated at consistently high levels (ranging from a "low" of $+.77$ for the "flexibility" rating to a high of $+.99$ for the "intelligence" rating). These results suggest that both groups' causal assessments were produced in a similar way, namely, by applying or generating similar causal theories. At any rate, it is clear that the actors' private access to their own mental experiences did not cause their explanations to differ much from those that they could have produced on the basis of their theories alone.

The more important results are the relative accuracy of the actors' and the observers' assessments and the specific functional relationships for which they were accurate or inaccurate. Figure 9.1 illustrates the basic finding: Actors, as a group, were "accurate" only to the extent that observers were similarly accurate. In cases in which the observers' general theories were appropriate (as in predicting that good academic credentials would lead them to infer high intelligence), the actors were quite accurate in reporting the influences on their own judgments. In cases in which the observers' predictions were inaccurate (for example, in predicting that academic credentials would enhance liking or in failing to predict that an expected meeting would enhance ratings of the applicants' sympathy and flexibility), actors' reports were similarly inaccurate.

Correlations between the actors' reports of the effects of the various factors and the actual effects of the factors were extremely high for the intelligence judgment ($r = .94$) but essentially nil for the other judgments ($r = -.31$, $+.14$ and $+.11$, respectively, for "liking," "flexibility," and "sympathy"). Not surprisingly in view of the high correlations between the

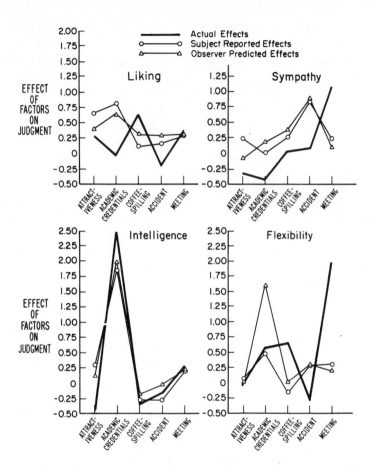

Fig. 9.1 Effects of manipulated factors on judgments, subjects' report about the effects of the factors, and observers' predictions about the effects of the factors. From Nisbett and Bellows, 1977.

actors' and the observers' assessments, the correlation between the observers' predictions and the actual effects on the actors were similarly high for the "intelligence" rating and similarly low for the other three ratings.

The results provide no evidence that actors made any use whatever of their memories for the mental events and processes that produced their judgments. Instead, like the observers, they appeared to rely on their theories about what factors influence the judgments. The results also make it clear that such theories range from highly accurate, in the case of factors influencing the intelligence judgment, to totally inaccurate, for all of the other judgments.

The Nisbett and Bellows results are quite striking, but there are two caveats. The between-subject design of the study made it impossible to assess the accuracy of the individual subjects' causal reports. It could be that, despite the failure of subjects as a group to distinguish between effective and ineffective manipulations, particular subjects may have reported accurately the influences on their own judgments. Smith and Miller (1978), in a critique of the study, seemed to argue that such accuracy did in fact occur. They reanalyzed the Nisbett and Bellows data and reported a pattern of low but significant correlations showing that those subjects who reported that a given factor had raised their rating on a given dimension tended to be those subjects whose rating on that dimension was relatively high.

Smith's and Miller's conclusion that the data provide evidence of introspectively accomplished accuracy is premature. Subjects who recognized their rating on a particular dimension to be relatively high may simply have been more likely to conclude that they had been positively influenced by *any* specified factor present than would subjects who gave low ratings on that dimension. By the same token, any *observer* also would have been more likely to assert that a given factor X heightened judgment Y in cases in which Y was relatively high than in cases in which Y was relatively low. Neither actors nor observers in such cases would have manifested any "introspective awareness" beyond that in simply recognizing that their particular judgment was, in fact, relatively high or relatively low, for example, that they liked the target a lot or didn't particularly like her.

It also should be noted that very low or zero correlations between extremity of judgment and rated influence of various factors also would be nonprobative and would not establish *lack* of introspective awareness. If a particular subject gave high ratings on a particular judgment and then asserted that most or all of the particular factors about which he was asked were noninfluential, he might be quite correct in those assertions. His high rating might have been produced by factors the experimenter failed to list on the questionnaire. Correlational analyses cannot settle matters one way or the other.

Despite the nonprobativeness of the data they marshalled in support of their contention, Smith and Miller could still be right in their assertion that individual subjects might have been correct in their reports and that their accuracy was based on some kind of private access not available to observers. We shall return to these possibilities later, in a general discussion of the question of actors' accuracy.

Our second caveat about the Nisbett and Bellows results is that they cannot be taken as typical of the accuracy to be expected generally for reports of interpersonal judgments. The investigators deliberately used implausible, counterintuitive effects suggested by previous research on interpersonal judgments, while taking no corresponding pains to include representative, intuitively plausible effects. The investigators could have improved the actors' overall accuracy by including more effects, like the relationship between academic performance and perceived intelligence, for which the objective data and the actors' theories were likely to correspond. It should be noted that there is no reason to assume, however, that such a strategy would have improved the actors' accuracy *relative to that of the observers.*

THE ACCURACY OF CAUSAL ACCOUNTS
IN EVERYDAY LIFE

This caveat returns us to our chief concern: How accurate, in general, are our causal explanations in daily life? There is a sense in which this question can never be answered. It even seems, on the surface, like a question one ought not to ask, since no amount of experimentation could ever indicate more than that such accounts are sometimes right and sometimes wrong. There are, however, some useful things that can be said about the question.

First, it should be emphasized that in all the research by Nisbett, Wilson and their colleagues, the experimental setting contained many plausible "decoy" factors. Subjects were asked only about the effects of a few actually effective stimulus factors and of a few plausible decoy factors. Had subjects been asked about the influence of every conceivable factor—the presence of a dust mote on the ceiling, the tenor of current U.S. relations with China, the effects of the subject's breakfast eaten three days before—subject accuracy, at least in percentage terms, would rapidly have begun to approach 100 percent. Viewed from this perspective, our causal reports in everyday life are very accurate indeed: Almost all genuinely ineffective factors, of which there are infinitely many, will be denied as having been influential.

This is not very encouraging, though, because the research to date makes it clear that it is child's play to generate decoy factors that people will falsely assert to have been influential and similarly easy to manipulate genuinely influential stimuli that people will deny to have been influential. We then have only to ask the question, "Does everyday life often present us with situations comparable to those in which Nisbett and Wilson placed their subjects?" Different readers will come to different conclusions about this question. Our own view is that the answer is a resounding "Yes." Life is fully as inventive as social psychologists are. We hum a tune because we heard a snatch of it on the radio a few minutes ago and not necessarily because it has deep personal meaning for us. We choose a sports jacket in part because it was not the first one the salesperson pulled off the rack, and not exclusively because of its style, fabric, and fit. Our overall affective reaction to a person influences, without our knowledge, our evaluation of the individual attributes of that person. When we are deeply affected by a book or a movie we sometimes will single out inconsequential factors as having contributed to its impact and sometimes will ignore consequential factors. (Indeed, a chief reason for reading critics is to get a "second opinion" about what factors influenced us and in what way.)

This view of the accuracy of our causal accounts has become controversial (see, for example Smith & Miller 1978; Ericcson & Simon 1978). This is not the place to attempt a rebuttal of the criticisms of Nisbett's and Wilson's thesis, but it would be instructive to examine some of the major criticisms to see whether they cause us to doubt that people sometimes will be as inaccurate in their causal accounts in daily life as they have proved to be in the laboratory.

We may group these criticisms under four major headings: (1) It is Nisbett and Wilson who are wrong in their causal accounts. They focus on their experimental manipulations in asking their subjects about causal influences, but subjects focus, quite rightly, on the mediating mental events that occur as a *consequence* of these manipulations and not on the manipulations themselves. (2) Nisbett and Wilson delayed in asking their subjects about their mental processes until much too late. Had they used "think-aloud" techniques (Newell and Simon, 1972) or some other immediate probe, much more accuracy might have been found. (3) Nisbett and Wilson used between-subject designs. Had they used within-subject designs, much more accuracy might have been found. (4) Nisbett and Wilson examined relatively trivial behaviors. Had they examined matters of greater import to the subjects, subjects would have been more accurate. We will discuss each of these objections, particularly as they concern the question of the accuracy to be expected of causal assessments in daily life.

Manipulations versus Mediators

Undoubtedly Nisbett's and Wilson's manipulations never *directly caused* any of the effects they examined. Instead, the manipulations produced effects on the subjects, in the form of various mental events, and these mental events in turn produced the behavioral effects. The most obvious example is provided by the position effect study in which, it will be recalled, subjects failed to recognize the functional relationship between the left-to-right position of a garment and their own rating of that garment. Probably "position" had such an influence, at least in part, because it determined the order in which the various items were examined. Order of examination, in turn, may have influenced a score of factors and processes, including the amount of time spent examining each item, various sensory thresholds, and perhaps the subjects' decision criteria and judgment rules. Thus, the subjects' reports (for example, I liked item 4 because it "felt softest" or "seemed most carefully constructed") may actually be accurate. What such a subject is not recognizing is the role that the experimenter's manipulation had played far earlier in the causal chain (for instance, the influence of "position" on "examination time," which influenced "thresholds, associations, and decision criteria," which ultimately influenced subjective experience of "softness" or "care in construction"). Thus the subjects may indeed have had introspective access to important mediating events, that is to the last "links" in the causal chain.

Assuming such introspective access (and remember it is only an assumption and not a demonstrated fact), how accurate or discerning has the subject been? There is no satisfactory answer, unless we have a prior notion of which links in the causal chain we deem a "fair test" of the subjects' access. When John says he married Jane in part because he thinks she is "understanding" and "beautiful," shall we challenge his assertion by pointing out that he thinks she is understanding because he has gotten to know her well and that if she hadn't lived next door he wouldn't have gotten to know her well? Shall we say that he "really" married her because of spatial proximity, (Festinger, Schachter, & Back 1950)? Shall we point out that pure sexual passion has strongly influenced his perceptions of her beauty, just as previous sexual deprivation initially influenced his subjective experience of being sexually attracted to her?

The point should be clear. Every causal sequence is extremely complex—one might say that is is infinitely complex—and it would be extremely difficult to demonstrate that someone is totally accurate or totally inaccurate about such a sequence. The proper question for our concerns is this: Is the actor aware that particular responses are functionally related to particular stimuli or situational factors, however many or complex the links? Though we cannot prove that an actor's own causal report is wrong—if by "wrong" we mean that the antecedent sentiment, idea, thought, or whatever did not occur — we can, however, prove that by normal standards of discourse, his causal analysis is inadequate or incomplete. That is, a subject can be shown to ignore or deny the influence of some factor that was necessary to produce his response in a given situation. If the error involves functional relationships about which no one has ever claimed introspective insight—for example, the relation between the structure of a molecule of liquid and subjective experience of taste—then the demonstrated failure of introspection is trivial. But if the "error" involves a common functional relationship, typical of the sorts of "causes" and "effects" about which we assume ourselves to be knowledgeable, then the demonstration is far from trivial. Such errors will lead us to say and do unwise things about potential changes in our environment. The possibility that we are not entirely wrong when we deny the direct influence, on our judgments, of position, order of presentation, proximity, contrast, or general evaluation of the object, is cold comfort. If such factors do influence our behavior, albeit through a highly mediated causal chain, we are likely to get into trouble if we believe they do not; even if there is some sense in which our claim is logically defensible.

Retrospective versus Concurrent Accounts

As Nisbett and Wilson themselves acknowledged, the closer the time of a causal inquiry is to the actual occurrence of the mental process, the more likely it is that the causal account will be accurate. This should be true, if for no other reason, because memory of genuinely influential events may decay over time, especially of any events not transferred from short-term to long-term memory. It should be clear, however, that a report about mental events is not the same thing as a report about mental processes, even under the limiting temporal case of "think-aloud" procedures. Access to process is not a matter of milliseconds but of definitions. By the definition we prefer, there can be no such thing as direct observation of mental processes, any more than there can be direct observation of physical processes. In both cases, it is only events that are observed. Beliefs about process—beliefs about the way in which one event influenced another—are always the product of inference and not of direct observation.

From the standpoint of our central concern with the accuracy to be expected in everyday life, it is clear that the temporal criticism of Nisbett's and Wilson's thesis scarcely is applicable. Their subjects were typically asked about the causes of their behavior immediately after it occurred and never more than a few minutes after. Thus the accuracy that they found can be regarded as something close to the maximum that would normally be obtained for comparable behaviors in daily life. Whatever the merits of the temporal argument for theoretical issues concerning access, the argument cannot be used to support the view that causal accounts in daily life generally would be expected to be more accurate than those in the laboratory.

Between versus Within Designs

Almost all of the Nisbett and Wilson studies used a between design. This allowed the experimenters to determine whether, overall, a given manipulated factor had an effect, which in turn allowed them to assess whether the subjects in a particular experimental condition were, overall, accurate in their assertions or denials of the influence of a factor to which they were exposed.

Two criticisms can be aimed at this strategy. The first is that such a design can never reveal whether an individual subject was accurate or not. Even if there were individual differences in accuracy, these would be of interest only if it could be shown that they were systematic. Even then it would not affect either the conclusions about accuracy for subjects in general, or the contention that such accuracy as exists is based on the accuracy of subjects' theories.

A second criticism of the between design is that subjects were being denied information that would have been pertinent to causal accounts. This is perfectly true, but exactly what information were they being denied? The most obvious answer is that the subject was denied knowledge of what his response would have been had he also participated in one or more of the other experimental conditions. If the response were different and all factors but one were held constant, then this would surely have been enormously helpful to the subject in detecting the causal role of the manipulated factor. But would we want to say that such a helpful hint came from introspection? Any observer could reach the same conclusion as the actor did, by simply attributing the behavior to that distinctive factor with which it was observed to covary. It is actually the between design that maximizes the potential advantage of the actor over any observer, because it leaves the actor's private introspective advantages intact. The within design makes public most of the additional clues it provides.

More importantly, from the standpoint of our main concern, the question to ask is whether it is the between design or the within design that comes closer to capturing the essence of everyday life judgments. We would argue that it is clearly the between design which comes closer. We know a warm Belgian psychology instructor or a cold Belgian psychology instructor, not two physically identical Belgian psychology instructors, one of whom is warm and one of whom is cold. We read literary selections as they are written, not once with a particular passage included and once with the passage deleted. We select a sports jacket after seeing a series of sports jackets in the order ABCD and not after seeing them in the order DBAC on Tuesday, BCDA on Wednesday, and so on. A stockbroker recommends IBM over other stocks which differ on a dozen dimensions from IBM, not IBM over another stock identical to IBM in all respects save one. A man never steps into the same stream twice, and life itself has a between design.

Important versus Trivial Behaviors

The claim can be made that for life's most important judgments, matters are quite different from what they are for the relatively inconsequential matters examined by Nisbett and Wilson. For an important decision, we may mull over the alternatives in a highly conscious, ruminative way, compare alternatives feature by feature, and so forth. We are sympathetic to this view (though we should note that others, particularly those holding a psychodynamic view, generally argue that matters are the opposite, and it is often life's most important decisions about which we are likely to be deluded). It does seem likely to us that, other things being equal, the more important a judgment is, the more likely we are to engage in cognitive processes that are sufficiently explicit and articulated to provide better than average clues about which factors are most important to the judgment. The argument is at most a quantitative one, however, and we can envision no mechanism by which importance alone could do more than amplify the "signal" coming from the influential factors and dampen the "noise" coming from the noninfluential ones. The question is an empirical one. Fortunately, we are able to report a particularly relevant study which speaks both to the question of accuracy in very important judgments and to the question of accuracy when a within design is used.

Weiss and Brown (1977) studied the accuracy with which women subjects could identify influences on their mood states. Their procedure was quite simple. They asked their subjects to report each day for a two-month period the quality of their moods that day, and to keep track of several factors that might potentially influence mood state. These included amount of sleep the night before, the weather, general state of health, sexual activity, stage of the menstrual cycle, and the day of the week.

At the end of the data-gathering period, the participants filled out a final set of items asking them about their perceptions of the relative impact on their mood of the factors they had monitored daily for two months. In order to derive corresponding "objective" weights for each of these factors, the investigators performed multiple regression analyses on the mood score for each subject. As the reader probably can foresee, there is no totally satisfactory way of assessing the relative contributions of each antecedent or "predictor variable" to the outcome variable (that is, "good mood" score). Nevertheless, the investigators were able to derive values that could be interpreted as indicators of the percent of total variance in mood explained by each predictor variable (with some, but not totally adequate, control for the other predictor variables). These values then could be treated as "objective weights" for the correlates of each subject's mood which, in turn, could be compared with the subjective weights the participants had reported in the follow-up questionnaires.

There were great discrepancies between the *objective* weights, determined by multiple regression analysis for the entire group of subjects, and the average *subjective* weights reported by the subjects. For instance, objectively, "day of the week" accounted for a substantial proportion of the variance in subjects' report of mood, while "amount of sleep" tended to be a rather poor predictor. Subjectively, "sleep" was rated on the average as the single most important factor, while day of the week was rated as relatively unimportant. Indeed, overall, the correlation between the objective weights and the subjective weights was slightly negative!

The finding of no accuracy in the group data is similar to the accuracy levels found by Nisbett and Wilson on the basis of their simple between-subject designs. But the special feature of the Weiss and Brown within-design study is the opportunity it provided to look more closely at the self-insight revealed by individual subjects. It was possible to examine the correlation between subjective and objective weights for each individual and thereby determine whether the participants whose moods *objectively* covaried most with a particular factor also were those whose *subjective* reports retrospectively gave that factor the greatest weight.

These correlational analyses revealed little if any evidence of insight into the correlates of emotional fluctuations. Four of the six correlations yielded positive, but far from statistically significant, correlations—ranging from a high of $+.127$ and $+.108$ (for "stage of the menstrual cycle" and "orgasm," respectively) to a low of $+.04$ and $+.01$) (for "health" and "sleep," respectively). Two of the six factors (that is, "day of the week" and the "weather"), on the other hand, yielded *negative* correlations and by conventional statistical criteria *significantly* so. That is, the more the subject's mood covaried with day of the week or weather, the less likely she was to give weight to these factors in her retrospective report. Thus subjects erred in assessing the impact of various determinants of their mood fluctuations, mistaking strong influences for weak ones or vice versa, and even failing to distinguish between positive influences and negative ones.

If subjects' impressions of the correlates of their moods do not reflect objective experience, then what do they reflect? The reader by now will be quite prepared for the answer. Weiss and Brown conducted a follow-up study in which they simply asked a group of undergraduates to fill out a short questionnaire on mood determinants. The questionnaire asked them to consider the case of an alleged participant in a psychological study of mood fluctuation and to estimate what impact would be exerted on the participant's daily mood by various factors, that is, weather, sexual activity, day of the week, and so on. The relative weightings predicted by these "observers" were virtually identical to those reported by the participants. In fact, the only difference in the ordering of the mood determinants was in "weather" and "day of the week." The participants ranked them third and fourth respectively, while the "observers" ranked them fourth and third respectively, a result that made the observers slightly more "accurate" than the participants themselves were.

The implications of such data seem obvious. Participants' daily experience of emotional ups and downs and their concomitants even the daily recording of these events—gave them no advantage in estimating the correlates of their moods. In a sense, these data seem inevitable given people's covariation detection capacities. That is, weak objective covariations are difficult, if not impossible, to detect in the absence of a previous theory, and illusory correlations reflecting one's theoretical biases are quite apt to be falsely "detected." The only new thing in the present data is the demonstration that any access to private mental events and processes that the actor might enjoy provides no prophylaxis against such errors.

From a practical standpoint, however, the data go far beyond this. They suggest that people's guesses about causality for the very most important outcomes are as faulty as their guesses about inconsequential outcomes. Simply put, they suggest that people do not know what makes them happy and what makes them unhappy.

The Weiss and Brown study thus addressed three questions that could be fairly directed toward the Nisbett and Wilson studies. (1) Does importance of the judgment guarantee accuracy? (2) Does a within design, in which subjects are exposed to many levels of the same factor, guarantee accuracy? (3) Does individual assessment, as opposed to the assessment of group means, allow us to demonstrate accuracy? The answer to all three questions would appear to be no.

We turn, finally, to a question left unanswered in the studies by Nisbett and Wilson and by Weiss and Brown: When *do* the actor's introspective insights lead him to be more accurate than the observer.

ACTORS' UNIQUE SOURCES OF INSIGHT AND ERROR

We have argued strenuously that actors' insights into the causes of their behavior are best regarded as inferences rather than as privileged or "direct" observations of the workings of their mental machinery. We do not deny that actors may know a great deal that observers do not know and that much of this knowledge is directly relevant to the accuracy of their causal analysis. Although a full treatment of this topic would take us far afield and expand an already long chapter beyond reasonable limits, we can summarize some of these "unique" sources of knowledge.

1. Let us begin by noting the obvious. Many stimuli and also many responses are to a degree ambiguous, that is, they may *mean* different things to different people. The actor often enjoys unique knowledge of the meaning he attaches to a stimulus or to his own behavior. Moreover, as the generation of gestalt social psychologists were quick to emphasize, such subjective accounts of stimuli and responses often may be crucial to understanding and explaining the actors' behavior. The observer, or the scientist who manipulates the objective features of the actors' environment, may simply lack the necessary insights about how the relevant stimuli or responses as they are perceived or interpreted by the actor.

The actor who names his firstborn "Jason," or chokes up when he hears

Smoke Gets in Your Eyes, or writes a check to the American Cancer Society, knows a great deal about the idiosyncratic meanings or associations relevant to his behavior. Sometimes this idiosyncratic knowledge arises simply because the actor recalls the past experiences that plausibly dictate the present meaning of particular stimuli or responses; sometimes it arises because he consciously experiences a particular chain of thoughts or associations. We do not imply that the actor *always* has special insight into meaning or full access to associative networks, only that he *sometimes* has such insight or access and that when he does he enjoys a potential advantage in causal analysis.

2. In many contexts the actor's unique knowledge may concern not the particular stimulus or response but knowledge of his own history and future goals. That is, he may know a great deal about his tastes, his priorities, his motives, his aspiration level, his self-regulation strategies, and sometimes even his decision criteria or weighting functions (see Slovic's and Lichtenstein's 1971 review). John may know that he is trying to save money for a ski weekend in Colorado or that he cares a lot about good service and does not mind having to drive a long way to reach a restaurant. Jane may know that she has promised herself to lose twenty pounds before next Christmas or to stop pestering her secretary about small matters. Again, in each case such knowledge is potentially relevant in helping the actor to understand his or her otherwise surprising actions in a variety of everyday situations.

3. Finally, the actor often has much knowledge of his past behavior in a variety of circumstances. This knowledge may provide a marked inferential advantage. If Jane knows she accepted John's dinner invitation but not George's and knows that both suitors proposed very similar dinner and after-dinner plans, she is at a marked advantage in assigning proper causal weight to suitor versus proposal (at least in comparison to either George or John, who may be ignorant of each other's fate). More generally, the actor often enjoys advantages over the observer by virtue of knowing information pertinent to Kelley's (1967) ANOVA variables of consistency or distinctiveness.

We may summarize all three sorts of advantages enjoyed by actors by saying that the intuitive scientist's task in causal analysis is akin to that of a detective, and, in that role, the actor enjoys privileged access to many "clues." The actor can, however, largely forfeit this advantage by simply sharing his knowledge or "clues" with the observer—that is, by telling the observer what the stimulus means to him, what his aspirations and priorities are, or how he responded in previous situations that share certain common or distinctive features with the one under consideration, and so forth. In such cases, we argue once again that the actor's and the observer's causal assessments will be similar. We should hasten to add that an abundance of clues is only sometimes advantageous to the detective, and, by the same token, the actor's additional knowledge—of associations, priorities, past experiences, and the like—is only sometimes an advantage in causal analysis. More specifically, the actor's unique knowledge is *disadvantageous* in many circumstances that the reader should now be able to predict on the basis of previous chapters. If the actor's causal theories about the relevance or impact of particular stimulus meanings are incorrect, then possession of privileged information about such associations or connotations can be disadvantageous. If a new parent's preference in names for a newborn child is determined by simple familiarity (Zajonc, 1968) then access to a rich associative network may place the parent at a disadvantage to those observers whose *only* clue is the knowledge that "the name 'Jason' seems a pretty popular choice for parents around here in the last few years."

The actor's unique access to additional cues or information also may prove to be more an inferential drawback than an asset if the antecedents of which he is uniquely aware are more salient than they are causally influential. The middle-aged man who becomes involved in an affair with a younger woman may be well aware of the popularly accepted theories of such liaisons. He even may be willing to apply such causal theories (for example, "male menopause," "the search for reassurance concerning one's sexuality," "fear of the approaching loss of youth," "compensation-seeking upon recognizing that one's greatest ambitions are out of reach") to *other* people who have engaged in similar relationships. But when explaining his *own* actions, the actor is apt to rhapsodize about a newly appreciated ability to smell flowers, about the sudden discovery of an "inner self," or about the welcome uproar of long-quiescent viscera. As a result, the actor will insist that he alone "understands" his actions and that his case is unique in its determinants, while his friends who do not share his access to private thoughts and feelings shake their heads at his "self-delusions."

In short, the actor's unique ability to introspect will aid the goal of self-insight only to the extent that the products of such introspection are roughly as causally relevant as they are available and vivid, and only to the extent that they reflect accurate theories of why people like himself, or people in general, behave as they do.

When will the actor's causal accounts be more accurate than the observer's? The answer is straightforward enough in the abstract: When the actor's data and theories are superior, he will be more accurate, when either is inferior he may be less accurate. Who is more often correct? Undoubtedly it is the actor, since he normally possesses more complete data. But, as we hope we have made clear, the data are far less important to the generation of causal accounts than the lay scientist is wont to presume, and superior access to data is in any case a two-edged sword. A corollary is that, on those occasions when the observer possesses a superior *theory*, it is normally the observer who has the advantage.

SELF-KNOWLEDGE AND SELF-IMPROVEMENT

We should close by pointing out the relevance of this chapter to the larger concerns of the book. We have claimed that people's inferences about the world are made using strategies that are often less than optimal, and sometimes woefully inadequate. We know from previous experience that some people are inclined to criticize our arguments on the grounds of introspection: "Well, I know *I* don't think that way." It should be clear that this chapter may be regarded as an extended reply to such a critic. The critic's introspections are not the court of last resort. They provide clues only, and clues that may be misleading, as to the workings of our minds. Thus a member of a graduate admissions committee may assert that he is making decisions by using a rough mental equivalent of a regression formula having factors *A, B, C,* and *D* with approximate weights 4, 3, 2, and 1. He may flatly deny that he ever engages in "persona matching" or is subject to contrast effects or to halo effects. We are saying that his assertions and denials should be treated as, at best, plausible hypotheses that are subject to contradiction by data. (The reader who wishes to demur from this conclusion would be advised to read Slovic's and Lichtenstein's 1971 review of the degree of correspondence that is to be expected between expert judges' assertions about the weights they apply to various factors in making professional decisions and the weights they can be shown empirically to employ.)

A still more important implication of this chapter is that our claims of the limits of introspection suggest a very serious roadblock on the path to inferential self-improvement. If our cognitive processes were transparent to us, then it would be easy to replace less optimal inferential strategies with superior ones. But if, as we have claimed, the nature of our cognitive processes can only be known to us only through the use of inferential strategies prone to the same sources of bias and error as those we wish to examine, then the learning of superior strategies necessarily must be seriously impeded. We discuss this question at more length in chapter 12.

SUMMARY

Our ability to know ourselves is more limited and more subject to error than common-sense beliefs would suggest.

People's characterizations of their own dispositions, though difficult to assess objectively, clearly reflect a heavy reliance on theories about themselves. Self-characterizations often seem to persist despite contradictory data.

Knowledge of one's own emotions and attitudes, though commonly believed by the layperson (and many philosophers) to be "direct" and certain, has been shown to be indirect and prone to serious error. Such knowledge is based in large part on inferences about the causes of behavior. Frequent errors in the self-ascription of emotions and attitudes would appear to be inevitable, given the inadequacy and inaccuracy endemic to causal explanations of one's own behavior.

People's causal accounts explaining their own behavior have been shown in a wide variety of settings to be: (1) often empirically wrong, (2) little different from the accounts of observers working from impoverished information and without benefit of the introspective clues available to the actor, and (3) based more heavily on causal theories than on the observation of mental events.

Whether most causal accounts in daily life are as prone to error, are as similar to those of minimally informed observers, and are as heavily dictated by theory as those examined in the laboratory, is unknown and perhaps unknowable. Perhaps the most that can be said with confidence is that a higher fraction of such daily life accounts may be characterized by these qualities than common sense would suggest or than would be congenial to one's sense of security and control.

10

psychodynamics versus psychologic

> The mind is always the dupe of the heart.
>
> *La Rochefoucauld*
>
> Every erroneous inference, though originating in moral causes, involves the intellectual operation of admitting insufficient evidence as sufficient.
>
> *John Stuart Mill*

Like La Rochefoucauld, we believe that many inferential errors and acts of folly can be traced to motivational or emotional causes, though the connections may be subtler than most laypeople and many social scientists seem to recognize. But the claim that it is always, or even usually, the passions that lead the mind astray seems to us to go much too far. Often, the sources of inferential error are primarily cognitive or informational. And, as Mill asserts, "moral" causes of inferential error—that is, causes involving wishes, values, or motives—are never sufficient; they require the collusion of intellectual shortcomings in the acquisition or evaluation of evidence.

HOT VS. COLD COGNITION: AN HISTORICAL PERSPECTIVE

The preceding chapters presented substantial evidence of imperfect rationality in human judgment and behavior. But the observation that people, even highly intelligent people, can think and act irrationally is scarcely new.

The distinctiveness of the present perspective lies primarily in the relative weight placed on "intellectual" or informational causes of irrationality, as opposed to motivational ones.

Robyn Dawes (1976), in an essay that has greatly influenced the present chapter, pointed out that psychologists from Aristotle to Freud conceived of personality as being organized hierarchically. Though differing as to the number and precise nature of the various levels of personality, most thinkers classified the intellectual functions as somehow "higher" than emotional or motivational ones. Personally or socially destructive behaviors then are regarded as the result of "intrusions" of the "lower" functions into the proper province of the higher ones.

The "intrusion" view of human folly is parsimonious only to the extent that normal or unimpassioned intellectual functioning is held to approach perfect rationality. Much of this book has questioned the facility with which people manage the purely intellectual tasks of collecting and analyzing evidence. Given these shortcomings, the rule of parsimony would seem to require that we hesitate before postulating additional, extra-intellectual agencies in accounting for judgmental failures in those cases where the errors seem to be congruent with the person's needs or values.

We have no wish to deny that people's needs and motives are important to personal and social dysfunctions. But, like many contemporary psychologists, we believe that motivational constructs have been too readily and indiscriminately invoked to explain failings that are at the least importantly aided, and perhaps even largely determined, by cognitive shortcomings. Such debasement of the coinage of motivational constructs, we feel, has limited our understanding of both motivational and cognitive processes and undermined our appreciation of the often subtle interactions between these processes.

The recent intellectual history of the contest between motivational and nonmotivational approaches is instructive. Both of the major "schools" in early twentieth-century psychology—psychoanalytic and behaviorist—featured primarily motivational theories. Behavior, as Leventhal (1970) pointed out, was seen by both schools to be the product of motivational forces, instincts, need states or drives. From this perspective, everything the organism does can be seen as instrumental. All behaviors, not only overt actions but also perceptual and cognitive responses, are the potential handmaidens of need states.

This "motivational imperialism" was challenged early on by Tolman, who maintained that some responses, notably learning responses, take place in the absence of any pressing biological drive state. The ensuing battle generated more heat than light, and most psychologists regard the question of "unmotivated learning" as unresolved and perhaps unresolvable.

The next battleground was the "New Look" enterprise in the field of perception following World War II. The New Look proponents were confident that perceptions could be shown to be influenced massively by needs, wishes, values, fears, and other motivational factors. Poor people would perceive coins as larger than rich people would, because of the greater value of coins to the poor. Hungry people would see food in tachistoscopically presented stimuli (or sometimes "defend" against seeing food), whereas satiated people would not. Ego-threatening stimuli would be perceived less readily than nonthreatening stimuli would, and so forth.

Although the initial demonstrations of such phenomena seemed promising, many theorists were quick to counter with nonmotivational interpretations of the same phenomena. Two arguments consistently were emphasized in these counterattacks (cf. Erdelyi 1974). One argument pursued the distinction between motivational influences on *overt* reports and parallel influences on *covert* perceptions or private experiences. Proponents of the nondynamic view refused to accept overt verbal reports as evidence of true covert perceptions. The other argument emphasized that experience, familiarity, and other purely "informational" factors could account for the same findings that had been cited initially as evidence of motivational influences. Higher "perceptual thresholds" for obscene words, for example, were interpreted as reflecting merely the lower frequency with which such words appeared in print and hence their lower familiarity and poorer discriminability.

The critics of the New Look research first seemed to carry the day, as the impact of motivational factors on perceptions generally proved to be slight and unreliable (once potentially contaminating nonmotivational artifacts were removed or controlled), with large effects confined almost exclusively to perceptions of highly impoverished or highly ambiguous stimuli. More recent reviewers (for example, Erdelyi 1974) questioned that early verdict, and a new generation of investigators relying on new and more sophisticated techniques has revived the debate. It remains to be seen whether persuasive evidence for the New Look phenomena will be found for motive states that are less than intense or for stimuli that are of low ambiguity.

The most recent arena for the debate over the intrusion of motives into higher order processes has been in social psychology. In the arena of attitude change, McGuire (1960) contributed one demonstration experiment that was highly promising for the motivational "intrusion" view. McGuire showed that change in a given belief (the "minor premise" in a logical syllogism) is heightened when that belief is logically connected to a conclusion that the subject deems desirable, and is attenuated when it is logically connected to a conclusion that the subject deems undesirable. Unfortunately, with very few exceptions (for example, Dillehay, Insko, and Smith 1966), neither this elegant demonstration nor the more general issues it raises have been followed up by subsequent investigators.

It has been in contemporary attribution theory that the interaction between motivational and intellectual processes has been most vigorously pursued. Though Heider was the founder of the highly cognitive research area of causal attribution, he himself was a proponent of the "intrusion" view. In fact, he gave precedence to motivational over cognitive considerations in his statement of the criteria for selection of a causal attribution: "(1) the reason has to fit the wishes of the person, *and* (2) the datum has to be plausibly derived from the reason" (1958, p. 172).

The second of Heider's criteria has been documented repeatedly by numerous attribution researchers, including Jones and Davis (1965), Kelley (1967, 1971a), Weiner (1974), and McArthur (1972, 1976). The first criterion of "wish-fulfillment" has suffered a different fate. It has received very mixed empirical support, and, perhaps inevitably in view of the history we have outlined, the contest between the motivational and nonmotivational interpretations of research findings has been far more spirited than conclusive.

In social psychology, the debate has been called one between proponents of "hot" versus "cold" cognition or between "psychodynamics" versus "psychologic" (Abelson, 1968). We would digress too far to review all of the evidence on the most recent version of this controversy. We will sketch two illustrative domains in which the controversy currently is raging: a debate over the existence of self-serving or ego-defensive biases in the attribution process, and a similar debate over the motivational versus nonmotivational basis for racial and ethnic prejudice.

SELF–SERVING BIASES
IN CAUSAL ATTRIBUTIONS

There are few beliefs more deeply ingrained in the perspectives of both laypeople and professionals than the notion that people tend to explain the causes of their own behavior, to themselves as well as to others, in a self-serving manner. People are presumed to be mightily inclined to attribute their successes to ability and their failures to bad luck, their good deeds to superior character and their bad deeds to compelling circumstance.

Overt Statements versus Covert Beliefs

We shall discuss some of the difficulties accompanying any attempt to establish that a given attribution which preserves or enhances the attributor's positive view of himself is biased by self-serving motives. First, we should note one very obvious conceptual problem that plagues almost all research in this area. This is the difficulty, first identified by critics of the New Look tradition, of distinguishing motivational effects on covert perceptions or judgments from motivational effects on overt public behavior (cf. Ross,

1977b). Obviously, no one disputes that public attributional statements are influenced by a variety of motives, including the desire to maximize one's own outcomes and the wish to be well regarded by one's peers. Depending on the particular context, the actor may show self-aggrandizement or self-denigration, undue harshness in evaluating others or great charity, without any corresponding biases in private perceptions. The question is and always has been: Can *perceptual* and *cognitive* processes be biased by such motives?

The problem of inferring covert judgments from overt responses is not unique to the attribution domain, but it is apt to be particularly troublesome there because there are strong and conflicting motives that may prompt the actor to be less than candid in his public assessments. The motives for claiming more credit than one believes to be one's due are obvious enough. But inflated and overly flattering self portraits can get one into trouble. Few motive states are as intense as the embarrassment occasioned by the public failure to live up to one's self-announced merits. Immodest, overly modest, or accurate public attributions all may be consequences of motivational factors, and none can be taken as evidence of correspondingly biased private perceptions. Since there are good reasons to assume that people often are powerfully motivated to offer accurate or even overly modest attributions concerning their outcomes, it does not seem surprising that the evidence (reviewed by Miller and M. Ross, 1975) suggests that self-serving biases in reported causal attributions are weak, if indeed they are present at all.

Wishes versus Theories in "Self-Serving" Attributions

Most researchers have attempted to demonstrate self-serving biases by showing asymmetries in judgment, that is, asymmetries in attributions of success versus failure, asymmetries in the attributions of actors versus uninvolved observers, or asymmetries in the attributions for outcomes that are high versus low in their relevance to the actor's self-concept. Many published studies have failed to show the expected asymmetries. Indeed, laboratory evidence (and much anecdotal evidence as well) leaves little doubt that in some situations actors hold themselves more responsible for failures than for successes (see Ross, Bierbrauer & Polly 1974). Undeniably, there are many studies in which actors do seem to take more responsibility for successes than for failures, and there even are a few studies in which actors seem to assign credit or blame for their outcomes in a more charitable fashion than observers. Even if one overcomes the objection that the actors' private perceptions in such studies may not correspond to their public reports, most such findings, as we shall see, can readily be explained in nonmotivational terms.

Consider, for example, the individual who has ample reason to regard himself as competent at a given task, but fails in a particular attempt to perform that task. Is he showing a "motivational" bias if he attributes the failure to task difficulty or to chance rather than to a new-found incapacity to perform the task? Or is he showing a standard *nonmotivational* bias of the type discussed in chapter 8, that is, the willingness to assimilate data about the self to a theory about the self?

As Ross pointed out, in most performance tests of the type used in outcome attribution studies:

> Success . . . is likely to be anticipated and congruent with the actor's past experience, whereas failure may be unanticipated and unusual. Similarly, successful outcomes are intended and are the object of plans and actions by the actor, whereas failures are unintended events which occur in spite of the actor's plans and efforts. (1977a, p. 182)

Thus, a quite dispassionate review of the evidence available to the actor often would serve to support the view that expected and intended success was self-produced while unexpected and unintended failure was situationally produced.

Even though observers may reverse this pattern of attributions, it hardly proves the actor's differing perceptions to be ego-defensive. The actor may be uniquely aware that he previously has been successful in similar tasks, that he was exerting great effort, or that changes in strategies were accompanied by improved performance, and accordingly may find it logically compelling that his success was self-produced. The observer may prefer a situational explanation of success not because he is disinterested but because he is ignorant of the actor's "privileged" information. By the same token, the actor's attributions could prove *less* self-flattering than could the observer's in circumstances in which the information uniquely available to the actor logically warranted such seemingly "counterdefensive" assessments.

Perhaps the most surprising aspect of the work on self-serving biases in attributions is the astonishingly uncritical reaction it has received from so many professional researchers. Data patterns that were congruent with the postulated motivational bias were accepted at face value by investigators, when a little thought should have sufficed to reveal the existence of equally plausible nonmotivational interpretations of the same findings. One wonders how strongly the theory of self-serving bias must have been held to prompt such uncritical acceptance of empirical evidence.

We should emphasize that, like Miller and M. Ross (1975), we have no desire to argue that convincing evidence of self-serving biases will *never* be found. On the contrary, the authors have a hunch that they personally have erred suspiciously often in the direction of benign self-ascriptions. Researchers less credulous and more sophisticated than those in the past may yet succeed in establishing relatively convincing evidence of these biases in at least some domains, although the "track record" of those who have sought decisive demonstrations of motivational effects must temper any such optimism.

The Basic Antinomy

We doubt that careful investigation will reveal ego-enhancing or ego-defensive biases in attribution to be as pervasive or potent as many laypeople and most motivational theorists presume them to be. The basis for our doubt was described well by Jones and Gerard (1967). These authors point out that there is a "basic antinomy" between Heider's "wish fulfillment" and "data-fitting" criteria for causal attribution. The *costs* of willy-nilly distortions in perception are simply too high to make them a cure-all for the disappointed or threatened perceiver. In general, misperceptions make us less able to remedy the situations that threaten us or give us pain than do accurate perceptions. In a sense, they poorly serve the goals of maximizing pleasure and minimizing pain in the *long term*, even if the immediate cost is the necessity of facing some disagreeable truths. This argument, obviously, applies not only to the relatively narrow domain of causal attributions but to all perception and cognition. The rodent scampering through a field might receive short-term relief if it could perceive the hawklike figure flying overhead as an unthreatening dove, but natural selection surely must deal harshly with such unrestrained subservience of reality to wishes. By the same token, the student who would treat all triumphs as reflective of his true abilities and all failures as irrelevant to those abilities must ultimately face far more pain, disappointment, and embarrassment than if he acted on less flattering attributions.

Our disagreement is not with the Freudians, for they generally have recognized that defense mechanisms are not brought into play every time one encounters an aversive fact. The Freudians emphasized the costs, both in terms of psychic energy and long term adaptation, that accrue from heavy reliance on defense mechanisms. They argued that the use of perceptual and cognitive defenses is essentially restricted to circumstances in which particular thoughts are too painful or too threatening to be handled in any other way. Like most Freudians, we doubt that the standard laboratory manipulations (which typically involve telling an actor that he has failed at some task or has been bested by a peer) involve a serious enough threat to prompt the mobilization of drastic "defensive" measures. We are far more impressed by anecdotal and clinical evidence of individuals who cling to reassuring beliefs in the face of seemingly overwhelming evidence when the immediate cost of changing those beliefs threatens to be devastating.

Our disagreement, perhaps, is only with those Neo-Hullians who have been too willing to equate perceptual and cognitive responses with those instrumental actions that can be shaped by immediate rewards and punishments. Or perhaps we have no quarrel with any real motivational "school." For surely no sophisticated Hullian forgot that responses reflect, at least in part, long-term reinforcement prospects, that even infrahuman organisms can curb the tendency to seek immediate pleasure without regard for the prospects of long-term adaptation. Perhaps the only legitimate target for our complaints should be the many investigators in this tradition who have thoughtlessly embraced facile lay assumptions about the role of motive states in perception and cognition.

Informational Sources of Self-protective Beliefs

How then shall we account for the apparent pervasiveness of people's tendency to hold unwarrantedly positive views of their own attributes? We already have stressed the extent to which self-serving attributions, when they exist, may be based on a relatively dispassionate assimilation of data to theories about the self. We may add to this that the available evidence itself may be biased to support self-serving attributions without the necessary intervention of any motivational distortions in the *interpretation* of the evidence. Consider the following vignette, by Bertrand Russell, which Heider (1958) approvingly quoted to illustrate the self-serving nature of explanations for failure.

> I am, we will say, a playwright; to every unbiased person it must be obvious that I am the most brilliant playwright of the age. Nevertheless, for some reason, my plays are seldom performed, and when they are, they are not successful. What is the explanation of this strange state of affairs? Obviously, that managers, actors, and critics, have combined against me for one reason or another. The reason, of course, is highly creditable to myself: I have refused to kowtow to the great ones of the theatrical world, I have not flattered the critics, my plays contain home truths which are unbearable to those whom they hit. And so my transcendent merit languishes unrecognized. (Russell 1930, p. 68.)

In our opinion, Russell's failed playwright has been not exposed but savaged. Anyone who has known a failed playwright (or musician or scientist) recognizes that such an individual normally has available much information that would be consistent with a self-ascription of talent despite current failure. He normally has a history of early success (minimally school and college success) in his chosen field, and has been told by friends (who may share his tastes as well as wishing to please him) that the very works that are disregarded by the public have great merit. The playwright's agent, producers, and financial backers are apt to have impressions of the playwright and his works that also are atypically positive (or else it would not be they who chose to represent him, or to invest their reputations or money in bringing his work before the public).

Though our playwright's *perceptions* may be free of motivational biases, his *behavior* is apt to reflect such biases and thus to expose him to atypically positive, but vivid and compelling, evidence of his talent. Notably, he is apt to spend more time with his admirers than with his critics, to seek out those who share rather than ridicule his artistic views and analysis of his failures.

Other nonmotivational factors further conspire to support the failed playwright's self-serving perceptions. It is indisputable that in the theater and elsewhere a good deal of trash does meet with popular success, and that deserving work is sometimes recognized only after its author is dead or in dotage. It is then easy for the playwright to assimilate the available evidence into a familiar "script" or schema that places a positive interpretation on his fate, for example, the "genius before his time," whose light will burn brightly when the panderers to popular taste are forgotten.

Finally, there are factors reflecting no inferential shortcoming at all. Rewards are imperfectly correlated with merit. Every successful scientist of our acquaintance acknowledges the role of good fortune at every career juncture, from being assigned to the right adviser at the right time, to bumping into the right problem at the propitious moment. One eminent psychologist we know characterizes his career as a series of iron gates banging down behind him as he ambles blindly down the corridor of success getting into a prestigious graduate school just before they stopped admitting people of his meager qualifications, getting an excellent first job just before the competition for such jobs became fierce, and so on. Unless we wish to call these beliefs on the part of successful scientists "counterdefensive," we have little need to label the complementary beliefs of failed scientists or artists "defensive." It seems more parsimonious to say that both successful and unsuccessful people believe, with good justification, that career outcomes are imperfectly correlated with effort or talent.

Let us emphasize again that we have no wish to deny that people, including Russell's playwright, are motivated to see themselves in the best possible light. We even share Russell's and Heider's suspicion that this motive can sometimes color, indeed even inspire, a pattern of attributions not uniquely dictated by the available data. We merely dispute the existing laboratory evidence for such a bias, and deny that such biases are solely or even largely responsible for all judgments that are on the surface self-serving. When motivational biases exist, moreover, we suspect that they rarely fly in the face of reality. They are usually supported, even encouraged, by the available evidence.

Where motivational biases undoubtedly do play a role, is in shaping the actor's behavior, in prompting him to expose himself to more pleasant and favorable evidence, in making him reluctant to expose himself to less flattering evidence, and in encouraging other actions that by accident or by design serve to ease the pain of failure or to heighten the pleasure of success. Thus an individual can say quite correctly that "the people I know seem to like my work," while being blind to the fact that it is in part for that very reason that he knows them.

ETHNIC PREJUDICE: HEARTS OR MINDS?

Perhaps no cognitive tendency is more universally attributed to motivational, emotional, or spiritual defects than is racial or ethnic prejudice. Prejudice is denounced from the pulpits of clerics, journalists, and social psychologists alike as a derangement of the passions, as a triumph of the heart over the intellect. Serious reflection on the topic (and the serious reflections to which we are most indebted in this section are those of Icheiser, 1949 and McCauley, in press) raises questions as to whether the right organ has been singled out for blame.

What is the Motive Behind Stereotypes?

First, what exactly is the motive for prejudice? Marxists will have a ready answer: It is economic self-interest or, less politely, greed. Whites are prejudiced against blacks because such prejudice justifies their exclusion from fair economic competition. Gentiles are prejudiced against Jews because of their economic success. Of course, "envious" anti-Semitism works best for contemporary America, where Jews have been economically successful; in earlier periods in Europe and America the prejudice must have had a different basis, perhaps the "exclusion from competition" motive. Many non-Marxists are skeptical of the economic self-interest theory precisely because of this sort of facility. Skepticism should be increased by a consideration of prejudices against groups (for example, Turks, Buddhists, and so on) whose economic position in America is unexceptional or unknown or otherwise irrelevant to the prejudiced individual's fate in the competition for access to goods and services.

Is prejudice perhaps a product of fear, a holdover from early man staring grimly out of his cave at the suspicious stranger? It seems true that, in contemporary America at least, many whites are deeply afraid of blacks and vice versa. But are Americans typically afraid of Jews? or Poles? or Turks?

Can sheer malevolence be the answer—the marauding tribesman in us, substituting thoughts and words for the sticks and stones of earlier eons? This

interpretation is perhaps the least plausible of all because there are few unam-
bivalent stereotypes: Blacks are labeled as stupid, lazy, and criminal, but they
also are characterized as strong and athletic, and as having rhythm and soul.
Jews are said to be crafty, clannish, and loud, but they also are said to be intelligent and unusually willing to care for their own unfortunates. Some
ethnic stereotypes, moreover, are substantially more favorable than unfavorable: The stereotype of the English, for example (excepting of course the
Irish version of the stereotype), is on balance rather enviable.

A second serious problem with the "hearts" hypothesis of prejudice is
that the stereotypes held by the various group members themselves often differ little from those held by the larger society. Self-stereotypes often may
accentuate the positive, but they rarely are unrecognizably different from
those of the outgroup. When self-stereotypes are actually negative—as
negative, in some cases, as outgroup stereotypes are—the "hearts"
hypothesis does not falter; it simply postulates "self-hate" as the explanation
for the negative self-characterization.

Perhaps the most serious problem with the hearts hypothesis is that it
fails to acknowledge that there are "stereotypes" for almost every category of
people. There are stereotypes of librarians, engineers, prostitutes, professors,
old people, young people, Baptists and Rotarians; people who wear beards or
beads, people who wear grey flannel suits or hard hats, people who drive
Cadillacs or Volkswagens, people who jog and people who have swimming
pools. Are these stereotypes all to be seen as subservient to economic motives,
or fear, or malevolence towards strangers? If not, why should ethnic or
regional stereotypes uniquely be singled out as passion-produced? Surely it
is simpler and more reasonable to look to mechanisms which might apply
equally well to both affect-laden and affect-free stereotypes.

Such a search inevitably takes us from the heart to the head, the place
where we normally look to understand the formulation and perseverance of
generic beliefs, not just beliefs about blacks or Turks or librarians, but also
about oak trees or restaurants or elephants.

Theory vs. Data in the Formation
and Maintenance of Stereotypes

The main origins of stereotypes about people, whether pejorative or
otherwise, seem clear enough. People believe that blacks are lazy or that Jews
are clannish because some person (or cartoon, joke, television program,
story, or song) told them so. Indeed, if we take the implications of chapter 5
seriously, there are not really many alternative possibilities. For, even if the
stereotype enjoyed some empirical validity, and even if the person had
enough information to generate the stereotype, people's covariation detection

capacities are far too crude to allow any such purely "data-based" discovery. The most unreasoning bigot would have to concede that the condition of virtually perfect covariation (to say nothing of ideal data storage and display) necessary for data-based covariation detection is not met in his "data" associating particular personality traits with particular races or ethnic groups.

It should be noted that interesting recent work by Hamilton and his colleagues does suggest that some erroneous ethnic stereotypes might be "data-driven" in part. Their research shows that when members of group A are more numerous than members of group B, and when desirable behaviors are more frequent than undesirable behaviors, the (distinctive) undesirable behaviors will be reported, erroneously, to be more characteristic of (distinctive) group B than of group A (Hamilton and Gifford 1976; Hamilton 1976; also Rothbart and colleagues 1978). Such an "illusory correlation" mechanism may well play a role in majority group beliefs about minorities. We suspect, however, that it is cultural transmission in its various forms that is chiefly responsible for sowing the seeds of prejudice.

Beyond the problem of their origins, how do stereotypes persist so strongly? Often they seem to survive in the absence of any data whatsoever, as in the case of stereotypes of Turks, and, for many people, of Texans, Poles, Jews, or blacks as well. People may quite reasonably presume that the culture which has provided them so economically with so many truths about covariations and functional relationships also has got the facts right in this case. (Or more accurately perhaps, people may not examine the original bases for their stereotypes any more than they scrutinize other culturally transmitted beliefs.)

In the event that the individual does have some data it is very unlikely that the data will serve to disconfirm the belief. To begin with, the individual is likely to encounter at least some entries in the "present/present" cell (cf. chapter 5). And people are inclined to give such cases exclusive, or at least disproportionate, weight. One of the present authors, on his first trip to Italy, spent most of his time in Rome. The closest he had come previously to direct encounters with Italians (other than Italian-Americans) had been his exposure to comedies about Sicilians, on the order of the film *Divorce Italian Style*. Though he was thrilled by the sights of Rome, he was somewhat disappointed by the Romans themselves. Svelte, sophisticated urbanites, they seemed "unrepresentative" of Italians. On a bus taken for a side trip outside Rome, however, the author saw an obese, warm, demonstrative woman clucking over her brood of four children. Now the author was able to leave Italy content that he had finally seen a "real" Italian, and indeed he felt reassured that at least the "real" Italians were very much as he had thought them to be.

Subtler, perhaps, are those cases in which the maintenance of a stereotype is abetted because that stereotype enjoys a kernel of, if not truth, at least fact. The same author mentioned above recently took a lengthy tour of

Scandinavia. One day, at a railroad station, he and his wife had been prowling for some minutes among the lockers looking for an empty one. Finding one at last, the author shouted to his wife: "Hey, there's one over here." Before the echo had died, the author realized that his was the only voice he had heard raised during several weeks of traveling in Scandinavia. Such an incident might legitimately help to confirm the Scandinavians' stereotype of Americans as loud. We suspect, however, that minimal confirmation of any part of a stereotype is taken by the stereotype-holder as evidence for the whole set of connotatively or semantically linked traits embraced by the stereotype. Thus, the incident might have served to "validate," for Scandinavians present in the rail station, a much broader stereotype than one involving simple loudness (that is, the stereotype of Americans as uncouth, uncultured, boorish, and overbearing, perhaps even materialistic or imperialistic).

In addition to the availability of at least some confirming cases (in anecdotes or media portrayals, even if sometimes not in personal experience), the whole panoply of mechanisms discussed in chapters 4 and 8 may be expected to come into play. Biased assimilation of evidence—coding and storing ambiguous data in a manner that serves to bolster one's theory or stereotype—is one mechanism that students of prejudice have noted repeatedly. The adult black, observed sitting on a park bench at 3 P.M. on a Wednesday might be coded as unemployed, lazy, and probably on welfare, whereas a white observed in similar circumstances would more likely be given the "benefit of the doubt"; that is, to be coded as enjoying a day off, relaxing before beginning work on the night shift, or even as being the innocent victim of recession layoffs.

Other, less familiar mechanisms of a type described in chapter 8 may play a role. The propensity to form causal explanations seems particularly relevant here. Such a propensity may have even greater impact on the perceptions of the person who would deny his bigotry than on the person who would seek to justify it. For instance, it is the "classic liberal" who hastens to formulate situational or societal explanations for the "phenomena" that figure in racial stereotypes (for example, blacks are not inherently lazy, or unmotivated, or criminally inclined; it all is a result of the "culture of poverty" or of the "father-absent syndrome" or of the "anomie born of oppression and powerlessness"). Whether justified or not, such explanatory "theories" potentially can do much to maintain stereotypes in the face of logical or empirical challenges (cf. Bennett 1978).

Finally, we should not ignore the fact that stereotypes, like other beliefs, are *acted* upon. The maintenance of a stereotype may take on a genuinely motivational character when the actor calls upon the stereotype to justify actions of seeming unfairness. Even more importantly, some stereotypes have the capacity to become self-fulfilling. The willing worker denied a job because of a stereotype suggesting he will be lazy becomes a prime candidate for the park bench and therefore a seeming justification for the stereotype that helped to place him there.

We have argued that there is no compelling reason to assume that ethnic stereotypes differ in their origin or nature from any other kinds of stereotypes, or for that matter from any other beliefs, good or bad. This is not to say that stereotypes, once held, cannot lead to *effects* with motivational significance. As Brown (1965) pointed out, the belief in ethnic differences can fuel resentment once conflict occurs. More importantly, stereotypes can and do lead to damaging behavior toward individuals. Ethnic stereotypes and the actions they promote, in short, undeniably have pernicious consequences. We believe it is for this reason that their *causes* are so widely believed to be pernicious.

Irrational Beliefs About Human Irrationality

Consider again the employer who fails to hire a black person because of his race. He undeniably harms that person. In the mind of the observer the harmful action may readily be attributed to a corresponding harmful intent or malevolent disposition. The employer's motives then are seen as evil, and the origin of the stereotypes which he uses to justify his action also seems to be evil.

It is simplistic and unnecessary to make either inference. Socially dysfunctional discrimination in hiring may no more reflect evil motives than personally dysfunctional consumer preferences do. But for most social observers, relatively mundane processes of the sort that make people persist in their choice of laundry detergents simply seem unrepresentative as potential causes of an effect as manifestly evil as the impoverishment and degradation of a racial group. People are often outraged, in fact, when it is suggested to them that evil actions can have their origins in anything other than evil motives, as witness the reaction to Hannah Arendt's (1965) thesis of "the banality of evil." She suggested that Adolph Eichmann, the man who oversaw the extermination of European Jewry, was a mere bureaucrat, a man with no greater passion for eliminating Jews than another bureaucrat might have for shipping the mail. To people who believe that motives must match acts, such a thesis is unacceptable.

In short, it is the employment of the representativeness heuristic and the susceptibility to the fundamental attribution error that produce psychodynamic theories of human irrationality. If destructive social actions must reflect correspondingly evil motives, then psychodynamic theories become essential. Similarly, if favorable opinions about oneself must reflect a correspondent motive to hold such favorable opinions, then the ascription of self-serving biases and ego-defensive motives would seem inevitable. By the same token, the existence of highly negative self-evaluations must be attributed to masochism and self-hate. We are reminded of the psychoanalyst who accused patients who came late of hostility, those who came early of defensiveness, and those who came on time of compulsiveness. In fact, we are reminded of psychoanalytic theory.

PSYCHOANALYSIS, PSYCHODYNAMICS, AND THE REPRESENTATIVENESS HEURISTIC

The previous chapter and this one have dealt with topics that until recently have been the almost exclusive preserve of psychoanalytic theory. It seems fitting, therefore, to conclude this chapter by discussing the relationship between the view of human inference and error offered in this book and the orthodox psychoanalytic view.

In *Mind and Emotion* (1975), Mandler predicted that cognitive psychologists soon would rediscover psychoanalytic constructs but would find it convenient and even necessary to use a more modern terminology for them. In our opinion, two of the more basic ideas in this book do amount to a rediscovery of two of the most important ideas with which Freud's name and the psychoanalytic tradition are associated. One of these is the notion that much of mental life is inaccessible to introspection, that is, is unconscious. We share this viewpoint with psychoanalytic thinkers (and with Mandler) though, as we soon will make clear, our view of the reasons for lack of access to some of the facts of mental life, and our view of the possibility of increasing that access, differ from traditional psychoanalytic views.

Representativeness and Associative Networks

The second fundamental idea has no real name in psychoanalytic terminology, although it involves an aspect of "primary process" thinking. It has a modern name, however. To us, the cornerstone, the chief contribution, and the Achilles heel of psychoanalytic thought all are one—Freud's discovery, for it was his, of the enormous importance to mental life of the representativeness heuristic. Most thoughtful psychologists probably would agree with Freud that (a) one thing can stand for another, in waking life and in dreams; (b) the link between the symbol and the thing that it "stands for" is their similarity on some salient dimensions, however idiosyncratic, illogical, or bizarre those dimensions might be; and even (c) that the individual then may behave toward the symbol in the same way he would behave toward the thing itself.

From his analysis of Little Hans to his account of slips of the tongue in every-day life, Freud is most convincing, and his brilliance is most apparent, when he assumes the mantle of detective and pursues the trail of representativeness-based associations.

Freud not only pointed to the importance of the representativeness heuristic in daily life; he also provided a technique for discovering what stands for what in the mental life of a given person. This technique is free association, in which the patient is instructed to say everything that comes into his mind without censorship or concern for logical connections. The assumption behind the technique, congruent with general psychological assumptions since nineteenth century British associationism, was that the order in which verbal material is produced by such a process is not random or arbitrary but instead reflects similarities and causal connections in the mind of the individual. When, immediately after speaking of his analyst, the pa-tient then speaks about a traffic policeman he has seen the day before, the analyst presumes the idea of analyst to be connected with that of policeman by some notion of representativeness, similarity, or "standing for" in the mind of the patient. Nothing in current psychological theory or research casts doubt on the validity of such a presumption, and there is much that supports it.

A major problem with the assumption (even in Freud's hands, but especially in the hands of many followers) is the uncertainty of criteria for determining when it is the patient's associative networks that have been laid bare and when it is the analyst's. The lack of such criteria is especially evident in such dubious exercises as the psychoanalysis, based on fragmentary and secondhand reports, of historical figures whom the analyst has never met. The same theory and methods that yielded Freud's most compelling analytic insights underlie the analyst Abrahamsen's (1977) "discoveries" about Richard Nixon. The ten year old Nixon apparently was proud of his ability to mash potatoes so smoothly that there were no lumps. Potatoes, Abrahamsen solemnly observes, were a substitute for people.

To our knowledge, psychoanalysis has never adequately dealt with the problem of identifying whether a given link exists in the head of the patient or only of the analyst, and this weakness has been responsible, perhaps more than any other, for exposing the Freudian tradition to scholarly skepticism. A psychoanalyst whose name is widely known to American psychologists and to the broader intellectual community once was heard to muse, at a case con-ference: "Hmm, the patient used the word 'handle' several times. Do we have a problem with masturbation here?" Was this a brilliant analytic in-sight, or was it merely a reflection of the cognitive processes and associations of the eminent analyst? We suspect the latter. As the father of the psychoanalytic tradition himself once remarked, "sometimes a cigar is only a cigar." Unfortunately he did not pass on the rules for making such discriminations to many of his most outspoken disciples.

Representativeness and Causality

The problem of authenticating the analyst's guesses about the patient's connotative networks pales in significance beside a far more devastating weakness. This was Freud's tacit assumption that the scientist could discover the true causes of human behavior by what amounts to an exercise of the representativeness heuristic: Behavior, once its "real" meaning was uncovered by the analyst, could be traced to correspondent motive states and dispositions. In making this assumption, Freud risked elevating the fundamental attribution error to the status of a scientific principle. The wish was to be father to the deed, and all deeds were to be traced to wishes with recognizable parental features. So committed was Freud to this strategy for causal analysis that he was led, by witnessing the slaughter of World War I (and by the newly observed clinical syndrome of masochism), to incorporate into his theory the notion of the death instinct. Like all events, the phenomenon of young men marching off to a likely death in the muddy, stinking, trenches of that war required a dynamic explanation. Since cause must mirror effect, and the effect was death, the cause must be a wish for death.

The enormous popularity of Freudian theory probably lies in the fact that, unlike all its competitors among contemporary views, it encourages the layperson to do what comes naturally in causal explanation, that is, to use the representativeness heuristic. Psychoanalytic theory shares with lay views not only a general causal analytic strategy, but specific assumptions about causality for particular types of events as well. The Chapmans' work, discussed at length in chapter 5, illustrated the remarkable overlap between the analyst's beliefs about covariation between signs and symptoms and the verbal associations and naive theories of the layperson.

It might be objected that at least some of the specific causal hypotheses of psychoanalytic theory do not correspond to lay hypotheses, most notably the great causal significance attached to childhood sexuality. This is true, but while the theory of childhood sexuality was shocking and at odds with some contemporary views of children, it did not completely violate representativeness criteria. On the contrary, childhood sexual experience is highly representative as a general causal factor both because of its significance (sexuality is very important, thus a good causal candidate with respect to magnitude for many equally important effects) and its timing (things that happen early should be formatively important, hence causally important). In addition, once one entertains the theory that sexuality determines behavior of all sorts, it is child's play (pun intended) to generate sexual explanations through the use of the representativeness heuristic. For example, the author now is using his *pen* trying to make a *mess* of what he finds *repellent* in psychoanalytic theory, while simultaneously trying to *retain* what he finds *attractive* in the theory.

The Unconscious and Repression

The authors share with psychoanalytic theorists the view that much, if not most, of mental life is inaccessible to conscious experience. In the view of the authors, however, what is unconscious is normally unconscious for the simplest of reasons: People lack the machinery for bringing the relevant facts into conscious purview. We often do not know why we like or dislike another person for the same reason that we do not know why we perceive an object to be at a given distance. The processes that produce affective judgments, like the processes that produce judgments of depth, are neither verbal in nature nor directly accessible to introspection.

The psychoanalytic account is quite different: In Freud's opinion, much (though not most) of what is inaccessible has been repressed. Unpleasant facts are unavailable to the person because the person does not wish to know them. Such a conclusion is the natural consequence of the theory's reliance on the representativeness heuristic and its susceptibility to the fundamental attribution error. An act must be produced by a correspondent motive; hence the "act" of not knowing an unpleasant mental fact must be due to a desire not to know it.

We do not wish to argue that there is no such thing as repression. We personally do not doubt that people sometimes "deny" the existence of threatening facts and exert psychic energy in their attempts to avoid recognizing them (although, like Erdelyi & Goldberg 1978 we are far more impressed by clinical evidence than by purported demonstrations in the laboratory). We suspect, however, that people normally fail to recognize the existence of painful psychological facts for the same reason that they fail to recognize painless ones—because they are inaccessible. When the painful fact is pointed out to the individual, he may deny its existence for the same reason that subjects in the Nisbett and Wilson studies denied the existence of quite painless facts—because they are implausible.

Our view also differs from the psychoanalytic view on the question of how to make the individual aware of unconscious material. Freud was quite explicit on this point:

> If we communicate to a patient some idea which he has at one time repressed but which we have discovered in him, our telling him does not remove the repression nor undo its effects, as might perhaps be expected from the fact that the previously unconscious idea has now become conscious. On the contrary, all that we shall achieve at first will be a fresh rejection of the repressed idea. At this point, however, the patient has in actual fact the same idea in two forms in two separate localities in his mental apparatus: first, he has the conscious memory of the auditory impression of the idea conveyed in what we told him, and, secondly and side by side with this, he has—as we know for certain—the

unconscious memory of his actual experience existing in him in its earlier form. Now in reality there is no lifting of the repression until the conscious idea, after overcoming the resistances, has united with the unconscious memory-trace. Only through bringing the latter itself into consciousness is the effect achieved. (Freud 1915/1959, p. 108)

Freud believed that direct access to normally unconscious facts was a possibility. There is a "memory-trace" to which the therapist's suggestion can be connected. In our view, there normally would be no memory-trace to be primed, excited, or retrieved. The unconscious fact, whether unpleasant or not, can only be inferred, not discovered. An example may clarify this difference of opinion. Behavior therapists Stuart and Davis (1972) believe that many husbands of the obese women whom they treat have an investment in their wives' unattractive states. The husband may have struck a tacit bargain: Your obesity for my impotence (or my alcoholism, or my failure in my profession). The weight loss of the wife therefore is often threatening to such a man and he sabotages the diet ("I really liked you better the way you were").

The man who feels threatened by his wife's increasing attractiveness might benefit from becoming "aware" of this fact. The Freudian view would seem to be that such insight can be accomplished if, and only if, the therapist's assertion makes contact with the client's repressed knowledge of the fact. In our view, there generally is no such knowledge to be "contacted." If the client is to be made aware of his hidden motive, it must be made plausible to him. The therapist might note for the client, for example, that his last two big benders were associated with his wife's successful attempts at weight loss, or that the client seems oddly concerned with the cost of a new, smaller size wardrobe, and so forth. In short, the therapist must present evidence that the client will have difficulty in explaining plausibly if he does not resort to the therapist's hypothesis.

Undoubtedly, the patient will not yield without offering substantial "resistance," and undoubtedly such resistance, which may take the form of offering alternative explanations and "contradictory data," is in part defensive. But note that the therapist's hypothesis is, in fact, also *implausible* in view of lay theories about husbands, wives, and feminine attractiveness. The lay view is that men like to be married to the most attractive women possible. A desire to have an unattractive wife is, especially to psychologically unsophisticated people, a notion fully as odd as it is threatening. The "discovery" of its truth, if it is made, is an inference from the available data, for the patient just as it is for the therapist. The resistance to such discoveries is no more remarkable than the "resistance" of any formal scientist to unusual propositions challenging a firmly entrenched theory.

It is interesting to speculate whether therapists might encounter less resistance to their interpretations if they were to acknowledge that it might be caused by something other than ego defensiveness. A client who is told that he is "resisting" an interpretation only in order to protect himself and that he could "see" the psychological facts for himself if he were willing, seems likely to continue the struggle. He might be less inclined to resist if he were told that, though the interpretation seems unlikely in view of common-sense notions about human behavior, and though his psychological states can no more be "seen" by the client than by the therapist, such an interpretation seems most consistent with the facts available to both the client and the therapist.

SUMMARY

Although errors in inference or behavior sometimes seem to reflect motives, informational or intellectual factors are often implicated in such errors. When self-serving motives such as ego defensiveness or ego enhancement are influential, the effect seldom is due to "direct" distortion of perception or judgment. Rather, the mediating role of *behavior,* which indisputably is influenced by the actor's motives, but also indisputably changes the nature of the information available to the actor, seems crucial in a great many cases.

Attempts to demonstrate conclusively the effects of motives on covert perceptual, cognitive, or inferential processes have a long and far from encouraging history in psychology. Classic learning theorists, and researchers testing the "New Look" hypothesis, encountered the difficulties both of ruling out nonmotivational interpretations for seemingly motivational phenomena and of proving that there were motivational effects on covert processes rather than merely on overt responses. Two current debates seem to be resurrecting the same issues and ultimately the same interpretative difficulties: One debate is on the role of self-serving biases in the attribution of positive versus negative personal outcomes. The other is on motivational versus cognitive sources of racial and ethnic prejudice.

Examination of these topics suggests that motivational interpretations, despite their intuitive appeal, are hardly demanded by the evidence. In both cases nonmotivational factors seem sufficient to account for most of the phenomena. In the case of so-called ego-defensive biases in attribution, it is clear that actors usually hold preconceptions and possess evidence that on purely intellectual grounds would seem to justify, if not demand, asymmetric responses to success and failure. In the case of prejudice, it seems clear that stereotypes of ethnic or racial groups are similar to the schemas or theories that encapsulate socially based knowledge of many other categories of people, objects, or events. Most important, the *persistence* of unwarranted stereotypes despite logical or evidential attack seems quite explicable by nonmotivational processes. These include the assimilation of available information to preconceptions, the formation of causal theories, and the bolstering effect of belief-relevant behavior, all of which conspire to give stereotypes the illusion of impressive empirical support.

To us, the real phenomenon to be explained is the widespread and generally uncritical acceptance of motivational explanations for erroneous and damaging beliefs. People's use of the representativeness heuristic in general, and their susceptibility to the fundamental attribution error in particular, seem to be reflected in their tendency to embrace motivational explanations.

Psychoanalytic theorists have recognized, as other theorists sometimes have overlooked, that unbridled distortion of perceptual and cognitive processes are generally held in check by the organism's need to respond adaptively to its environment. They also have offered unique insights into the complex, often "representativeness-based" links between covert processes and overt responses. But proponents of psychoanalysis seem seriously compromised by their *own* willingness to link behavior to underlying needs, wishes, or motives on the basis of relatively crude resemblance criteria.

11

assessing the damage

Many people vigorously protest the view of human inferential abilities presented in this book. They argue that people's inferential triumphs are far more impressive, and far more typical, than their failures. Dramatic successes such as placing astronauts on the moon, cracking the genetic code, and unlocking the secrets of the atom, and the less dramatic ones that permit us to enjoy a generally harmonious and comprehensible world, do raise some important questions. How can our species' unparalleled inferential accomplishments be reconciled with this book's seemingly unflattering portrait of lay inference? More to the point, perhaps, have the present authors been unfair in their choice of research and anecdotes? Have we sensitized the reader to instances of inferential folly and thereby fostered highly distorted estimates of the ratio of failures to successes that might be revealed in a more exhaustive or less biased survey? Most important, would such a survey show normatively inappropriate inferences to be restricted largely to contexts in which such errors are inconsequential or even functional for the layperson?

Such questions about the actual damage done by the strategies and tactics of lay inference are the focus for this chapter.

RECONCILING INFERENTIAL
TRIUMPHS WITH INFERENTIAL FAILURES

The Triumphs: Collective and Nonintuitive

Although the challenge to reconcile our point of view with moon landings and the like is somewhat playful, it does force us to begin our assessment of damage by emphasizing how seldom is human society totally at the mercy of intuitive inferential strategies. Humans did not "make it to the moon" (or unravel the mysteries of the double helix or deduce the existence of quarks) by trusting the availability and representativeness heuristics or by relying on the vagaries of informal data collection and interpretation. On the contrary, these triumphs were achieved by the use of formal research methodology and normative principles of scientific inference. Furthermore, as Dawes (1976) pointed out, no single person could have solved all the problems involved in such necessarily collective efforts as space exploration. Getting to the moon was a joint project, if not of *idiots savants,* at least of savants whose individual areas of expertise were extremely limited—one savant who knew a great deal about the propellant properties of solid fuels but little about the guidance capabilities of small computers, another savant who knew a great deal about the guidance capabilities of small computers but virtually nothing about gravitational effects on moving objects, and so forth. Finally, those savants included people who believed that redheads are hot-tempered, who bought their last car on the cocktail-party advice of an acquaintance's brother-in-law, and whose mastery of the formal rules of scientific inference did not notably spare them the social conflicts and personal disappointments experienced by their fellow humans.

The very impressive results of organized intellectual endeavor, in short, provide no basis for contradicting our generalizations about human inferential shortcomings. Those accomplishments are collective, at least in the sense that we all stand on the shoulders of those who have gone before; and most of them have been achieved by using normative principles of inference often conspicuously absent in everyday life. Most importantly, there is no logical contradiction between the assertion that people can be very impressively intelligent on some occasions or in some domains and the assertion that they can make howling inferential errors on other occasions or in other domains.

The Failures: Limited to the Laboratory?

The complaint that the present authors have been unfair and unrepresentative in their "sampling" is less easily dismissed. More than once the suspicion has been voiced that investigators working in this tradition have a sharp eye for the occasional judgmental frailty and that they craftily construct laboratory experiments to exploit such lapses. The implication is that the investigators are trying to pass off a few puckish demonstrations as a faithful portrait of human inferential incapacity.

In some ways we would plead guilty to at least a muted version of this charge. Indeed, one goal of this chapter will be to flesh out the "biased sampling" objection and explore the possibility that the actual everyday damage done by the layperson's shortcomings may be relatively slight. However, complaints about the heavy use of laboratory demonstrations occasionally carry a further implication. They sometimes imply that it is *only* in the laboratory that one can demonstrate the overutilization of intuitive strategies or the underutilization of normative ones. We adamantly reject this view. We insist that the errors demonstrated in the laboratory and chronicled in this book are the ingredients of individual and collective human tragedy.

Our impatience with critics who would dismiss the laboratory evidence as the hothouse products of devious experimenters is based on our belief that such critics fail to compare the pitfalls faced by the subject in the laboratory tasks with those that the same person is likely to face in everyday behavioral or judgmental dilemmas. As we noted at several points, the laboratory procedures often lead to an *underestimation* of the magnitude of particular inferential failings. One example is the crucial task of detecting covariation. Recall that the laboratory tasks almost always presented subjects with already "prepackaged" and highly "processed" data. By contrast, in everyday experience, observers must decide for themselves which data are pertinent and how they are to be sampled, must resolve any ambiguities in coding, must store and retrieve the data, and must find a way to aggregate and display the data.

Or recall the research on the layperson's tendency to maintain impressions or beliefs after their evidence base has been thoroughly discredited. In the laboratory, the discrediting manipulations were completely decisive and they followed almost immediately upon the initial receipt of the evidence. In the real world, discrediting is rarely either immediate or incontrovertible. Typically, attacks on the evidence that prompted initial beliefs are themselves subject to alternative interpretation and to refutation. Even when seemingly decisive attacks occur, they are apt to take place only after the individual has had considerable opportunity to process new evidence in the light of his beliefs and sometimes even to reinforce his beliefs with consonant behavior.

Perhaps the most important of the ecologically unrepresentative advantages enjoyed by the laboratory subject is that experimenters typically make it explicitly clear that they are soliciting inferences or judgments from the subject. In everyday life, many inferential errors might be eliminated, or at least reduced, if the "subjects" were to recognize explicitly that they were, in fact, engaged in making an inference. The individual who hears a cocktail party anecdote about an automotive lemon, or sees a volcano while on vacation, or passes an able-bodied individual sitting on a park bench in midday, is not told: "Here is some evidence. Now answer the following questions about the conclusions that can be drawn on the basis of such evidence." But many laboratory procedures go even further than that in coaxing subjects to be on their best inferential behavior. Subjects are explicitly told that the experiment is a *test* of inferential or judgmental skills.

Our greatest impatience with those who suggest that systematic inferential failings are restricted to exotic laboratory contexts stems from the regularity with which everyday experience seemingly parallels the relevant laboratory findings. President Lyndon Johnson led his country into a futile war by evoking potent social schemas of Munich-like capitulation, falling dominoes, aggressive foreign hordes, and bullies who had to be taught a lesson. Every day, people make harmful and damaging judgments about themselves, or harmful judgments about their spouses even to the point of severing marriages, because they wrongly attribute current crises to stable personal dispositions instead of to transient situational pressures. Deserving job candidates are daily denied jobs by personnel managers (and university committees) who see no reason to doubt that the vivid data provided by thirty-minute personal interviews and stress-laden "job talks" reveal new truths that were somehow obscured in pallid résumés, test scores, or letters of recommendation. Civic and state leaders regularly refute charges of police brutality or deplorable prison conditions on the basis of their "samples" of police behavior or their personal tours of penal institutions. Between the Age of Enlightenment and the middle of the nineteenth century, thousands and perhaps millions of people died at the hands of physicians whose opportunities to witness empirical covariations between treatments and outcomes did not destroy their confidence in the therapeutic effects of such practices as blood-letting. As the twentieth century begins to draw to a close, intelligent people make a multimillion-dollar industry of astrology and fill the pockets of quacks and self-styled gurus who promise to cure medical, personal, or social ills.

People, in short, do not suddenly assume a mantle of credulity or ignorance when they walk into the laboratory. On the contrary, there is reason to believe that they wear their Sunday best when they enter the psychologist's sanctum.

Finally, we wish to stress two additional points concerning generalizability from the laboratory to everyday life. Many of the laboratory studies have been replicated in non-laboratory contexts and in settings where subjects did not even know that they were participants in an experiment. This is true both for many studies in the attribution tradition and for many studies in the judgment tradition. Sometimes it is children who are the subjects, taking part in what they believe to be standard classroom activities; sometimes it is expert professionals who are the subjects (for example, in the Chapmans' work), innocently giving the investigator what they believe to be simply "information" about their professional practices or inferential strategies; and sometimes the subjects are the standard college sophomores, but participating in what they believe to be a test not of themselves but of some new psychological instrument or institutional procedure. In such cases, one is generalizing not from the laboratory to everyday life, but from one slice of everyday life to another.

We are often confronted with the suggestion that results from studies like those discussed in this book might be quite different if subjects were paid for judgmental accuracy, the implication being that subjects care so little about their performance in the inferential tasks presented to them that they give slipshod, off-the-cuff answers. The suggestion never ceases to surprise us, especially when it comes, as we must admit it often does, from our fellow professional psychologists. It makes us wonder if such psychologists have ever chatted with their own subjects about their experiments and their subjects' reactions to them. As we have just argued, we find that our subjects take their participation very seriously indeed and care a great deal about the sensibleness of their responses, so much so that it would never have occurred to us to attempt to improve subject performance by monetary incentives. Nevertheless, we have occasionally offered such incentives, and so have Kahneman and Tversky and many other investigators, in order to be able to confront skeptics with something more convincing than gasps and arm-waving. In general, incentives for accuracy produce no systematic effect on accuracy. Such incentives sometimes cause judgments to change in such a way as to maximize subjects' expected *payoff*, but even this effect is the exception. Subjects call it as they see it, and money does not seem to much affect their eyesight.

Although we vehemently dispute the suggestion that serious inferential errors are restricted to the laboratory, we cannot deny that readers could have been misled somewhat by the emphasis of earlier chapters. We happen to share the critic's view that people may not make as many inferential errors as one might assume from a simple list of the inferential failings that have been demonstrated.

In fact, some critics might be surprised by how much we are willing to concede: We believe it is possible that most people may get through most of their days without making *any* major inferential errors leading to untoward behavioral consequences. This concession is not very reassuring, since it takes only a few such errors to seriously disrupt individual and collective social existence. But if, as we suspect, inferential errors of major consequence are relatively infrequent in everyday life, it is worth considering what it is that protects the intuitive scientist from paying the potential costs of his shortcomings. We focus on four such potentially mitigating factors: (a) intuitive strategies may typically serve us fairly well even when they are, strictly speaking, normatively inappropriate; (b) many of the most important inferences are collective, and the errors of the group may be prevented by a single person; (c) different shortcomings may sometimes cancel each other out; and (d) the behavioral consequences of erroneous judgments typically may be muted.

We wish to make it clear at the outset of our discussion that we are in no way recanting our belief that people regularly make serious inferential errors and that they sometimes pay very dear for these errors. We merely wish to assert that there may be a good many factors at work that serve to limit the damage and that may even operate in such a way as to encourage the survival of nonoptimal inferential strategies.

WHEN INTUTIVIE STRATEGIES SERVE US WELL

As we have emphasized at many junctures, our everyday or "intuitive" strategies serve us well in many judgmental contexts. The availability heuristic does help us form accurate estimates of frequency or likelihood in many domains, that is, in those domains in which the perceptual or memorial salience of objects or events is not distorted by factors irrelevant to the probability of their occurrence. The availability heuristic helps us to judge, accurately and immediately, that there are more Chinese restaurants in Palo Alto than in Ann Arbor (we remember seeing more), and that the new Albanian restaurant in the suburbs is more likely to go bankrupt than the new McDonalds in the shopping plaza (we can more readily construct a scenario for failure).

Similarly, the representativeness heuristic, for all the judgmental folly it can inspire, is a prompt and faithful servant in a great many domains, particularly where objects or events are characterized by properties that are both unique and invariant. Thus, we do not confuse oak trees with telephone poles, or Anglican bishops with door-to-door salesmen. And people whose business it is to know about trees do not confuse oaks with maples; nor do people whose business it is to know about prelates confuse bishops with abbots.

Our schemas and theories similarly stand us in good stead most of the time. Generic knowledge typically is well founded—in someone else's experience even if not always in our own—and it normally serves as an automatic guide to effective behavior. This is particularly true in the many cases in which events and event sequences are simple and invariant. Thus we all learn early, and seldom need to be reminded, that switches turn on lights, and hot things burn. Even relationships that are only near invariant (for example, transgressing the rules of powerful people results in punishment if the transgression is discovered; apologies and soft answers turn away wrath) are readily learned by observation or instruction and may serve as near-infallible guides for behavior.

As we have emphasized, heuristics and knowledge structures do sometimes lead people astray when they are overextended or misapplied. Even then, the resulting errors often are inconsequential and are readily forgiven by those with whom we interact. Rarely is it the case in social dealings that a "miss is as good as a mile." If we temporarily mistake a bishop for an abbot, or for that matter an engineer for a librarian, there are few social consequences. When there *would* be consequences—if we started asking the engineer about the Dewey decimal system for classifying books—we usually have our error quickly pointed out to us.

Thus, as we have emphasized at many points, people's intuitive inferential strategies are probably used appropriately and effectively in the great majority of cases. In many cases where they are not strictly appropriate, they may nevertheless yield answers that are similar or identical to those that would be produced by more appropriate strategies. And in many of the remaining cases, where answers are in fact wrong, environmental feedback may force a ready revision. Finally, the "cost" of intuitive strategies is generally so low, relative to that of more formal strategies, that it seems distinctly possible that the long range "economics" of their habitual, preferential use is well in balance, even allowing for fairly high frequency, in absolute if not in relative terms, of their disadvantageous consequences.

WHEN IGNORANCE OF NORMATIVE RULES MAY COST US LITTLE

As we often have stressed, ignorance of the normative rules of inference can result in gross and painful errors, small errors, or no errors at all, depending on the nature of the judgment. It might be useful, however, to speculate about which normative rules generally can be ignored with little cost and which cannot. Considerations of space prohibit us from undertaking a full review of all the normative rules discussed in the book. We shall restrict ourselves to three—one rule, that of the law of large numbers, for which we suspect people may pay a surprisingly low cost for ignorance; one rule, namely the requirement of random or unbiased samples, for which we suspect the cost of ignorance may be distressingly high, and one rule, namely the requirement to revert to base rate or central tendency when highly diagnostic target information is lacking, for which the questions about costs are complex and difficult to resolve but also highly illuminating.

Sample Size

People have little understanding of the relationship between the size of a sample and its faithfulness in reflecting the characteristics of the population from which it was drawn. For certain sophisticated problems of statistical inference this ignorance can be fatal, but in a great many everyday contexts it may be far less costly than the formal statistician might imagine.

Consider the case of a student who must make course selections for the coming semester and who wishes to consult a sample of past student evaluations. For the sake of simplicity let us assume: a) that some proportion (P) of the relevant population liked the course "better than average" while the remainder (1–P) liked it "less than average"; b) that the student's objective is to select a given course if, and only if, the *majority* of the population liked it "better than average"; and (c) that the probability that the student in question personally will like a given course is identical to the population proportion who like the course.

Figure 11.1 summarizes the consequences of four different decision strategies that the student might consider adopting. The first strategy is choosing or rejecting a course without regard to any sample of peer opinion at all, that is, just flipping a coin and taking the course if the coin shows "heads" and not taking it if the coin shows "tails." The second strategy is consulting a single, randomly sampled student and taking the course if the student liked it, and not taking it if the student didn't like it. The third strategy is a bit more complex but it may offer a good approximation of the way many people actually would operate in the course selection problem. It consists of consulting *two* students and taking the course if both liked it, not taking the course if neither liked it, and sampling a third and decisive case (a "tiebreaker") if the first two disagreed.[1] The fourth strategy is the conservative (and costly) extreme of sampling the entire population and then taking or not taking the course depending on the majority evaluation.

The left portion of each panel in Figure 11.1 presents the degree of "normative correctness" of the decisions that would result from these four

---

[1] This "two cases plus tiebreaker" strategy is essentially equivalent to that of sampling three cases (in which no "tie" is possible), except that the former strategy specifies that the effort and expense of a third case be avoided when the first two cases have agreed and hence have already determined one's decision.

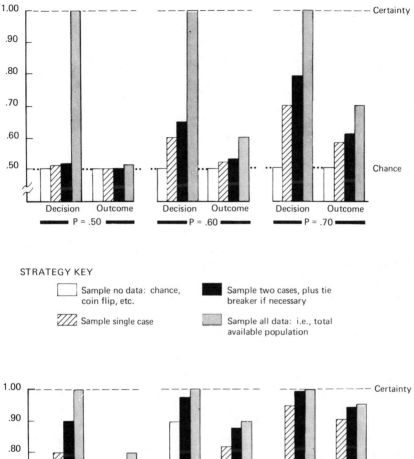

STRATEGY KEY

☐ Sample no data: chance, coin flip, etc.

▨ Sample single case

■ Sample two cases, plus tie breaker if necessary

▨ Sample all data: i.e., total available population

Fig. 11.1 Probabilities associated with normatively correct decision (DECISION) and personally advantageous outcome (OUTCOME): A comparison of four sampling strategies across varying population proportions (P).

strategies (that is, the likelihood that the student will, as a result of using the strategy, take a course that the majority likes or avoid a course which the majority dislikes). It is immediately clear that the strategies of consulting a "single case" or consulting "two cases plus a tiebreaker" fare quite badly when P is near .5, but serve quite well when P approaches unity (or zero). In other words, if there is high consensus about the course, the strategy of asking one student, or asking two students plus a tiebreaker when necessary, generally leads to normatively correct decisions. For example, if 80 percent of the previous students liked (or disliked) the course, the strategy of sampling a single case rather than relying on a coin flip increases the probability of a normatively correct decision all the way from .5 to .8; the strategy of sampling two cases and a tiebreaker raises it almost to .9. Any additional sampling the student could do, up to the extreme of sampling *all* previous students, could only raise the likelihood of a correct decision from .9 to 1.0. This pattern becomes even clearer when the population proportion shifts from .8 to .9. Now, informal sampling strategies become overwhelmingly attractive. In fact, the likelihood of making an incorrect decision with the "two plus tiebreaker" strategy is .03, lower than the .05 level beloved by social scientists. On the other hand, if only 60 percent of the population of former students liked or disliked the course, the use of a single case or even two or three cases would do the prospective student little good. Sampling a single case instead of relying on chance would only raise the likelihood of a normatively correct decision from .5 to .6, and the "two plus tiebreaker" strategy would raise it only to .65.

The outcomes summarized so far are merely a specific demonstration of what every statistician knows about the relationship between "power" and sample size. Strong statistical differences or "effects" are revealed in small samples but weak ones generally are not. If a social scientist wanted to know definitely whether the majority of the students liked a course—that is, if he wanted to be certain before deciding upon a hypothesis that predicted P to be greater than .5—he would be incompetent indeed if he used the "one case" or "two cases plus tiebreaker" strategy and thereby ran a high risk of failing to detect small but real "effects."

But our student's concern is not simply to make normatively correct decisions. What the student wants is to maximize the likelihood of personally advantageous outcomes. That is, the student wishes to know the impact of each of the four sampling strategies on the chances of the decision leading to one of the two desirable outcomes—taking a course that he will like or avoiding a course he would have disliked.

The right portion of each panel of Figure 11.1 presents the likelihoods of actually obtaining a desired outcome, and they can be summarized quite succinctly. Large samples *never* prove to be very helpful. When there is high consensus, small samples do almost as good a job of optimizing personal outcomes as very large samples do. When there is low consensus, small samples are of little value, but under such conditions *large samples also are of little value.* The reason for this is simply that when the population has a fairly even division of opinion, a normatively correct decision offers little likely advantage over an incorrect one.[2]

One particular "extreme case" deserves special mention. When there is virtually total consensus (or, more generally, whenever one samples from a population that has virtually no variability), the sampling of a single case is tremendously helpful. Thus the traveler benefits enormously when he asks directions from a single local resident rather than relying upon a "coin flip." Similarly, the curious individual who wishes to know the number of teeth in a horse's mouth, and wishes to do so with data rather than guesswork or logical deduction, will be served very well by "sampling" a single horse.

Our suspicion is that people behave very much as the implications of our extended example would dictate. When in doubt about a course of action for which data might be helpful, one generally samples a case, or two, or even three when the first two cases disagree. Whether one consults a second case after sampling a first depends on prior expectations of the degree of variability to be found among sampled cases.

We should not forget that people's decision-making strategies are sometimes confidently based on data samples that are even less probative, and "smaller" even than the N of 1 in the "sample one case" strategy above: Students sometimes select a course not on the advice of a friend who has attended it through an entire term but on the basis of a friend's "sample" of the first day of class; and people sometimes confidently infer on the basis of a five-minute conversation at a party that, despite her reputation, Jane is a bore.

We therefore should not lose sight of the fact that reliance upon very small samples is sometimes not a reasonable strategy. If the same behavioral choice is to be faced many times, or if the cost of errors is likely to be compounded, the effort or expense involved in securing large samples may well be justified. If statistics based on large samples are available at no extra cost, they are surely preferable to single cases or statistics based on more limited

---

[2] Note that the probability associated with personally advantageous outcomes represents the sum of two products; it is the probability of the student deciding to take the course times the probability he would like it, *plus* the probability of the student deciding not to take it times the probability he would not like it. Consider, for example, the case in which $P = .8$, and the sampling strategy requires the sampling of two students plus a "tiebreaker" if necessary. A personally advantageous outcome results *either* if the student's sampling strategy leads him to the normatively correct decision to take the course $[P = .8^2 + 2(.8)^2(.2) = .896]$ and he then finds himself in the majority that likes it ($P = .8$), *or* if his strategy leads to the normatively incorrect decision to avoid the course ($P = .2^2 + 2(.8)(.2)^2 = .104$) but he nevertheless is in the minority that would have disliked the course ($P = .2$); that is, the probability of a personally advantageous outcome in this instance is $(.896)(.8) + (.104)(.2) = .738$.

samples. If we are interested in the relative prices of four-bedroom houses in comparable Palo Alto and Ann Arbor neighborhoods, or if we want to know the size of fully grown Great Danes, or if we want to choose between the Western at the Roxy or the comedy at the Bijou, we will probably be as accurate as we need to be if we simply consult a couple of new home buyers, dog owners, or movie goers. But if we want to operate mortgage or insurance companies, or if the costs of a wrong judgment are very great, we had better continue to heed the advice of the formal statistician. Even if our interests are limited to a single, less-than-urgently important decision, we ought to use the best data that are freely available to us.

The question of what constitutes the "best" data available goes beyond the issue of sample size to that of sample bias. Hence, our next topic.

Sample Bias

Although the damage resulting from faith in *small* data samples often may be both limited in magnitude and justified by the savings in effort, the case seems quite different when we turn our attention to the question of faith in *biased* data. Here, ignorance or credulity can have serious costs, even though, as we shall see, people are not without defenses. Chapter 4 examined the laboratory evidence showing people's insensitivity to the perils of biased data. We should like to supplement this evidence with some additional, anecdotal examples.

The Ann Arbor author of the present book had been eating in an excellent restaurant in Palo Alto with the Palo Alto author of the book. "Alas" (or some similar expression of dismay), said the Ann Arbor author, "among all the other advantages of Northern California over Southern Michigan, it hardly seems fair for your restaurants also to be so much better." "What do you mean?" retorted the Palo Alto author, "I've yet to get a bad or overpriced meal in Ann Arbor, and let me assure you I've had plenty of both in Palo Alto." Both authors then mused about their disagreement, each searching for the source of his colleague's misperception. Clever scientists that they are, it took the authors only a few minutes to solve the mystery of the discrepant perceptions: Each author had quite deliberately, as befits a host, presented the other with a sample of local restaurants that was extremely biased with respect to quality and price. Tourists in large cities often have a related, but opposite, experience. They sample eateries at random—or worse, they sample tourist traps at random—and then conclude that the restaurant situation in that city is terrible, far inferior to that in their own towns where one can get a good, reasonably priced meal "just by going to Luigi's" or "just by driving to that little out-of-the-way place on Busby Boulevard."

Our real-world examples of susceptibility to biased data could be multiplied indefinitely. The bachelor and the married man who each feel undue envy because of the "data samples" that each makes available to (or hides from) the other, is one familiar example. The two mothers, each of whom is surprised to hear her own child described by the other as an obedient and cooperative little angel instead of a quarrelsome little savage (because each samples "home" behavior of her own child but "visiting" behavior of the other child) offer another example.

In sum, for the case of sample bias, unlike that of sample size, it is not difficult to cite real-world examples of inferential errors that have nontrivial consequences. The source of the errors, moreover, can be extremely difficult to track down, even for the formally-trained scientist.

The conclusion should not be overstated, however. A little thought suggests that people sometimes have healthy defenses against biased data.

Protection Against Mendacious or Self-Interested Informants

It seems likely that we are fairly well protected against presentations of biased evidence by the patently self-interested informant. Few people are likely to be enticed by the new butcher shop's offer to sell "100 pounds of beef at less than wholesale prices" when the proprietor emerges from the back room with a lovely steak and says "most of the meat is already packed but this piece is pretty typical of what you'll find in your 100 pound order." Similarly, few consumers are willing to accept paid testimonials as accurate indicators of the satisfaction one could expect from the use of a given product or service.

People seem also to have a healthy skepticism about statistics presented by politicians, government or industrial apologists, salespeople, and others who have an obvious motive to persuade. "You can prove anything with statistics" or "There are lies, damn lies, and statistics" are two popular expressions of such skepticism. People often seem to have, however, a better appreciation of the professional spokesman's ability to pick and choose among statistics than of his ability to pick and choose among concrete cases that are summarized in such statistics. Thus, the economic advisor who assures the country that the seasonally adjusted unemployment rate has decreased by two-tenths of a percentage point may be greeted with cynical eye rolling, but a TV news item about a single aerospace worker who has landed a good job after three months of unemployment may renew many viewers' optimism.

The "Atypical Situation" Script

The "mendacious informant" script is perhaps the most general and familiar schema which offers protection to people, but there are many others. Most professors, for instance, have learned that the sample of behavior offered by freshman advisees in their first meeting is not a random or representative one. If the student appears inarticulate, indecisive, or even unintelligent, experienced advisors typically recognize that the student's performance may be biased by his nervousness and uncertainty about the interaction. Unfortunately, as we noted earlier, most of these same professors are not similarly experienced in dealing with job candidates. They do not give the same benefit of the doubt to poor performances, or withhold enthusiasm in the case of an unusually polished performance, when a new Ph.D. presents a job talk. The problem partially may lie in the opportunity for subsequent verification. Over the years, scores of advisees have proved themselves far more sensible and talented than the first interview might have suggested. Job candidates who are not hired, however, disappear from immediate view, and if they do prove successful it is usually several years later, at which time their success can be attributed to growth and experience rather than to the very qualities that were obscured in the job interview situation.

Thus, the mere fact that a situation is atypical does not guarantee a recognition of this fact and a consequent reluctance to take the data at face value. Nevertheless, it seems clear that atypicality is often recognized, especially when feedback occurs, and some protection against bias therefore results.

The "Discrepancy from Expectations" Cue

There are many causal explanations or schemas on which people may draw when a particular performance differs from expectations. If a world-class tennis champion loses in straight sets to an unknown, if one's star pupil does miserably on an exam, if a normally witty and charming guest is morose at one's dinner party, or if a great dancer performs far below par, people do not normally accept the evidence at face value and drastically revise their previous impressions. Instead, they readily generate causal theories or scripts involving factors such as illness, personal problems, or overwork.

What people seem to lack is a *general* vigilance about the possibility of biased data. Although they respond to unexpected outcomes by entertaining the possibility of sampling bias, they do not entertain such a possibility so readily for expected or neutral outcomes. Although they are sensitive to the fact that motivated communicators may offer them biased samples, they are far less aware that quite disinterested people, with no particular motive or desire to mislead, may also present biased data. Many role- and situation-specific biases offer no salient cues about the distortions they produce in the available evidence. Finally, as many of our examples and much of the research shows, people do not seem to realize that their particular niches in the universe may funnel unrepresentative evidence or information to them in a thousand different domains.

It is hard to avoid the conclusion that people suffer a great deal from their failure to understand the possibilities that exist for data bias, and for their failure to understand in general terms just how much damage can be done by such bias. The "special purpose" scripts and cues that prompt recognition of bias seem to us to be missing in many if not most cases where the available data are sufficiently biased to guarantee erroneous inferences.

Reliance on Target Information
Over Base Rates and Central Tendencies

People's inclination to ignore base rates and central tendencies and to focus almost exclusively on potentially diagnostic information about the "target case" is well documented. What is less clear is how costly this tendency might be and what degree of protection people might have against it.

Equal or Unknown Base Rates

As we noted in chapter 2, the tendency to ignore base rates obviously is without consequences when the base rates in question are roughly equal. This is true for some natural categories; there are roughly equal numbers of men and women, Frenchmen and Englishmen, sociology professors and history professors. The tendency is also without consequences when base rates are unknown and unobtainable.

But there are many decisions for which the base rates in question are known and do have predictive value. On such occasions, it is folly to disregard the base rate. Sometimes one must decide on the relative weights that should be placed, respectively, on discouraging base-rate and encouraging target-case information, or vice versa. Should the hot prospect for quarterback be given the huge bonus he seeks, which otherwise could be used to buy veteran performers of known abilities, given that: a) in background and appearance, he is the spitting image of the erstwhile great Joe Namath, but b) a perusal of the records would show that only 10 percent of the "prospects" who are signed to bonuses ever become members of the starting team? Should Horace Snade, the convicted murderer who has served twenty years of a life term be granted parole given that: a) his crime was a particularly heinous one and his prison record has been marked by fights and an uncooperative attitude towards guards, but b) 90 percent of paroled murderers who have served as long as Snade have made a success of their paroles? It is to such dilemmas (and to the many related parametric problems in which the individual must recognize the need to make predictions that are appropriately "regressed" toward the mean) that people are most vulnerable.

Highly Diagnostic Target Information

There is an important, special case in which inattention to base rates or central tendencies has little practical significance. When information about a target case is highly diagnostic, that is, when the covariation between target features and outcome categories is virtually perfect, people's overreliance on representativeness criteria may cost them very little. Even the subjects in Kahneman's and Tversky's (1973) classic demonstration would have been safe in ignoring base rates for engineers versus lawyers if they had been told that one of the target cases worked for a firm that designed computer circuits and displayed a bumper sticker on his car reading "Kiss me, I'm an engineer." The base rates would not be literally irrelevant to an exact determination of probabilities, even in such a case. In terms of the "odds," the relative likelihood of engineer in such a case is much greater if engineers are common than if they are uncommon in the relevant population. But for *practical* purposes, the difference is between a very, very high likelihood and virtual certainty—a difference that would generally matter little. Similarly, if the correlation between two variables is .95, it will do little harm if the individual making the prediction fails to be regressive at all—that is, unless his concern is testing an exact scientific hypothesis, or making an actuarial prediction for insurance purposes, or some other prediction where the marginal gains for precision are very great.

Causality and Concreteness

As we noted in chapter 7, there is good reason to believe that, even in the absence of a general sophisticated understanding of Bayes' theorem or of regression phenomena, people may be sensitive to base rates in many specific contexts. When people can place a causal interpretation on the base rate, or when they have experienced the base rate concretely, they can make substantial use of it. Perhaps the great majority of problems which are properly regarded as involving a contest between base-rate and target-case information are characterized by one or both of these factors. When three year old Jennifer announces that she saw a tiger on the playground, her parents will have a strong recognition, on grounds of concrete experience and well-founded causal theory, that the base rate for tigers in the neighborhood cannot be set aside in favor of their young informant's testimony, no matter how impassioned it may be.

Novel vs. Recurrent Decisions

An important implication of the considerations above is that, for many judgments of a recurrent nature, people may come to appreciate the relevance of base rates, if not in general terms then at least in concrete, "scripted" terms which can allow effective use of the base rate. With enough immediate feedback, and suitable conditions of presentation, people can show very fine sensitivity to base rate information (cf. Hammond and others 1975). The manager of a professional athletic team, the graduate student adviser, the horse breeder, are all likely to come to recognize that hot prospects often stumble and dark horses sometimes take the lead. Similarly, people whose job it is to make predictions about product sales, the weather, or stock performance seem to reach a kind of humility or conservatism that is functionally equivalent to regressiveness. The very tendencies of which we were critical in chapter 8, for example people's penchant for unchecked causal theorizing, may serve the purpose of generating maxims and rules of thumb that are regressive in their force ("These hot shots often get too much praise and attention, and then they slack off and stop working as hard").

The range of circumstances in which people are seriously hobbled by their lack of a general appreciation of base-rate and regression considerations may be relatively narrow. These circumstances may be summarized on the basis of the preceding discussion: (a) when the judgment is a novel one and the individual has had no concrete experience with the relevant base rates and no opportunity to generate causal theories about them, and (b) when base-rates are known to be unequal and target-case information is not actually diagnostic. The number of such occasions may be large in absolute terms but sufficiently small in relative terms to render people's ignorance of base-rate considerations less surprising, and the resulting damage less severe, than might be implied by our discussion in earlier chapters.

And The Reverend Bayes
May Have To Give a Little Ground Too

The layperson's failure to be a doctrinaire Bayesian may in the near future seem to be even less of a mystery than it does at the present time. The mathematician Shafer (1976) and the measurement theorists Krantz and Miyamoto (1980) recently have begun to develop a normative theory of inference which seems able to handle the same range of problems covered by Bayesian theory. It is beyond the scope of this book (not to mention the competence of its authors) even to outline this theory. One of its central features, however, is its deliberate nonutilization (or heavy discounting) of the base rate in many problems where the Bayesian insists on its full employment.

As of the writing of this book, it does not appear that much if any of the Kahneman-Tversky research or normative analysis of specific problems would be called into question by this new non-Bayesian position. But it is important to note that the Bayesian analysis of problems quite similar to typical Kahneman-Tversky problems has been sharply criticized. It is also of great interest that the new, "Shaferian" theory appears to correspond more closely to intuitive principles and to actual lay inferential practice than does Bayesian theory.

INFERENCE AS A COLLECTIVE ENTERPRISE

Cultural Transmission of Knowledge

There are several senses in which people protect each other from the inferential errors to which they might otherwise be prone. Perhaps the most important is that we all are the beneficiaries of a tremendous amount of knowledge built up by past and present "experts," cultural specialists operating in subfields of inquiry. Much of the knowledge that is most important to survival and effective functioning does not require original inferential work. Corporation executives are not thrown upon their own resources for estimating most of the parameters that play an important role in their decisions. Tourists need not try to estimate for themselves the quality of restaurants from their external features, and browsers need not judge books by their covers. People do not have to try to estimate whether they are in any danger from smoking cigarettes by observing the illness and mortality rates of their acquaintances.

The fact that a certain amount of culturally supplied information is incorrect, or is erroneously applied, does not detract from the fact that an enormous amount of inferential work is done for us by other people who work at least with more information than we have, and often with normatively correct procedures of inference as well.

Novel Inferences and Social "Quality Control"

Novel or "first-time" inferences in daily life are subject to social verification procedures in much the same way that new scientific findings may be scrutinized by the scientific community. The more public is the forum in which the inference is presented, the larger is the number of potential critics. These critics may possess knowledge or may be able to offer arguments that either support or cast doubt on the inference.

It would be extremely interesting to know how many of the inferential errors reported in this book would survive intact after an open discussion among groups of ten or twelve subjects. Our guess is that most of the errors would at least be substantially reduced. Even if only one individual in the group were able to come up with a normatively correct answer, providing that he could offer persuasive arguments in favor of it, the group would be likely to shift their answers in the normatively correct direction. The evidence on group vs. individual problem-solving efficacy (e.g. Kelley & Thibaut, 1954; Davis, 1973; Vinokur and Burnstein, 1978) suggests that, in general, group solutions are superior to individual solutions, though this conclusion must be heavily qualified by noting that the extra time taken by groups is sometimes not cost-effective, and, even more importantly, that for some problems and some group compositions, *less* accurate solutions may result from group than from individual problem-solving (see, for example, Janis & Mann 1977). It should not be taken for granted that, for all the sorts of problems discussed in this book, group discussion would serve to reduce errors; though it seems likely that it would do so for most.

Correctness versus Consensus

It is important to note that, for many beliefs and inferences, it is probably as important that they be shared as that they be correct. Harmonious social interaction often may depend more on consensus about the world than on accuracy. It does not really matter whether both of us call a spade a spade or both of us call it a shovel or even a spoon, as long as each knows what the other means and agrees to use the implement in the same way. It is chastening to be reminded how much harmony is possible in closed, primitive societies whose cosmologies are a patchwork of figment and error. Even those societies which harbor extremely erroneous and dangerous assumptions about causality (for example, a belief in witchcraft) may pay a surprisingly small price for their shared misconceptions.

COMPENSATORY ERRORS

It seems distinctly possible that the effect of some erroneous inference processes may be compensated for by other erroneous processes, so that the net result is more benign than one might expect from the individual contributions to that result. We discussed one case of directly compensating biases in chapter 7 in our discussion of the "dilution effect."

Nisbett and his colleagues (Nisbett and Zukier, 1979; Zukier, 1979;

Nisbett and Lemley, 1979), it will be recalled, showed that when subjects are asked to make predictions about target cases based on a combination of "diagnostic" and "nondiagnostic" information about the targets, both types of information tend to be used in a normatively inappropriate fashion. The diagnostic information is treated "nonregressively" while the nondiagnostic information is treated, in effect, as if it were diagnostic of "averageness." The net result of these two opposing or compensating errors often is a prediction that mimics the one that would result from the more appropriate strategy of ignoring the nondiagnostic information and treating the diagnostic information in a properly regressive fashion.

Other examples of directly compensating errors may be cited. For instance, in domains where outcomes are due to some combination of ability and opportunity, predictions about these outcomes are apt to reflect the influence of both the "fundamental attribution error" and a version of the "gambler's fallacy." The former encourages people to assume that outcomes reflect stable dispositions of the actor and hence that future outcomes generally will resemble past ones. The latter makes individuals believe that the future somehow compensates for unusual outcome patterns by reversing those patterns ("Joe has been riding high, but he is surely heading for a fall," or "After all that Sally has been through, she is due for a few good breaks.") Taken together, the net effect of these two biases may be the eminently reasonable prediction that an actor's future outcomes will resemble his past outcomes, but be less extreme.

The assumption that errors may cancel each other out, that two inferential wrongs miraculously produce an inferential right, may seem Panglossian and facile, and we are reluctant to press the point without more specific evidence. Less facile perhaps, is the more general and essentially statistical argument that if a reasonably large number of independent biases operate, the net error that results is bound to be less than the sum of their individual effects.

It may be the case that two erroneous but countervailing inferential rules may be invoked by the same problem features often enough that the impact of any given erroneous rule is softened considerably. It is even possible that some erroneous inferential rules are reinforced by feedback or experience precisely *because* they habitually combat the consequences of others. Particular inferential shortcomings may be neutralized and may therefore survive if they typically occur in contexts in which there are compensatory biases.

Perhaps even more often, a given problem may trigger two or more normatively incorrect inferential procedures which produce two or more *different* conclusions. Such a conflict, in turn, may prompt a more thorough and normatively appropriate inferential strategy, or referral of the problem to experts. It seems likely that, in general, the more consequential the inference is, the more likely it is that such "reserves" will be called up in the event of conflicting judgments.

INFERENCE AND BEHAVIOR

Perhaps the most important source of protection from the errors produced by intuitive strategies is that ill-advised inferences do not necessarily result in ill-advised behavior. Sometimes, erroneous inferences may have no behavioral consequences or may have consequences indistinguishable from those that would follow from correct inferences. Even when the behavioral consequences are different from those of correct inference, those consequences nevertheless may have equal or greater utility.

Incorrect Inferences with No Behavioral Costs

It seems clear that many inferences have no behavioral consequences or at any rate result only in inconsequential behavior. In fact, it seems likely that this is true for the great majority of our beliefs and inferences, whether correct or incorrect. Inferences about the relative frequency of maple trees versus oak trees, or bishops versus abbots, or about the proportion of unemployed persons, blue-eyed persons, or antiabortion advocates, normally lack behavioral implications for the actor. Only seldom are people called upon to act in accordance with beliefs about covariation, such as those concerning the temperament of redheads or the thriftiness of Scots. Many erroneous inferences about causality also lack important behavioral implications. Only emperors and would-be sodomites were ever likely to act on the belief that sodomy causes earthquakes. The belief that rain dances cause rain produces behavior no more dangerous than dancing in dry weather (safer than, for instance, singing in the rain).

In our discussions of people's beliefs about causality, we have stressed the pervasiveness of the fundamental attribution error. It is easy to see the personal and social damage that can be produced when people act on their erroneous beliefs that their insomnia, their marital discord, or the unemployment of blacks is best understood in exclusively dispositional rather than in situational terms. Nevertheless, it seems clear that many dispositional inferences have the same behavioral implications as situational ones do. The decorous behavior of bankers, the authoritative manner of doctors, and the avuncular manner of clergymen may, perhaps, best be understood as the product of certain role and situational constraints. But behavior toward such individuals will be no less appropriate, in most instances, if people are guided by the erroneous belief that the behavior of such individuals is the product of underlying personality traits.

Many behaviors have the desired effects on the environment even though causal theories about the mediation of the effects may be erroneous. For example, many effective agricultural and medical procedures are applied in the absence of a correct causal theory. Many social or business strategies also are effective in spite of their origins in an incorrect theory. The general manager who refuses to yield to the sensational rookie's contract demands because he fears that such quick rewards will prompt complacency and a resulting sophomore slump, does just as well as one whose statistical knowledge suggests to him the second-year performances after exceptional first-year performances will, on the average, regress somewhat to the mean.

Incorrect Inferences with Relatively Desirable Consequences

It is perhaps a dangerous notion that error can sometimes result in more useful or desirable behavior than truth can. Yet it seems clear that this is sometimes the case.

A decision theory expert told us of an interesting demonstration he performed with the top executives of a large U.S. corporation. He described several potential new products to half of the executives and then asked them to rate their quality. He described the same products to the other half of the executives and asked them to predict how well the products would do on the market. The market success predictions perfectly mirrored the quality evaluations. Then the executives were asked how well, *in general,* one can predict market performance from product quality. "Oh," said the executives, "you can't predict well at all. You can come up with a terrific new product and the competition can come up with the same thing 10 percent cheaper. Or you can turn out a lousy product that somehow catches fire." (For more formal demonstrations of the same phenomenon, see Tversky and Kahneman, 1978).

The concrete predictions of the executives showed the typical, normatively incorrect pattern of prediction, that is, a heavy use of the representativeness heuristic to the exclusion of regression considerations. The executives' abstract generalizations about the relationship between predictor variables and outcomes, in contrast, showed a normatively correct understanding of the limits of predictability. Consider the probable effect of the normatively incorrect (that is, nonregressive) predictions in the case of a particular highly promising product. Will the behavioral consequences be untoward? It is easy to imagine the "disaster scenario": Unduly impressed by the excellence of the new product, the executives invest a huge proportion of the company's resources in it. Then the competition does indeed produce the same product for less, and our first company is left hanging on the brink of bankruptcy. On the other hand, imagine that the executives act "prudently," on the basis of their normatively correct understanding of the difficulty of predicting performance from quality. The complementary "disaster" is perhaps equally easy to spell out: With insufficient resources invested in the product, its development is delayed, and due to insufficient advertising, dissemination of knowledge of its existence is retarded. The "imprudent" competition, meanwhile, rushes a similar but inferior and more expensive product to market where it quickly catches fire and, because of market inertia, retains dominance indefinitely. Our original company loses out, and prudent executive heads roll.

This point about prediction errors and behavior may be generalized: People sometimes may require overly optimistic or overly pessimistic subjective probabilities to goad them into effective action or prevent them from taking dangerous actions. Thus, it is far from clear that a bride and groom would be well advised to believe, on their wedding day, that the probability of their divorce is as high as .40. A baseball player with a batting average of .200 may not be best served, as he steps up to bat, by the belief that the probability that he will get a hit is only .2. The social benefits of individually erroneous subjective probabilities may be great even when the individual pays a high price for the error. We probably would have few novelists, actors, or scientists if all potential aspirants to these careers took action based on a normatively justifiable subjective probability of success. We also might have few new products, new medical procedures, new political movements, or new scientific theories.

We do not wish to dwell on the dangerous notion that people's actions may better be guided by error than by truth. Since we believe that the opposite is generally the case, our last chapter is devoted to exploring the means by which people might be encouraged to abandon normatively incorrect inference procedures in favor of normatively more correct ones.

SUMMARY

People may fare rather better in their everyday life than might be expected from a survey of laboratory evidence or from the emphasis of this book. This state of affairs does not reflect any inherent difficulties in the tasks studied in the laboratory. On the contrary, careful analysis suggests that the laboratory tasks probably give the participant ecologically unrepresentative *advantages*. Instead, the everyday damage from inferential shortcomings is probably limited by several factors that have not been studied often in laboratory settings.

Despite their lack of "rigor," intuitive strategies serve people quite well in many contexts. Judgmental heuristics and knowledge structures are often well founded and helpful guides to inference. Ignorance of normative principles may have small costs for many everyday inferential tasks, even if their costs are prohibitively large for more formal scientific judgments. Reliance on very small samples, for instance, is a highly efficient or "cost-effective" procedure for many familiar tasks. Reliance on biased samples, by contrast, is a potentially lethal failing, although even here people are sometimes protected by domain-specific cues and by causal scripts. The potential costs of people's general willingness to ignore base rates in favor of diagnostic information, even diagnostic information of uncertain value, are similarly limited by people's access to culturally transmitted or experientially based insights about particular phenomena.

Perhaps most important of the defenses is the collective nature of many inferential tasks. Wiser, more experienced, or more formally trained experts have passed on their insights and are often available to challenge the most blatant and most important of our erroneous inferences. In addition, two or more heads, even nonexpert heads, are generally better than one, so the collective solving of problems normally should produce inferences superior to those of the individual working in isolation.

It seems possible that peoples' inferential shortcomings may cancel each other out to some degree, and result in judgments approximating the outcome of more normatively correct procedures. Finally, the layperson is protected because erroneous inferences do not necessarily lead to maladaptive behavior. Often, incorrect judgments have no behavioral implications at all, and occasionally the costs of incorrect judgments may be less than the costs of more normatively correct ones.

12

improving human inference: possibilities and limitations

> Philosophical decisions are nothing but the reflections of common life, methodized and corrected.
>
> *David Hume.*

We have identified a number of shortcomings in everyday inference—shortcomings that, for the most part, can be traced either to people's over-reliance on primitive judgmental heuristics or to their inattentiveness to conventional normative considerations. We also have discussed some of the factors that may limit the damage done by such shortcomings. Now it is time to supplement these diagnoses and prognoses with some discussion of "treatment." When should treatment be undertaken and when should the patient simply be left alone? What can be done to reduce the incidence and seriousness of inferential maladies? What factors make the therapeutic task more difficult?

In the first section of the chapter we note some important differences between the primarily "applied" concerns of the layperson and the pure scientific concerns of the formal researcher, differences that cannot be ignored in assessing the normativeness of the layperson's procedures. Next, we discuss some of the considerations that determine when it is advisable to substitute more formal inferential strategies for intuitive ones. We then consider educational techniques that might help to give the layperson a better understanding of those formal strategies and of the logical or statistical principles that underlie them. Finally, we discuss some of the barriers that frustrate efforts to improve everyday human inference.

THE STATUS OF THE LAYPERSON:
PURE SCIENTIST OR APPLIED PRACTITIONER?

Throughout the book we have held lay inferences up to the rigorous standards of formal scientific inquiry. In the particular examples we have focused on, we believe that these standards were reasonable. As we first noted in chapter 4, however, only rarely does the layperson function in a role that is completely analogous to that of the *pure* scientist. The layperson is more nearly an *applied* scientist, and as such the normative rules governing formal inquiry in the pure sciences often are poorly suited to his purposes. The pure scientist seeks to understand the basis of lawfulness in the social or physical world around him. He is (or at least he should be) willing to make great sacrifices of time and energy in the interests of exactness and certainty; for his is a collective endeavor lasting far longer than his own life, and both the costs of his errors and the dividends realized on his insights are apt to be multiply compounded.

The applied scientist, by contrast, is concerned less with the underlying nature of reality than with the pliability of the real world, less with discovering and understanding new phenomena or higher order regularities than with determining which phenomena or regularities can be used in solving immediate practical problems. The applied scientist whose job is to get a satellite in orbit around one of Jupiter's moons may know that the lack of a solution to the classic "many-body" problem is making the task more difficult, but it scarcely follows from this that he should put aside his computer approximations to tackle the many-body problem. By the same token, the intuitive scientist whose immediate concerns are predicting and controlling other people's behavior can hardly await, or personally try to bring about, the emergence of a basic understanding of human perception, thinking, or motivation. For the applied scientist, fundamental problems are to be finessed, not solved; and fundamental inquiry, with its exacting standards and demands, is an unaffordable luxury.

It could be argued that it is not even to the applied scientist that the layperson should be compared, but rather to the practitioner—to the physician, carpenter, or weather forecaster. Unlike the applied scientist, the practitioner normally does not invent solutions to problems. Instead, he selects solutions worked out by the most skilled and ingenious of the applied scientists who have preceded him. Costly research to collect new data or invent new solutions will pay commensurate dividends only under rather special circumstances.

The goals of the informal scientist often dictate procedures that would be highly counter-normative for the formal one. We have already noted one such instance of differing normative prescriptions in chapter 4. There, we contended that the layperson, like any practitioner using a prior theory, but unlike the formal scientist intent on testing one, should allow the theory to govern the interpretation of ambiguous data. A thorough review of the differing goals of pure and applied science, and of the resulting differences in normative prescriptions, would take us far beyond the scope of this chapter and the competence of the present authors. One further example, however, is worth mentioning because it so clearly points to the difference in priorities and strategies. We noted in chapter 4 how willing people seem to be to make inferences based on data they know to be biased. We also noted that it is often extremely difficult to determine the nature and extent of the bias that exists in a given data sample or alternatively, to collect unbiased data. The conventional response of the formal scientist to such a state of affairs seems clear enough: move on to another, more "tractable" problem. But what of the layperson? The requirement of action in the real world (where "no action" can be a highly costly "response") is apt to prohibit such a pristine stance. Often, the layperson *must* proceed. He can only hope that the inferential damage wrought by any potential bias is slight, and try to minimize such damage by avoiding undue certainty.

The requirement of action is not the only difference between the demands placed on the pure scientist and those placed on the lay practitioner. The layperson often must be guided by goals that are quite distant from issues of epistemic correctness. These include the need to maintain comity with one's fellows by sharing their perceptions of social reality, and a concern for fairness and justice. (For a brilliant analysis of the competition between epistemic and extra-epistemic considerations in the arena of the law, see Tribe, 1971.)

In short, it seems evident that any normative theory of lay inference must differ, even in its outlines, from the prescriptive theories that guide scientific inference. Such a "regulative" theory for the layperson (cf. Goldman, 1978), if and when it finally emerges, will undoubtedly contain principles that capture the spirit of almost all formal principles of inference. But it will contain much more than those principles, and the additional considerations will sometimes take precedence over the formal ones.

It should be clear, therefore, that in discussing ways of improving lay inference it is not our intent to bind the layperson to the exclusive use of formal scientific rules and procedures. We even think that formal scientists are too often shackled by such procedures. Formal inferential methods, as Kuhn (1962) and others have noted, primarily serve the goals of verification and communication and suffice only for the conduct of so-called normal science. The "rules" governing the more crucial tasks of hypothesis generation and discovery have not been developed; but we believe that when they are, they will bear a strong family resemblance to the intuitive strategies of the layperson (cf. Polanyi, 1958).

Our purpose therefore is less to proscribe the use of intuitive strategies than to foster a recognition of their limits and to enlarge the layperson's repertoire to at least *include* the more formal strategies. Whether the individual will find it advisable to substitute formal strategies for informal ones in a given instance, as we shall see, is a matter of relative costs and benefits.

COSTS AND BENEFITS OF FORMAL VS. INTUITIVE STRATEGIES

Many judgments and decisions are so manifestly trivial and routine that no rational person would consider using anything like formal inferential methods. Consider the behavior of the person confronted with the list of thirty-six flavors in his neighborhood ice-cream parlor. He may simply "order what I always order, chocolate" or he may browse through the list in search of some flavor that meets some sufficiency criterion or evokes some resonant chord ("The woman before me ordered Banana Nut Supreme and she said 'yum' when she took her first taste" or "I'm in the mood for something totally new and I've never tried Boysenberry Surprise" or "I love Coconut Cream Pie, so why not Coconut Cream Sherbert.") If no flavor gains primacy over its competitors through such simple and informal procedures, the intuitive scientist may vacillate or delay, typically feeling foolish at having tarried so long in so inconsequential a decision. But surely he will not, and should not, resort to more formal decision-making strategies such as polling a random sample of customers, inquiring about specific ingredients to determine whether his schema-based assumptions are warranted, or assigning utilities and associated probabilities for each flavor.

At the other extreme, some decisions are so important that exclusive use of purely intuitive strategies seems highly inadvisable. Normally, such decisions as what home or car to purchase, whether or not to change careers, or whether to begin to raise a family, should be undertaken with the use of the best data and inferential strategies at one's disposal. (See Wheeler and Janis, 1980 for a lay-oriented guide to such "vital decision-making"). Even for important judgments, however, one should be loath to legislate blanket decision rules, as the following anecdote attests.

One of the authors recently found himself seated on an airplane next to the comptroller of a major U.S. corporation. The gentleman was quite charming and intelligent; that is to say, he inquired with apparent interest about the author's research activities. In the ensuing conversation, the author trotted out his Volvo-Saab chestnut, adding the homily that, of course, the normatively correct way to proceed in such a decision as a car purchase is to attend chiefly to the opinions of experts and to the distilled experience of large numbers of owners. "Not for me," said the comptroller. "The way I buy a car is that I see a picture in, say *U.S. News and World Report,* and then call up the dealer and order one in green or blue or whatever color I think I'd like."

The author stammered out something like "to each his own," and quickly changed the subject. On reflection, however, the author came to recognize the extent to which the executive's simple judgment procedure ("if it looks good, buy it") faithfully reflected his priorities and expected utilities. For the executive, in sharp contrast to the author, the purchase price of a car is *not* a very serious cost. If the car proved unsatisfactory, it simply could be traded in at a loss of one or two thousand dollars (probably tax-deductible) for something else that caught his eye. He would not miss the money, and the time and effort he spent replacing one car with another would be minimal; probably a phone call or instruction to a subordinate would suffice. Unlike the author, he certainly would not exhaust any time or patience, or engage in self-recriminations, if the car turned out to be a "lemon."

There also are cost-effectiveness considerations beyond time, money, and cognitive work. For the comptroller, a new car might be a symbol of wealth and status and a source of pleasure. To consult a host of facts and figures, to calculate marginal benefits, probable fuel costs, and resale values, and so on, might well diminish that pleasure. In fact, such activities might seem perilously close to those of his everyday professional life. The author, by contrast, does not (at least to his knowledge) derive much symbolic satisfaction from the purchase of an automobile. Beyond furnishing anecdotal material for his professional musings, the car he drives is chiefly a means of conveyance and a potential drain on his resources. In essence, he can "afford" to assume a pinched-nose accountant's role when purchasing a car. Indeed, in view of the largely nonpecuniary nature of his profession's rewards, and his own commitment to be as rational as possible in making important purchases, he can hardly "afford" to do otherwise.

The relativity of rational consumerism extends in both directions on the wealth continuum, of course. The same author recently confided to a graduate student friend that, on a single weekend, after consulting one expert and doing a minimal amount of comparative shopping, he had decided to junk his old malfunctioning stereo system and replace it with a far more expensive one. The student was aghast! (''Did you ever hear the Volvo-Saab story,'' she chided.) The author had no shortage of defenses and excuses, mostly the difficulties and the marginal advantages of trying to find the One Best Speaker System or the Ideal Turntable. But the stereo anecdote makes exactly the same points as the car purchase anecdote does. The potential costs and utilities of following more normatively appropriate decision strategies—in the marketplace, but in other arenas as well—depend on the life situation, values, and resources of the decision-maker. More generally, one should not lightly criticize or recommend ''treatment'' for the seemingly nonnormative character of another's judgments. For the illness may often be more bearable for the individual—that is, offer a better ratio of benefits to costs—than the cure.

In introducing the question of cost-effectiveness, we have relied on consumer decisions for illustrative purposes because the costs and benefits of both formal and informal decision strategies in such cases are apt to be readily discernible to the reader. The same issues obviously arise in nonconsumer decisions or judgments. (''Shall I walk the dog before or after supper?'' ''Shall I phone Fred and congratulate him on his promotion or will he think I'm trying to be ingratiating?'' ''Shall I kiss Jane goodnight or might she misinterpret?'' ''Should I drop out of the graduate program in psychology and apply to law school?'') In each case, the decision about whether even to consider the relative merits of more formal versus less formal decision strategies is apt to be dictated by the apparent importance or triviality of the benefits that might result from more formal inferential strategies.

It should be emphasized that the costs of time and effort associated with relatively formal strategies for inference or decision-making are not always higher. Even beyond their potentially greater dividends, their cost sometimes may be quite a bit lower than the costs associated with intuitive strategies. For example, the mechanical application of simple regression formula for student selection seems to achieve better results (in terms of traditional reliability and validity criteria) than the laborious intuitive methods applied by expert judges and decision makers (Dawes, 1979). Even if the simple formula merely equaled the performance of expert judges, of course, it could be defended on grounds of cost alone. As Slovic (1976) and others have noted, even a very expensive ''start-up'' operation (establishing empirical regression weights, and so on) can pay enormous dividends when recurrent, conceptually identical decisions are modeled formally. Kahneman and Tversky (in press), as well as Slovic, have outlined some of the procedures that can greatly improve these recurrent judgment tasks.

Even non-recurrent, unique decisions sometimes can be made more efficiently with relatively formal strategies than with the combination of intuition and informal data collection that sometimes are brought to bear (often with accompanying obsession) in making important life choices. This is particularly true when some highly valid data are readily available, but vivid and non-probative data abound. The decision about which college to attend, or which car to purchase, are cases in point. Objective information compiled by experts is readily available and it is easy to review that information in light of one's priorities. The informal options—carefully poring over brochures, discussing the matter ad nauseum with one's friends and family, making personal visits to see the various cars or campuses with one's own eyes—are far more exhausting of one's resources and far more likely to make one the victim of happenstance, ill-founded advice, or the ingratiating individual whose primary objective is to "sell" the prospective client.

In considering the "cost-effectiveness" of formal versus informal strategies, it is important not to lose sight of costs and benefits that might be social or psychological, and difficult to express in terms of time, money, or other economic desiderata. For instance, the tasks of carefully compiling evidence, making decision criteria explicit, and so on, may be relatively pleasurable or esteem-enhancing for one individual and relatively noxious and ego-deflating for another individual. The likelihood that one will be forced to justify one's decision to others, or even to oneself, may tip the scales in favor of a more formal strategy, even if other costs and benefits are relatively equal. On the other hand, the exclusive use of a cut and dried formula for certain decisions, for example, personnel decisions, might have costs—in terms of appearing cold, rigid, and inhuman—that would offset gains in efficiency and validity, or even in objectivity and fairness. Only the decision maker, mindful of particular priorities and values, can assess the appropriate weight to give such social and psychological factors.

A final point about cost-effectiveness is that the sheer importance of the outcomes that will follow from a decision is not a sufficient justification for costly inferential strategies, whether formal or intuitive in nature. The game show contestant told to choose either the red box or the blue box, knowing only that one box contains a $10,000 check and the other an old shoe, will profit little from formal inferential strategies. There are some decisions that, although of critical importance, have outcomes that are unknowable in principle or that are presently indistinguishable in terms of their overall costs and benefits. In such cases, a flip of the coin may be the most cost-effective strategy available.

Our "decision-theoretic" analysis of informal versus formal strategies makes it clear that the normative questions, as always, are more difficult than first meets the eye. We cannot maintain that people should always use more formal strategies, even for inferential problems of great importance. Nevertheless, the present analysis indicates that people often are well advised to choose more formal strategies. Such choices can be made most rationally by people who enjoy a clearer understanding of the advantages of formal inferential strategies—and of the major failings of informal strategies—than our educational system now provides.

PROGRAMS TO IMPROVE INFERENTIAL STRATEGIES

Knowledge of inferential principles and failings, and skill in applying that knowledge, does not guarantee correct inferences. But it can greatly reduce the likelihood of error in at least some domains of judgment and can reduce the likelihood at least marginally in a great many more. We therefore consider it advisable to teach formal inferential principles to as wide a public as possible. Two questions present themselves. First, how can the information best be taught? Second, how effective are even the most energetic and well-conceived attempts at education likely to prove?

Preconditions of Change

It seems important to establish a more receptive climate for the educational undertaking we advocate. People must be persuaded that they are prone to inferential errors that are highly recognizable and codifiable. They must be given greater motivation to attend closely to the nature of the inferential tasks that they perform and to the quality of their performance. This book (following the lead of Newell and Simon, Kahneman and Tversky, Slovic and Lichtenstein, Dawes, and others) has taken a step in this direction. Although we have addressed a narrow and uncharacteristically sophisticated audience, the first returns on our own efforts seem encouraging. We have found that university students at all levels who are exposed to the material in this book are stimulated and intrigued. They readily recognize themselves in our portrait of the error-prone intuitive scientist. Daniel Kahneman, who has begun a program of education in inferential strategies and shortcomings directed at high school students, reports similar experiences. Indeed, he suspects that his initial efforts may have been carried a bit too far, as many of the students became so convinced of their inferential incapacity that they despaired of mastering more appropriate techniques. Our experience in this regard has been somewhat similar. It is easier to shock audiences into a recognition of their susceptibility to error or bias than it is to reassure them of their already formidable defenses and their capacity for improvement.

Teaching Statistics

Many of the inferential principles central to the education we are proposing can be appreciated fully only if one has been exposed to some elementary statistics and probability theory. (Some exposure to research methodology and philosophy of science also would help.) Perhaps no subjects are more inappropriately excluded from the curricula of primary and secondary schools than these. Some fifty years ago, H. G. Wells expressed the opinion that it would shortly be recognized that the teaching of statistics was as central to the production of an educated citizenry as the teaching of reading and writing. He was wrong in his prediction, but that is to our discredit, not his.

The present authors lack the necessary background or expertise to speculate about the best methods for introducing school children to inferential problems and concepts. But every course, from history and civics to science or even to arithmetic, surely provides some opportunity for introducing the concept of "biased data" and the notion that our preconceptions structure and potentially distort what we see, understand, and remember. One logical place for exploring these concepts, and many more sophisticated ones (such as the existence and nature of regression phenomena), is within the context of an introductory statistics course. In our opinion, elementary statistics and probability theory should be introduced at least as early as secondary school. Needless to say, we would advocate statistics courses geared less to significance testing and other concerns of social science majors, and more to everyday problems of informal inference and judgment. In any case, statistics should be taught in conjunction with material on intuitive strategies and inferential error of the sort presented in this book. It seems to us that this would have the advantages both of clarifying the underlying principles of statistics and probability and of facilitating an appreciation of their applications to concrete judgmental tasks. We are pleased to note that a statistics text emphasizing judgmental heuristics and the contest between intuitive and formal inferential strategies is currently being prepared by W. H. Dumouchel and D. H. Krantz (1979) of the University of Michigan. We are also pleased to report that initial student response to that approach seems very positive.

Teaching by Concrete Illustrations
and Vivid Anecdotes

We have characterized the intuitive scientist as being highly responsive to concrete, vivid, and anecdotal information. If this characterization is correct, it has clear implications for educational strategy in general and for educating people about inferential strategies and shortcomings in particular.

Because we believe this, we have loaded our book with such material in the hope that it would make the ideas easier to comprehend and allow them to be generalized more readily to other concrete inferential tasks. We have done so with no little trepidation about the degree to which we have exposed ourselves to the charge of exploiting, in our own arguments, the very shortcomings against which we warn our readers. We believe that there is nothing contradictory or hypocritical in our position. We offer in our defense Brickman's (1978) observation that concrete, anecdotal material is essential for comprehension (or, in Brickman's term, for "phenomenological reality") and that it is only the inferential or putatively evidential use of such information that is dubious.

The particular anecdotes and thought experiments presented in this book, we should note, are not the best aids to comprehension and generalization for all constituencies. They have been chosen specifically for an audience of social scientists and academicians, and probably will be of less value to other types of audiences. A decision-theory expert told us that in consulting with large corporations, he has learned to present examples and case histories that overlap as much as possible in their concrete elements with those that the executives use in their own work, even if those concrete elements are "logically" irrelevant. He recounted an experience of telling the executives of a computer corporation about a problem faced by a rubber company that was formally similar to one confronting the computer executives. The response was a wall of blank stares. At last one executive replied uncomfortably, "Well, that's the rubber industry, here we deal with computers."

Lest the reader decide that corporation executives are unusually prone to be victimized by the representativeness heuristic, let us recall Colonel House's testimony about President Woodrow Wilson, the ex-academic, who on the very eve of World War I was fretting about the possibility of war with *England*. House reported that Wilson had this fear because the English were currently searching American ships illegally just as they had before the War of 1812 and during the presidency of James Madison, "the only other Princeton alumnus" to occupy the White House.

Illustrations both of inferential error and of correct applications of formal inferential strategies thus should be tailored to one's audience. By presenting people with a large number of concrete examples drawn from their daily experiences, they ultimately can be led to construct new knowledge structures— schemas, scripts, standard operating procedures,—and the like that generalize and abstract the conceptual elements common to the examples.

Maxims and Slogans: The Fortune Cookie Didactic

It is apparent that everyday inference is not governed by schematized, concrete experience alone. Judgmental maxims and slogans (a bird in the hand. . .; as the twig is bent . . . and so on) are so ubiquitous that they probably serve at least to communicate recommended strategies and perhaps even to guide the performance of particular inferential tasks. We have tried our hand at inventing (and borrowing from social science terminology) some useful slogans for didactic purposes. Many of these were presented elsewhere in the book; others now are added that convey similarly important messages. Since we are new to the business of sloganeering, most of our maxims leave much to be desired from a literary standpoint. We trust that this reflects only the authors' limitations and not any inherently greater difficulty in expressing truth than in expressing half-truths or errors.

IT'S AN EMPIRICAL QUESTION. This is a slogan known and used by most social scientists. It means many things, all of which are likely to point those who use it in a helpful direction. Sometimes it means "This is a question whose resolution can be reached only by consulting or generating data." Sometimes it is the social scientist's gentle reminder that one should place limited confidence in any theoretical proposition that lacks a sound empirical footing, no matter how plausible the proposition may seem on purely a priori grounds. For most social scientists, there is a solid groundwork of professional experience behind this slogan, as so many of society's and of one's own personal theories have turned out, in the crucible of empirical test, to have no support. Perhaps that is why there are so few social scientists, at least of our acquaintance, who work constructively with data and yet remain extreme ideologues. The conduct of social science research, like the pursuit of philosophical inquiry, is apt to make one tentative about all of one's social theories. We have argued that people hold many social theories that are simply wrong, that they hold many partially correct theories with too great confidence, that they often apply theories erroneously beyond their appropriate domains, and that they often substitute a read-out of theory for an appraisal of data even when the relevant data can be obtained readily. Thus we believe that the social scientist's slogan "It's an empirical question" prompts a needed corrective to the layperson's natural confidence in theory. The slogan does not have the passion of Lord Cromwell's cry, "I beseech you, in the bowels of Christ, think it possible you may be wrong." But a thorough appreciation of the meaning of the slogan may result in a greater willingness to question the certainty of one's views.

WHICH HAT DID YOU DRAW THAT SAMPLE OUT OF? It might be useful to have this slogan at one's fingertips for those occasions when questionably sampled evidence is adduced in support of some proposition. Thus, a reference to the characteristics of Tennessee Williams to support a proposition about homosexuals, or a generalization about Russians adduced from observations of Brezhnev or Baryshnikov, could immediately be challenged. The slogan might also be useful to confront those who argue against uncongenial statistics with "counterexample" cases. It seems likely to us that a thorough grounding with a minimum of formal statistical training, in the meaning of the slogan could bestow on the layperson one of the inferential defenses of the social scientist. By the same token, the layperson could readily be made to appreciate the inferential power of data samples that are drawn *randomly*. Then, perhaps, fewer people would scoff at the Gallup Poll that, on the basis of only a few hundred interviews, predicts defeat for their candidate. And, by understanding the "hat" slogan, they would take less comfort from the huge crowds shown cheering their candidate in the nightly news.

OKAY, WHAT DO THE OTHER THREE CELLS LOOK LIKE? For this slogan to make any sense, the hearer must be familiar with the logic of the 2 / 2 contingency table. In our opinion, this knowledge ought to be imparted long before the college level. Although necessary, such abstract knowledge is insufficient to guarantee normatively appropriate responses to covariation propositions. Social scientists usually are not as readily victimized by data on the order of, "Well, I know lots of people who were cured of all sorts of things by chiropractors," as laypeople are. But we find that even well-trained social scientists are apt to respond to such observations with a logically inadequate request for data from only one or two other cells ("Yes, but how about the people who didn't get cured?" or "What about the people who got better without treatment?") Our slogan may not come trippingly off the tongue, but a maxim or rule of thumb is needed which makes it clear that there are indeed four separate observations that must be considered for even the simplest case of covariation assessment. Again, a number of concrete and memorable illustrations will be necessary to drive this point home and increase the likelihood of its application to new cases.

BEWARE OF THE FUNDAMENTAL ATTRIBUTION ERROR. (Or, for a less hortatory tone: Consider the actor's situation before jumping to conclusions about his dispositions). This slogan is not universally endorsed by social scientists. Instead, it has been a battle cry for one group of social scientists—an alliance of role-theory sociologists, behaviorists, and experimental social psychologists—challenging a second group—an alliance of psychodynamic psychologists and trait-theory personologists. (The divisions, however, are not as simple as this implies. A brilliant psychodynamic, but fundamentally situationist view of psychopathology and treatment possibilities, for example, is offered in Haley's *The Uncommon Therapy,* 1973. Behaviorism, on the other hand, can be, and in its early days often was, associated with a strong dispositionalist or "individual difference" viewpoint.)

By now it is obvious to the reader that the situationist battle cry is our own and that we would like to hear it from the lips of the layperson as well. We suspect, moreover, that few of our colleagues, regardless of their theoretical camp, would deny that the injunction often can provide the layperson with a useful perspective. It sanctions, moreover, a number of useful special-purpose maxims that express the same underlying thought ("What would you have done if you were in his shoes?" or "There but for the grace of God go I.") Each of these maxims points in the direction of role demands or situational determinants of behavior, and each tacitly counsels against inappropriate dispositional interpretation. In our experience, the broad injunction adds something to the specific maxims. It warns against hasty behavior-based inferences about personal characteristics even for those cases in which the exact nature of the situational forces and constraints is not immediately apparent.

YOU CAN ALWAYS EXPLAIN AWAY THE EXCEPTIONS. In our experience, the layperson has difficulty recognizing that people's explanatory powers are so keen, and the possibilities for alternative interpretation are typically so rich and varied, that exceptions only seldom pose problems for any general theory or rule. Even the social scientist in the conduct of professional inquiry has far too little appreciation of this fact. It has only been in writing this book, in fact, that the authors have become at all self-conscious about explaining away exceptions to their favorite theories and generalizations. This maxim, or something like it, should help to warn the scientist against too vigorous a defense of his pet theories, just as it should caution the layperson who is guilty of the same offense.

FURTHER INFERENTIAL MAXIMS AND THEIR GENERATION. The authors must resist the temptation to restate, this time in fortune-cookie fashion, all of the theses of the preceding chapters. A few more maxims, however, are offered without elaboration, in the hope that they will both jog the reader's memory and encourage the generation of newer and better ones.

Methinks I detect the availability (or representativeness) heuristic at work.
That's a vivid datum (or that's a striking "man-who" statistic) all right, but I'll still consult the base rates, thank you.
Now look at the same data from the vantage point of our theory (or their theory), instead of yours.
You're bolstering your theory with "processed information" instead of "raw data."
Before considering a fancy causal explanation, how about considering simple regression?

The authors would love to see the generation of inferential maxims become a popular diversion for epistemologists and social scientists. Brevity, "punchiness," and wit should be the chief desiderata. One simple technique we recommend for would-be inferential epigrammatists is the inversion or qualification of popular (but normatively suspect) maxims already in the public domain. For example: "You can lie with statistics, but a well-chosen example does the job better." Three further examples, designed to startle people into an appreciation of the regression phenomenon, are offered below. (And let him who is without doggerel cast the first bone.)

As ye sow, so shall ye reap . . . but generally less so.
As the twig is bent . . . so the tree is slightly and occasionally inclined.
Nine stitches in time do save, at least on average, a stitch or two.

OVERCOMING THE BARRIERS TO CHANGE

The preceding section tacitly conveys our conviction that the quality of human inferences and judgments can be improved. Without this conviction, our proposals for education would have little point. But how much improvement can be expected, even from the best of educational programs? The first answer must be that we do not and cannot know; it is, indeed, "an empirical question."

A second, somewhat less noncommital answer, is that we suspect that the possibilities for change, for particular types of inferences in particular domains, range from almost nil to very great. We do not anticipate, for example, much change in people's susceptibility to the power of theories, and other knowledge structures, to bias their interpretation of events. Most bias of this type is automatic and reflexive, and we have argued that in any case such "bias" generally promotes rapid, efficient and correct coding of events. Only rarely, we suspect, will people be able to separate the wheat among their knowledge structures from the chaff. By the same token, we do not expect any real improvement in people's ability to assess covariation. Under most circumstances, this requires mental operations that are simply beyond our intuitive, informal capacities. About the most that can be expected in this area is that people can be made to recognize their incapacities and to be dubious of any covariation theories that are not based on the systematic collection and analysis of appropriate data.

At the other extreme, there are some inferences, in at least some domains, for which we expect that very great improvement will prove possible. A general familiarity with the ideas in this book should provide people with substantial defenses against certain kinds of argumentation based on manifestly flawed evidence, or on dubious and facile causal theories. And understanding of the general idea of regression should bestow similar advantages, at least under circumstances where people recognize explicitly that they are making predictions. The magnitude of gains from each of these insights should at least approximate the gains attained from an understanding of the gambler's fallacy or an appreciation of the distinction between dependent and independent events.

Our optimism about the magnitude of ultimate change is tempered by several factors. It seems to us that there are several very general and very serious barriers in the path to change. To some extent these barriers may limit the degree of change to be expected in any area. To some extent they may best be regarded as challenges that must be surmounted, or at least sidestepped, if the most exciting prospects for change are to be realized. We will speculate about three major barriers: (a) our inability to directly observe our cognitive processes, (b) our susceptibility to inferential errors when confronted with particularly vivid and personally-relevant information, and (c) our general tendency to be overly confident about whatever judgments and inferences we have happened to reach.

Inferences About Our Inferences

A distressing limit is placed on our ability to improve our inferences by our lack of introspective insight or self awareness. Having no window on our cognitive processes, we cannot simply note flaws and correct them in accordance with our normative insights. Instead, we must infer indirectly, on the basis of spotty and imperfect evidence, what those processes are. As chapter 9 made clear, the opportunities for self-delusion are legion. We are likely to reject the possibility that our judgments have been guided by some foolish procedure on the grounds that it is *implausible* that we would use such a procedure. One may go so far as to speculate that a given cognitive procedure is likely to be misidentified or unrecognized precisely to the degree that it is inappropriate or foolish.

Actually, matters may be even more unsettling than this. Work by Bem and McConnell (1970) and by Goethals and Reckman (1973) indicates that peoples' judgments may change in the absence of any recognition that a change has occurred. Particularly unnerving is the latter investigators' demonstration that subjects' opinions of such an important issue as the "bussing" of school children could be shifted from pro to con (or con to pro), by an eloquent speaker, without the subjects' recognition that their opinions had changed at all. If the shift in judgment itself is hidden from view, then the chances of recognizing the inappropriateness of an inferential strategy underlying that shift seem slim indeed.

On the other hand, even if it is agreed that we often fail to recognize that an inference has occurred, and can only guess at inferential procedures when we do recognize that an inference has taken place, matters are not quite hopeless. Whenever we find that we have made a decision or judgment that seems surprising (either surprising to ourselves or to others who know us well), then a more formal and self-conscious inferential strategy can be pursued. The result frequently will prove to be the unmasking of a familiar culprit—a lazy use of the representativeness heuristic, inattentiveness to sampling bias, or reliance on dubiously relevant schemas or scripts.

A Tverskian anecdote offers a concrete illustration. Tversky had accepted an invitation to attend a conference. Shortly after he had done so, a colleague happened to ask him why he had accepted the invitation when he had refused so many others. Tversky heard himself giving plausible, that is, "representative" reasons for attending a conference ("I'm interested in the topic," "There will be some interesting people there"), but they sounded curiously flat to him. Once alone, he began to review the seemingly appropriate justifications that he had offered. The topic? He was not really all that interested in it and never had been. The people? A few moderately interesting people, but no one exceptional, certainly no one both exceptional and otherwise inaccessible enough to justify the trip. The time or circumstances? Inconvenient really, a bad time to be trotting off to a distant conference; no possibility even of combining the trip with other, more necessary, undertakings. Hmm. There *had* been that glossy brochure about the conference site. An elegant hotel, a sandy beach, girls in bikinis, crystal clear water (all of which he would be able, at best, merely to watch from the window of the conference room as the meetings droned on). Hmm. "Dear Professor Smith: I had hoped to be able to attend your conference in Majorca this April. Unfortunately . . . "

In other words, we often are given clues, frequently in the form of questions asked by other people, to the fact that we hold some opinion, or have chosen some course of action, that does not seem reasonable in light of the evidence and arguments that we currently can muster. Sometimes there will be a tipoff, like Tversky's sudden memory of the glossy brochure; but even when we cannot immediately uncover the culprit, a more formal appraisal may result in the discovery of some violation of normative inferential principles or sensible decision strategy.

Vivid Data and Inferences About the Self

An unfortunate but important implication of the speculations offered in chapter 3 is that the judgments and inferences that are of greatest personal importance to the individual may be the ones that can least be touched by the normative considerations discussed in this book. The more vivid the data that people confront, and the more affect-laden or personally relevant the issues with which they deal, the less likely it may be that higher-order inferential routes—of the sort we are trying to improve—will be used in the evaluation of evidence. This is true to such an extent that people may have different standards of rationality, indeed even different standards of sanity, for inferences that touch deeply on the self than for those that pertain to other matters. Consider two examples.

One of the authors recently read an essay written by a young professional woman discussing the problems of balancing a new career and a new baby. Along the way, the woman mentioned incidentally that for a long time after the birth of her baby she had felt like a bad mother because she had had an inverted nipple and had been unable to breast feed successfully. The "reasoning" underlying such feelings is of course manifestly flawed, but it does not lead one to conclude that the woman in question was irrational. But consider how one would judge a woman who said, "I feel that Elaine is a bad mother" and then explained her feeling by saying, "Well, she has an inverted nipple and can't breast feed her baby." Such an observation would prompt a strong suspicion that the speaker was out of her mind.

Or consider the plight of a person who has persuaded a visiting relative to take a later flight home than originally planned so that they could enjoy a relaxed dinner beforehand. The relative agrees, takes the later flight, and as a consequence dies in a horrible crash. Inevitably, the grieving survivor would express guilt and anguished self-castigation over "causing" the death. This would not be surprising and would not raise doubts about his inferential competence. Now suppose, on the other hand, that an uninvolved observer, perhaps a neighbor of the survivor, were similarly to castigate and blame the survivor for his role in the tragedy. We would label him a fool or a madman.

These examples make it clear that inferences about matters that touch deeply upon the self have a unique status. They seem to call upon cognitive structures that are less normative and more primitive than those that figure in less personal inferences. Moreover, such structures cannot readily be superseded by more logical ones. When other people point out to the individual that his inferences or feelings are distorted and erroneous, he may accept this intellectually but scarcely be affected by it emotionally. That is, he may recognize his error, and realize that he would not have made a similar judgment about anyone else, but still remain trapped by his feelings and by the primitive inferential processes underlying them.

These observations are hardly original insights into human nature. If matters were otherwise, psychotherapists could be replaced by logicians. The relevance of the observations to the question of the perfectibility of inference processes should be clear, however. It is the most personally important inferences that are the least likely to be affected by the pallid, normative principles discussed in this book. This does not mean that no improvement at all can be expected for this critical class of inferences. To understand intellectually that one has made an erroneous inference surely can convey some advantages. The half-life, as it were, of the more primitive inferences may be reduced, so that when the vividness of the initial evidence has paled, the superior inferences may gain precedence at an earlier point than would otherwise have been the case. Even while still in the grip of the more primitive inferences, the individual may be able to anticipate relief and forestall self-destructive actions. To go beyond such small comforts, however, we would have to deny much of what we said about the vividness criterion in chapter 3.

It is not only the most personally relevant information that has a profound, often too profound, impact on our inferences. Informational concreteness, firsthandedness, even the skill of the transmitter of the information, all threaten to undermine the intuitive scientist's analyses. Once again, there are limits to the value of understanding the importance of sample size or of understanding the logical irrelevance of some of the factors that contribute to the vividness of a given piece of evidence. We cannot easily "will" ourselves to attend to or remember pallid inputs to the same degree as we do vivid ones. The formal scientist has evolved strategies that guarantee the noting and recording of all data deemed relevant on a priori grounds, strategies that strip such data of their extraevidential features. Can the layperson, or the scientist when he is functioning like a layperson, similarly free himself of the tyranny of his senses? Often the answer is yes! People sometimes can take preventive measures.

To return to one of the authors' favorite examples, consider again the ritual in which applicants for academic jobs meet their prospective colleagues and then culminate their visit with a "job talk." Under some circumstances, the "extra" information (information beyond that conveyed in résumés, letters of recommendation, published and unpublished papers, and so on) offered by the applicant's visit might more profitably be avoided than purchased. The limitations of the interview technique as a predictive tool have been demonstrated repeatedly. It has proved largely useless for predicting success in undergraduate or professional school, success in the Peace Corps, and performance in various jobs, including scientific occupations. There is no compelling reason to presume that the academic job interview is any more valid as a predictor than are interviews for other jobs or roles. However, if the arguments of chapters 2 and 3 are given credence, there is little likelihood that the candidate's prospective colleagues will be able to resist giving the vivid interview "data" far more weight than it merits. Confronted with a living, breathing, candidate who poorly matches their "hot-shot psychologist" persona—one who seems nervous, confused, too eager to please, too wrapped up in dissertation details and insufficiently inclined to explore the fascinating intellectual pathways they suggest—they may find it difficult to hire that candidate even if the other evidence offers testimony of excellence that they recognize in the abstract to have far more diagnostic value than the job talk or interview data. They may even sharply revise their estimates of their previously esteemed colleagues who tried to dump this manifest incompetent on them!

It seems to us that search committees sometimes would be best advised to forgo the interview process altogether. This would be the case, for example, where one candidate stands head and shoulders above the others on the basis of the "folder." To interview in such a case, and to risk losing the candidate because the hapless person fails to match the committee members' personae, is to place more weight on the validity of interview procedures than either measurement theory or the extant evidence could justify. There is another, less drastic remedy. One can commit oneself, before a candidate's visit, to a fixed weighting scheme in which the interview is assigned only a limited number of "points" out of the total to be awarded. In such a case, the remaining points should be awarded before the visit, so that the recommendations, papers, academic awards, and so on, cannot be "reevaluated" in the light of one's new "insights" about the candidate.

In most everyday judgments, the best advice, and the best normative strategy is simpler. If one knows that one cannot avoid giving a particular datum far more weight than is justified by its probative value, then by all means one should avoid that datum and rely only on the evidence that, in dispassionate moments, one would rate as most useful for the inferential task at hand. The person considering which college to attend, or considering which car to buy, would do well to throw away glossy brochures and avoid personal visits to campuses or showrooms that are likely to provide only the highly biased, but vivid, presentations of those who are simply trying to sell their product.

SOCIAL VERSUS INDIVIDUAL EPISTEMIC GAINS. One implication of the preceding discussion is that the potential for collective inferential improvement may far outstrip the potential for individual improvement. We are likely to be better able to see the motes in our brothers' eyes than to see the beams in our own. Two people on a search or admissions committee together are perhaps more likely to catch each other in the act of persona matching than to catch themselves. In determining the accuracy of government gas mileage estimates, Congressman Jones is perhaps more likely to question the relevance of the gas mileage of Congressman Smith's neighbor's Blatzmobile than is Congressman Smith.

Greater social than individual gains also can be anticipated on the basis of the simple mathematical argument discussed in chapter 11. The larger the number of people who take part in an inferential procedure, the greater the likelihood that at least one person will have a normatively superior strategy. Assuming that the possessor of a superior strategy should be able to gain at least some supporters (particularly if the participants have been trained to appreciate normative considerations) this should guarantee that groups can be led to use more normative strategies even when individuals cannot. Indeed, committees and the institutions that they serve can put any increase in inferential sophistication to use by formalizing their decision-making procedures according to the normative consideratons they have come to appreciate. All of the institutional decision-making domains we have discussed, including student and employee selection, parole decisions, sales predictions, and public officials' policy decisions, could so benefit.

Collective, institutional, and recurrent judgments are the ones which seem most capable of improvement. The "debiasing" procedures discussed by Kahneman and Tversky (in press) and by Slovic (1976) are particularly appropriate for such judgments, and the barriers against change which we have discussed seem much weaker for such judgments.

THE ALL-TOO-FUNDAMENTAL ATTRIBUTION ERROR. For one type of error that people commit, our own personal experience makes us doubt that much improvement is to be expected. The reader will not be surprised, we trust, to

hear the authors confess that in most of their everyday inferences about people they cannot escape the "fundamental attribution error." Just as we were
before we became professional psychologists and before we read Lewin,
Heider or Mischel and began to spread their gospel, we are inveterate trait
theorists or "dispositionalists" in most of our social dealings. We still think of
the individuals in our lives as being chronically and transsituationally nice or
not nice, honest or dishonest, dependent or independent. This is not to say
that our quasi-public verbal behavior has not changed. We do not enjoy having our colleagues and students say, in effect, "Nah, nah, fundamental attribution error." So we have driven the error underground, so to speak,
where it undoubtedly continues to guide our judgments to an extent that we
believe, intellectually, to be insupportable.

On the other hand, each of us can think of isolated instances, depressing-
ly infrequent to be sure, in which our judgments and behavior seem to have
been influencd by our intellectual position on these issues. There have been
occasions when we were able to temper otherwise undoubtedly overconfident
predictions, and occasions when we have taken actions concerning students
and employees that were guided by the recognition that undesirable behavior
might be situationally rather than dispositionally produced. Again, we find
that these intellectually preferable judgments seems to occur in inverse proportion to the vividness and self-relevance of the behaviors (and of the people)
we are judging. But it does seem to us that there has been at least some gain
in our personal lives and still more in the relatively dispassionate arenas of
our professional lives.

Broadening of Inferential Confidence Limits

Epistemologists from Bacon to Russell are agreed on a fundamental and
pervasive human failing that we alluded to at several points in this book,
although we have not given it a chapter or section of its own. This failing is
the tendency toward overconfidence in one's judgments, toward greater certainty about one's assessments, theories, and conclusions than closely reasoned
analysis could possibly justify. The empirical evidence (see reviews by
Einhorn and Hogarth, 1978; Fischhoff, Slovic & Lichentenstein, 1977;
Slovic, 1976) gives strong support to this generalization. We have tried at
various points (see chapters 6 and 8) to provide evidence for some of the
mechanisms that might produce misplaced confidence—from the failure to
recognize how much of one's understanding of the world is theory-based
rather than data-based, to the failure to understand the logic of regression.

Many philosophers seem to throw up their hands at the cocksure stance
of the layperson and place their hopes only in the formal analyses of the
philosopher or scientist. Perhaps this pessimism is justified. But the authors

nurse the hope that this book, and the general orientation it presents, may offer more than just another edict from ivory-tower types who enjoy the luxuries of caution and conservatism. If people have a clearer notion about the kinds of judgments and inferences that are likely to show error, and a clearer idea about the kinds of mechanisms that prompt such error, perhaps their ill-founded certainty might be shaken. We will review some of those error-producing mechanisms with a view toward showing their relevance to the problem of overconfidence.

KNOWLEDGE STRUCTURES AND THE VARIABILITY OF THE ENTITY. One of the oldest and most persistent criticisms of human inference is the accusation that once people have applied a particular label to a given object (and thereby applied a specific knowledge structure to it), their subsequent presumptions about the object are apt to owe too much to that label and too little to any actual observations about the unique object. The General Semantics movement that enjoyed something of an intellectual vogue in the 1950s and 1960s provided perhaps the latest voice for such misgivings, with its insistent warnings about the dangers of Aristotelian thinking, and its reminders that ''mother #1 is not mother #2'', that ''mother #1 at time 1 is not mother #1 at time 2'', and so forth. The present viewpoint, we feel, adds something to such warnings. It suggests the kinds of object categories that we are particularly likely to be overconfident about. For example, it leads us to expect more errors and more severely misplaced confidence in judgments when the category in question lies in the social rather than the physical domain. The reason is obvious: Bigot #1 is far less likely to resemble bigot #2 or the ''prototypic bigot'' than oak tree #1 is likely to resemble oak tree #2, or the ''prototypic oak tree,'' and so forth. The semanticists' point readily can be made in more statistical or probabilistic terms: The variance in the characteristics of objects to which we have applied the *same* knowledge structures is usually *greater* than we are likely to assume while, conversely, the variance in objects to which we have applied *different* knowledge structures (especially if those objects happen to be people) is likely to be *less* than we assume.

THEORIES AND THEIR JUSTIFICATION. An important step in reducing people's overconfidence would be taken by leading them to recognize that their interpretations of events, rather than being simple read-outs of data, are inferences that make heavy use of theory. Once one recognizes that the same data would look quite different, and could easily support different beliefs, if those data were viewed from the vantage point of alternative theories, the groundwork for a humbler epistemic stance has been laid. Such a recognition invites people to consider the logical or empirical status of their prior theories and to adjust their confidence accordingly. When the theory is well-founded, its heavy use in the interpretation of ambiguous events is correspondingly justified. But when the origin of the theory is dubious, its role in governing the interpretation of data must be severely circumscribed.

This book has offered many clues which might help people to identify theories that are suspect and are therefore unlikely to merit heavy use in the interpretation of data. For example, informal theories of covariation normally should be considered suspect, as should *ad hoc* causal theories, especially those that seem to involve heavy reliance on the representativeness heuristic.

EXTREME JUDGMENTS AND PREDICTIONS. A better understanding of the nature of regression should prompt caution about extreme judgments and predictions, that is, about precisely those judgments and predictions that are most likely to be wrong and to result in disadvantageous behavior. An appreciation of regression should serve to make people stop and reconsider whenever they find that they have arrived at an extreme assessment: Is the theory underlying my assessment sufficiently well-grounded? Is my data sample sufficiently large and free of bias to justify my extreme departure from the central tendency of the population of objects or events about which I have made my assessment?

THE ROLE AND RESPONSIBILITIES
OF THE SOCIAL SCIENTIST

It is not only the layperson who is frequently overconfident. It is appropriate for us to conclude this book by pointing to the damage that can be done when it is social scientists who are inappropriately confident—particularly when they are overconfident in their efforts to guide effective policy making.

In urging the teaching and frequent use of more normatively appropriate inferential strategies, we also are urging an important role for the social scientist. It has been social scientists (and philosophers) who have sought to identify inferential shortcomings and to develop more normatively appropriate methods for collecting and analyzing data, for testing theories, and for integrating information in the service of decision making. It is social scientists, moreover, who serve as executors of the rich legacy of theory and data accumulated through the exercise of formal inferential strategies. One of our goals in writing this book has been to provide a rationale for giving a larger role to the formally trained scientist—in arbitrating disputes over existing facts, in designing strategies for discovering new facts, and in evaluating the conflicting theories generated by the exercise of 'intuitive" science.

The lofty position we are advocating for the social scientist necessarily carries with it some important responsibilities and restrictions. We are all too aware of the destructive influence that social scientists can have, and have had, in justifying and even initiating ill-advised and pernicious social policies. (Kamin's 1975 documentation of the part that psychologists played in furnishing a "scientific" rationale for the exclusionary immigration policies initiated in the United States during the 1920s is one particularly shocking example.)

Regrettably, it is inevitable that social scientists sometimes will be wrong in characterizing particular social problems and in predicting the impact of particular social remedies. But the damage, to our profession as well as to the society it serves and seeks to understand, can be curtailed considerably. Perhaps most imperative is the need to show greater candor and humility. We must learn to distinguish clearly, in our public statements as in our professional writing, what is known from what it is reasonable to presume, what it is reasonable to presume from what it is possible to make an educated guess at, and what it is possible to make an educated guess at from what it is possible only to guess at. In other words, we must learn to be more forthright in specifying when we are speaking as formal scientists, "ex cathedra," as it were, willing and able to defend our contentions against the exacting and conservative standards that our science demands, and when we are speaking essentially as intelligent laypeople or "intuitive" scientists.

We also must be more willing to concede that it is as methodologists and not as theorists that we are most able to contribute. Seldom can we look to the findings and theories of our field to discover a firm basis for policy decisions. What we *can* do is help to find better ways of designing and evaluating social programs. We can defend the long term advantages of well-controlled experiments over "cheaper" and more politically expedient designs. We can help to justify and design the best possible methods for data collection. Most important, we can champion the cause of normative inferential strategies, and warn against the dangers of purely intuitive ones, when the issues addressed are both empirical and of pressing social concern.

SUMMARY

The inferential goals of the layperson are best compared not to those of the pure scientist but to those of the applied scientist or practitioner. The rules of pure scientific inquiry thus provide only a rough and approximate guide to lay inferential strategy, and it will sometimes be proper to set them aside in favor of procedures that facilitate action or that better serve extraepistemic goals.

The decision to substitute a relatively formal inferential strategy for a relatively informal one, or vice versa, is dictated by cost-benefit considerations. Decisions of little consequence generally will, and should, be guided by intuitive strategies. At the other extreme, recurrent decisions with important consequences generally should be made with the aid of the best normative strategies available, even if these are relatively costly.

Programs of secondary and higher education should be revised to provide people with a better grounding in formal inferential rules. Statistics and probability theory should be taught at least as early as secondary school, and curricula should feature discussion of the contrast between formal and informal intuitive strategies. Providing concrete, anecdotal examples of intuitive errors and teaching judgmental maxims also should be helpful.

Though the mood of the book is optimistic about prospects for the improvement of human inference, it must be recognized that there are serious barriers to change. People cannot examine directly their inferential procedures and discover their flaws; the very most important personal judgments are apt to prove particularly impervious to logical insights; and people are apt to be so confident about most of their judgments that they are disinclined to examine them for the possibility of error.

Social scientists, especially in the role of social advocates, are often open to the same charge of misplaced certainty as the layperson. If social scientists are to be worthy of the role that we advocate, they must specify when they are speaking as formal scientists and when they are speaking only as intuitive scientists.

references

ABELSON, R. P. Psychological implication. In R. P. Abelson, E. Aronson, W. J. McGuire, T. M. Newcomb, M. J. Rosenberg, & P. H. Tannenbaum (Eds.), *Theories of cognitive consistency: A sourcebook*. Chicago: Rand McNally, 1968.

ABELSON, R. P. Script processing in attitude formation and decision making. In J. S. Carroll & J. W. Payne (Eds.), *Cognition and social behavior*. Hillsdale, N.J.: Lawrence Erlbaum, 1976.

ABELSON, R. P. *Scripts*. Invited address to the Midwestern Psychological Association, Chicago, May 1978.

ABRAHAMSEN, D. *Nixon vs. Nixon: An emotional tragedy*. New York: Farrar, Straus, & Giroux, 1977.

AJZEN, I. Intuitive theories of events and the effects of base-rate information on prediction. *Journal of Personality and Social Psychology*, 1977, *35*, 303-314.

ALLPORT, G. W. *The nature of prejudice*. Reading, Mass.: Addison-Wesley, 1954.

AMABILE, T. M. *Investigations in the psychology of prediction*. Unpublished manuscript, Stanford University, 1975.

ANDERSON, C., LEPPER, M. R. & ROSS, L. *Theory perseverance*. Unpublished manuscript, Stanford University, 1979.

ANDERSON, N. H. Averaging versus adding as a stimulus-combination rule in impression formation. *Journal of Experimental Psychology*, 1965, *70*, 394-400.

ANDERSON, N. H. Two more tests against change of meaning in adjective combinations. *Journal of Verbal Learning and Verbal Behavior*, 1971, *10*, 75-85.

ANDERSON, N. H. *The problem of change-of-meaning*. Center for Human Information Processing Technical Report, June, 1974.

ANDERSON, N. H., & JACOBSON, A. Effect of stimulus inconsistency and discounting instructions in personality impression formation. *Journal of Personality and Social Psychology*, 1965, *2*, 531-539.

ARENDT, H. *Eichmann in Jerusalem: A report on the banality of evil.* New York: Viking, 1965.

ARKIN, R., & DUVAL, S. Focus of attention and causal attributions of actors and observers. *Journal of Experimental Social Psychology*, 1975, *11*, 427–438.

ASCH, S. Forming impressions of personality. *Journal of Abnormal and Social Psychology*, 1946, *41*, 258–90.

BACON, F. *The new organon and related writings.* New York: Liberal Arts Press, 1960. (Originally published, 1620.)

BARBER, B. *Science and the social order.* New York: Collier, 1952.

BARTLETT, F. C. *Remembering.* Cambridge: Cambridge University Press, 1932.

BECK, A. T. *Depression: Clinical, experimental, and theoretical aspects.* New York: Harper & Row, 1967.

BEM, D. J. *An experimental analysis of beliefs and attitudes.* (Doctoral dissertation, University of Michigan) Ann Arbor, Mich.: University Microfilms, 1964, No. 64-12, 588.

BEM, D. J. An experimental analysis of self-persuasion. *Journal of Experimental Social Psychology*, 1965, *1*, 199–218.

BEM, D. J. Self-perception: An alternative interpretation of cognitive dissonance phenomena. *Psychological Review*, 1967, *74*, 183–200.

BEM, D. J. Self-perception theory. In L. Berkowitz (Ed.) *Advances in Experimental Social Psychology* (Vol. 6). New York: Academic Press, 1972.

BEM, D. J. Cognitive alteration of feeling states: A discussion. In H. S. London & R. E. Nisbett (Eds.) *Thought and feeling: Cognitive alteration of feeling states.* Chicago: Aldine-Atherton, 1974.

BEM, D. J., & ALLEN, A. On predicting some of the people some of the time: The search for cross-situational consistencies in behavior. *Psychological Review*, 1974, *81*, 506–520.

BEM, D. J., & FUNDER, D. C. Predicting more of the people more of the time: Assessing the personality of situations. *Psychological Review*, 1978, *85*, 485–501.

BEM, D. J., & McCONNELL, H. K. Testing the self-perception explanation of dissonance phenomena: On the salience of premanipulation attitudes. *Journal of Personality and Social Psychology*, 1970, *14*, 23–31.

BENNETT, C. The effects of the student's race, social class, academic history, and task performance on the teacher's expectations, causal attributions, and sentiments toward the student. Unpublished doctoral dissertation, University of Mighigan, 1978.

BERNE, E. *Games people play.* New York: Grove Press, 1964.

BIERBRAUER, G. *Effect of set, perspective, and temporal factors in attribution.* Unpublished doctoral dissertation, Stanford University, 1973.

BLOCK, J. *The Q-sort method in personality assessment and psychiatric research.* Springfield, Ill.: Charles C. Thomas, 1961.

BOBROW, D., & COLLINS, A. *Representation and understanding: Studies in cognitive science.* New York: Academic Press, 1976.

BORGIDA, E., & NISBETT, R. E. The differential impact of abstract vs. concrete information on decisions. *Journal of Applied Social Psychology,* 1977, *7,* 258–271.

BOWER, G. H. Mental imagery and associative learning. In L. Gregg (Ed.), *Cognition in learning and memory.* New York: Wiley, 1972.

BOWER, G., BLACK, J., & TURNER, T. Scripts in text comprehension and memory. *Cognitive Psychology,* in press.

BRICKMAN, P. Is it real? In J. Harvey, W. Ickes, and R. Kidd (Eds.) *New directions in attribution research.* (Vol. 2). Hillsdale, N.J.: Lawrence Erlbaum Associates, 1978.

BROWN, R. *Social psychology.* New York: Free Press, 1965.

BRUNER, J. S. Going beyond the information given. In H. Gulber and others (Eds.), *Contemporary approaches to cognition.* Cambridge, Mass.: Harvard University Press, 1957.

BRUNER, J. S., SHAPIRO, D., & TAGIURI, R. The meaning of traits in isolation and in combination. In R. Tagiuri & L. Petrullo (Eds.), *Person perception and interpersonal behavior.* Stanford, Calif.: Stanford University Press, 1958.

CANTOR, J. R., ZILLMAN, D., & BRYANT, J. Enhancement of experienced arousal in response to erotic stimuli through misattribution of unrelated residual arousal. *Journal of Personality and Social Psychology,* 1975, *32,* 69–75.

CANTOR, N., & MISCHEL, W. Traits as prototypes: Effects on recognition memory. *Journal of Personality and Social Psychology,* 1977, *35,* 38–49.

CANTOR, N., & MISCHEL, W. Prototypicality and personality: Effects on free recall and personality impressions. *Journal of Research in Personality,* in press.

CHAPMAN, L. J. Illusory correlation in observational report. *Journal of Verb Learning and Verbal Behavior,* 1967, *6,* 151–155.

CHAPMAN, L. J., & CHAPMAN, J. P. Genesis of popular but erroneous diagnostic observations. *Journal of Abnormal Psychology*, 1967, *72*, 193–204.

CHAPMAN, L. J., & CHAPMAN, J. P. Illusory correlation as an obstacle to the use of valid psychodiagnostic signs. *Journal of Abnormal Psychology*, 1969, *74*, 271–280.

CHRISTIE, R., & GEIS, F. L. (Eds.), *Studies in Machiavellianism*. New York: Academic Press, 1970.

COLLINS, B. E. Four components of the Rotter internal-external scale: Belief in a difficult world, a just world, a predictable world, and a politically responsive world. *Journal of Personality and Social Psychology*, 1974, *29*, 381–391.

CRANDALL, V. C., KATKOVSKY, W., & CRANDALL, V. G. Children's beliefs in their own control of reinforcements in intellectual-academic achievement situations. *Child Development*, 1965, *36*, 91–109.

CROUSE, T. *The boys on the bus*. New York: Ballantine, 1974.

D'ANDRADE, R. G. Trait psychology and componential analysis. *American Anthropologist*, 1965, *67*, 215–228.

D'ANDRADE, R. G. Memory and the assessment of behavior. In H. M. Blalock (Ed.), *Measurement in the social sciences*. Chicago: Aldine, 1974.

DAVIS, J. H. Group decision and social interaction: A theory of social decision schemes. *Psychological Review*, 1973, *80*, 97–125.

DAWES, R. M. Shallow psychology. In J. S. Carroll and J. W. Payne (Eds.), *Cognition and social behavior*. Hillsdale, N.J.: Lawrence Erlbaum Associates, 1976.

DAWES, R. M. The robust beauty of improper linear models in decision making. *American Psychologist*, 1979, in press.

DAWES, R. M., & CORRIGAN, B. Linear models in decision-making. *Psychological Bulletin*, 1974, *81*, 95–106.

DECI, E. C. Effects of externally mediated rewards on intrinsic motivation. *Journal of Personality and Social Psychology*, 1971, *18*, 105–115.

DE SOTO, C. B. The predilection for single orderings. *Journal of Abnormal and Social Psychology*, 1961, *62*, 16–23.

DILLEHAY, R., INSKO, C., & SMITH, M. Logical consistency and attitude change. *Journal of Personality and Social Psychology*, 1966, *3*, 646–654.

DIXON, N. F. *Subliminal perception: The nature of a controversy*. London: McGraw-Hill, 1971.

DORNBUSCH, S. M., HASTORF, A. H., RICHARDSON, S. A., MUZZY, R. E., & VREELAND, R. S. The perceiver and the perceived: Their relative influence on the categories of interpersonal cognition. *Journal of Personality and Social Psychology*, 1965, *3*, 434–440.

DOYLE, A. C. *The memoirs of Sherlock Holmes*. London: John Murray and Jonathan Cape, 1974. (Originally published, 1893).

DUMOUCHEL, W. H., & KRANTZ, D. H. *Statistics notes*. Unpublished manuscript, University of Michigan, 1979.

DUVAL, S., & WICKLUND, R. A. *A theory of objective self-awareness*. New York: Academic Press, 1972.

EDWARDS, W. The theory of decision making. *Psychological Bulletin*, 1954, *51*, 380–417.

EDWARDS, W. Conservatism in human information processing. In B. Kleinmuntz (Ed.), *Formal representation of human judgment*. New York: Wiley, 1968.

EINHORN, H. J., & HOGARTH, R. M. Confidence in judgment: Persistence of the illusion of validity. Psychological Review, 1978, *85*, 395–416.

ELLSWORTH, P., & ROSS, L. Intimacy in response to direct gaze. *Journal of Experimental Social Psychology*, 1975, *11*, 592–613.

ENZLE, M. E., HANSEN, R. D., & LOWE, C. A. Humanizing the mixed-motive paradigm: Methodological implications from attribution theory. *Simulation and Games*, 1975, *6*, 151–165.

ERDELYI, M. H. A new look at the New Look: Perceptual defense and vigilance. *Psychological Review*, 1974, *81*, 1–25.

ERDELYI, M. H., & GOLDBERG, B. Let's not sweep repression under the rug: Toward a cognitive psychology of repression. In J. H. Kilstrom & F. J. Evans (Eds.), *Functional disorders of memory*. Hillsdale, N.J.: Lawrence Erlbaum, 1978.

ERICCSON, K. A., & SIMON, H. A. *Retrospective verbal reports as data*. Unpublished manuscript, Carnegie-Mellon University, 1978.

EVANS-PRITCHARD, E. E. *Witchcraft, oracles and magic among the Azande*. Oxford: Clarendon, 1937.

FESTINGER, L. *A theory of cognitive dissonance*. Stanford, Calif.: Stanford University Press, 1957.

FESTINGER, L., SCHACHTER, S., & BACK, K. *Social pressures in informal groups: A study of human factors in housing*. New York: Harper & Row, 1950.

FISCHHOFF, B. Hindsight ≠ foresight: The effect of outcome knowledge on judgment under uncertainty. *Journal of Experimental Psychology: Human Perception and Performance,* 1975, *1,* 288–299.

FISCHHOFF, B., & BEYTH, R. "I knew it would happen"—remembered probabilities of once-future things. *Organizational Behavior and Human Performance,* 1975, *13,* 1–16.

FISCHHOFF, B., SLOVIC, P., & LICHTENSTEIN, S. Knowing with certainty: The appropriateness of extreme confidence. *Journal of Experimental Psychology: Human Perception and Performance,* 1977, *3,* 552–564.

FREEDMAN, R., & PAPSDORF, J. Biofeedback and progressive relaxation treatment of insomnia: A controlled all-night investigation. *Biofeedback and Self-Regulation,* 1976, *1,* 253–271.

FREUD, S. *Collected Papers* (Vol. 4). New York: Basic Books, 1959.

GARCIA, J., McGOWAN, B., ERVIN, F., & KOELLING, R. Cues: Their relative effectiveness as reinforcers. *Science,* 1968, *160,* 794–795.

GARCIA, J., McGOWAN, B. K., & GREEN, K. F. Sensory quality and integration: Constraints on conditioning. In A. H. Black & W. F. Prokasy (Eds.), *Classical conditioning II: Current research and theory.* New York: Appleton-Century-Crofts, 1972.

GEHRING, R. E., TOGLIA, M. P., & KIMBLE, G. A. Recognition memory for words and pictures at short and long retention intervals. *Memory and Cognition,* 1976, *4,* 256–260.

GIBSON, J. J., & PICK, A. D. Perception of another person's looking behavior. *American Journal of Psychology,* 1963, *76,* 386–394.

GOETHALS, G. R., & RECKMAN, R. F. The perception of consistency in attitudes. *Journal of Experimental Social Psychology,* 1973, *9,* 491–501.

GOFFMAN, E. *The presentation of self in everyday life.* New York: Doubleday, 1959.

GOLDBERG, L. R. The effectiveness of clinician's judgments: The diagnosis of organic brain damage from the Bender-Gestalt Test. *Journal of Consulting Psychology,* 1959, *23,* 25–33.

GOLDBERG, L. R. Differential attribution of trait-descriptive terms to oneself as compared to well-liked, neutral, and disliked others: A psychometric analysis. *Journal of Personality and Social Psychology,* 1978, *36,* 1012–1028.

GOLDBERG, P. Are women prejudiced against women? *Transaction,* April 1968, 28–30.

GOLDING, S. L., & RORER, L. G. Illusory correlation and subjective judgment. *Journal of Abnormal Psychology*, 1972, *80*, 249–260.

GOLDMAN, A. I. Epistemics: The regulative theory of cognition. *The Journal of Philosophy*, 1978, *75*, 509–524.

GOLDMAN, A. I. *Regulative epistemology and the psychology of doxastic states.* Unpublished manuscript, University of Michigan, 1979.

HALEY, J., *Uncommon therapy. The psychiatric techniques of Milton H. Erickson, M.D.* New York: Norton, 1973.

HAMILL, R., WILSON, T. D., & NISBETT, R. E. Ignoring sample bias: Inferences about collectivities from atypical cases. Unpublished manuscript, University of Michigan, 1979.

HAMILTON, D. L. Cognitive biases in the perception of social groups. In J. S. Carroll & J. W. Payne (Eds.), *Cognition and social behavior.* Hillsdale, N.J.: Lawrence Erlbaum, 1976.

HAMILTON, D. L. A cognitive attributional analysis of stereotyping. In L. Berkowitz (Ed.), *Advances in Experimental Social Psychology* (Vol. 12). New York: Academic Press, 1979.

HAMILTON, D. L., & GIFFORD, R. K. Illusory correlation in interpersonal perception: A cognitive basis of stereotypic judgments. *Journal of Experimental Social Psychology*, 1976. *12*, 392–407.

HAMILTON, D. L., & ZANNA, M. P. Context effects in impression formation: Changes in connotative meaning. *Journal of Personality and Social Psychology*, 1974, *29*, 649–654.

HAMMOND, K. R., STEWART, T. R., BREHMER, B., & STEINMAN, D. O. *Social judgment theory.* New York: Academic Press, 1975.

HANSEN, R. D., & DONOGHUE, J. M. The power of consensus: Information derived from one's own and others' behavior. *Journal of Personality and Social Psychology*, 1977, *35*, 294–302.

HARTSHORNE, H., & MAY, M. A. *Studies in the nature of character.* Vol. I. *Studies in deceit.* New York: Macmillan, 1928.

HASTIE, R., & KUMAR, P. A. Person memory: Personality traits as organizing principles in memory for behavior. *Journal of Personality and Social Psychology*, 1979, *37*, 25–38.

HATVANY, N., STRACK, F., & ROSS, L. *Effects of the discredited "keywitness." A surprising exception to the "perseverance effect."* Unpublished manuscript, Stanford University, 1979.

HEIDER, F. Social perception and phenomenal causality. *Psychological Review,* 1944, *51,* 358–373.

HEIDER, F. *The psychology of interpersonal relations.* New York: Wiley, 1958.

HIGGINS, E. T. & RHOLES, W. S. Impression formation and role fulfillment: A "holistic reference" approach. *Journal of Experimental Social Psychology,* 1976, *12,* 422–435.

HIGGINS, E. T., RHOLES, W. S., & JONES, C. R. Category accessibility and impression formation. *Journal of Experimental Social Psychology,* 1977, *13,* 141–154.

HORNSTEIN, H. A., LaKIND, E., FRANKEL, G., & MANNE, S. Effects of knowledge about remote social events on prosocial behavior, social conception, and mood. *Journal of Personality and Social Psychology,* 1975, *32,* 1038–1046.

HOVLAND, C. I., JANIS, I. L., & KELLEY, H. H. *Communication and persuasion.* New Haven, Conn.: Yale University Press, 1953.

ICHEISER, G. Misunderstanding in human relations: A study in false social perception. *American Journal of Sociology,* 1949, *55,* 1–70.

JANIS, I. L. Stages in the decision-making process. In R. P. Abelson, E. Aronson, W. J. McGuire, T. M. Newcomb, M. J. Rosenberg, & P. H. Tannenbaum (Eds.), *Theories of cognitive consistency: A sourcebook.* Chicago: Rand McNally, 1968.

JANIS, I. L., & MANN, L. *Decision making.* New York: Free Press, 1977.

JAYNES, J. *The origin of consciousness in the breakdown of the bicameral mind.* Boston: Houghton-Mifflin, 1976.

JENKINS, H. M., & SAINSBURY, R. S. Discrimination learning with the distinctive feature on positive or negative trials. In D. Mostofsky (Ed.), *Attention: Contemporary theory and analysis.* New York: Appleton-Century-Crofts, 1970.

JENNINGS, D., AMABILE, T. M., & ROSS, L. Informal covariation assessment: data-based vs. theory-based judgments. In A. Tversky, D. Kahneman & P. Slovic (Eds.) *Judgment under uncertainty: Heuristics and biases.* New York: Cambridge University Press, 1980.

JENNINGS, D. L., LEPPER, M. R., & ROSS, L. *Persistence of impressions of personal persuasiveness.* Unpublished manuscript, Stanford University, 1979.

JONES, E. E. The rocky road from acts to dispositions. *American Psychologist,* 1979, *34,* 107–117.

JONES, E. E. The rocky road from acts to dispositions. *American Psychologist,* 1979, *34,* 107–117.

JONES, E. E., & DAVIS, K. E. From acts to dispositions: The attribution process in person perception. In L. Berkowitz (Ed.), *Advances in Experimental Social Psychology* (Vol. 2). New York: Academic Press, 1965.

JONES, E. E., & GERARD, H. B. *Foundations of social psychology.* New York: Wiley, 1967.

JONES, E. E., & GOETHALS, G. Order effects in impression formation: Attribution context and the nature of the entity. In E. E. Jones and others (Eds.), *Attribution: Perceiving the causes of behavior.* Morristown, N.J.: General Learning Press, 1972.

JONES, E. E., & HARRIS, V. A. The attribution of attitudes. *Journal of Experimental Social Psychology,* 1967, *3,* 1-24.

JONES, E. E., & NISBETT, R. E. The actor and the observer: Divergent perceptions of the causes of behavior. In E. E. Jones and others (Eds.), *Attribution: Perceiving the causes of behavior.* Morristown, N.J.: General Learning Press, 1972.

JONES, E. E., ROCK, L., SHAVER, K. G., GOETHALS, G. R., & WARD, L. M. Pattern of performance and ability attribution: An unexpected primacy effect. *Journal of Personality and Social Psychology,* 1968, *10,* 317-340.

JONES, J. M. *Prejudice and racism.* Reading, Mass.: Addison-Wesley, 1972.

KAHNEMAN, D., & TVERSKY, A. Subjective probability: A judgment of representativeness. *Cognitive Psychology,* 1971, *3,* 430-454.

KAHNEMAN, D., & TVERSKY, A. On the psychology of prediction. *Psychological Review,* 1973, *80,* 237-251.

KAHNEMAN, D., & TVERSKY, A. Intuitive prediction: Biases and corrective procedures. *Management Science,* in press.

KAMIN, L. G. *The science and politics of IQ.* New York: Halsted Press, 1975.

KANOUSE, D. E. Language, labeling, and attribution. In E. E. Jones, and others (Eds.), *Attribution: Perceiving the Causes of Behavior.* Morristown, N.J.: General Learning Press, 1972.

KATZ, D. The functional approach to the study of attitudes. *Public Opinion Quarterly,* 1960, *24,* 163-204.

KELLEY, H. H. The warm-cold variable in first impressions of persons. *Journal of Personality,* 1950, *18,* 431-439.

KELLEY, H. H. Attribution theory in social psychology. In D. Levine (Ed.), *Nebraska Symposium on Motivation* (Vol. 15). Lincoln: University of Nebraska Press, 1967.

KELLEY, H. H. Attribution in social interaction. In E. E. Jones and others (Eds.), *Attribution: Perceiving the causes of behavior.* Morristown, N.J.: General Learning Press, 1972. (a)

KELLEY, H. H. Causal schemata and the attribution process. In E. E. Jones and others (Eds.), *Attribution: Perceiving the causes of behavior.* Morristown: N.J.: General Learning Press, 1972. (b)

KELLEY, H. H. The process of causal attribution. *American Psychologist,* 1973, *28,* 107–128.

KELLEY, H. H ., & STAHELSKI, A. J. Social interaction basis of cooperators' and competitors' beliefs about others. *Journal of Personality and Social Psychology,* 1970, *16,* 66–91.

KELLEY, H. H., & THIBAUT, J. W. Experimental studies of group problem-solving and process. In G. Lindzey (Ed.), *Handbook of social psychology* Vol. II. Cambridge, Mass.: Addison-Wesley, 1954.

KELLY, G. *The psychology of personal constructs* (2 vols.). New York: Norton, 1955.

KELLY, G. Man's construction of his alternatives. In G. Lindzey (Ed.), *Assessment of human motives.* New York: Holt, Rinehart & Winston, 1958.

KELMAN, H. C. The human use of human subjects: The problem of deception in social psychological experiments. In A. G. Miller (Ed.), *The social psychology of psychological research.* New York: Macmillan, 1972.

KIESLER, C. A., COLLINS, B. E. & MILLER, N. *Attitude change: A critical analysis of theoretical approaches.* New York: Wiley, 1969.

KIESLER, C. A., NISBETT, R. E., & ZANNA, M. P. On inferring one's beliefs from one's behavior. *Journal of Personality and Social Psychology,* 1969, *11,* 321–327.

KRANTZ, D., & MIYAMOTO, J. *Non-Bayesian belief structures.* Unpublished manuscript, University of Michigan, 1980.

KRUGLANSKI, A. W. Endogenous attribution and intrinsic motivation. In M. R. Lepper & D. Greene (Eds.), *The hidden costs of reward.* Hillsdale, New Jersey: Lawrence Erlbaum, 1978.

KUHN, T. S. *The structure of scientific revolutions.* Chicago: University of Chicago Press, 1962.

LANGER, E. J. The illusion of control. *Journal of Personality and Social Psychology,* 1975, *32,* 311–328.

LANGER, E. J. The psychology of chance. *Journal for the Theory of Social Behavior,* 1977, *7,* 185–208.

LANGER, E. J., & ROTH, S. Heads I win, tails it's chance: The illusion of control as a function of the sequence of outcomes in a purely chance task. *Journal of Personality and Social Psychology,* 1975, *32,* 951–955.

LEFCOURT, H. M. Internal vs. external control of reinforcement revisited: Recent developments. In B. A. Maher (Ed.), *Progress in Experimental Personality Research* (Vol. 6). New York: Academic Press, 1972.

LEPPER, M. R., & GREENE, D. (EDS.). *The hidden costs of reward.* Morristown, N.J.: Lawrence Erlbaum, 1978.

LEPPER, M. R., GREENE, D., & NISBETT, R. E. Undermining children's intrinsic interest with extrinsic reward: A test of the overjustification hypothesis. *Journal of Personality and Social Psychology,* 1973, *28,* 129–137.

LEPPER, M. R., ROSS, L., & LAU, R. *Persistence of inaccurate and discredited personal impressions: A field demonstration of attributional perseverance.* Unpublished manuscript. Stanford University, 1979.

LERNER, M. J., & MATTHEWS, G. Reactions to suffering of others under conditions of indirect responsibility. *Journal of Personality and Social Psychology,* 1967, *5,* 319–325.

LEVENTHAL, H. Findings and theory in the study of fear communications. In L. Berkowitz (Ed.), *Advances in Experimental Social Psychology* (Vol. 5). New York: Academic Press, 1970.

LEWIN, K. *A dynamic theory of personality.* New York: McGraw-Hill, 1935.

LEWINSOHN, P. M., MISCHEL, W., CHAPLIN, W., & BARTON, R. Social competence and depression: The role of illusory self-perceptions. *Journal of Abnormal Psychology,* in Press, 1980.

LIBET, J. M., & LEWINSOHN, P. M. The concept of social skill with special reference to the behavior of depressed persons. *Journal of Consulting and Clinical Psychology,* 1973, *40,* 304–312.

LORD, C., ROSS, L., & LEPPER, M. R. Biased assimilation and attitude polarization: The effects of prior theories on subsequently considered evidence. *Journal of Personality and Social Psychology,* in press, 1979. Stanford University, 1979.

LUCHINS, A. S. Mechanization in problem solving: The effect of Einstellung. *Psychological Monographs,* 1942, *54,* 1–95.

LUCHINS, A. S. Experimental attempts to minimize the impact of first impressions. In C. I. Hovland (Ed.), *The order of presentation in persuasion.* New Haven, Conn.: Yale University Press, 1957.

MAHONEY, M. J. *Scientist as subject: The psychological imperative.* Cambridge, Mass.: Ballinger, 1976.

MAHONEY, M. J. *Psychology of the scientist: An evaluative review.* Unpublished manuscript, Pennsylvania State University, 1977.

MAHONEY, M. J., & DeMONBREUN, B. G. Psychology of the scientist: An analysis of problem-solving bias. *Cognitive Therapy and Research,* 1977, *1,* 229–238.

MANDLER, G. *Mind and Emotion.* New York: John Wiley & Sons, 1975.

MANIS, M., & DOVALINA, I. *Base rates can affect individual predictions.* Unpublished manuscript, University of Michigan, 1979.

MARKUS, H. Self-schemata and processing information about the self. *Journal of Personality and Social Psychology,* 1977, *35,* 63–78.

MAY, E. R. *"Lessons" of the past.* New York: Oxford University Press, 1973.

McARTHUR, L. Z. The how and what of why: Some determinants and consequences of causal attribution. *Journal of Personality and Social Psychology,* 1972, *22,* 171–193.

McARTHUR, L. Z. The lesser influence of consensus than distinctiveness information on causal attributions: A test of the person-thing hypothesis. *Journal of Personality and Social Psychology,* 1976, *33,* 733–742.

McARTHUR, L. Z. *Consensus and distinctiveness information effects on causal attribution as a function of the type of stimuli to which each pertains.* Unpublished manuscript, Brandeis University, 1978.

McARTHUR, L. Z. & POST, D. Figural emphasis and person perception. *Journal of Experimental Social Psychology,* 1977, *13,* 520–535.

McARTHUR, L. Z., & SOLOMON, L. K. Perceptions of an aggressive encounter as a function of the victim's salience and the perceiver's arousal. *Journal of Personality and Social Psychology,* 1978, *36,* 1278–1290.

McCAULEY, C. The concept of stereotype. *Psychological Bulletin,* in press.

McGUIGAN, F. J. The experimenter: A neglected stimulus object. *Psychological Bulletin,* 1963, *60,* 421–428.

McGUIRE, W. J. Attitudes and opinions. *Annual Review of Psychology,* 1966, *17,* 475–514.

McGUIRE, W. J. A syllogistic analysis of cognitive relationships. In M. J. Rosenberg, C. I. Hovland, W. J. McGuire, R. P. Abelson, and J. W. Brehm (Eds.), *Attitude organization and change.* New Haven, Conn.: Yale University Press, 1960.

MEEHL, P. *Clinical vs. statistical prediction.* Minneapolis: University of Minnesota Press, 1955.

MILGRAM, S. Behavioral study of obedience. *Journal of Abnormal and Social Psychology,* 1963, *67,* 371–378.

MILL, J. S. *A system of logic ratiocinative and inductive.* Toronto: University of Toronto Press, 1974. (Originally published, 1843.)

MILLER, A. G. (Ed.), *The social psychology of psychological research.* New York: Macmillan, 1972.

MILLER, A. G., GILLEN, B., SCHENKER, C., & RADLOVE, S. Perception of obedience to authority. *Proceedings of the 81st Annual Convention of the American Psychological Association,* 1973, *8,* 127–128.

MILLER, D. T., & ROSS, M. Self-serving biases in the attribution of causality: Fact or fiction? *Psychological Bulletin,* 1975, *82,* 213–225.

MINSKY, M. A framework for representing knowledge. In P. H. Winston (Ed.), *The psychology of computer vision.* New York: McGraw-Hill, 1975.

MISCHEL, W. *Personality and assessment.* New York: Wiley, 1968.

MISCHEL, W. Continuity and change in personality. *American Psychologist,* 1969, *24,* 1012–1018.

MISCHEL, W. Towards a cognitive social learning reconceptualization of personality. *Psychological Review,* 1973, *80,* 252–283.

MISCHEL, W., EBBESEN, E., & ZEISS, A. R. Determinants of selective memory about the self. *Journal of Consulting and Clinical Psychology,* 1976, *44,* 92–103.

MISCHEL, W., & GILLIGAN, C. Delay of gratification, motivation for the prohibited gratification, and responses to temptation. *Journal of Abnormal and Social Psychology,* 1964, *64,* 411–417.

NEISSER, U. *Cognition and reality: Principles and implications of cognitive psychology.* San Francisco: Freeman, 1976.

NEWCOMB, T. M. *Consistency of certain extrovert-introvert behavior patterns in 51 problem boys.* New York: Columbia University, Teachers College, Bureau of Publications, 1929.

NEWELL, A., & SIMON, H. A. *Human problem solving.* Englewood Cliffs, N.J.: Prentice-Hall, 1972.

NISBETT, R. E., & BELLOWS, N. Verbal reports about causal influences on social judgments: Private access versus public theories. *Journal of Personality and Social Psychology,* 1977, *35,* 613–624.

NISBETT, R. E., & BORGIDA, E. Attribution and the psychology of prediction. *Journal of Personality and Social Psychology,* 1975, *32,* 932–943.

NISBETT, R. E., BORGIDA, E., CRANDALL, K., & REED, H. Popular induction: Information is not always informative. In J. S. Carroll & J. W. Payne (Eds.), *Cognition and social behavior*, 1976, *2*, 227–236.

NISBETT, R. E., CAPUTO, C., LEGANT, P., & MARACEK, J. Behavior as seen by the actor and as seen by the observer. *Journal of Personality and Social Psychology*, 1973, *27*, 154–164.

NISBETT, R. E., HARVEY, D., & WILSON, J. *"Epistemological" coding of the content of everyday social conversations.* Unpublished manuscript, University of Michigan, 1979.

NISBETT, R. E., & LEMLEY, R. N. *The evil that men do can be diluted, the good cannot.* Unpublished manuscript, University of Michigan, 1979.

NISBETT, R. E., & SCHACHTER, S. Cognitive manipulation of pain. *Journal of Experimental Social Psychology*, 1966, *21*, 227–236.

NISBETT, R. E., & WILSON, T. D. Telling more than we can know: Verbal reports on mental processes. *Psychological Review*, 1977, *84*, 231–259 (a).

NISBETT, R. E., & WILSON, T. D. The halo effect: Evidence for unconscious alteration of judgments. *Journal of Personality and Social Psychology*, 1977, *35*, 250–256. (b)

NISBETT, R. E., & ZUKIER, H. *The dilution effect: Producing "regressive" predictions by exposure to nondiagnostic information.* Unpublished manuscript, University of Michigan, 1979.

NORMAN, W. T., & GOLDBERG, L. R. Raters, ratees, and randomness in personality structure. *Journal of Personality and Social Psychology*, 1966, *4*, 681–691.

ORNE, M. T. Demand characteristics and their implications for real life: The importance of quasi-controls. In A. G. Miller (Ed.), *The social psychology of psychological research.* New York: Macmillan, 1972.

ORVIS, B. R., CUNNINGHAM, J. D., & KELLEY, H. H. A closer examination of causal inference: The roles of consensus, distinctiveness, and consistency information. *Journal of Personality and Social Psychology*, 1975, *32*, 605–616.

OSGOOD, C. E., SUCI, G. J., & TANNENBAUM, P. H. *The measurement of meaning.* Urbana: University of Illinois Press, 1957.

OSKAMP, S. Overconfidence in case-study judgments. *Journal of Consulting Psychology*, 1965, *29*, 261–265.

PAIVIO, A. *Imagery and verbal processes.* New York: Holt, Rinehart, & Winston, 1971.

PETERSON, C. R., & BEACH, L. R. Man as an intuitive statistician. *Psychological Bulletin*, 1967, *68*, 29-46.

PIAGET, J. *La naissance de l'intelligence chez l'enfant.* Neuchatel et Paris: Delachau et Niestle, 1936.

POLANYI, M. *Personal knowledge: Toward a post-critical philosophy.* New York: Harper & Row, 1958.

POLANYI, M. *Science, faith and society.* Chicago: University of Chicago Press, 1964.

POPPER, K. R. *The logic of scientific discovery.* New York: Harper, 1959.

PRYOR, J. B., & KRISS, M. The cognitive dynamics of salience in the attribution process. *Journal of Personality and Social Psychology*, 1977, *35*, 49-55.

REGAN, D. T., & TOTTEN, J. Empathy and attribution: Turning observers into actors. *Journal of Personality and Social Psychology*, 1975, *32*, 850-856.

ROGERS, T. B., ROGERS, P. J., & KUIPER, N. A. *Recognition memory for personal adjectives: Some evidence for self-reference as an aspect of memory.* Unpublished manuscript, University of Calgary, 1978.

ROKEACH, M., & ROTHMAN, G. The principle of belief congruence and the congruity principle as models of cognitive interaction. *Psychological Review*, 1965, *72*, 128-142.

ROSCH, E. Principles of categorization. In E. Rosch & B. Lloyd (Eds.), *Cognition and categorization.* Hillsdale, N.J.: Lawrence Erlbaum, 1978.

ROSENTHAL, R., & JACOBSON, L. *Pygmalion in the classroom: Teacher expectation and pupils' intellectual development.* New York: Holt, Rinehart & Winston, 1968.

ROSS, L. The intuitive psychologist and his shortcomings. In L. Berkowitz (Ed.) *Advances in Experimental Social Psychology* (Vol. 10). New York: Academic Press, 1977. (a)

ROSS, L. Problems in the interpretation of "self-serving" asymmetries in causal attribution: Comments on the Stephen et al. paper. *Sociometry*, 1977, *40*, 112-114. (b)

ROSS, L. Afterthoughts on the intuitive psychologist. In L. Berkowitz (Ed.), *Cognitive theories in social psychology.* New York: Academic Press, 1978.

ROSS, L., AMABILE, T. M., & JENNINGS, D. *Theories, strategies, and shortcomings in the psychology of intuitive prediction.* Unpublished manuscript, Stanford University, 1976.

Ross, L, Amabile, T. M., & Steinmetz, J. L. Social roles, social control, and biases in social-perception processes. *Journal of Personality and Social Psychology*, 1977, *35,* 485–494.

Ross, L., & Anderson, C. Shortcomings in the attribution process: On the origins and maintenance of erroneous social assessments. In A. Tversky, D. Kahneman & P. Slovic (Eds.), *Judgment under uncertainty: Heuristics and biases.* New York: Cambridge University Press, 1980.

Ross, L., Bierbrauer, G., & Polly, S. Attribution of educational outcomes by professional and non-professional instructors. *Journal of Personality and Social Psychology*, 1974, *29,* 609–618.

Ross, L., Greene, D., & House, P. The false consensus phenomenon: An attributional bias in self-perception and social perception processes. *Journal of Experimental Social Psychology*, 1977, *13,* 279–301.

Ross, L., Lepper, M. R., & Hubbard, M. Perseverance in self perception and social perception: Biased attributional processes in the debriefing paradigm. *Journal of Personality and Social Psychology*, 1975, *32,* 880–892.

Ross, L., Lepper, M. R., Strack, F., & Steinmetz, J. L. *Social explanation* and social expectation: The effects of real and hypothetical explanations upon subjective likelihood. *Journal of Personality and Social Psychology*, 1977, *35,* 817–829.

Ross, L., Rodin, J., & Zimbardo, P. G. Toward an attribution therapy: The reduction of fear through induced cognitive-emotional misattribution. *Journal of Personality and Social Psychology*, 1969, *12,* 279–288.

Ross, L., Turiel, E., Josephson, J., & Lepper, M. R. *Developmental perspectives on the fundamental attribution error.* Unpublished manuscript, Stanford University, 1978.

Ross, M., & Sicoly, F. Egocentric biases in availability and attribution. *Journal of Personality and Social Psychology*, 1979, *37,* 322–336.

Rothbart, M., & Fulero, S. *Attributions of causality for important events: The profound motive fallacy.* Unpublished manuscript, University of Oregon, 1978.

Rothbart, M., Fulero, S., Jensen, C., Howard, J., & Birrell, B. From individual to group impressions: Availability heuristics in stereotype formation. *Journal of Experimental Social Psychology*, 1978, *14,* 237–255.

Rotter, J. B. Generalized expectancies for internal versus external control of reinforcement. *Psychological Monographs*, 1966, *80* (609).

RUBLE, D. N., & FELDMAN, N. S. Order of consensus, distinctiveness and consistency information and causal attributions. *Journal of Personality and Social Psychology*, 1976, *34*, 930–937.

RUMELHART, D. E. Understanding and summarizing brief stories. In D. LaBerge & S. J. Samuels (Eds.), *Basic processes in reading: Perception and comprehension*. Hillsdale, N.J.: Lawrence Erlbaum, 1976.

RUMELHART, D. E., & ORTONY, A. The representation of knowledge in memory. In R. C., Anderson, R. J., Spiro, & W. E. Montague, (Eds.), *Schooling and the acquisition of knowledge*. Hillsdale, N.J.: Lawrence Erlbaum, 1976.

RUSSELL, B. *The conquest of happiness*. London: Allen & Unwin, 1930.

SAINSBURY, R. S. Discrimination learning using positive or negative cues. *Canadian Journal of Psychology*, 1973, *27*, 46–57.

SALANCIK, G. R. Inference of one's attitude from behavior recalled under linguistically manipulated cognitive sets. *Journal of Experimental Social Psychology*, 1974, *10*, 415–427.

SALANCIK, G. R. Extrinsic attribution and the use of behavior information to infer attitudes. *Journal of Personality and Social Psychology*, 1976, *34*, 1302–1312.

SALANCIK, G. R., & CONWAY, C. Attitude inferences from salient and relevant cognitive content about behavior. *Journal of Personality and Social Psychology*, 1975, *32*, 829–840.

SCHACHTER, S. The interaction of cognitive and physiological determinants of emotional state. In C. D. Spielberger (Ed.), *Anxiety and behavior*. New York: Academic Press, 1966.

SCHACHTER, S. The assumption of identity and perpheralist-centralist controversies in motivation and emotion. In M. B. Arnold (Ed.), *Feelings and emotion*. New York: Academic Press, 1970.

SCHACHTER, S. *Emotion, obesity, and crime*. New York: Academic Press, 1971.

SCHACHTER, S., & SINGER, J. E. Cognitive, social and physiological determinants of emotional state. *Psychological Review*, 1962, *69*, 379–399.

SCHACHTER, S., & WHEELER, L. Epinephrine, chlorpromazine, and amusement. *Journal of Abnormal and Social Psychology*, 1962, *65*, 121–128.

SCHANK, R. C. *Conceptual information processing*. Amsterdam: North Holland, 1975.

SCHANK, R., & ABELSON, R. P. *Scripts, plans, goals and understanding: An inquiry into human knowledge structures.* Hillsdale, N.J.: Lawrence Erlbaum, 1977.

SELIGMAN, M. E. P. On the generality of the laws of learning. *Psychological Review,* 1970, *77,* 406–418.

SELIGMAN, M. E. P. *Helplessness: On depression, development and death.* San Francisco: W. H. Freeman, 1975.

SELIGMAN, M. E. P. Comment and integration. *Journal of Abnormal Psychology,* 1978, *87,* 165–179.

SHAFER, G. *A mathematical theory of evidence.* Princeton, N.J.: Princeton University Press, 1976.

SHEPARD, R.N. Recognition memory for words, sentences and pictures. *Journal of Verbal Learning and Verbal Behavior,* 1967, *6,* 156–163.

SHWEDER, R. Likeness and likelihood in everyday thought: Magical thinking in judgments about personality. *Current Anthropology,* 1977, *18,* 637–658.

SILVERMAN, I. *Motives underlying the behavior of the subject in the psychological experiment.* Paper presented at the Meeting of the American Psychological Association, Chicago, 1965.

SINCLAIR, U. *The jungle.* New York: Sinclair, 1906.

SKINNER, B. F. *Science and human behavior.* New York: Macmillan, 1953.

SKINNER, B. F. *Verbal behavior.* New York: Appleton-Century-Crofts, 1957.

SKLAR, L. Methodological conservativism. *Philosophical Review,* 1975, *84,* 374–399.

SLOVIC, P. Toward understanding and improving decisions. In E. I. Salkovitz (Ed.), *Science, technology and the modern navy: Thirtieth anniversary, 1946–1976.* Arlington, Va.: *Office of Naval Research,* 1976.

SLOVIC, P., FISCHHOFF, B., & LICHTENSTEIN, S. Cognitive processes and societal risk taking. In J. S. Carroll and J. W. Payne (Eds.), *Cognition and social behavior.* Hillsdale, N.J.: Lawrence Erlbaum, 1976.

SLOVIC, P., FISCHHOFF, B., & LICHTENSTEIN, S. Behavioral decision theory. *Annual Review of Psychology,* 1977, *28,* 1–39.

SLOVIC, P., & LICHTENSTEIN, S. Comparison of Bayesian and regression approaches to the study of information processing in judgment. *Organizational Behavior and Human Performance,* 1971, *6,* 649–744.

SMEDSLUND, J. The concept of correlation in adults. *Scandinavian Journal of Psychology,* 1963, *4,* 165–173.

SMITH, E. R., & MILLER, E. R. Limits on perception of cognitive processes: A reply to Nisbett and Wilson. *Psychological Review,* 1978, *85,* 355–362.

SNYDER, M., & CANTOR, N. *Testing theories about other people: Remembering all the history that fits.* Unpublished manuscript, University of Minnesota, 1979.

SNYDER, M., & SWANN, W. B. Behavioral confirmation in social interaction: From social perception to social reality. *Journal of Experimental Social Psychology,* 1978, *14,* 148–162.

SNYDER, M., TANKE, E. D., & BERSCHEID, E. Social perception and interpersonal behavior: On the self-fulfilling nature of social stereotypes. *Journal of Personality and Social Psychology,* 1977, *35,* 656–666.

STANDING, L., CONEZIO, J., & HABER, R. N. Perception and memory for pictures: Single-trial learning of 2500 visual stimuli. *Psychonomic Science,* 1970, *19,* 73–74.

STICH, S. P. *Beliefs and subdoxastic states:* Unpublished manuscript, University of Maryland, 1979.

STICH, S. P., & NISBETT, R. E. *Philosophy of Science.* In press, University of Michigan, 1979.

STORMS, M. D. Videotape and the attribution process: Reversing actors' and observers' point of view. *Journal of Personality and Social Psychology,* 1973, *27,* 165–175.

STRICKLAND, L. H. Surveillance and trust. *Journal of Personality,* 1958, *26,* 200–215.

STUART, R. B., & DAVIS, B. *Slim chance in a fat world: Behavioral control of obesity.* Champaign, Ill.: Research Press, 1972.

TAYLOR, S. E., & CROCKER, J. C. Schematic bases of social information processing. In E. T. Higgins, P. Herman, & M. P. Zanna (Eds.), *The Ontario Symposium on Personality and Social Psychology* (Vol. 1). Hillsdale, N.J.: Lawrence Erlbaum, 1980.

TAYLOR, S. E., & FISKE, S. T. Point of view and perceptions of causality. *Journal of Personality and Social Psychology,* 1975, *32,* 439–445.

TAYLOR, S. E., & FISKE, S. T. Salience, attention and attribution: Top of the head phenomena. In L. Berkowitz (Ed.), *Advances in Experimental Social Psychology* (Vol. 11). New York: Academic Press, 1978.

TAYLOR, S. E., FISKE, S. T., CLOSE, M., ANDERSON, C. P., & RUDERMAN, A. *Solo status as a psychological variable: The power of being distinctive.* Unpublished manuscript, Harvard University, 1979.

TAYNOR, J., & DEAUX, K. When women are more deserving than men: Equity, attribution, and perceived sex differences. *Journal of Personality and Social Psychology,* 1973, *28,* 360-367.

TESSER, A. Self-generated attitude change. In L. Berkowitz (Ed.), *Advances in Experimental Social Psychology* (Vol. 11). New York: Academic Press, 1978.

TESTA, T. J. Causal relationships and the acquisition of avoidance responses. *Psychological Review,* 1974, *81,* 491-505.

THOMPSON, W. C., REYES, R. M., & BOWER, G. H. *Delayed effects of availability on judgment.* Unpublished manuscript, Stanford University, 1979.

TOMKINS, A. Script theory: Differential magnification of affects. In H. E. Howes & R. A. Dienstbier (Ed.), *Nebraska Symposium on Motivation.* (Vol. 26). Lincoln, Neb.: University of Nebraska Press, 1979.

TRIBE, L. Trial by mathematics: Precision and ritual in the legal process. *Harvard Law Review,* 1971, *84,* 1329-1393.

TSUJIMOTO, R. N. Memory bias toward normative and novel trait prototypes. *Journal of Personality and Social Psychology,* 1979, *36,* 1391-1401.

TSUJIMOTO, R. N., WILDE, J., & ROBERTSON, D. R. Distorted memory for examplars of a social structure: Evidence for schematic memory processes. *Journal of Personality and Social Psychology,* 1979, *36,* 1402-1414.

TVERSKY, A. Features of similarity. *Psychological Review,* 1977, *84,* 327-352.

TVERSKY, A., & KAHNEMAN, D. Belief in the law of small numbers. *Psychological Bulletin,* 1971, *76,* 105-110.

TVERSKY, A., & KAHNEMAN, D. Availability: A heuristic for judging frequency and probability. *Cognitive Psychology,* 1973, *5,* 207-232.

TVERSKY, A., & KAHNEMAN, D. Judgment under uncertainty: Heuristics and biases. *Science,* 1974, *185,* 1124-1131.

TVERSKY, A., & KAHNEMAN, D. Causal schemata in judgments under uncertainty. In M. Fishbein (Ed.), *Progress in social psychology.* Hillsdale, N.J.: Lawrence Erlbaum, 1978.

VINOKUR, A., & BURNSTEIN, E. Depolarization of attitudes in groups. *Journal of Personality and Social Psychology,* 1978, *36,* 872-885.

WALSTER, E. Assignment of responsibility for an accident. *Journal of Personality and Social Psychology,* 1966, *3,* 73-79.

WALSTER, E., BERSCHEID, E., ABRAHAMS, D., & ARONSON, E. Effectiveness of debriefing following deception experiments. *Journal of Personality and Social Psychology,* 1967, *6,* 371-380.

WARD, W. D., & JENKINS, H. M. The display of information and the judgment of contingency. *Canadian Journal of Psychology,* 1965, *19,* 231-241.

WASON, P. C., & JOHNSON-LAIRD, P. N. *Psychology of reasoning: structure and content.* London: Batsford, 1965.

WATSON, J. B. *Behaviorism.* Chicago: University of Chicago Press, 1924.

WEBER, M. *The protestant ethic and the spirit of capitalism.* (T. Parsons, trans.). New York: Scribner, 1930. (Originally published, 1904.)

WEINER, B. (Ed.), *Achievement motivation and attribution theory.* Morristown, N.J.: General Learning Press, 1974.

WEINER, B., FRIEZE, I., KUKLA, A., REED, L., REST, S., ROSENBAUM, R. M. Perceiving the causes of success and failure. In E. E. Jones and others (Eds.), *Attribution: Perceiving the causes of behavior.* Morristown, N.J.: General Learning Press, 1972.

WEISS, J., & BROWN, P. *Self-insight error in the explanation of mood.* Unpublished manuscript, Harvard University, 1977.

WELLS, G. L., & HARVEY, J. H. Do people use consensus information in making causal attributions? *Journal of Personality and Social Psychology,* 1977, *35,* 279-293.

WHEELER, D., & JANIS, I. *Making vital decisions: A guidebook.* New York: Free Press, 1980.

WILSON, T. D., & NISBETT, R. E. The accuracy of verbal reports about the effects of stimuli on evaluations and behavior. *Social Psychology,* 1978, *41,* 118-131.

WITTGENSTEIN, L. *Philosophical investigations.* New York: MacMillan, 1953.

WYER, R. S., JR., & WATSON, S. F. Context effects in impression formation. *Journal of Personality and Social Psychology,* 1969, *12,* 22-33.

ZAJONC, R. B. Attitudinal effects of mere exposure. *Journal of Personality and Social Psychology Monograph Supplement,* 1968, *9,* (2, Part 2) 1-27.

ZANNA, M. P., & COOPER, J. Dissonance and the attribution process. In J. H. Harvey, W. J. Ickes, & R. F. Kidd (Eds.), *New directions in attribution research* (Vol. 1). Hillsdale, New Jersey: Lawrence Erlbaum, 1976.

ZIMBARDO, P. G. *Shyness: What it is, what to do about it.* Reading, Mass.: Addison-Wesley, 1977.

ZUKIER, H. *On the psychology of red herrings: The role of nondiagnostic information in predicition.* Unpublished manuscript, New School for Social Research, 1979.

name index

subject index

Ability inferences:
  causal explanation for, 183–86
  misconstrual of regression phenomena,
    161–65
  perseverance of, 176–79
  use of consensus information for,
    134–35
Access to mental events (*see* Awareness)
Accommodation of theories to data,
  168–69
Actors vs. observers:
  access to private experience, 195–96,
    223–25
  accuracy of causal accounts, 212–14
  and availability heuristic, 122–25
  belief perseverance, 177–78
  causal inferences, 22
  and consensus information use, 133
  divergent attributions of, 123–24
  and salience, 125
Anchoring:
  effects on judgments, 41–42
  failure to recognize effects of, 208
Anova model for attribution:
  factors in, 113–15
  introspective access to variables, 224
Assimilation:
  of data to theories, 168–69
  of information regarding self, 197, 233,
    235
Associative networks and representativeness, 242–43
Attitude change:
  fundamental attribution error in, 121
  resistance to, 169–72
Attribution:
  motivational vs. informational biases
    in, 231–37
  process in labeling own emotions,
    199–200
  theory, 5–6, 113–15
Availability heuristic:
  actors' vs. observers' use of, 123–25
  appropriate and inappropriate uses of,
    23
  and causal inference, 21–23, 122–27

and conditioning, 102–4
and data coding, 72, 74–76
defined, 18–19
and linguistic influences, 126–27
in probability estimation, 19–21
and schema arousal, 36–37
utility of, 254
Awareness:
  of causes of own behavior, 210–25
  and improvement of inferential strate-
    gies, 287–88
  of mental events and processes, 202–10
  and repression, 245–47
  and "think-aloud" procedures, 219
  within-subject vs. between-subject
Base-rate information:
  causal interpretation of, 264
  use in novel vs. recurrent decisions, 265
  use in prediction, 141–50, 156–60
  and use in probability estimation,
    25–26, 28
  use when rates are equal, unknown,
    known, 263–64
Basic Antinomy, 234–35
Bayesian analysis, 265–66
Behavior:
  and inference, 269–71
  as reflection of judgmental errors, 11
Beliefs (*see* Theories)
Categories:
  in physical vs. social domains, 38–39
  underlying schemas, 32–33
Causal explanation (*see* Causal inference)
Causal inference:
  by actors vs. observers, 22, 122–25
  and attribution theory, 5–6
  availability effects on, 21–23, 122–27
  and base-rate information, 264
  and chance-determined outcomes,
    135–37
  and consensus information, 130–35
  and culturally-shared algorithms,
    212–14
  and discrepancy from expectation,
    262–63
  dispositional vs. situational, 30–31